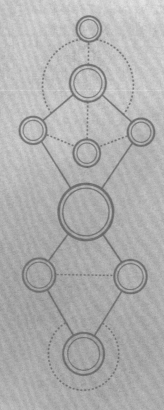

Writer: jonathan**HICKMAN**

Artist: dustin**WEAVER**

Color Artists: sonia**OBACK**
with rachelle**ROSENBERG** (#4), christina**STRAIN** (#4) & dustin**WEAVER** (#5-6)

Letterer: todd**KLEIN**

Cover Art: gerald**PAREL**

Assistant Editor: kathleen**WISNESKI**

Associate Editor: daniel**KETCHUM**

Editor: nick**LOWE**

S.H.I.E.L.D. CREATED BY **STAN LEE** & **JACK KIRBY**

COLLECTION EDITOR: **JENNIFER GRÜNWALD**
ASSISTANT EDITOR: **CAITLIN O'CONNELL**
ASSOCIATE MANAGING EDITOR: **KATERI WOODY**
EDITOR, SPECIAL PROJECTS: **MARK D. BEAZLEY**
VP PRODUCTION & SPECIAL PROJECTS: **JEFF YOUNGQUIST**
SVP PRINT, SALES & MARKETING: **DAVID GABRIEL**
SPECIAL THANKS TO **JEFF POWELL**

EDITOR IN CHIEF: **C.B. CEBULSKI**
CHIEF CREATIVE OFFICER: **JOE QUESADA**
PRESIDENT: **DAN BUCKLEY**
EXECUTIVE PRODUCER: **ALAN FINE**

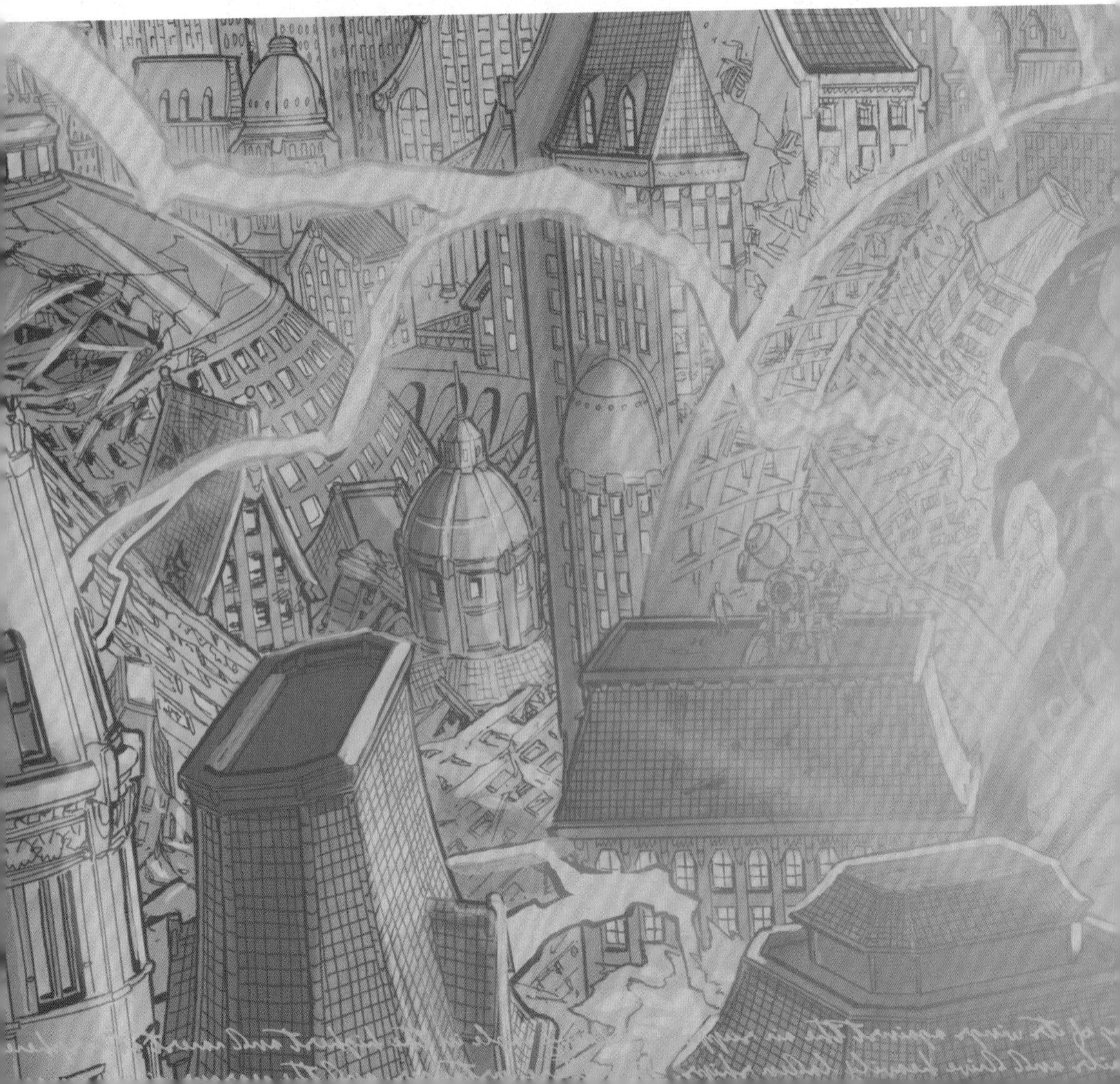

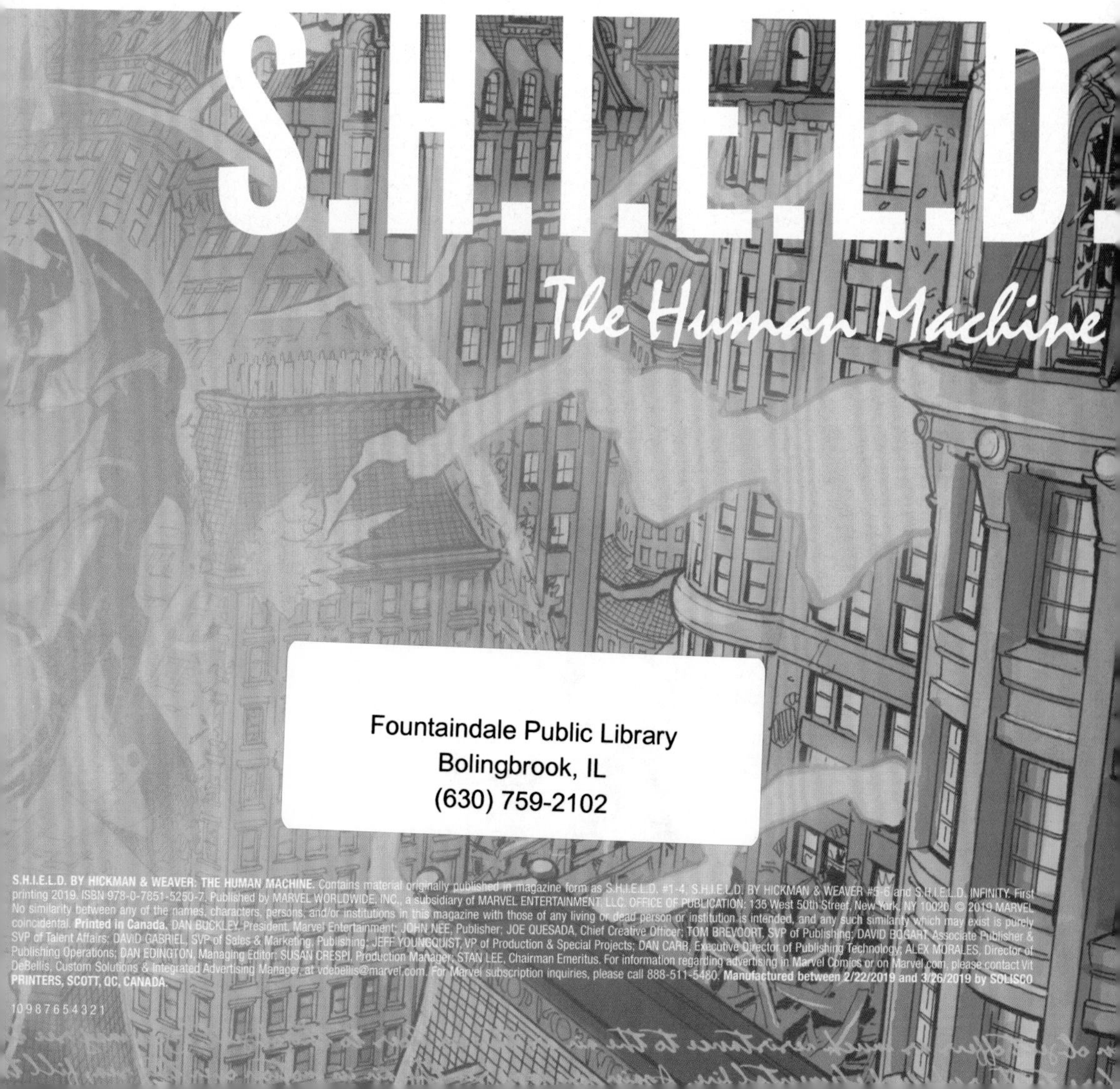

S.H.I.E.L.D.

The Human Machine

S.H.I.E.L.D. BY HICKMAN & WEAVER: THE HUMAN MACHINE. Contains material originally published in magazine form as S.H.I.E.L.D. #1-4, S.H.I.E.L.D. BY HICKMAN & WEAVER #5-6 and S.H.I.E.L.D. INFINITY. First printing 2019. ISBN 978-0-7851-5250-7. Published by MARVEL WORLDWIDE, INC., a subsidiary of MARVEL ENTERTAINMENT, LLC. OFFICE OF PUBLICATION: 135 West 50th Street, New York, NY 10020. © 2019 MARVEL No similarity between any of the names, characters, persons, and/or institutions in this magazine with those of any living or dead person or institution is intended, and any such similarity which may exist is purely coincidental. **Printed in Canada.** DAN BUCKLEY, President, Marvel Entertainment; JOHN NEE, Publisher; JOE QUESADA, Chief Creative Officer; TOM BREVOORT, SVP of Publishing; DAVID BOGART, Associate Publisher & SVP of Talent Affairs; DAVID GABRIEL, SVP of Sales & Marketing, Publishing; JEFF YOUNGQUIST, VP of Production & Special Projects; DAN CARR, Executive Director of Publishing Technology; ALEX MORALES, Director of Publishing Operations; DAN EDINGTON, Managing Editor; SUSAN CRESPI, Production Manager; STAN LEE, Chairman Emeritus. For information regarding advertising in Marvel Comics or on Marvel.com, please contact Vit DeBellis, Custom Solutions & Integrated Advertising Manager, at vdebellis@marvel.com. For Marvel subscription inquiries, please call 888-511-5480. **Manufactured between 2/22/2019 and 3/26/2019 by SOLISCO PRINTERS, SCOTT, QC, CANADA.**

10 9 8 7 6 5 4 3 2 1

Chapter One
"Terribilità"

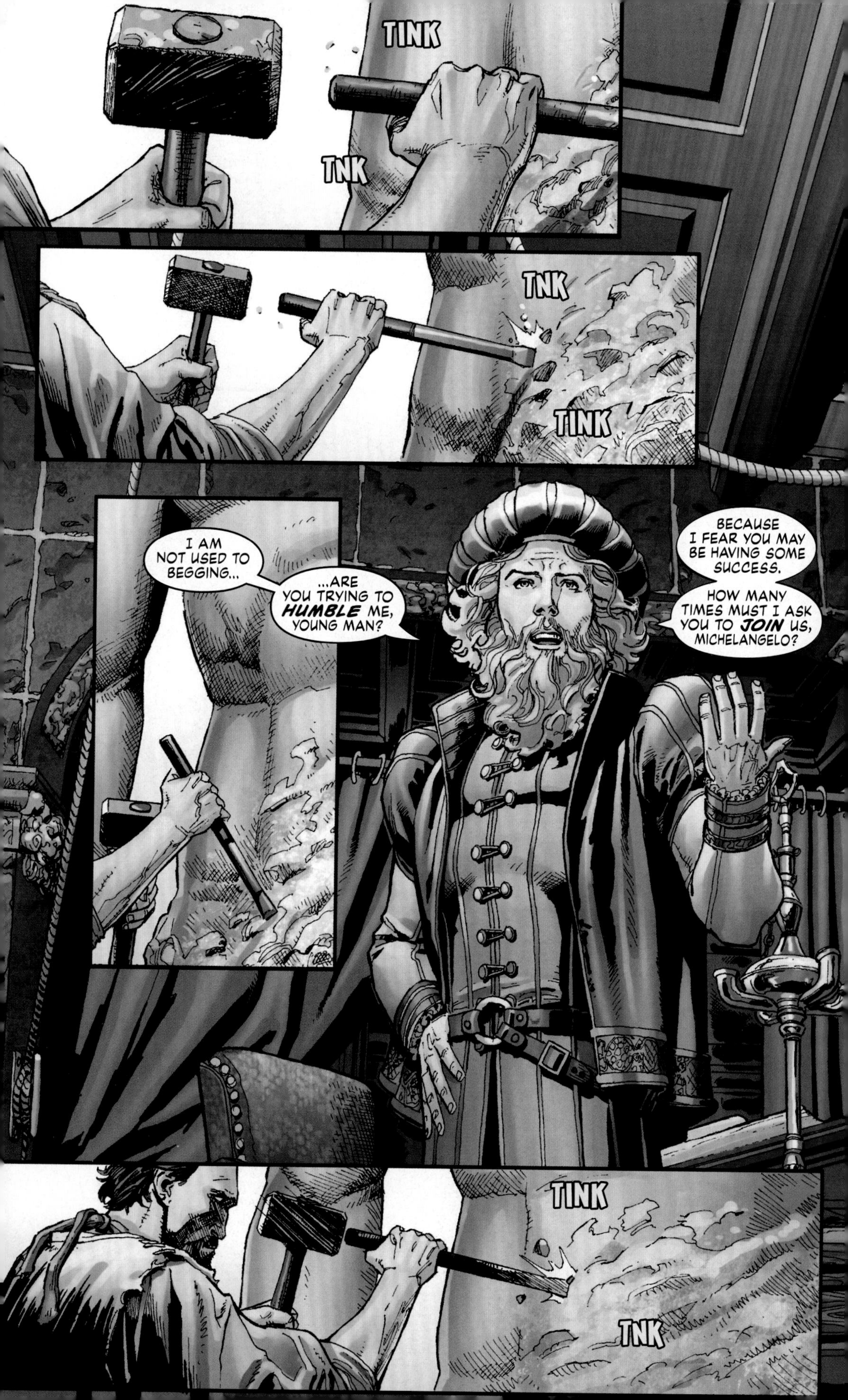
TINK
TNK
TNK
TINK
I AM NOT USED TO BEGGING...
...ARE YOU TRYING TO HUMBLE ME, YOUNG MAN?
BECAUSE I FEAR YOU MAY BE HAVING SOME SUCCESS.
HOW MANY TIMES MUST I ASK YOU TO JOIN US, MICHELANGELO?
TINK
TNK

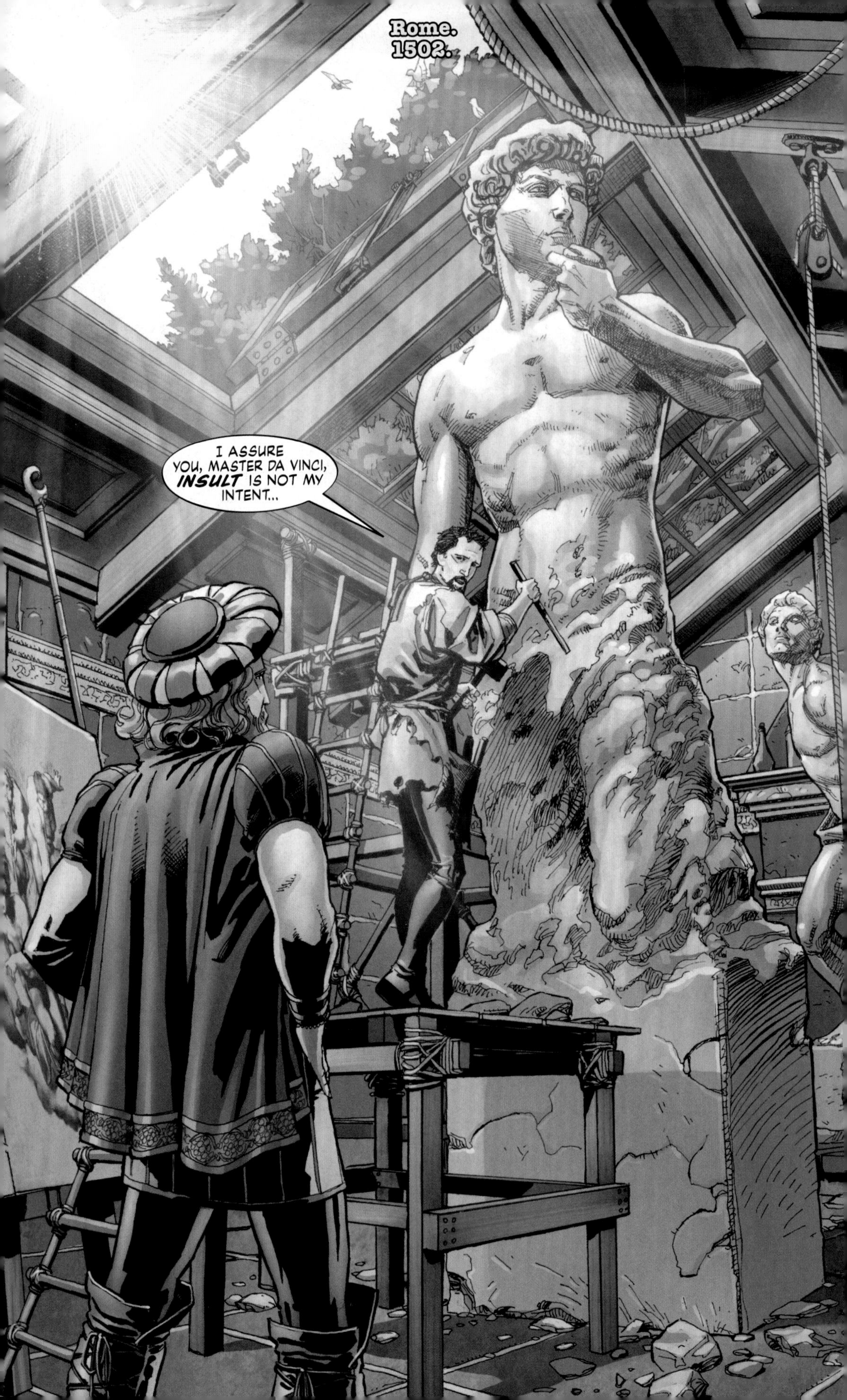
Rome.
1502.
I ASSURE YOU, MASTER DA VINCI, INSULT IS NOT MY INTENT...

Since Imhotep quelled the Brood invasion in 2620 B.C., one organization has taken it upon itself to safeguard the human race against the known and unknown. They are security, they are shelter... they are the Shield. This higher calling has been passed from generation to generation, from Imhotep to Leonardo Da Vinci to Galileo. And now, it is being passed to a young man named Leonid.

The High Council of Shield, in The Immortal City preserved deep below Rome, is ruled over by the immortal Sir Isaac Newton. He has instructed Leonid in the hidden history of the world. However, Newton's position as both leader of Shield and mentor to Leonid has been challenged by the return of Leonardo da Vinci. Representing two opposing philosophies, both da Vinci and Newton begin to amass followers...and conflict stirs between them, eventually erupting in battle.

And as Leonid tries to determine how to quell the conflict, he is met by another member of the Brotherhood: Michelangelo Buonarotti.

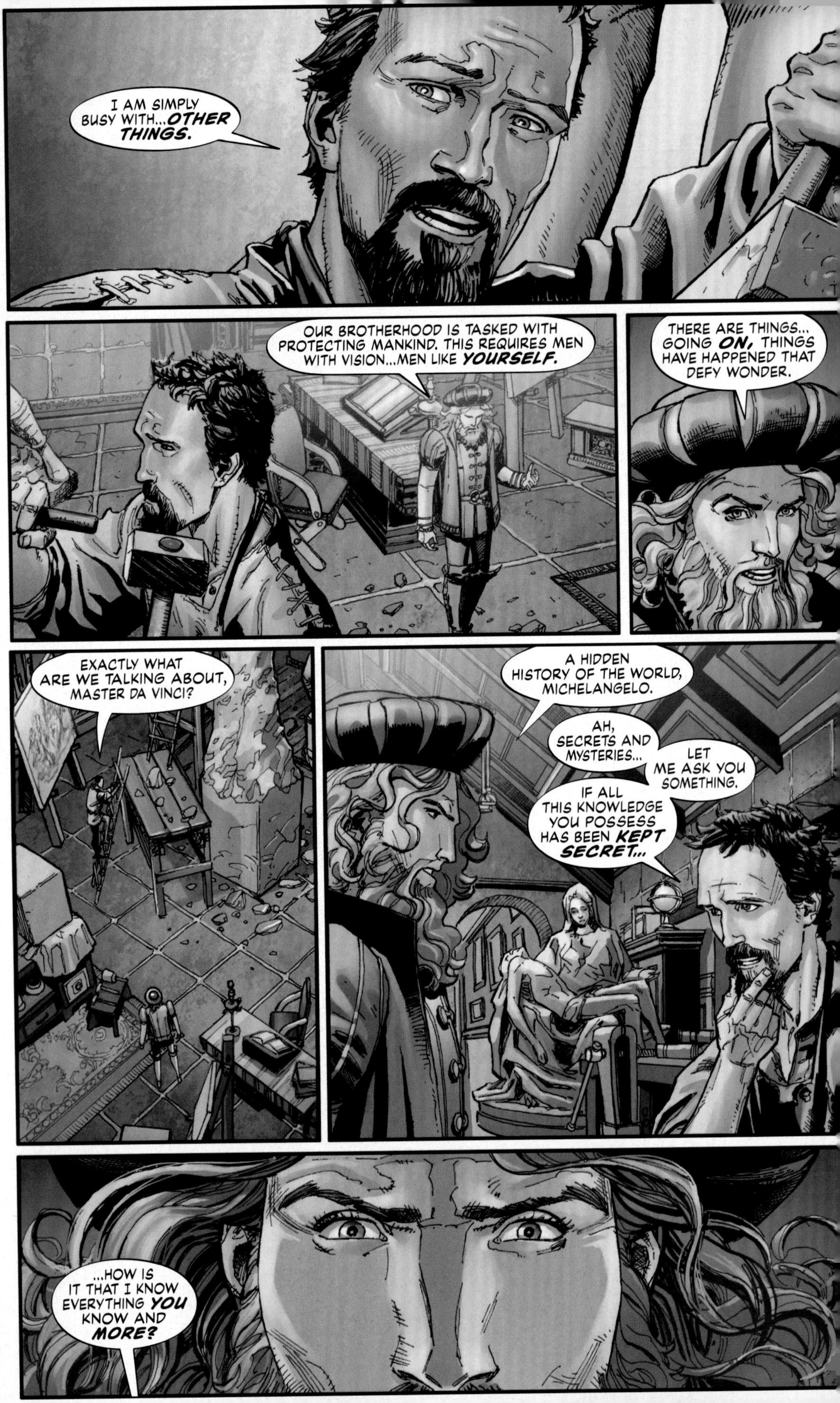
I AM SIMPLY BUSY WITH...OTHER THINGS.
OUR BROTHERHOOD IS TASKED WITH PROTECTING MANKIND. THIS REQUIRES MEN WITH VISION...MEN LIKE YOURSELF.
THERE ARE THINGS... GOING ON, THINGS HAVE HAPPENED THAT DEFY WONDER.
EXACTLY WHAT ARE WE TALKING ABOUT, MASTER DA VINCI?
A HIDDEN HISTORY OF THE WORLD, MICHELANGELO.
AH, SECRETS AND MYSTERIES...
LET ME ASK YOU SOMETHING.
IF ALL THIS KNOWLEDGE YOU POSSESS HAS BEEN KEPT SECRET...
...HOW IS IT THAT I KNOW EVERYTHING YOU KNOW AND MORE?

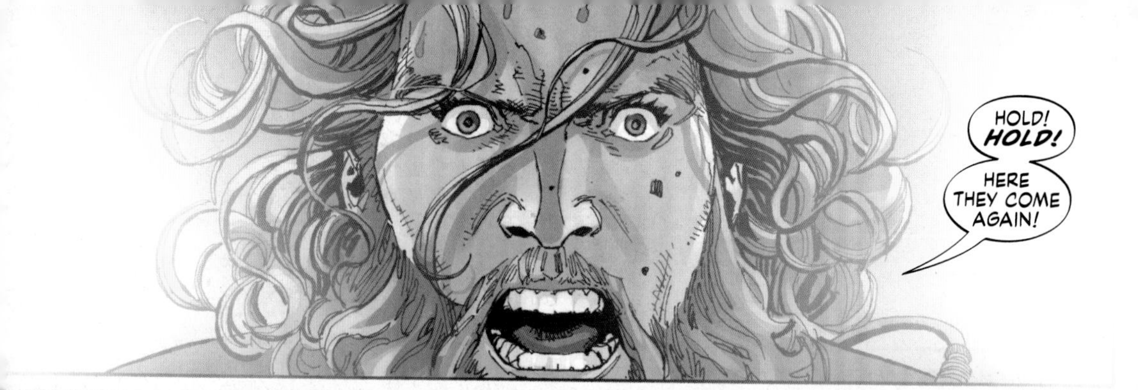
HOLD! HOLD!
HERE THEY COME AGAIN!

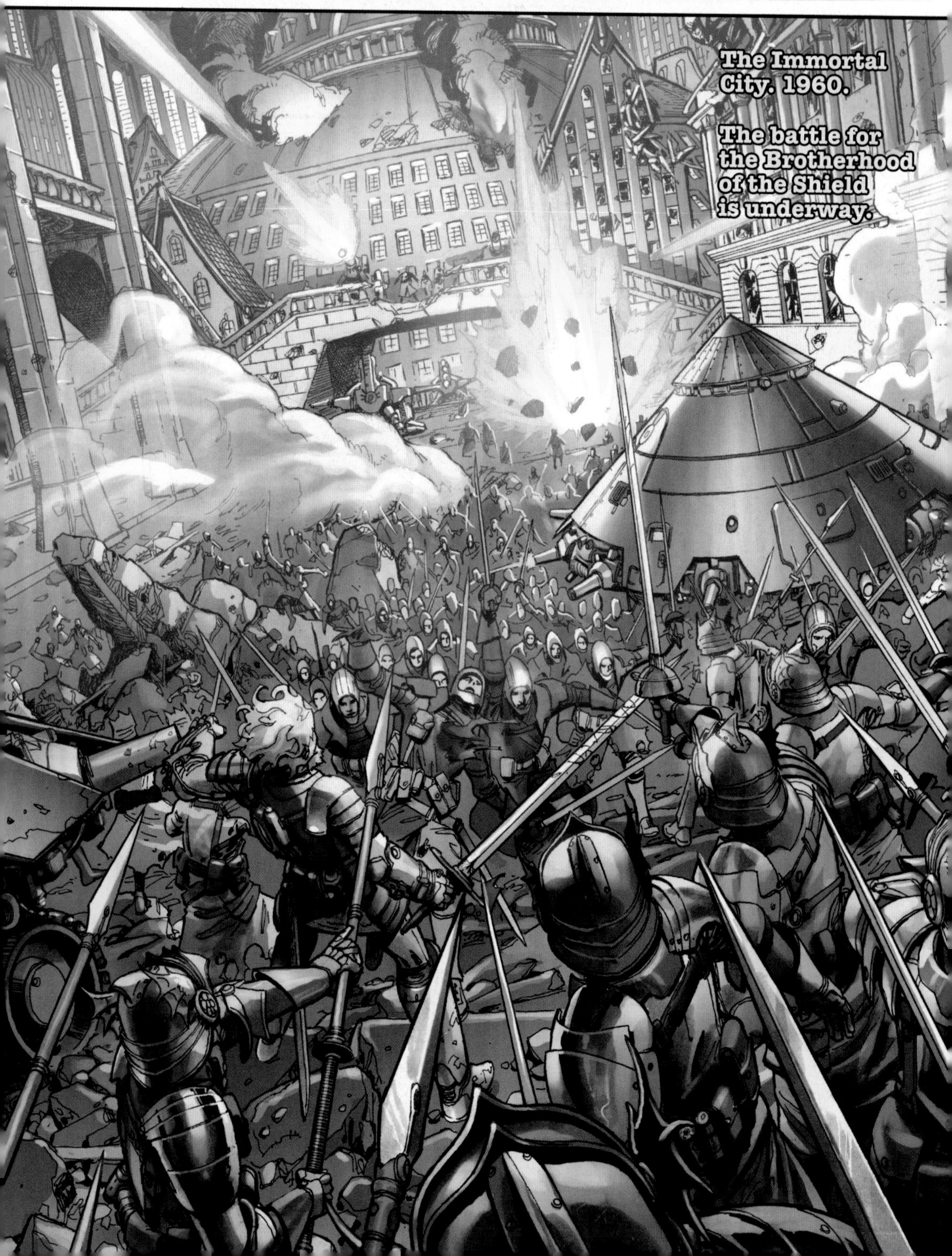
The Immortal City. 1960.
The battle for the Brotherhood of the Shield is underway.

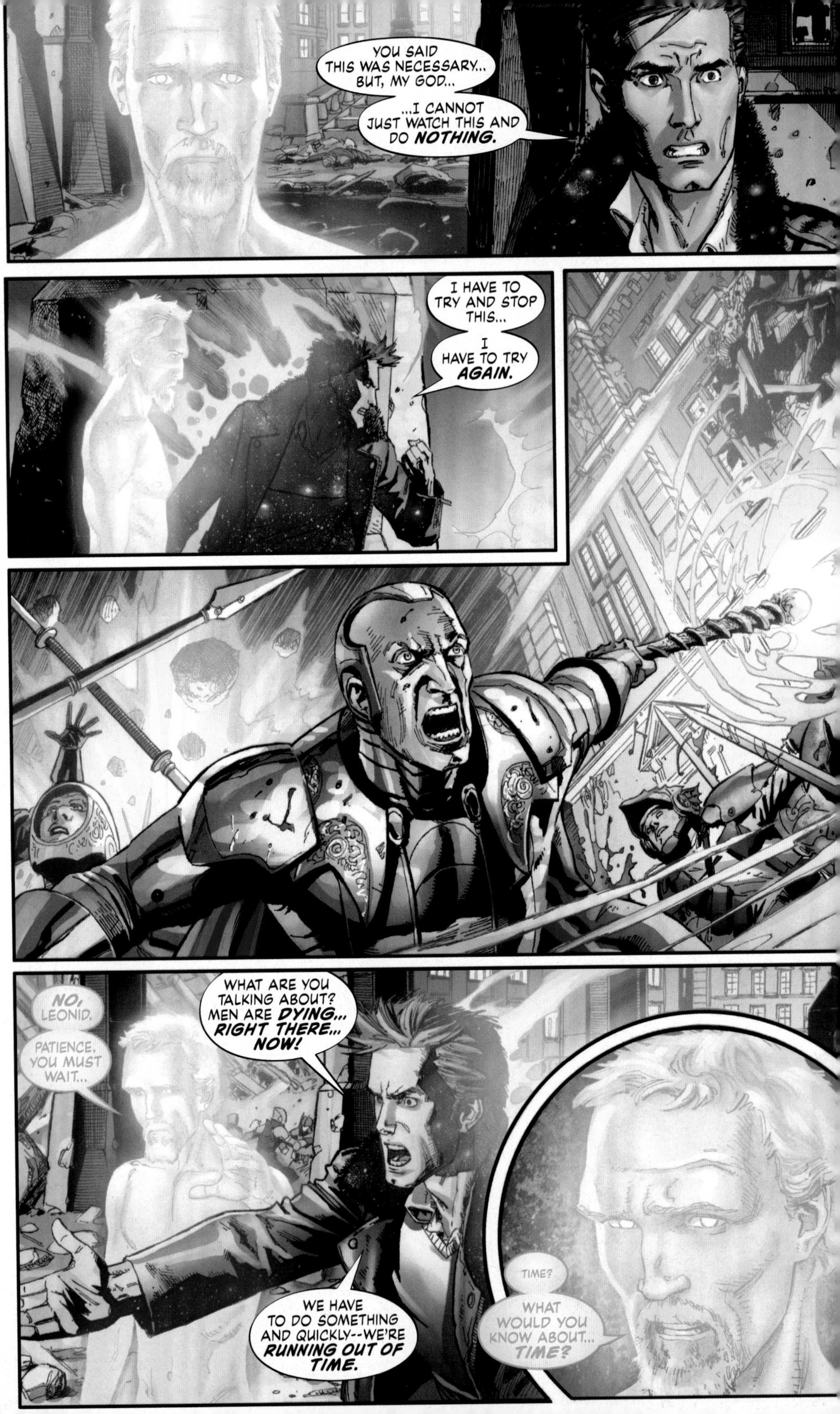
YOU SAID THIS WAS NECESSARY... BUT, MY GOD...
...I CANNOT JUST WATCH THIS AND DO **NOTHING.**
I HAVE TO TRY AND STOP THIS...
I HAVE TO TRY **AGAIN.**
NO, LEONID.
PATIENCE. YOU MUST WAIT...
WHAT ARE YOU TALKING ABOUT? MEN ARE **DYING... RIGHT THERE... NOW!**
WE HAVE TO DO SOMETHING AND QUICKLY--WE'RE **RUNNING OUT OF TIME.**
TIME?
WHAT WOULD YOU KNOW ABOUT... **TIME?**

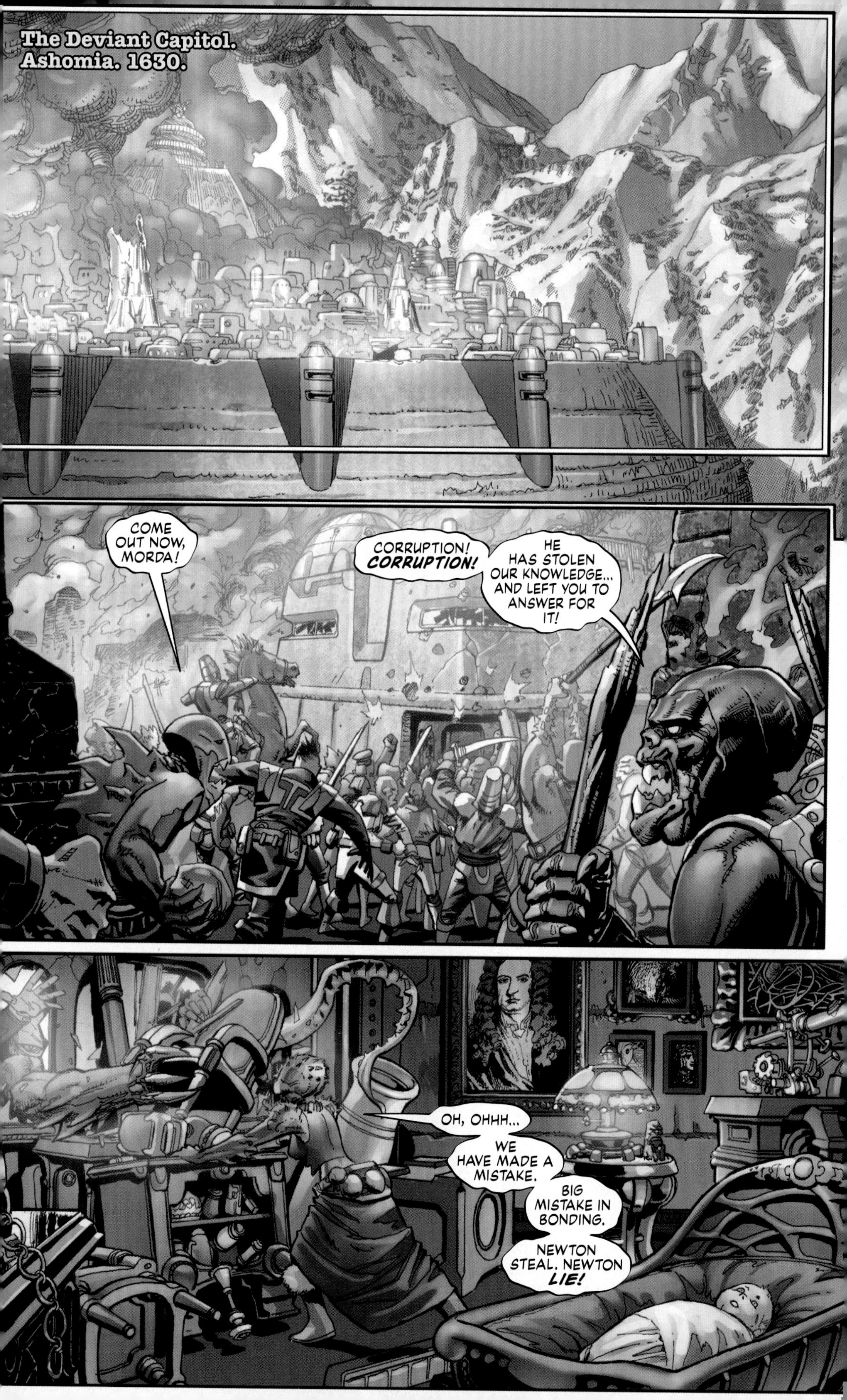
The Deviant Capitol.
Ashomia. 1630.
COME OUT NOW, MORDA!
CORRUPTION! CORRUPTION!
HE HAS STOLEN OUR KNOWLEDGE... AND LEFT YOU TO ANSWER FOR IT!
OH, OHHH...
WE HAVE MADE A MISTAKE.
BIG MISTAKE IN BONDING.
NEWTON STEAL. NEWTON LIE!

BAH!

MORE MAN! CORRUPTION!

I CUT YOU...AND GIVE TO OTHERS.

SAVE MORDA. SAVE BABY.

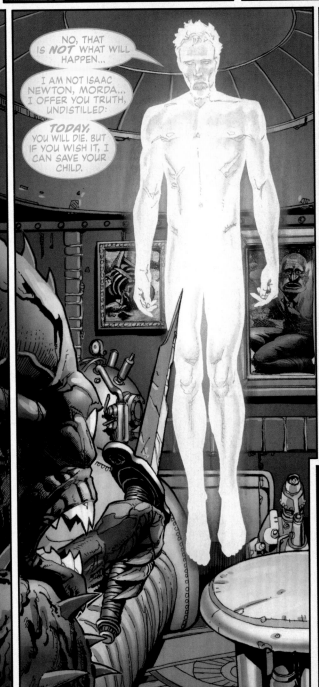

NO, THAT IS *NOT* WHAT WILL HAPPEN...

I AM NOT ISAAC NEWTON, MORDA... I OFFER YOU TRUTH, UNDISTILLED:

TODAY, YOU WILL DIE. BUT IF YOU WISH IT, I CAN SAVE YOUR CHILD.

SAVE BABY?

TAKE BABY?

PROMISE. NO NEWTON!

I CANNOT DO THAT.

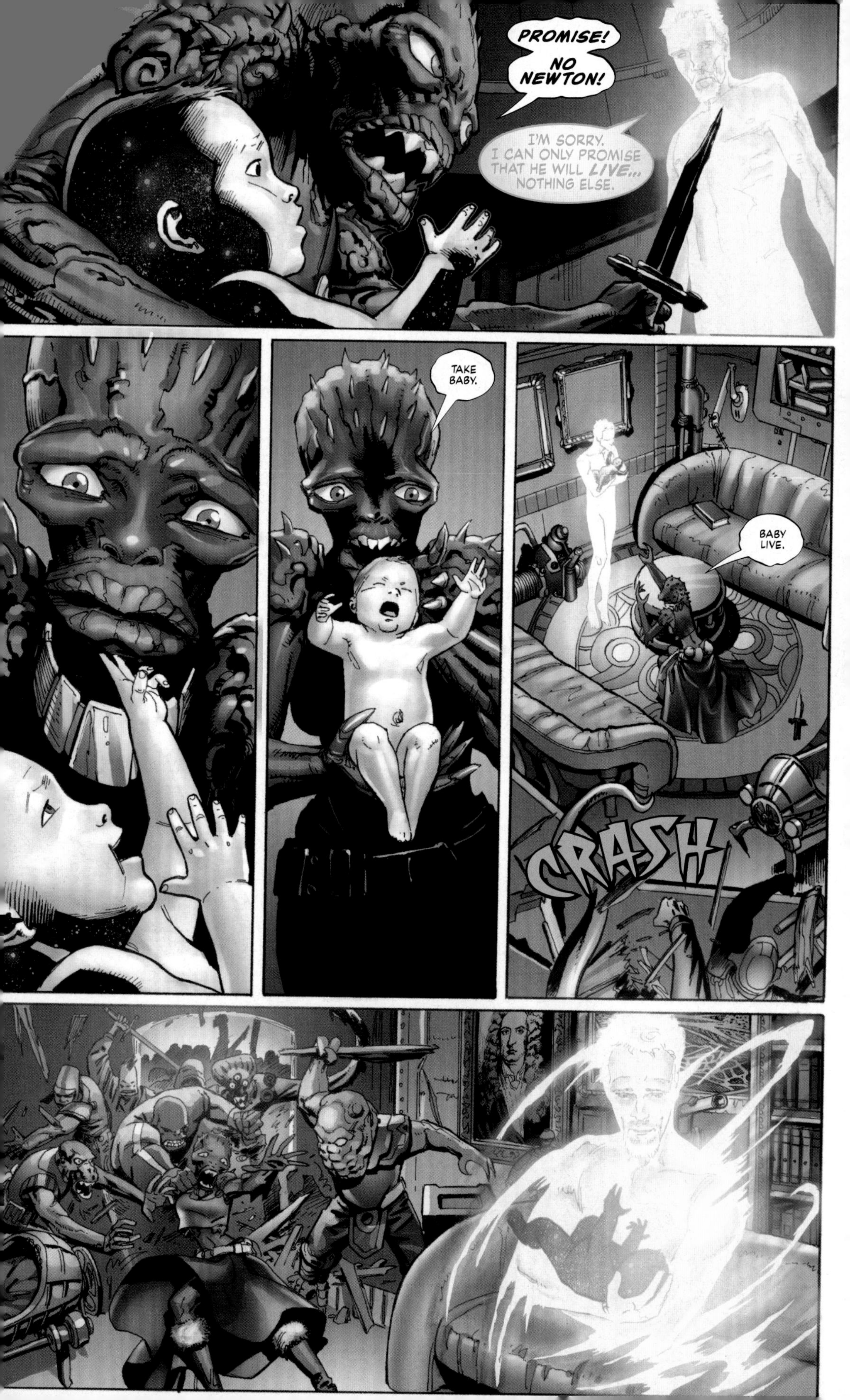

PROMISE! NO NEWTON!
I'M SORRY. I CAN ONLY PROMISE THAT HE WILL *LIVE*... NOTHING ELSE.
TAKE BABY.
BABY LIVE.
CRASH

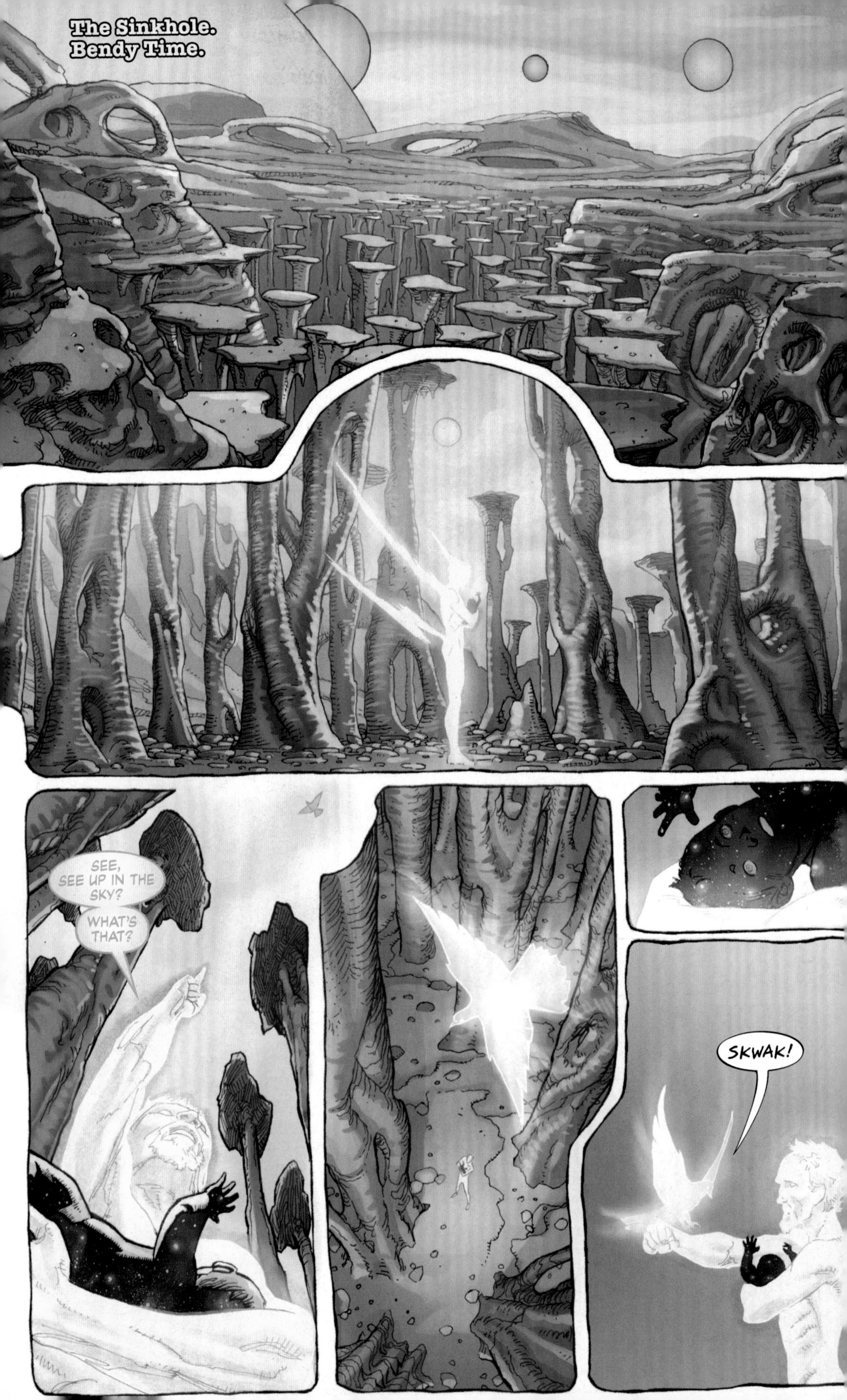
The Sinkhole.
Bendy Time.
SEE, SEE UP IN THE SKY?
WHAT'S THAT?
SKWAK!

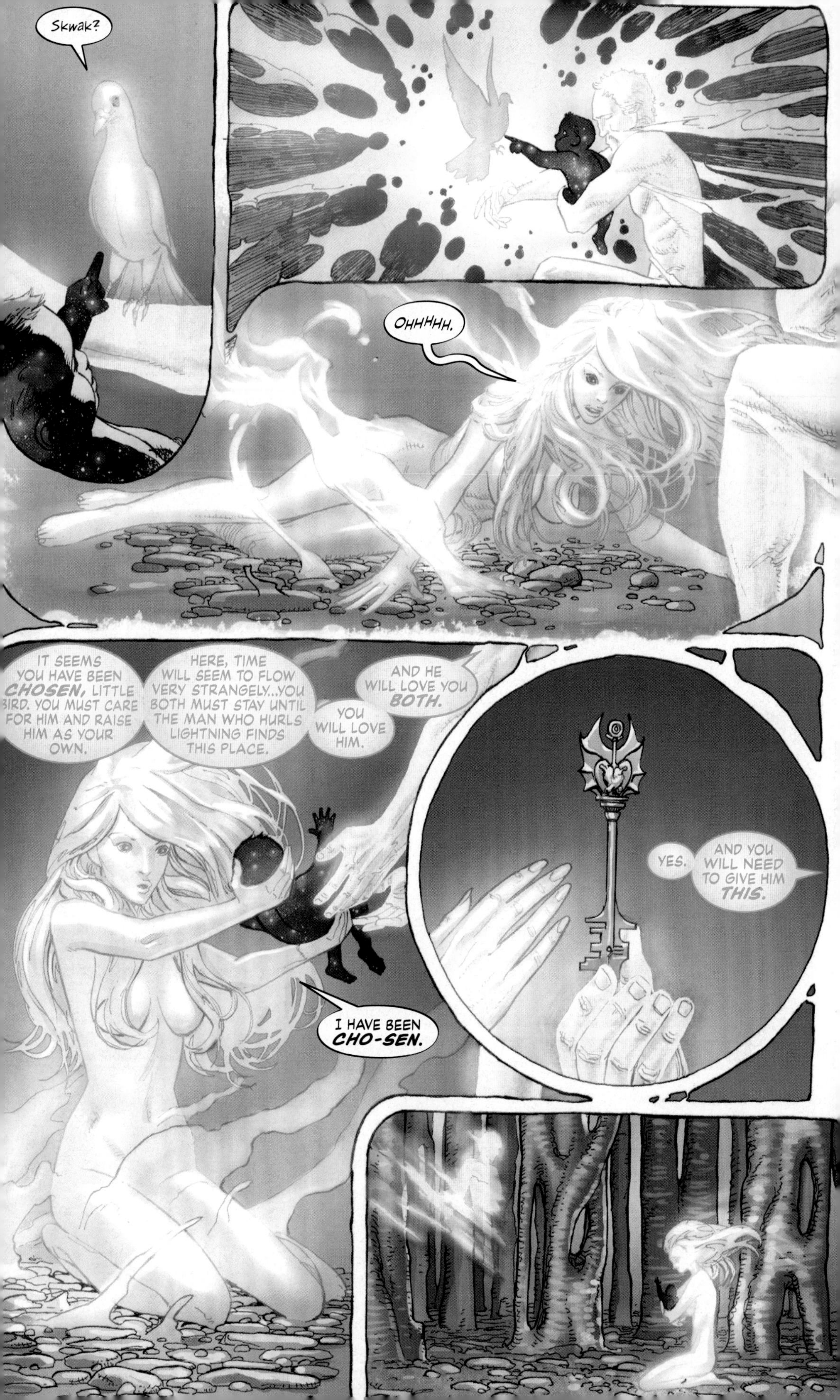
SKWAK?
OHHHHH.
IT SEEMS YOU HAVE BEEN CHOSEN, LITTLE BIRD. YOU MUST CARE FOR HIM AND RAISE HIM AS YOUR OWN.
HERE, TIME WILL SEEM TO FLOW VERY STRANGELY...YOU BOTH MUST STAY UNTIL THE MAN WHO HURLS LIGHTNING FINDS THIS PLACE.
YOU WILL LOVE HIM.
AND HE WILL LOVE YOU BOTH.
I HAVE BEEN CHO-SEN.
YES.
AND YOU WILL NEED TO GIVE HIM THIS.

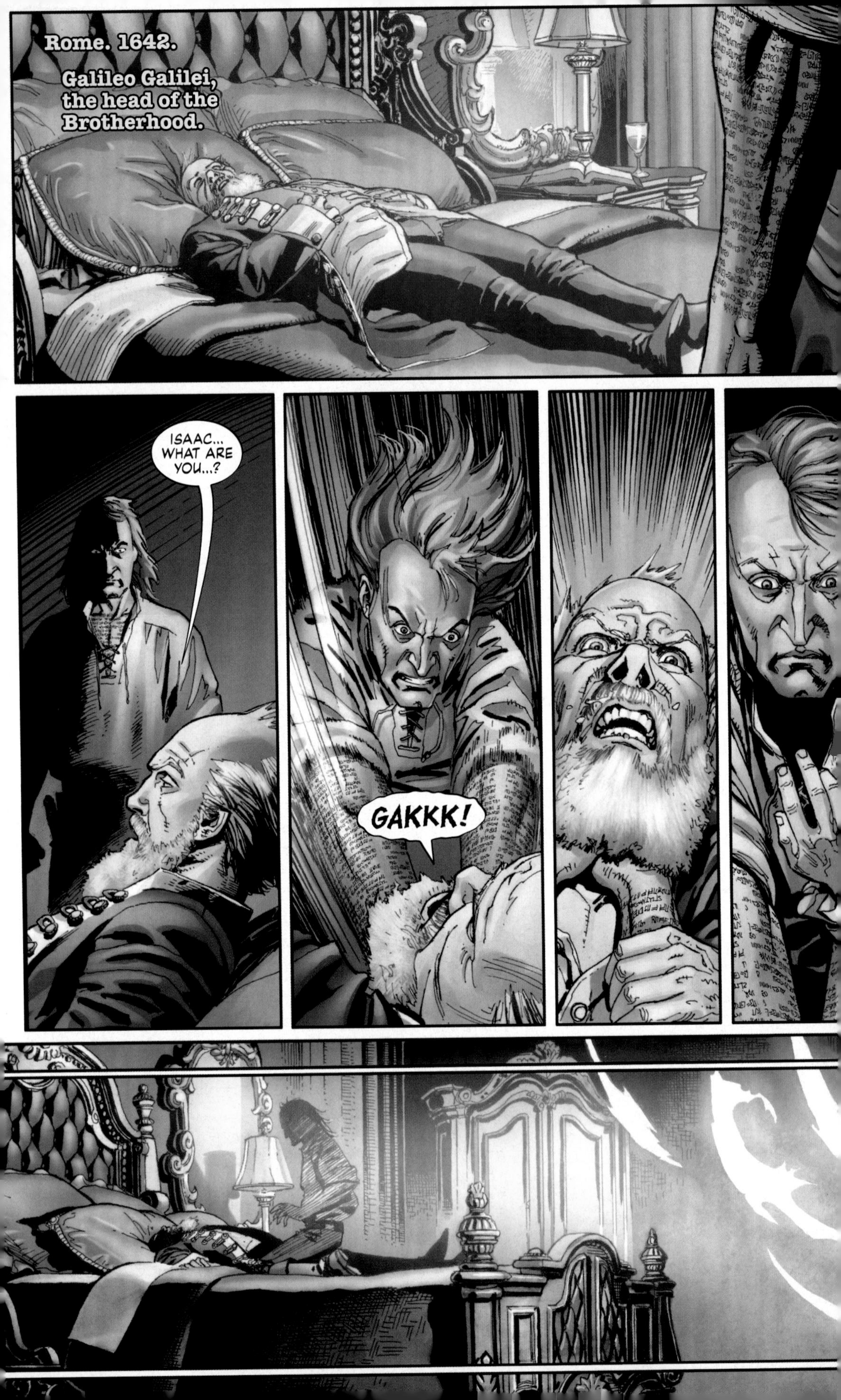
Rome. 1642.
Galileo Galilei, the head of the Brotherhood.
ISAAC... WHAT ARE YOU...?
GAKKK!

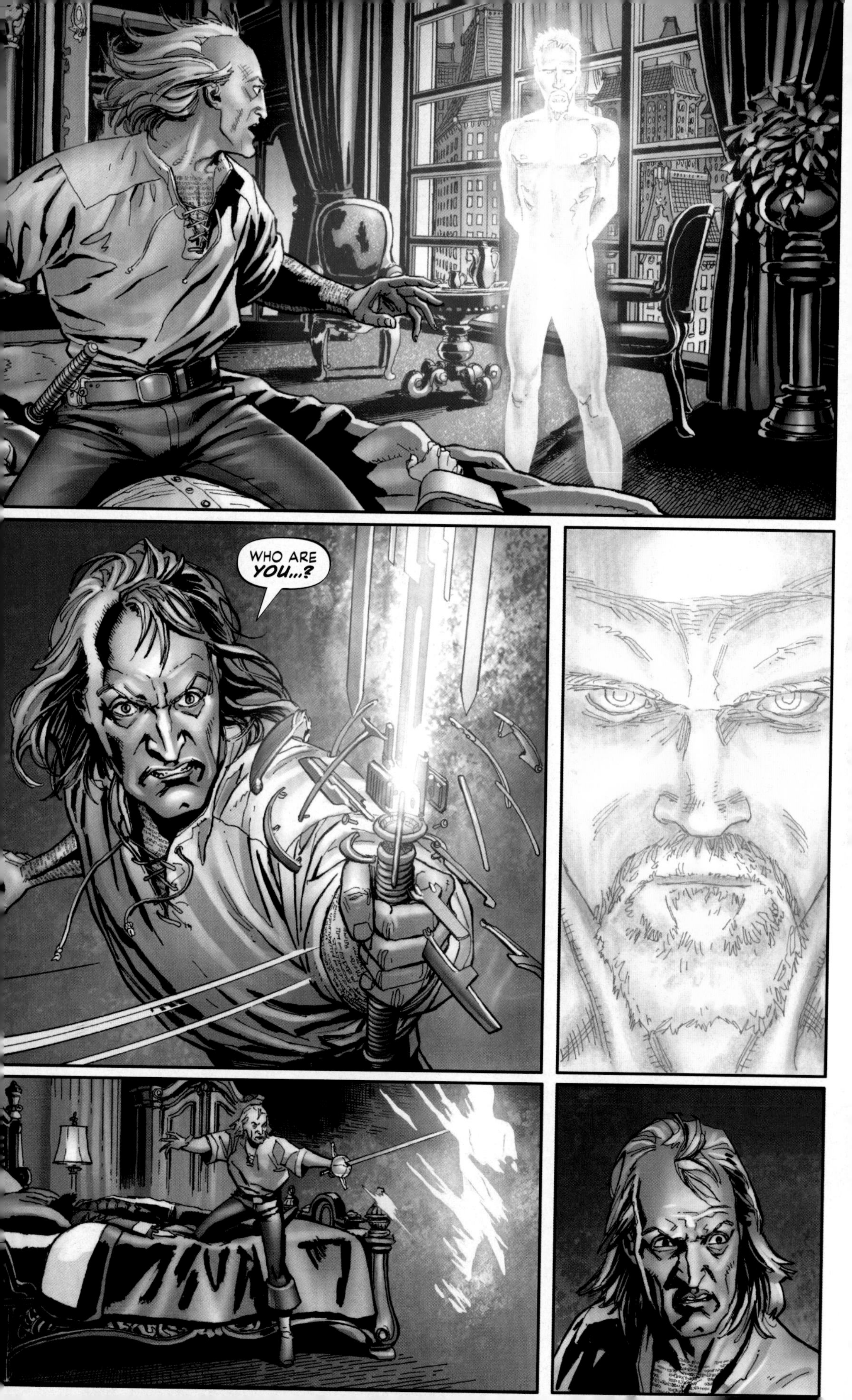
WHO ARE YOU...?

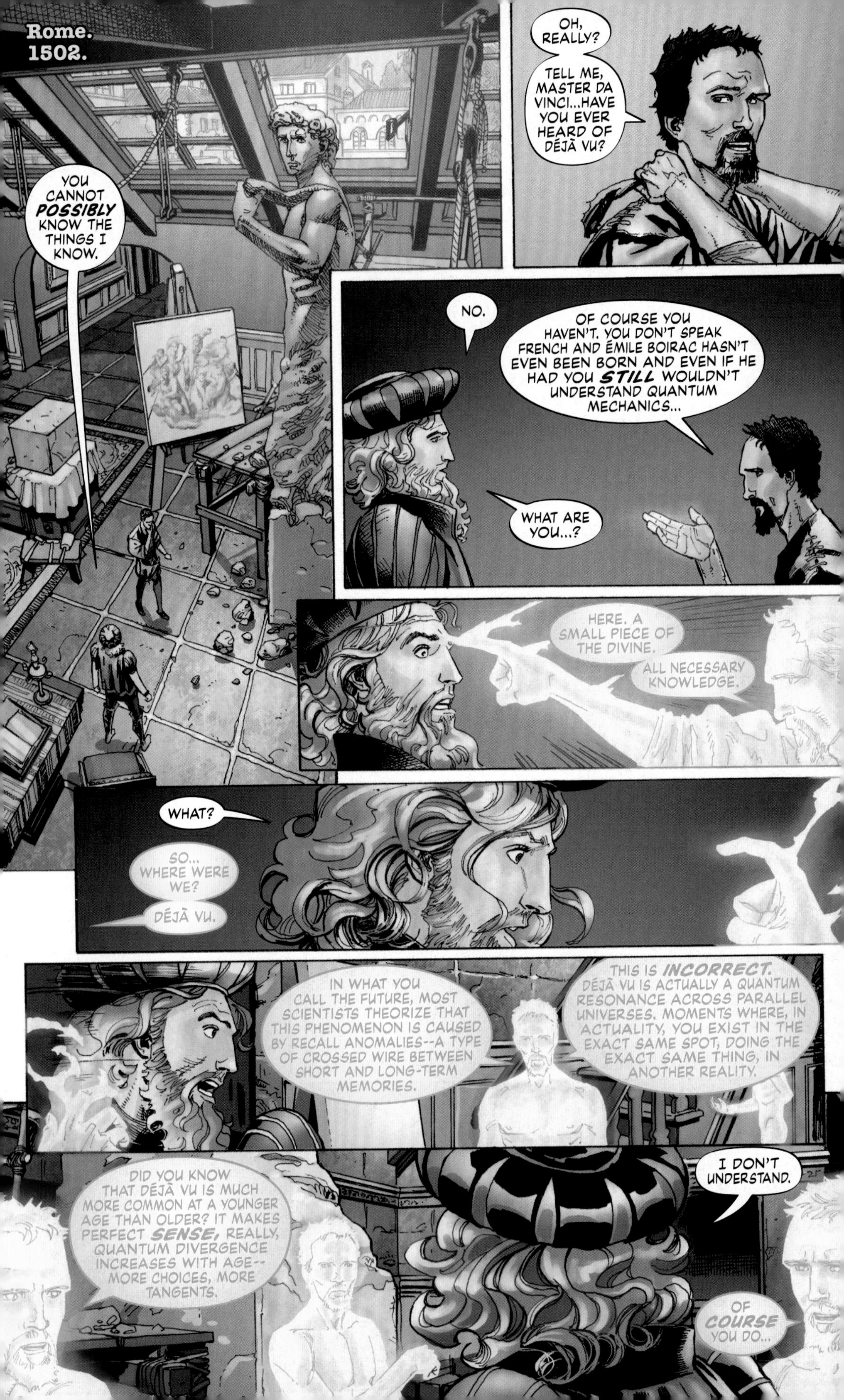

Rome.
1502.
YOU CANNOT POSSIBLY KNOW THE THINGS I KNOW.
OH, REALLY?
TELL ME, MASTER DA VINCI...HAVE YOU EVER HEARD OF DÉJÃ VU?
NO.
OF COURSE YOU HAVEN'T. YOU DON'T SPEAK FRENCH AND ÉMILE BOIRAC HASN'T EVEN BEEN BORN AND EVEN IF HE HAD YOU STILL WOULDN'T UNDERSTAND QUANTUM MECHANICS...
WHAT ARE YOU...?
HERE. A SMALL PIECE OF THE DIVINE.
ALL NECESSARY KNOWLEDGE.
WHAT?
SO... WHERE WERE WE?
DÉJÃ VU.
IN WHAT YOU CALL THE FUTURE, MOST SCIENTISTS THEORIZE THAT THIS PHENOMENON IS CAUSED BY RECALL ANOMALIES--A TYPE OF CROSSED WIRE BETWEEN SHORT AND LONG-TERM MEMORIES.
THIS IS INCORRECT. DÉJÃ VU IS ACTUALLY A QUANTUM RESONANCE ACROSS PARALLEL UNIVERSES. MOMENTS WHERE, IN ACTUALITY, YOU EXIST IN THE EXACT SAME SPOT, DOING THE EXACT SAME THING, IN ANOTHER REALITY.
DID YOU KNOW THAT DÉJÃ VU IS MUCH MORE COMMON AT A YOUNGER AGE THAN OLDER? IT MAKES PERFECT SENSE, REALLY, QUANTUM DIVERGENCE INCREASES WITH AGE--MORE CHOICES, MORE TANGENTS.
I DON'T UNDERSTAND.
OF COURSE YOU DO...

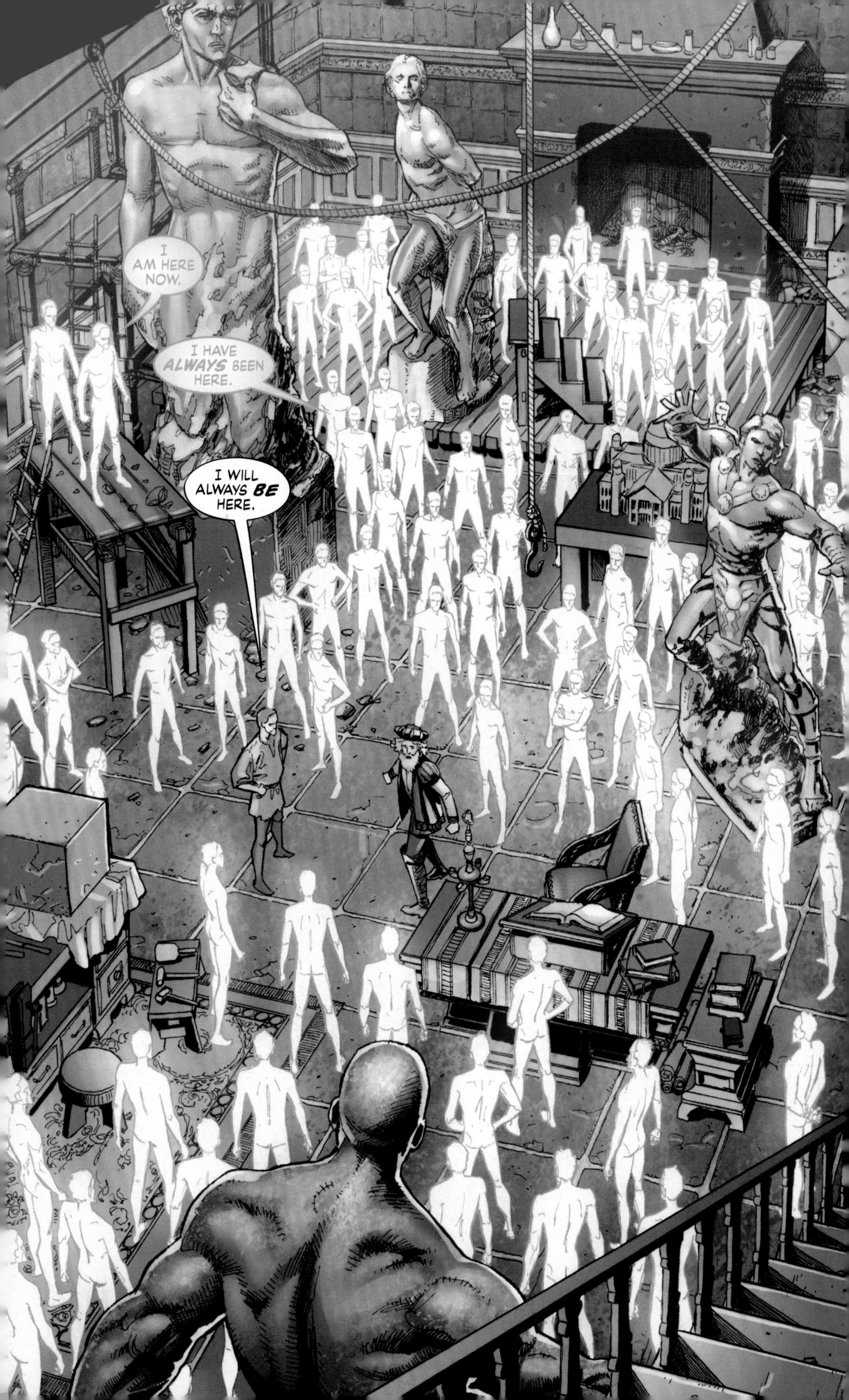
I AM HERE NOW.
I HAVE ALWAYS BEEN HERE.
I WILL ALWAYS BE HERE.

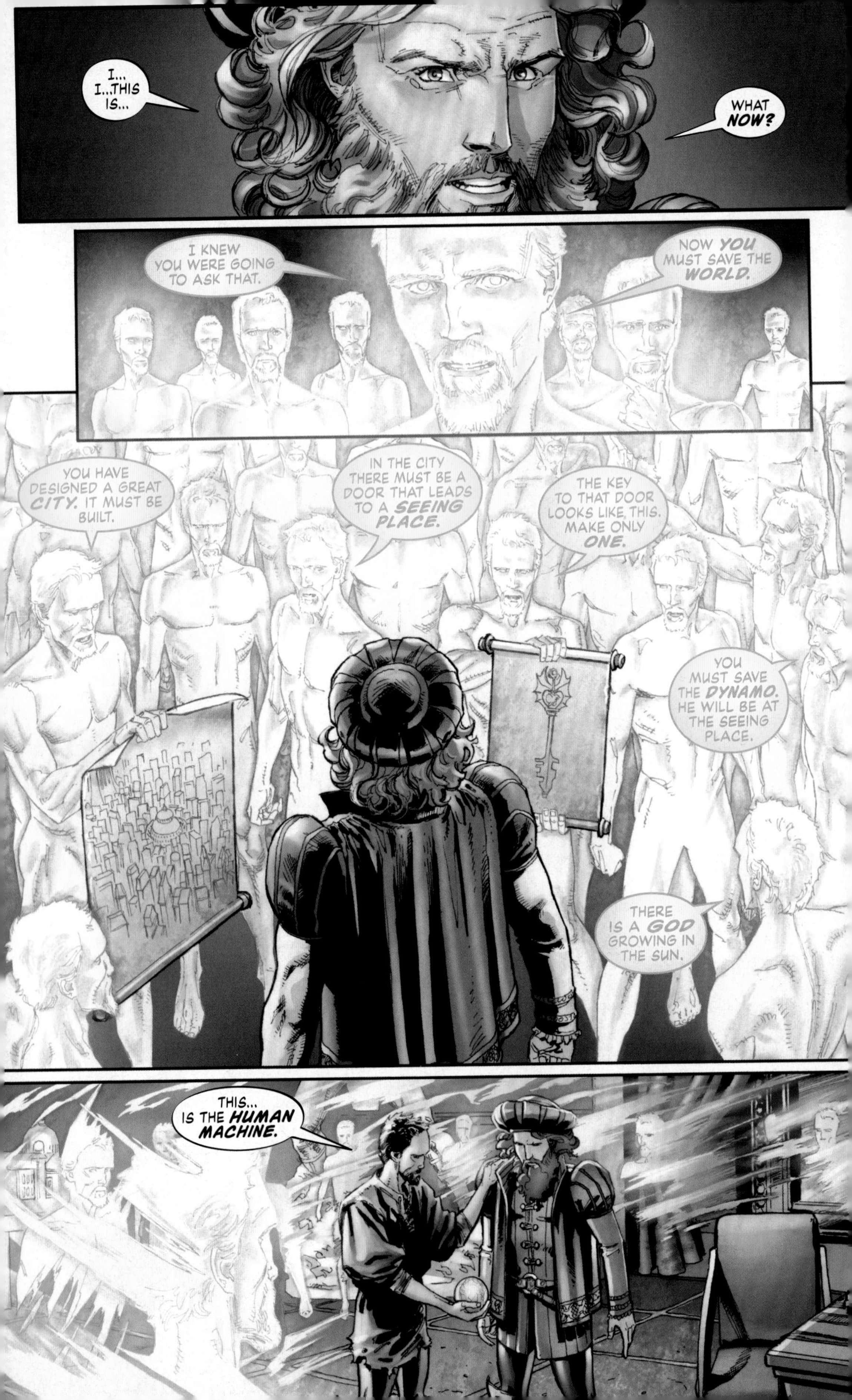
I... I...THIS IS...
WHAT NOW?
I KNEW YOU WERE GOING TO ASK THAT.
NOW YOU MUST SAVE THE WORLD.
YOU HAVE DESIGNED A GREAT CITY. IT MUST BE BUILT.
IN THE CITY THERE MUST BE A DOOR THAT LEADS TO A SEEING PLACE.
THE KEY TO THAT DOOR LOOKS LIKE THIS. MAKE ONLY ONE.
YOU MUST SAVE THE DYNAMO. HE WILL BE AT THE SEEING PLACE.
THERE IS A GOD GROWING IN THE SUN.
THIS... IS THE HUMAN MACHINE.

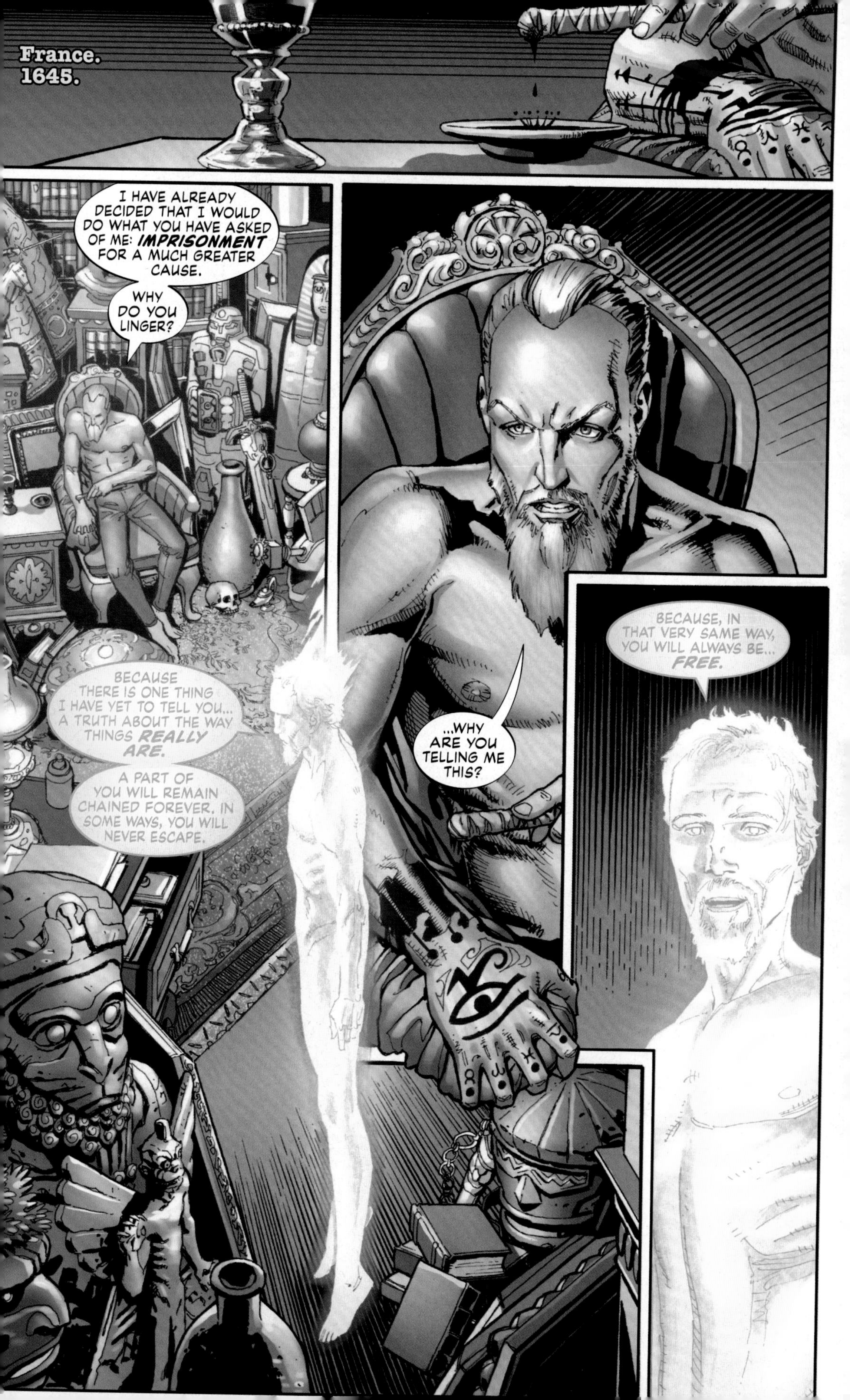
France. 1645.
I HAVE ALREADY DECIDED THAT I WOULD DO WHAT YOU HAVE ASKED OF ME: IMPRISONMENT FOR A MUCH GREATER CAUSE.
WHY DO YOU LINGER?
BECAUSE THERE IS ONE THING I HAVE YET TO TELL YOU... A TRUTH ABOUT THE WAY THINGS REALLY ARE.
A PART OF YOU WILL REMAIN CHAINED FOREVER. IN SOME WAYS, YOU WILL NEVER ESCAPE.
...WHY ARE YOU TELLING ME THIS?
BECAUSE, IN THAT VERY SAME WAY, YOU WILL ALWAYS BE... FREE.

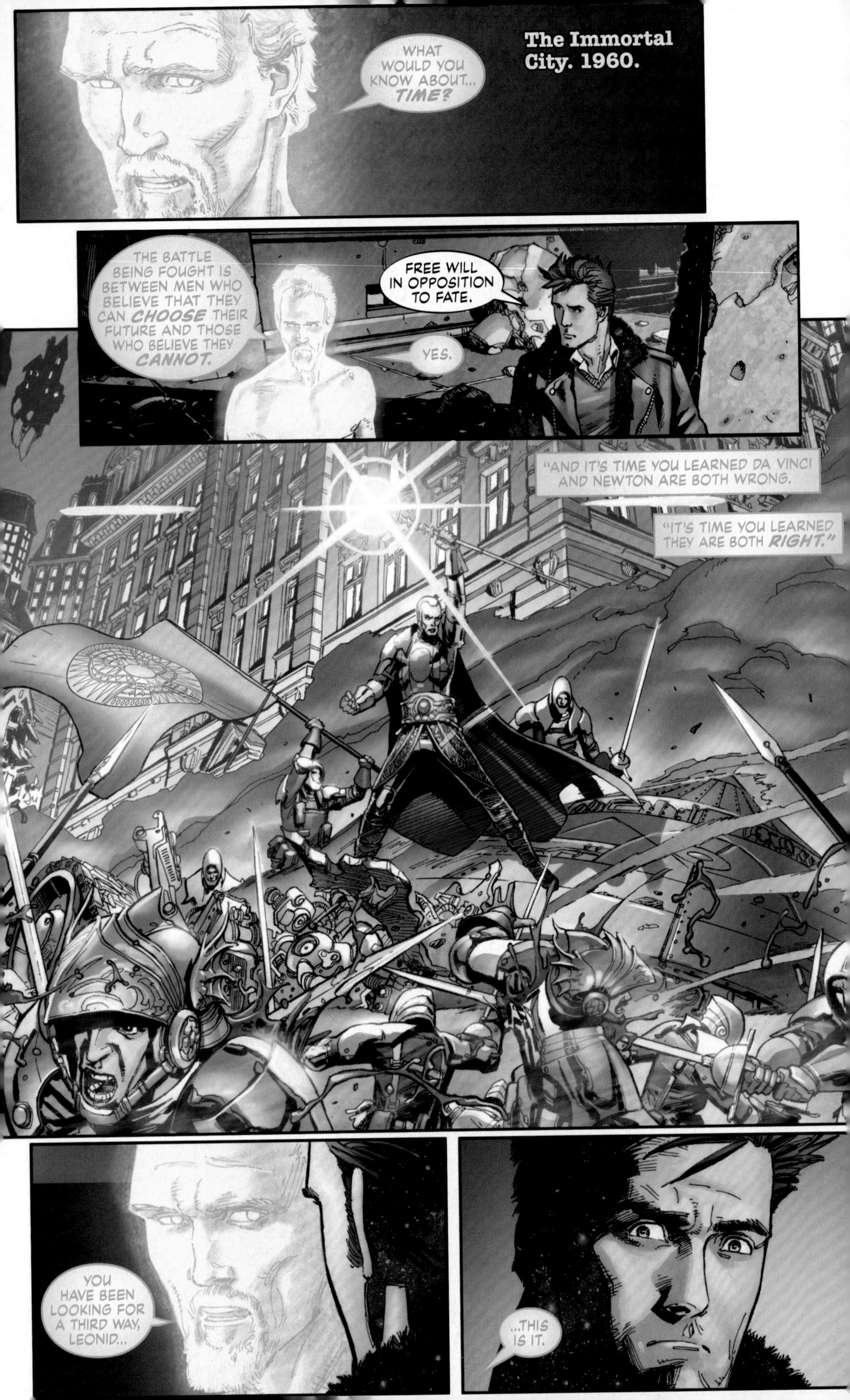
The Immortal City. 1960.
WHAT WOULD YOU KNOW ABOUT... TIME?
THE BATTLE BEING FOUGHT IS BETWEEN MEN WHO BELIEVE THAT THEY CAN CHOOSE THEIR FUTURE AND THOSE WHO BELIEVE THEY CANNOT.
FREE WILL IN OPPOSITION TO FATE.
YES.
"AND IT'S TIME YOU LEARNED DA VINCI AND NEWTON ARE BOTH WRONG.
"IT'S TIME YOU LEARNED THEY ARE BOTH RIGHT."
YOU HAVE BEEN LOOKING FOR A THIRD WAY, LEONID...
...THIS IS IT.

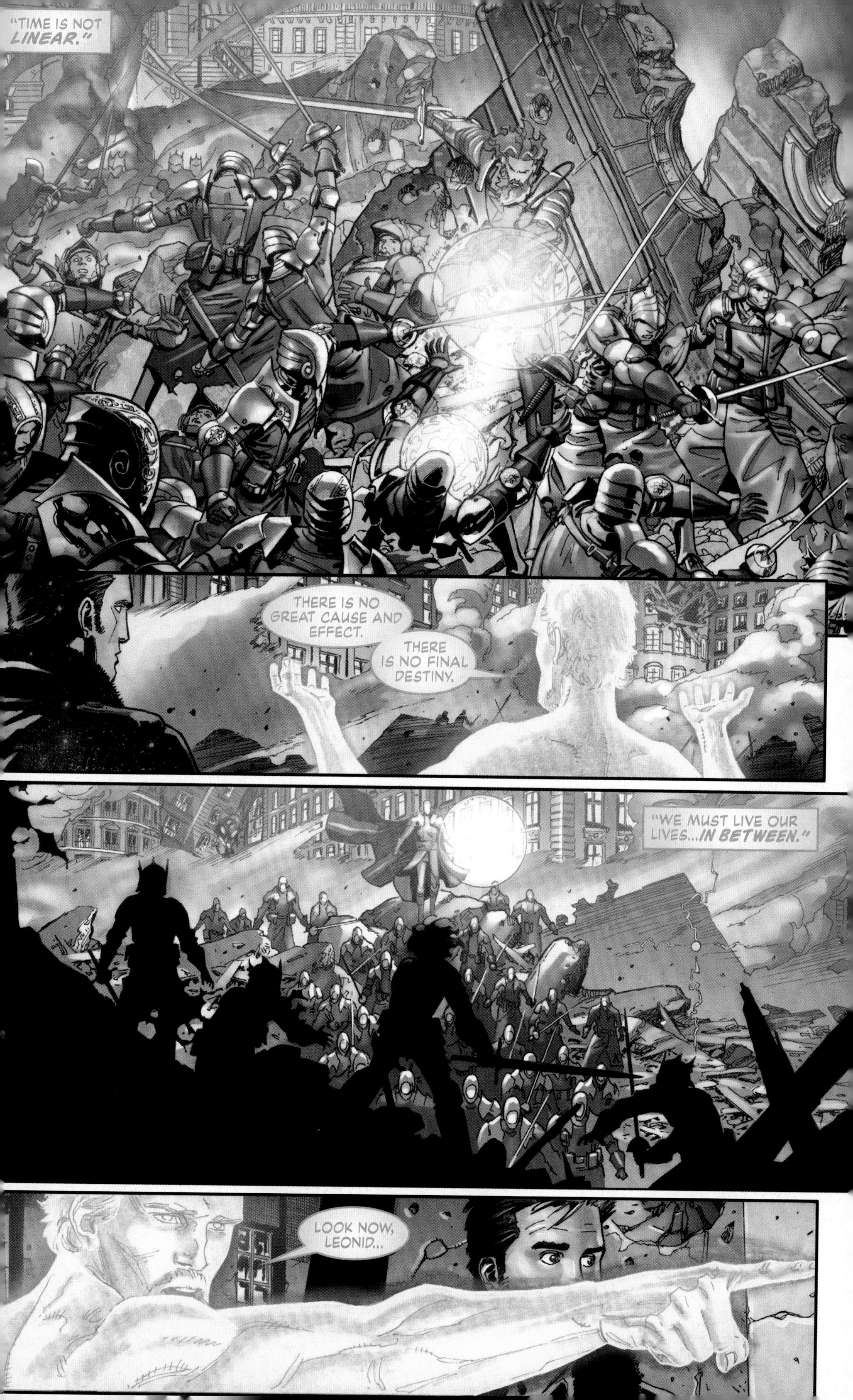
"TIME IS NOT LINEAR."
THERE IS NO GREAT CAUSE AND EFFECT.
THERE IS NO FINAL DESTINY.
"WE MUST LIVE OUR LIVES...IN BETWEEN."
LOOK NOW, LEONID...

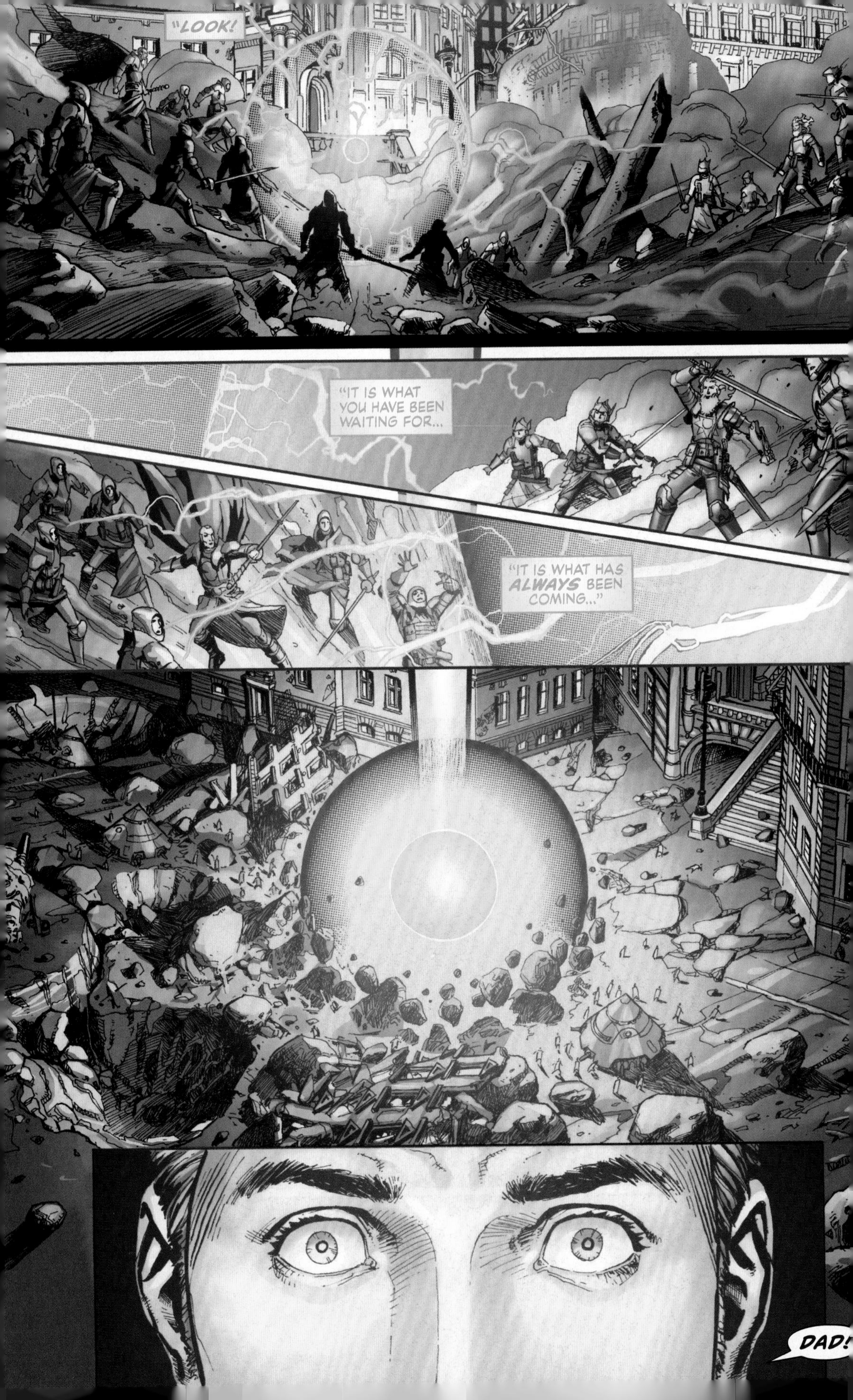
"LOOK!
"IT IS WHAT YOU HAVE BEEN WAITING FOR...
"IT IS WHAT HAS ALWAYS BEEN COMING..."
DAD!

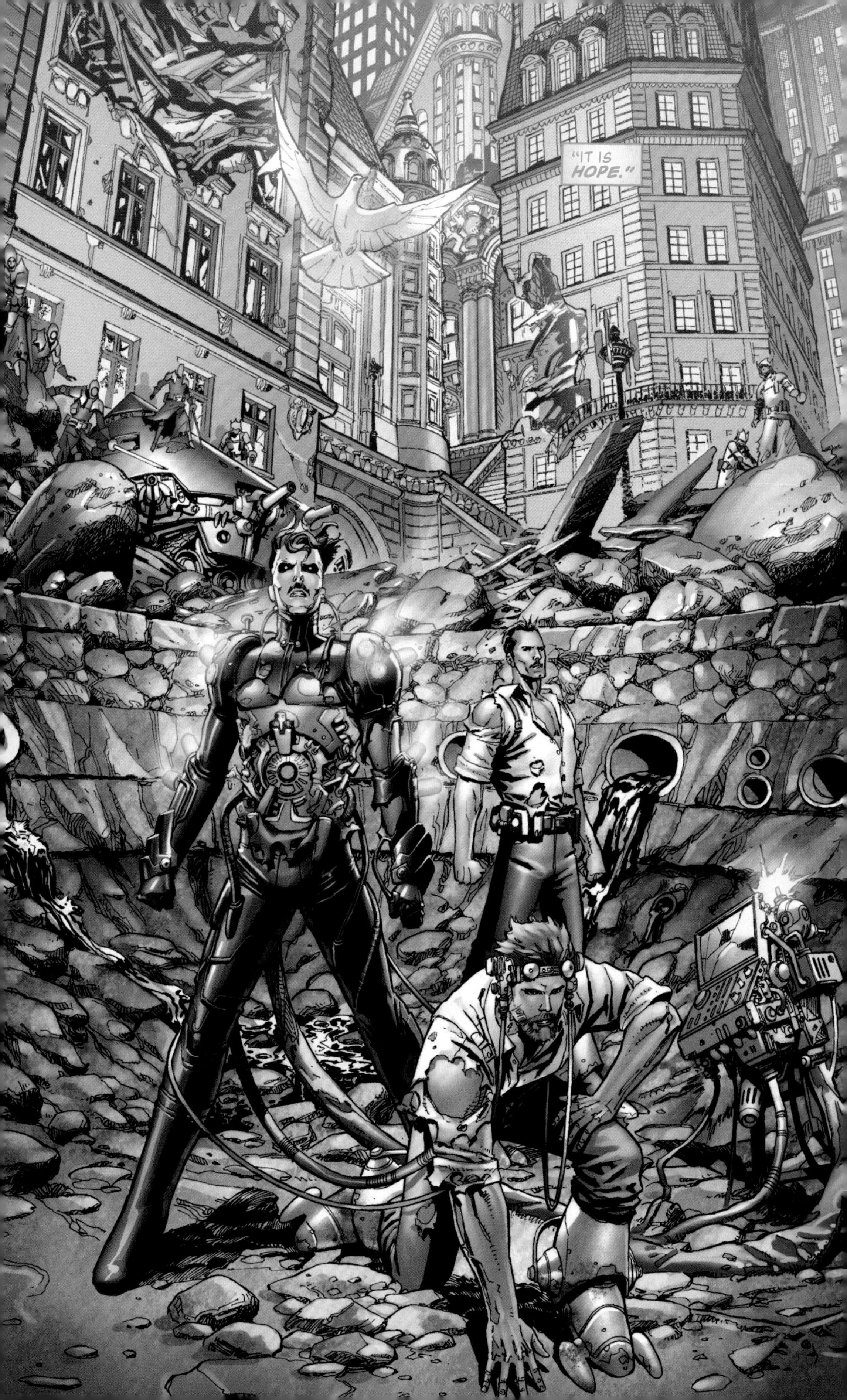
"IT IS HOPE."

Chapter Two

"Fire"

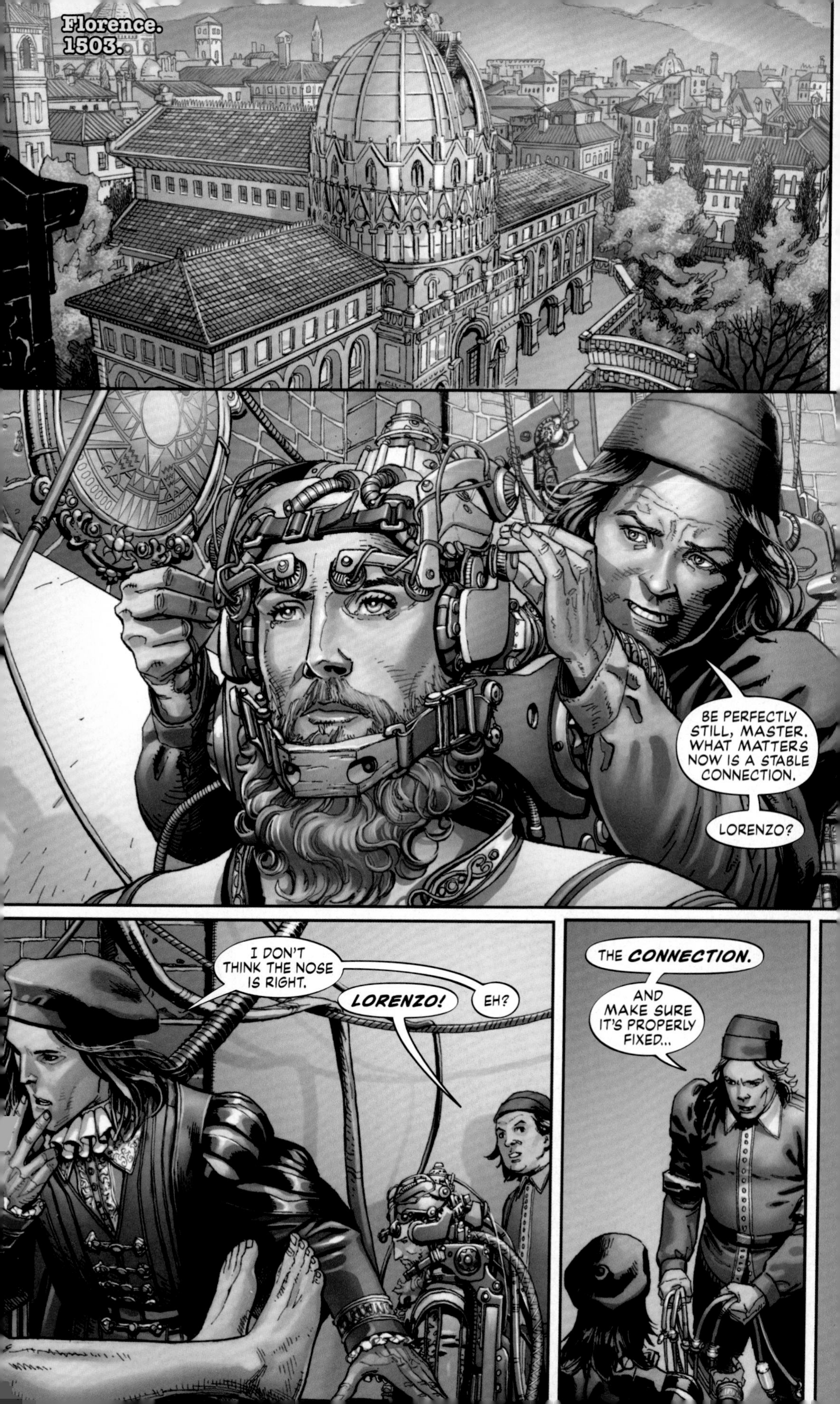
Florence.
1503.
BE PERFECTLY STILL, MASTER. WHAT MATTERS NOW IS A STABLE CONNECTION.
LORENZO?
I DON'T THINK THE NOSE IS RIGHT.
LORENZO!
EH?
THE CONNECTION.
AND MAKE SURE IT'S PROPERLY FIXED...

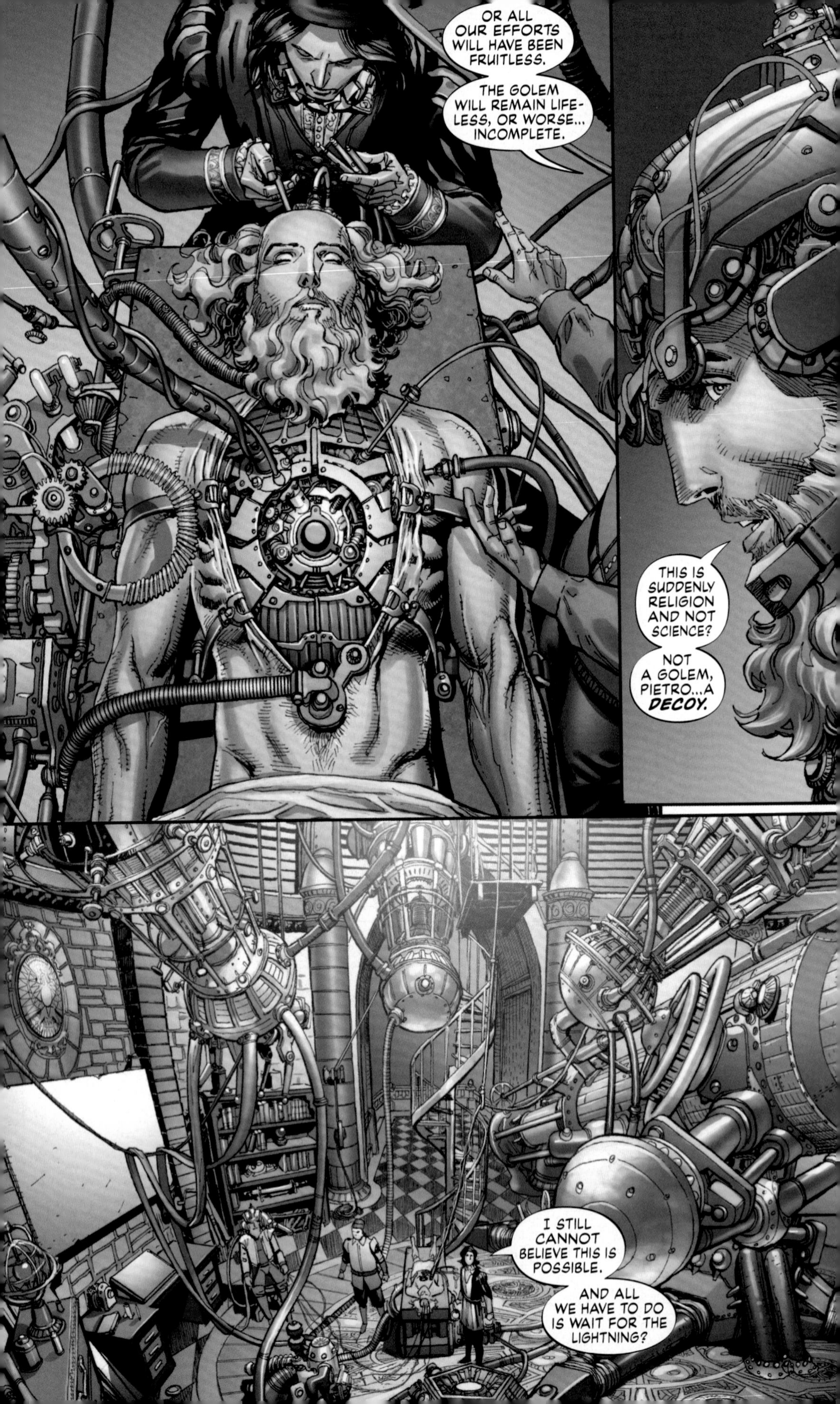
OR ALL OUR EFFORTS WILL HAVE BEEN FRUITLESS.
THE GOLEM WILL REMAIN LIFE-LESS, OR WORSE... INCOMPLETE.
THIS IS SUDDENLY RELIGION AND NOT SCIENCE?
NOT A GOLEM, PIETRO...A *DECOY.*
I STILL CANNOT BELIEVE THIS IS POSSIBLE.
AND ALL WE HAVE TO DO IS WAIT FOR THE LIGHTNING?

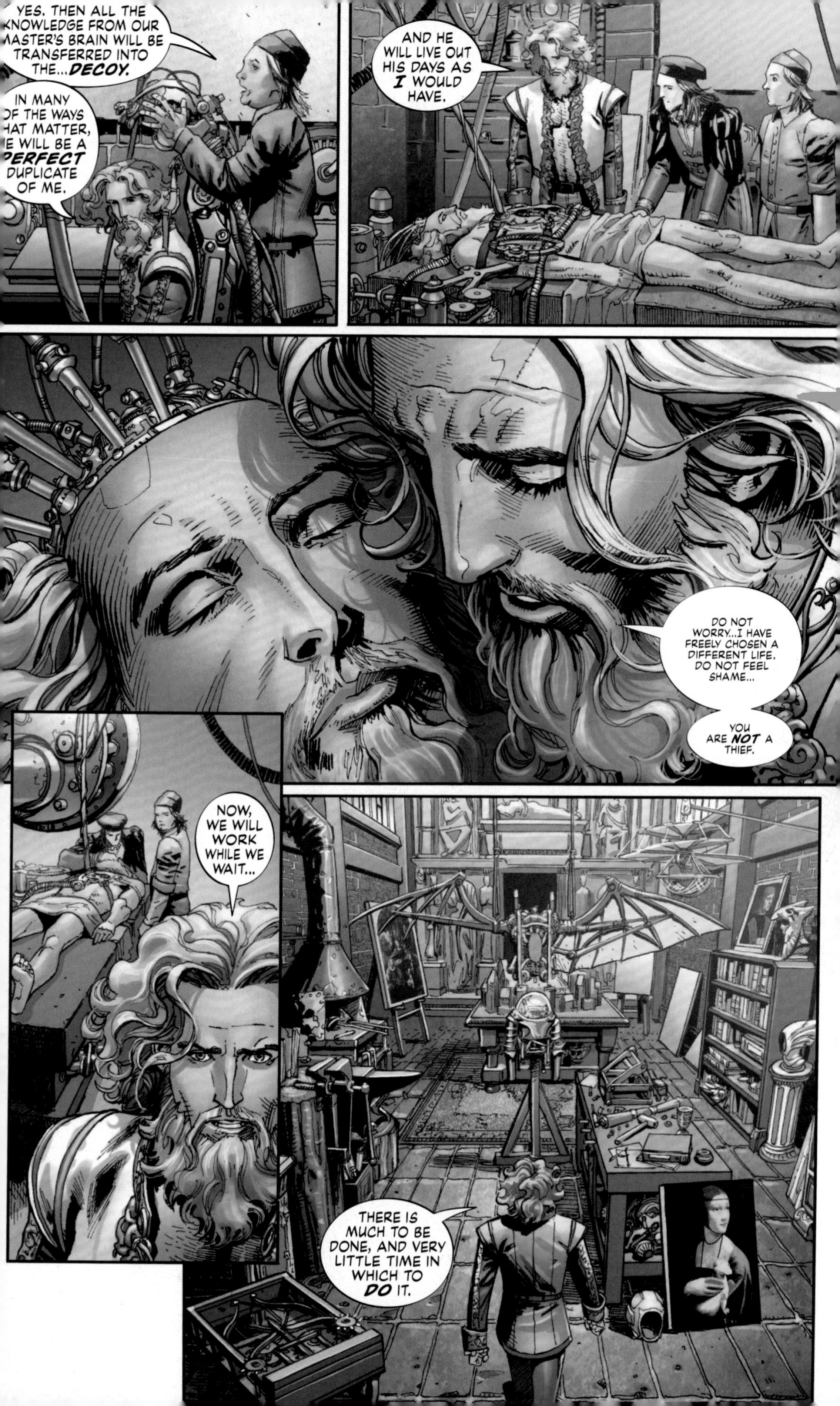
YES. THEN ALL THE KNOWLEDGE FROM OUR MASTER'S BRAIN WILL BE TRANSFERRED INTO THE...DECOY.
IN MANY OF THE WAYS THAT MATTER, HE WILL BE A PERFECT DUPLICATE OF ME.
AND HE WILL LIVE OUT HIS DAYS AS I WOULD HAVE.
DO NOT WORRY...I HAVE FREELY CHOSEN A DIFFERENT LIFE. DO NOT FEEL SHAME...
YOU ARE NOT A THIEF.
NOW, WE WILL WORK WHILE WE WAIT...
THERE IS MUCH TO BE DONE, AND VERY LITTLE TIME IN WHICH TO DO IT.

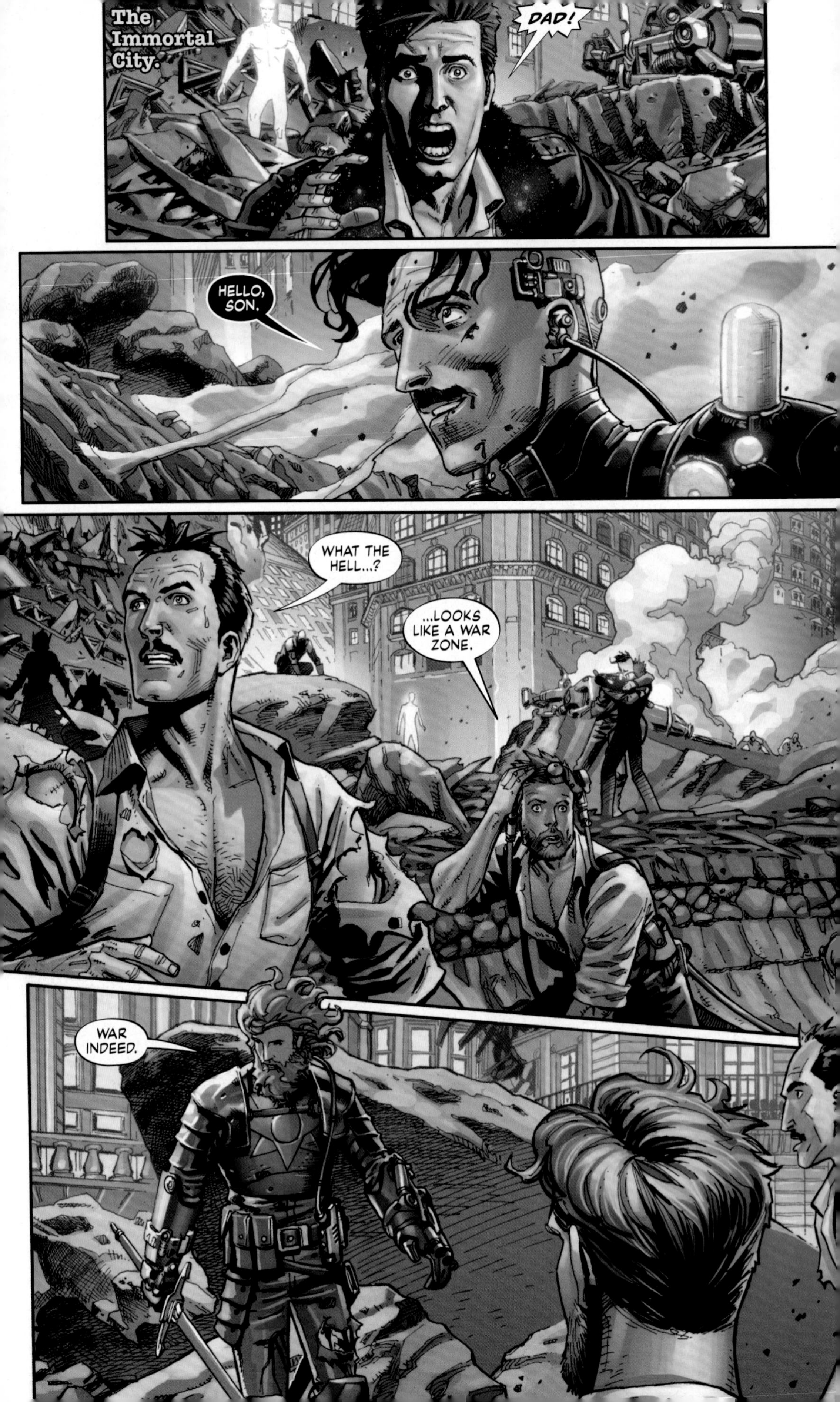
The Immortal City.
DAD!
HELLO, SON.
WHAT THE HELL...?
...LOOKS LIKE A WAR ZONE.
WAR INDEED.

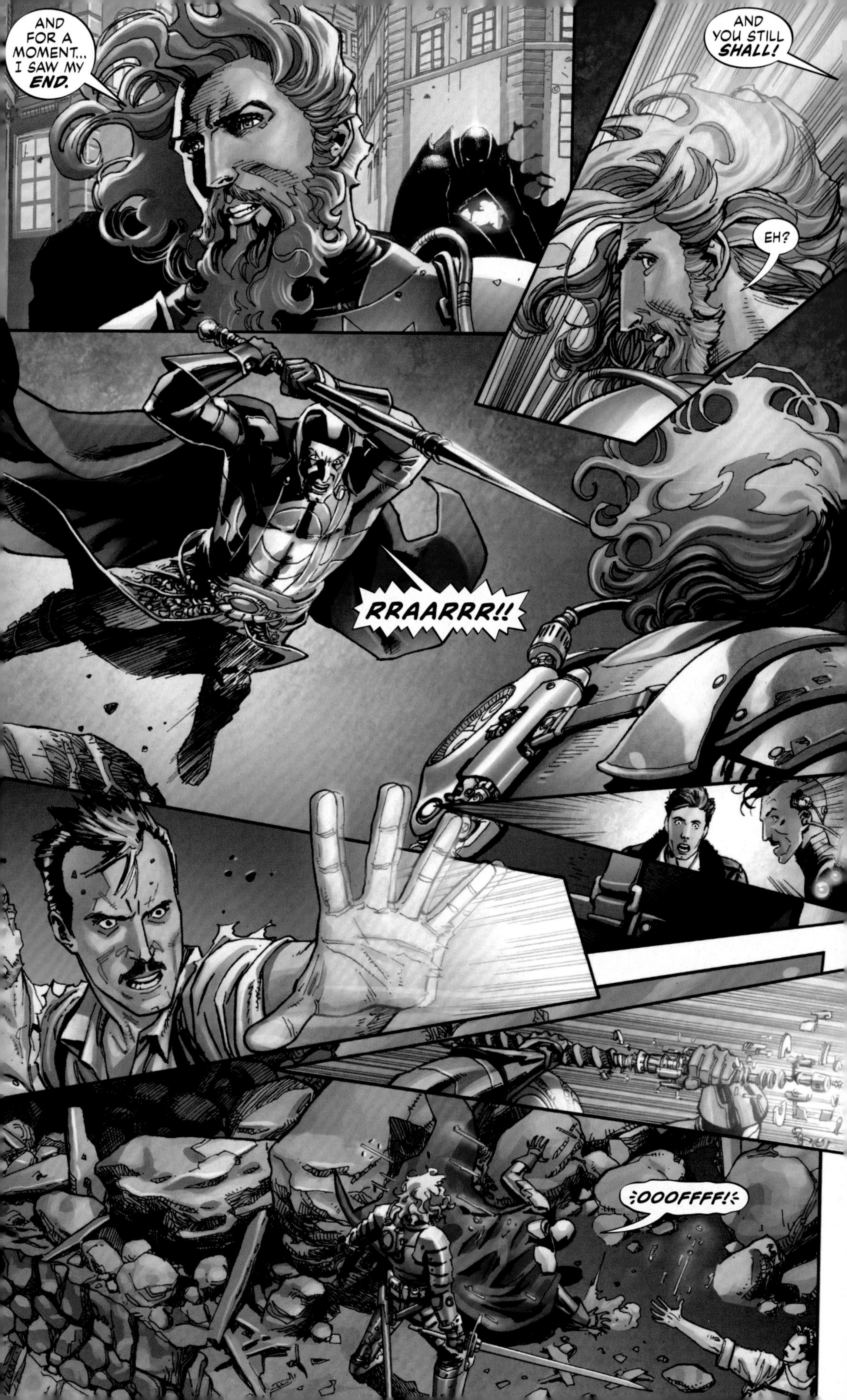
AND FOR A MOMENT... I SAW MY **END.**
AND YOU STILL **SHALL!**
EH?
RRAARRR!!
OOOFFFF!

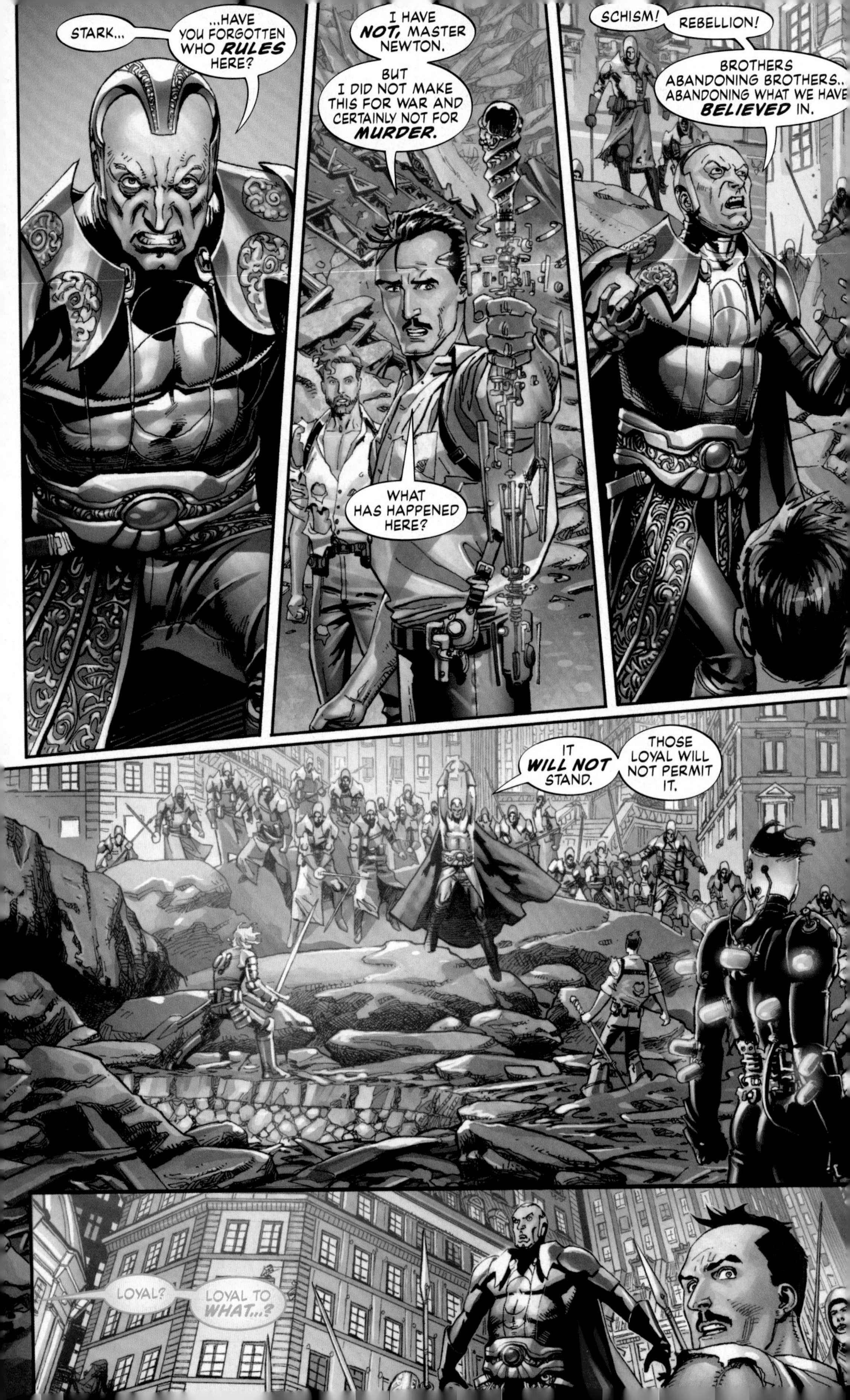
STARK...
...HAVE YOU FORGOTTEN WHO **RULES** HERE?
I HAVE **NOT,** MASTER NEWTON.
BUT I DID NOT MAKE THIS FOR WAR AND CERTAINLY NOT FOR **MURDER.**
WHAT HAS HAPPENED HERE?
SCHISM!
REBELLION!
BROTHERS ABANDONING BROTHERS.. ABANDONING WHAT WE HAVE **BELIEVED** IN.
IT **WILL NOT** STAND.
THOSE LOYAL WILL NOT PERMIT IT.
LOYAL?
LOYAL TO **WHAT...?**

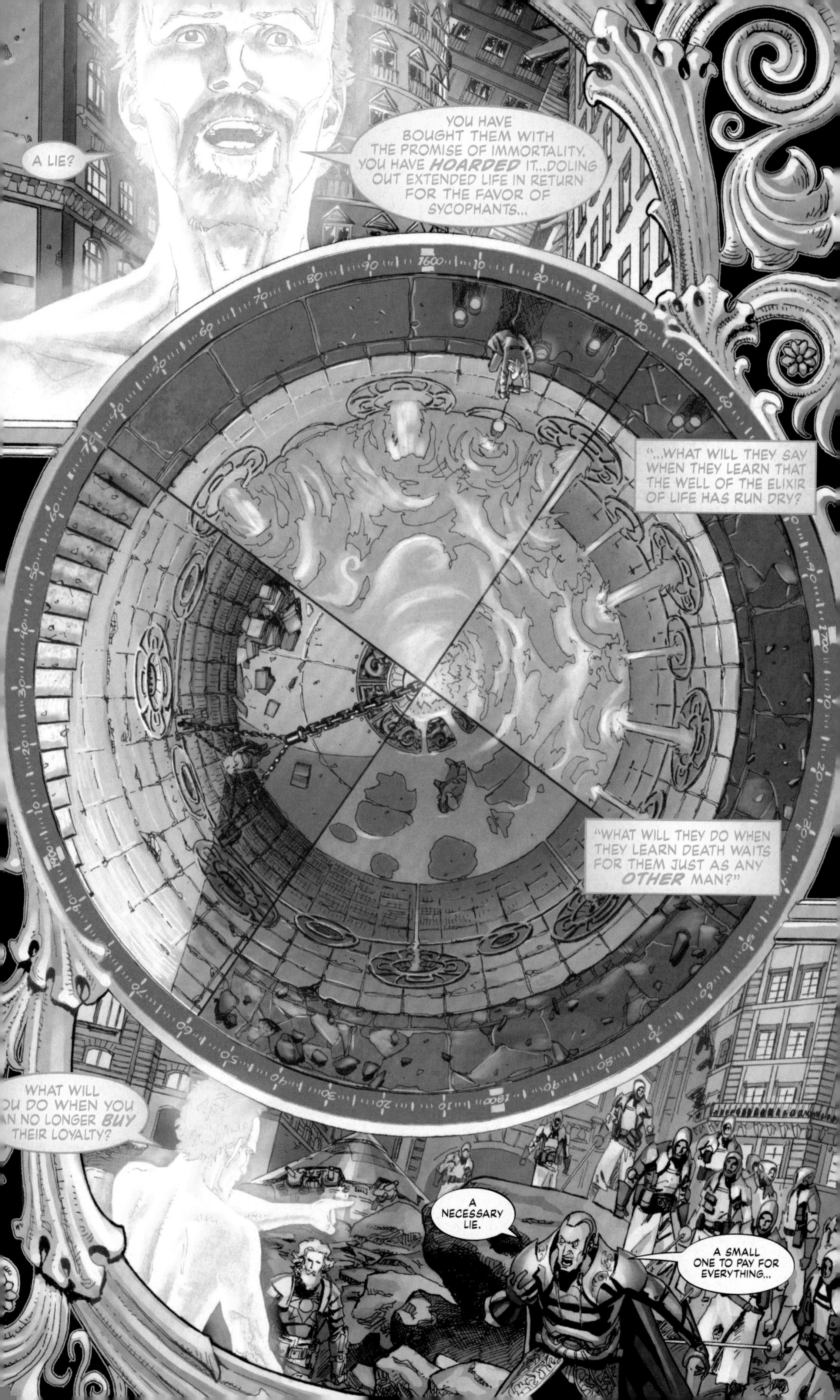

A LIE?
YOU HAVE BOUGHT THEM WITH THE PROMISE OF IMMORTALITY. YOU HAVE HOARDED IT...DOLING OUT EXTENDED LIFE IN RETURN FOR THE FAVOR OF SYCOPHANTS...
"...WHAT WILL THEY SAY WHEN THEY LEARN THAT THE WELL OF THE ELIXIR OF LIFE HAS RUN DRY?
"WHAT WILL THEY DO WHEN THEY LEARN DEATH WAITS FOR THEM JUST AS ANY OTHER MAN?"
WHAT WILL
A NECESSARY LIE.
A SMALL ONE TO PAY FOR EVERYTHING...

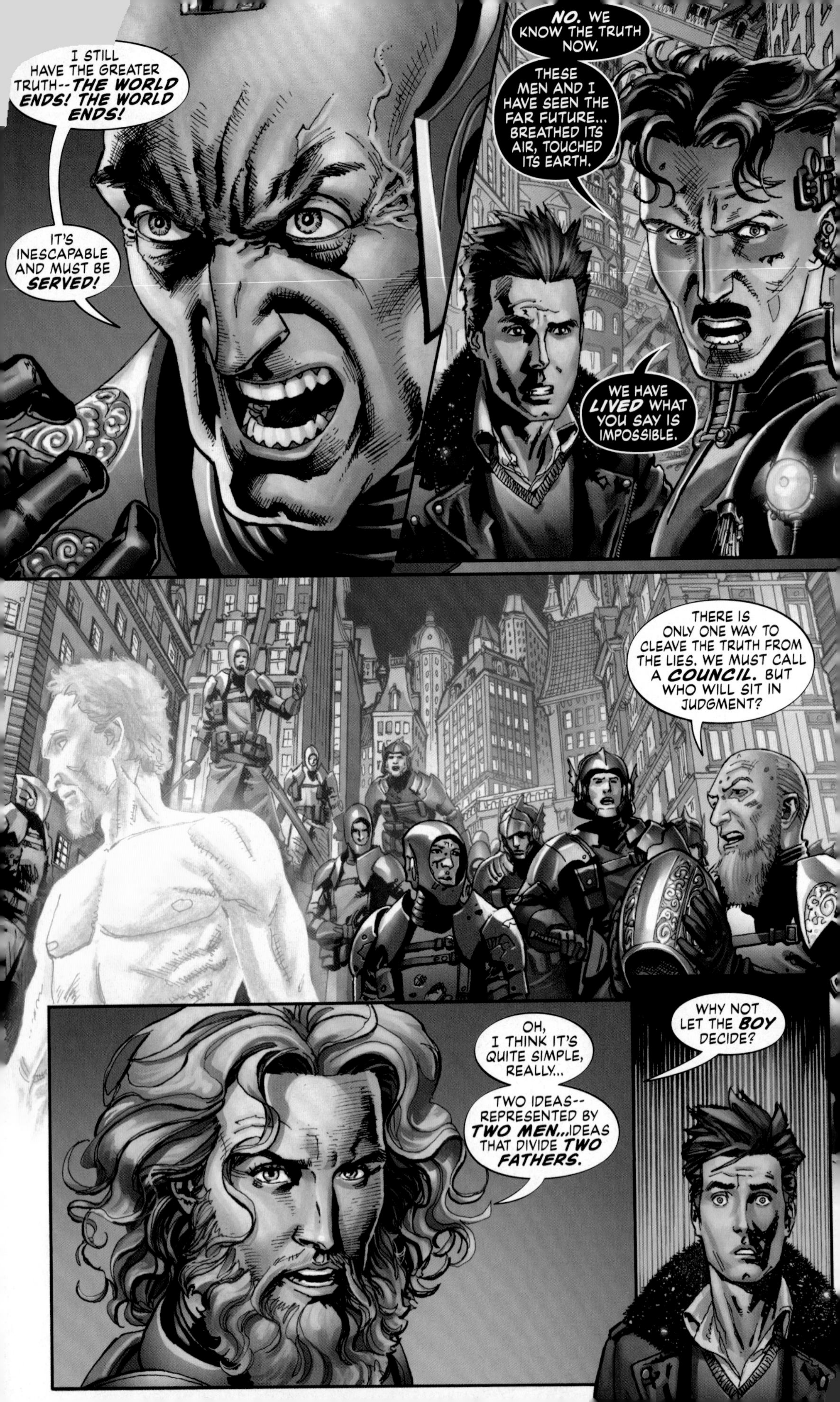
I STILL HAVE THE GREATER TRUTH--THE WORLD ENDS! THE WORLD ENDS!
IT'S INESCAPABLE AND MUST BE SERVED!
NO. WE KNOW THE TRUTH NOW.
THESE MEN AND I HAVE SEEN THE FAR FUTURE... BREATHED ITS AIR, TOUCHED ITS EARTH.
WE HAVE LIVED WHAT YOU SAY IS IMPOSSIBLE.
THERE IS ONLY ONE WAY TO CLEAVE THE TRUTH FROM THE LIES. WE MUST CALL A COUNCIL. BUT WHO WILL SIT IN JUDGMENT?
OH, I THINK IT'S QUITE SIMPLE, REALLY...
TWO IDEAS--REPRESENTED BY TWO MEN...IDEAS THAT DIVIDE TWO FATHERS.
WHY NOT LET THE BOY DECIDE?

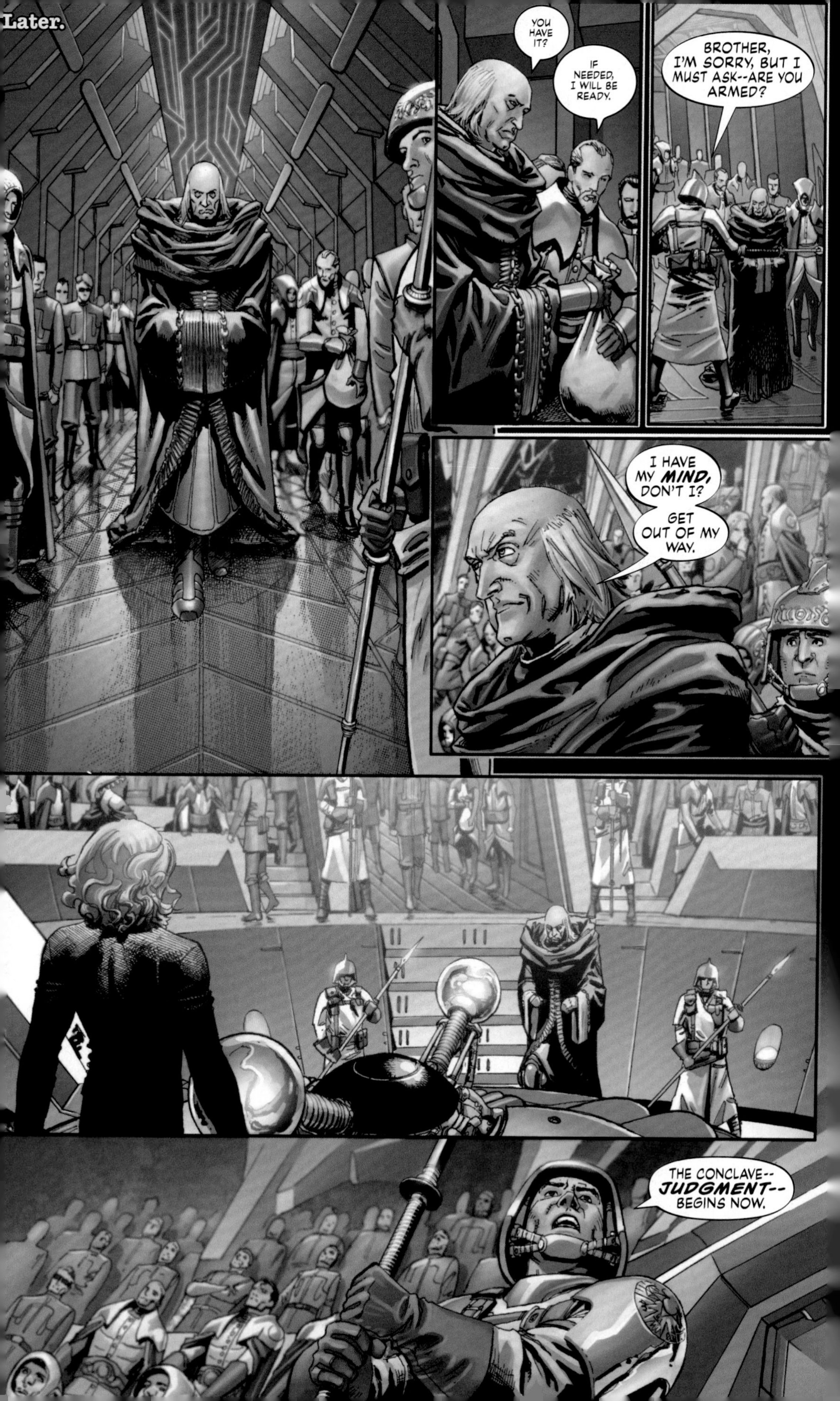

Later.
YOU HAVE IT?
IF NEEDED, I WILL BE READY.
BROTHER, I'M SORRY, BUT I MUST ASK--ARE YOU ARMED?
I HAVE MY MIND, DON'T I?
GET OUT OF MY WAY.
THE CONCLAVE-- JUDGMENT-- BEGINS NOW.

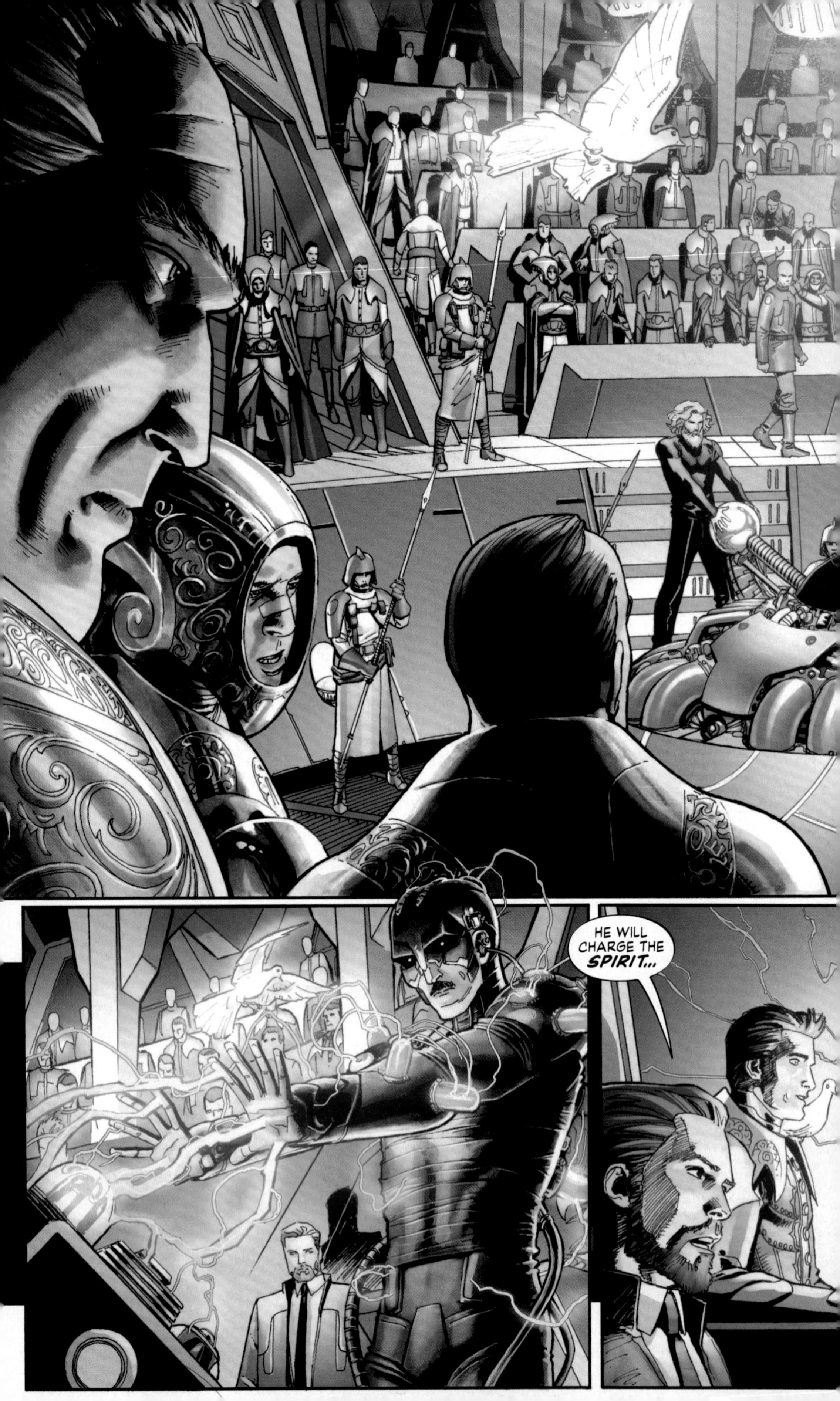
HE WILL CHARGE THE *SPIRIT*...

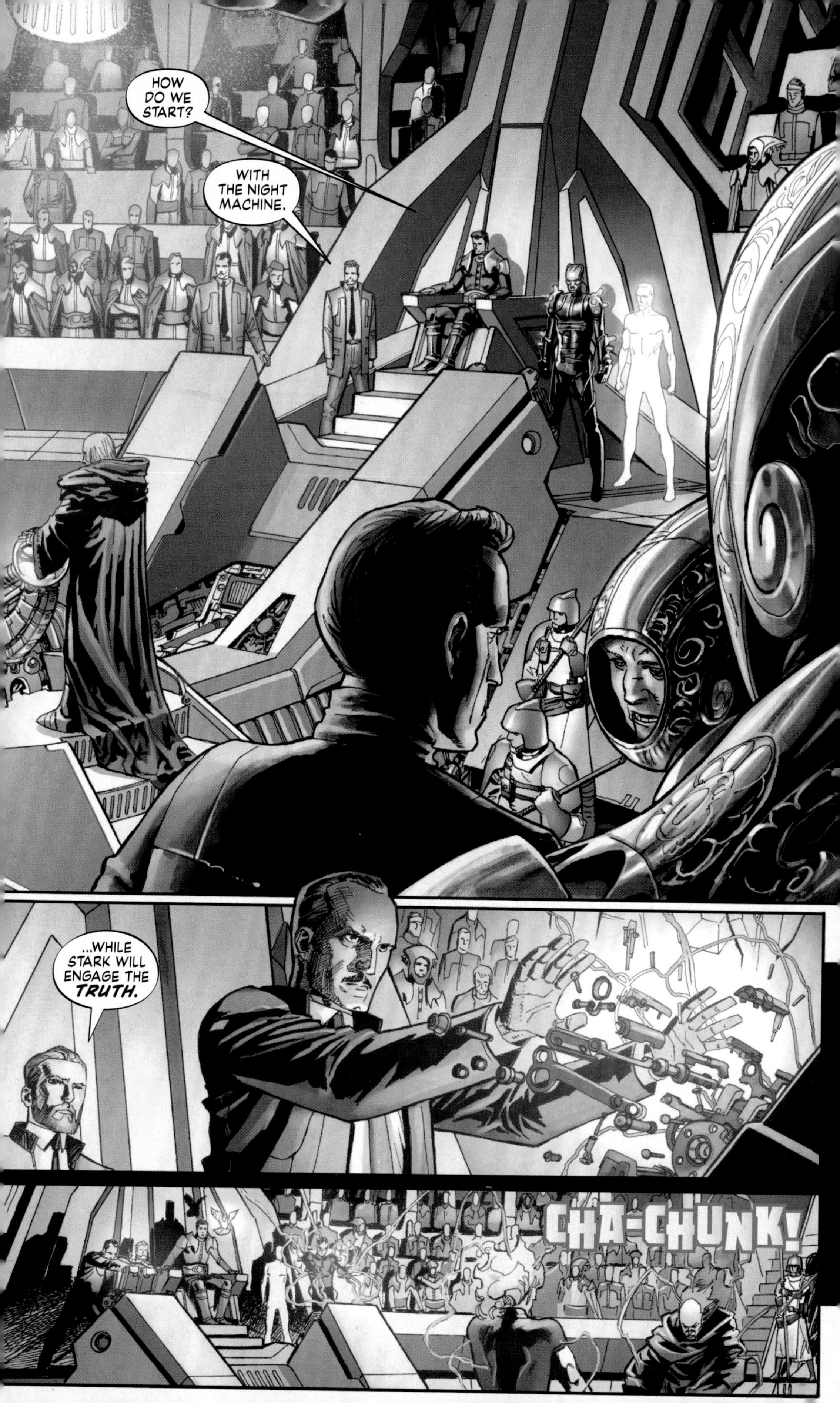
HOW DO WE START?
WITH THE NIGHT MACHINE.
...WHILE STARK WILL ENGAGE THE *TRUTH*.
CHA-CHUNK!

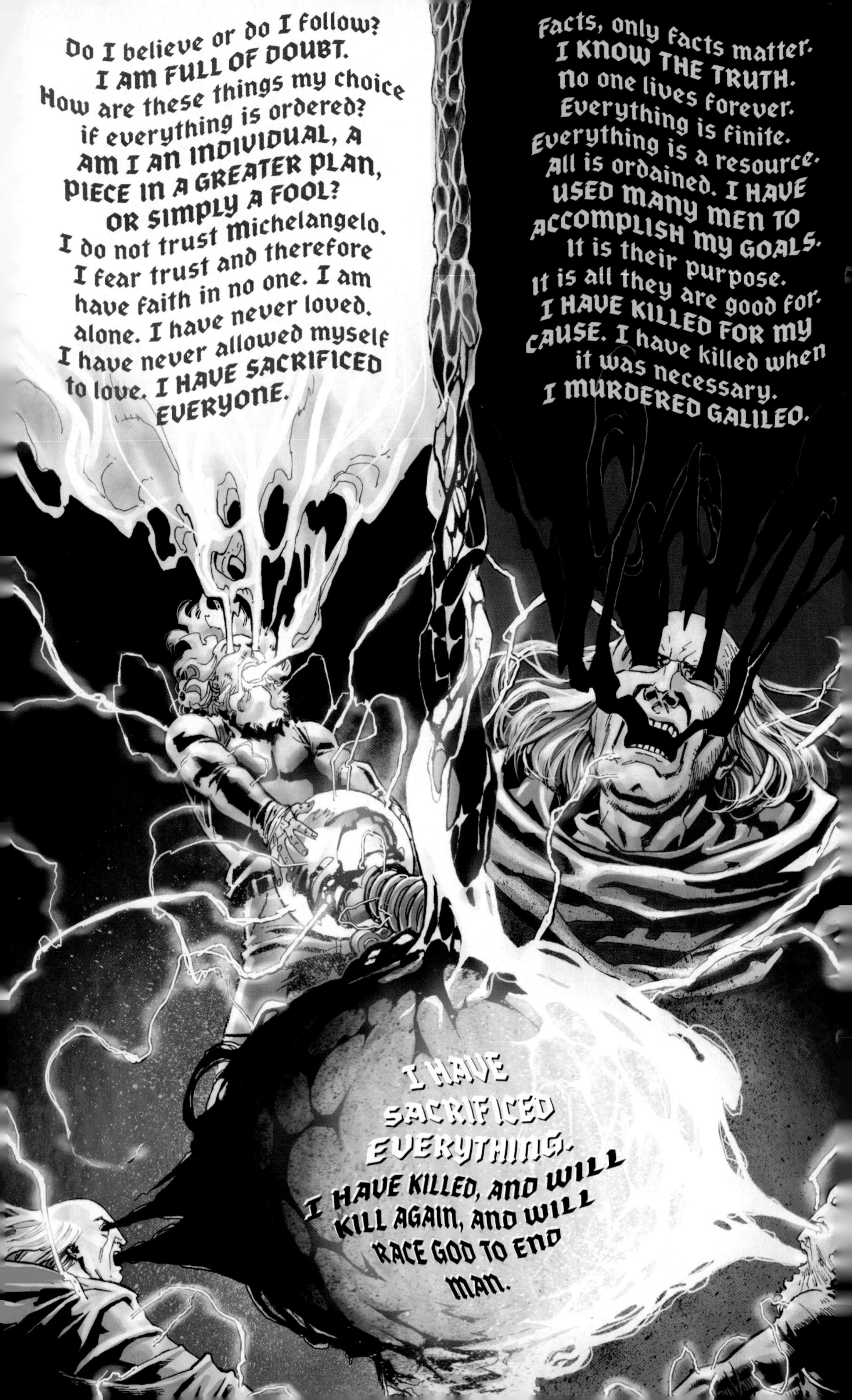
Do I believe or do I follow?
I AM FULL OF DOUBT.
How are these things my choice
if everything is ordered?
AM I AN INDIVIDUAL, A
PIECE IN A GREATER PLAN,
OR SIMPLY A FOOL?
I do not trust Michelangelo.
I fear trust and therefore
have faith in no one. I am
alone. I have never loved.
I have never allowed myself
to love. I HAVE SACRIFICED
EVERYONE.
Facts, only facts matter.
I KNOW THE TRUTH.
No one lives forever.
Everything is finite.
Everything is a resource.
All is ordained. I HAVE
USED MANY MEN TO
ACCOMPLISH MY GOALS.
It is their purpose.
It is all they are good for.
I HAVE KILLED FOR MY
CAUSE. I have killed when
it was necessary.
I MURDERED GALILEO.
I HAVE
SACRIFICED
EVERYTHING.
I HAVE KILLED, AND WILL
KILL AGAIN, AND WILL
RACE GOD TO END
MAN.

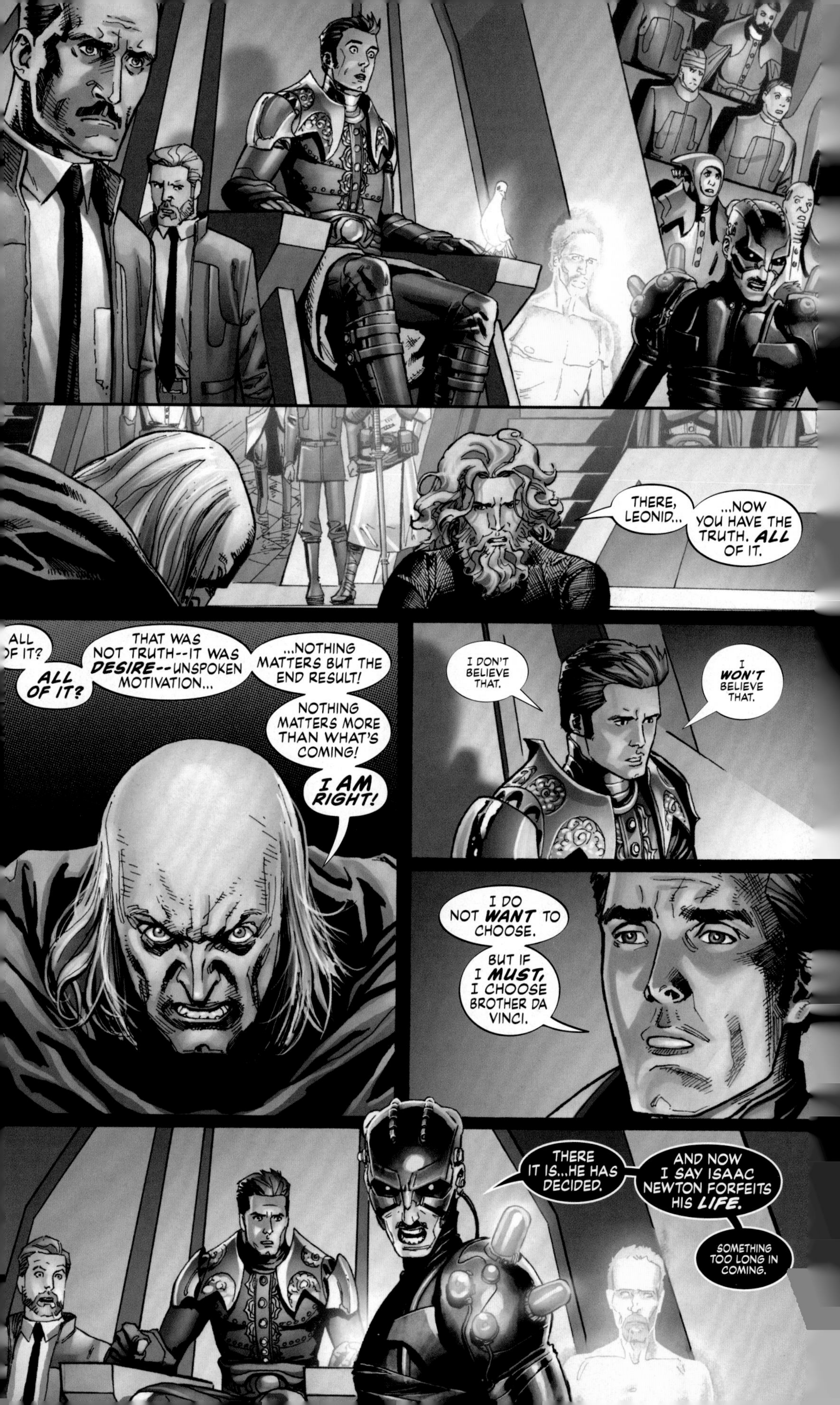

THERE, LEONID...
...NOW YOU HAVE THE TRUTH. ALL OF IT.
ALL OF IT?
ALL OF IT?
THAT WAS NOT TRUTH--IT WAS DESIRE--UNSPOKEN MOTIVATION...
...NOTHING MATTERS BUT THE END RESULT!
NOTHING MATTERS MORE THAN WHAT'S COMING!
I AM RIGHT!
I DON'T BELIEVE THAT.
I WON'T BELIEVE THAT.
I DO NOT WANT TO CHOOSE.
BUT IF I MUST, I CHOOSE BROTHER DA VINCI.
THERE IT IS...HE HAS DECIDED.
AND NOW I SAY ISAAC NEWTON FORFEITS HIS LIFE.
SOMETHING TOO LONG IN COMING.

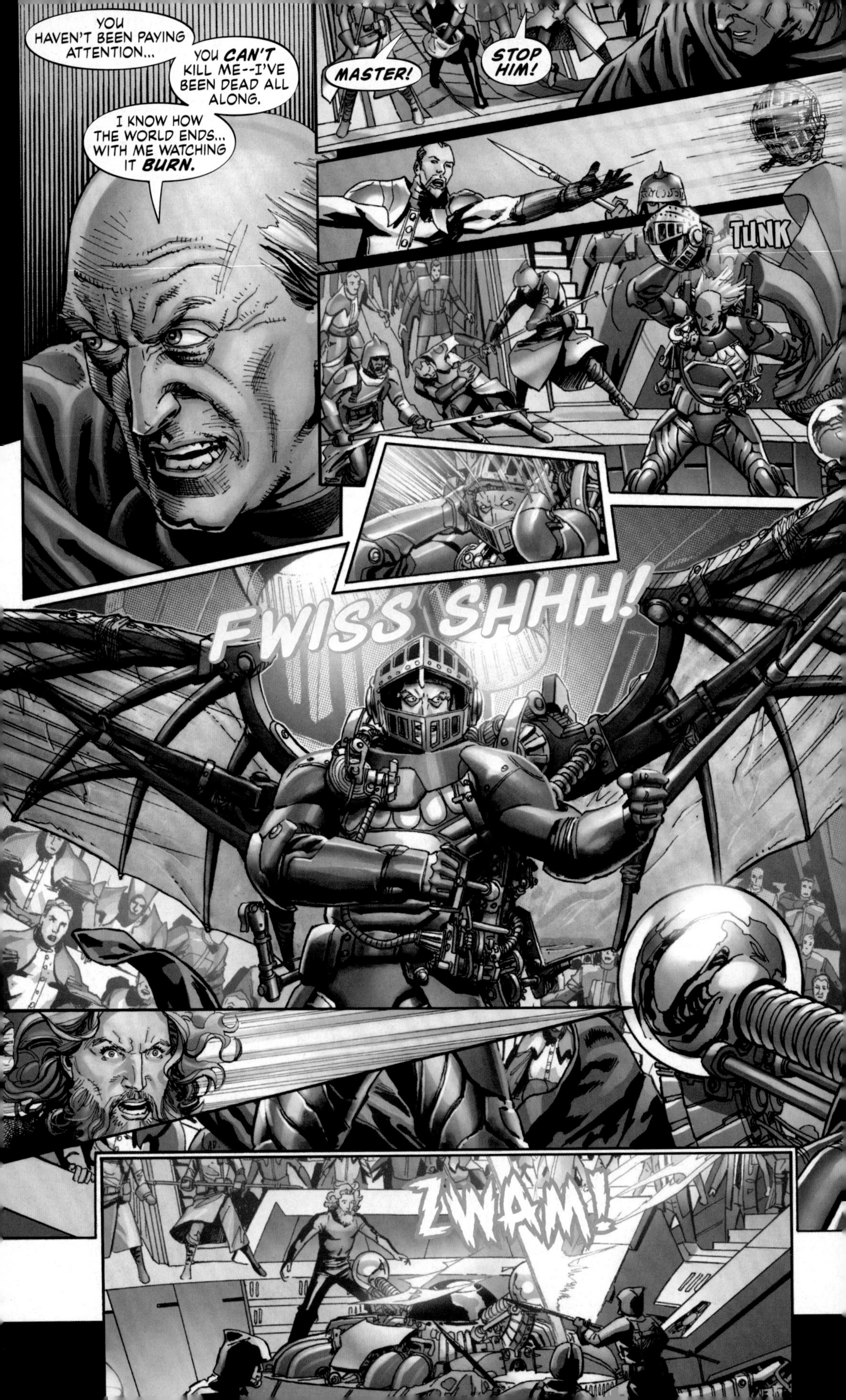
YOU HAVEN'T BEEN PAYING ATTENTION...
YOU **CAN'T** KILL ME--I'VE BEEN DEAD ALL ALONG.
I KNOW HOW THE WORLD ENDS... WITH ME WATCHING IT **BURN.**
MASTER!
STOP HIM!
TUNK
FWISS SHHH!
ZWAM!

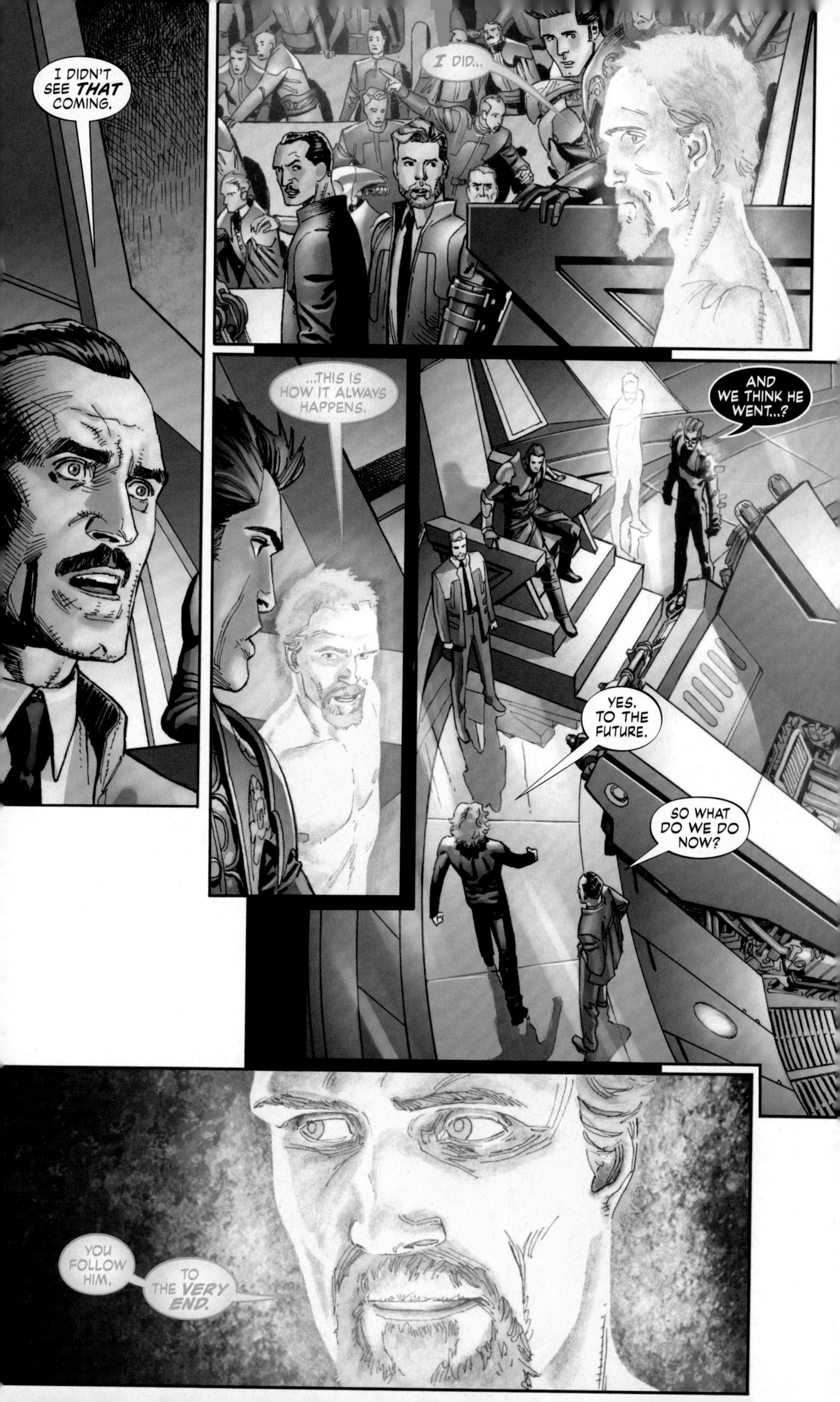
I DIDN'T SEE THAT COMING.
I DID...
...THIS IS HOW IT ALWAYS HAPPENS.
AND WE THINK HE WENT...?
YES. TO THE FUTURE.
SO WHAT DO WE DO NOW?
YOU FOLLOW HIM.
TO THE VERY END.

Later.

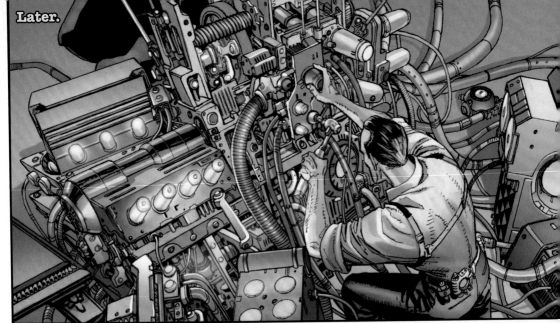

I STILL DON'T UNDERSTAND WHAT IT IS YOU'RE TRYING TO DO HERE.

CAN YOU HAND ME THAT?

THIS?

NO. THE OTHER...YES. THAT'S THE ONE.

SO, WHAT *IS* IT?

IT'S GOING TO BE A MESSAGE.

WE...

...I NEED TO LEAVE SOMETHING BEHIND.

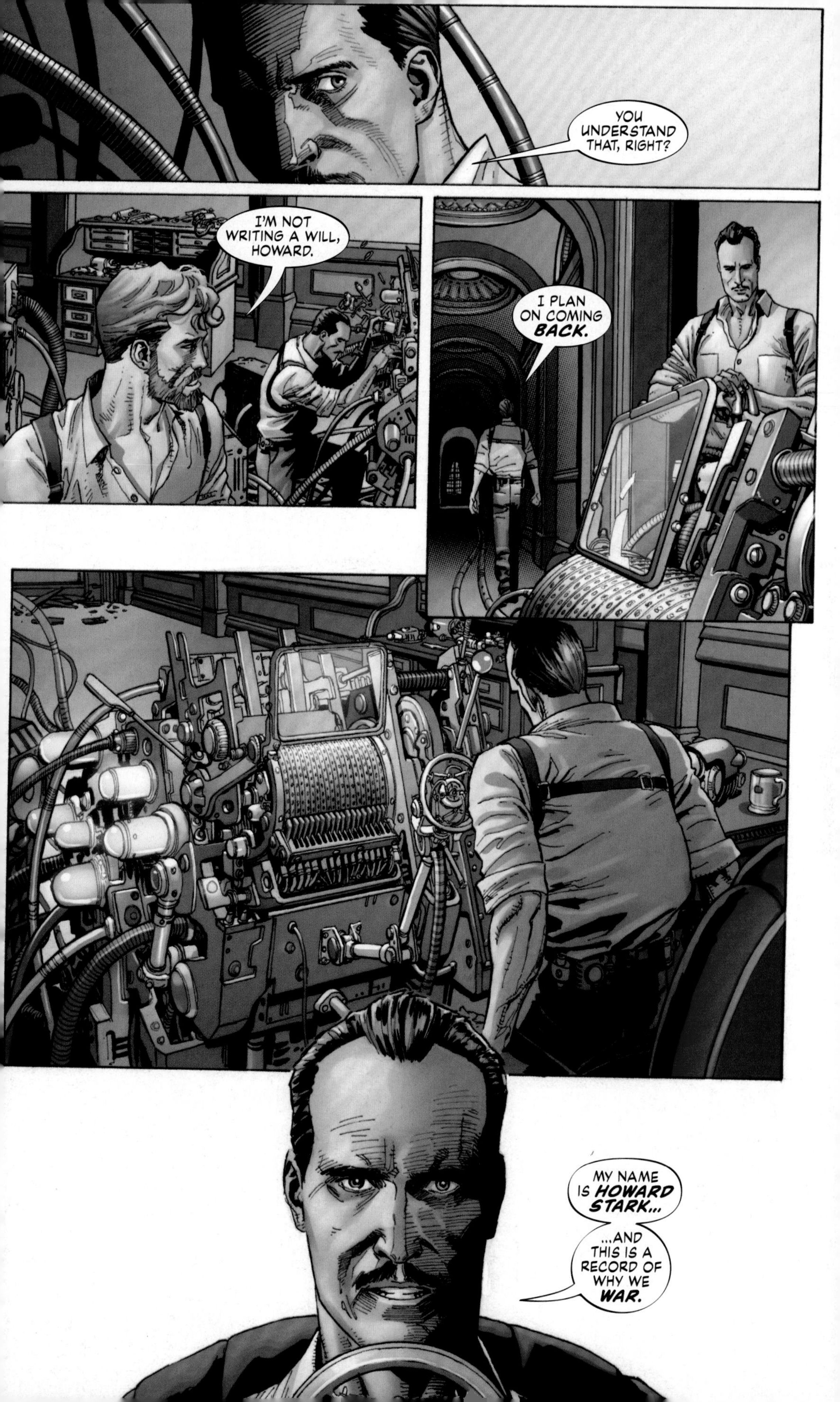
YOU UNDERSTAND THAT, RIGHT?
I'M NOT WRITING A WILL, HOWARD.
I PLAN ON COMING BACK.
MY NAME IS HOWARD STARK...
...AND THIS IS A RECORD OF WHY WE WAR.

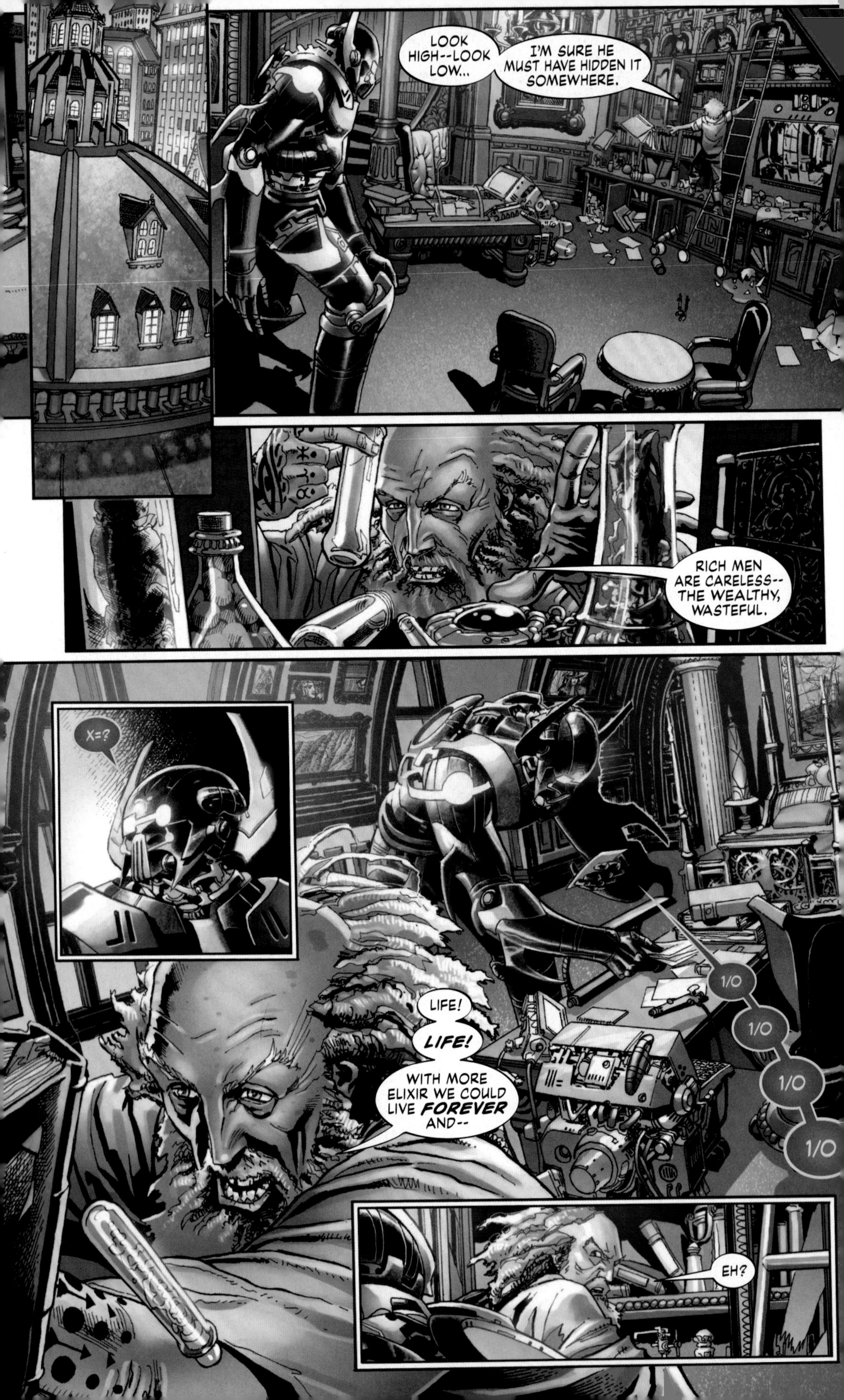
LOOK HIGH--LOOK LOW...
I'M SURE HE MUST HAVE HIDDEN IT SOMEWHERE.
RICH MEN ARE CARELESS-- THE WEALTHY, WASTEFUL.
X=?
LIFE!
LIFE!
WITH MORE ELIXIR WE COULD LIVE FOREVER AND--
1/0
1/0
1/0
1/0
EH?

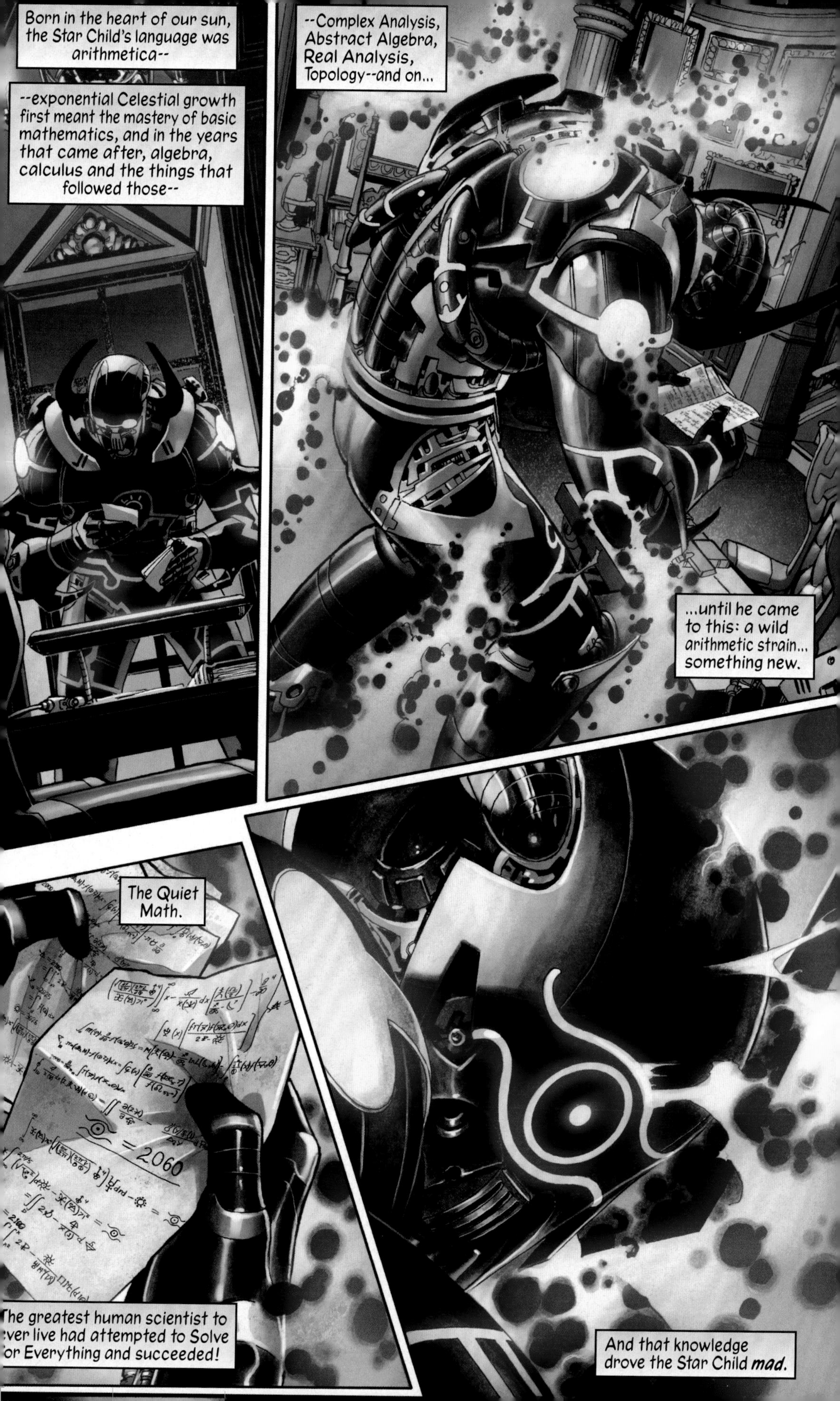
Born in the heart of our sun, the Star Child's language was arithmetica--
--exponential Celestial growth first meant the mastery of basic mathematics, and in the years that came after, algebra, calculus and the things that followed those--
--Complex Analysis, Abstract Algebra, Real Analysis, Topology--and on...
...until he came to this: a wild arithmetic strain... something new.
The Quiet Math.
2060
The greatest human scientist to ever live had attempted to Solve for Everything and succeeded!
And that knowledge drove the Star Child *mad*.

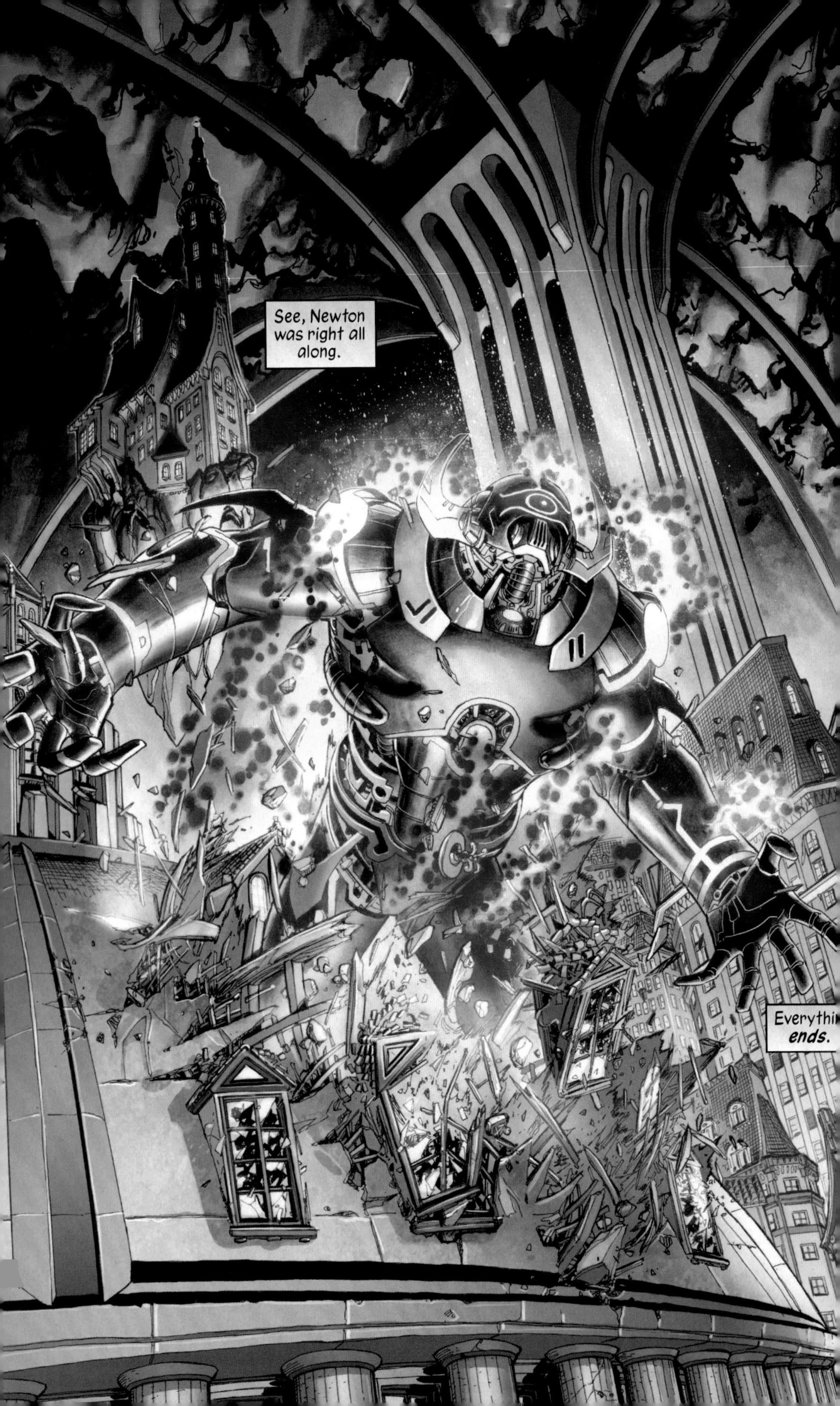
See, Newton was right all along.
Everythi
ends.

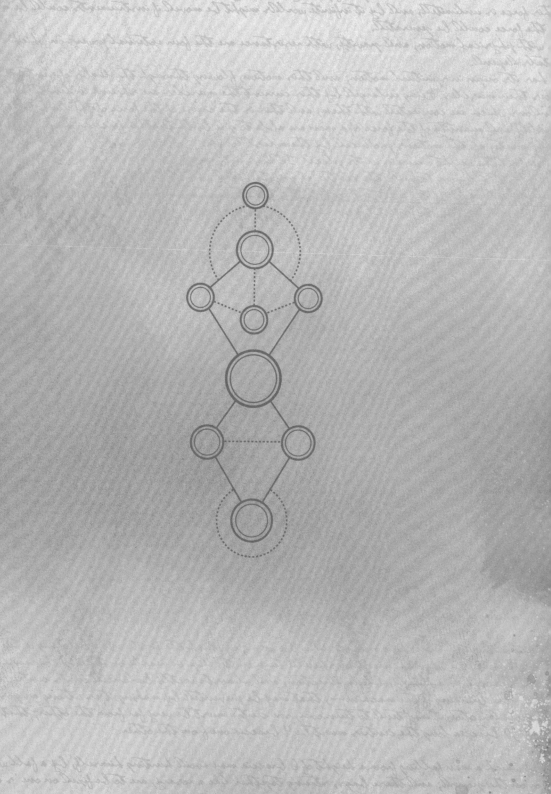

Chapter Three
"The Fall"

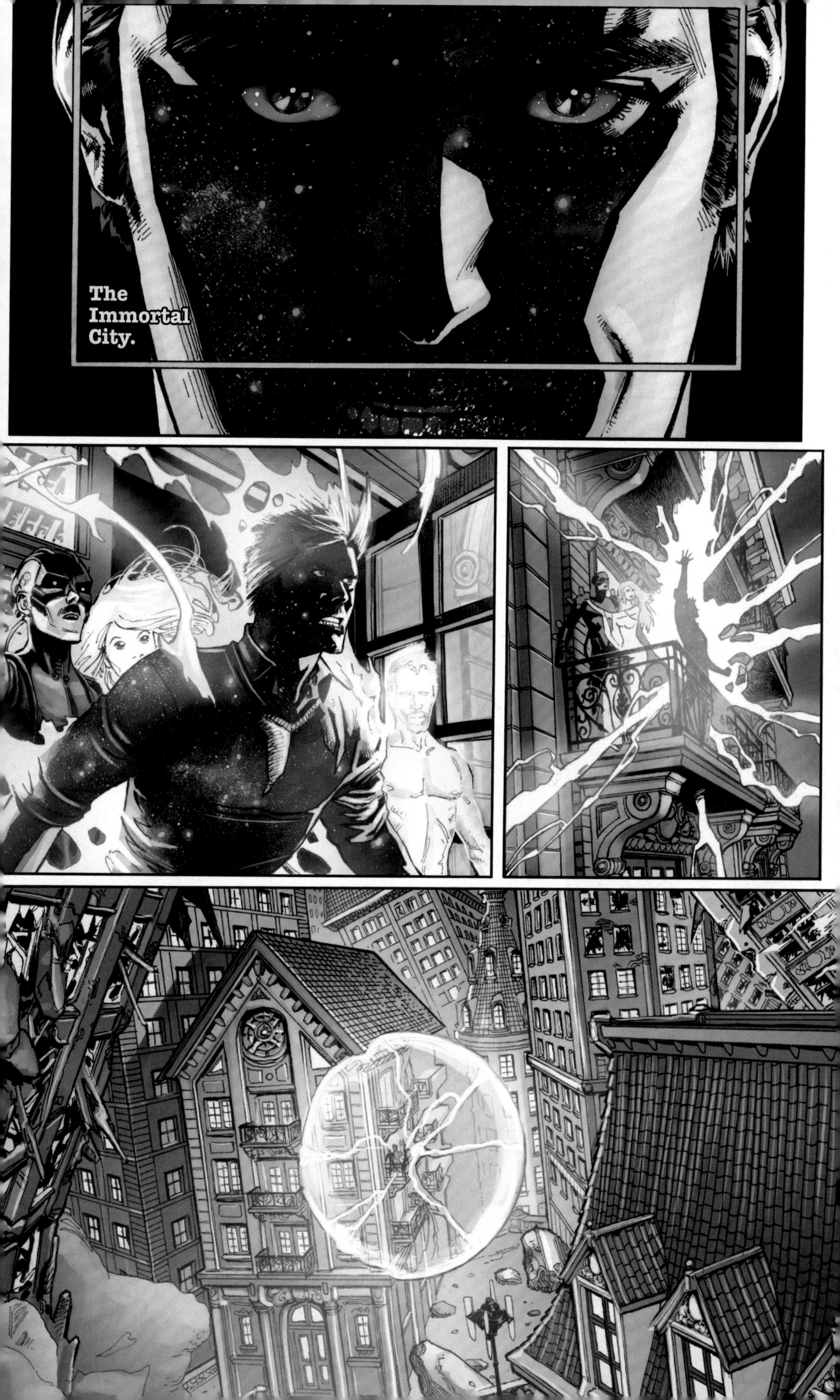
The Immortal City.

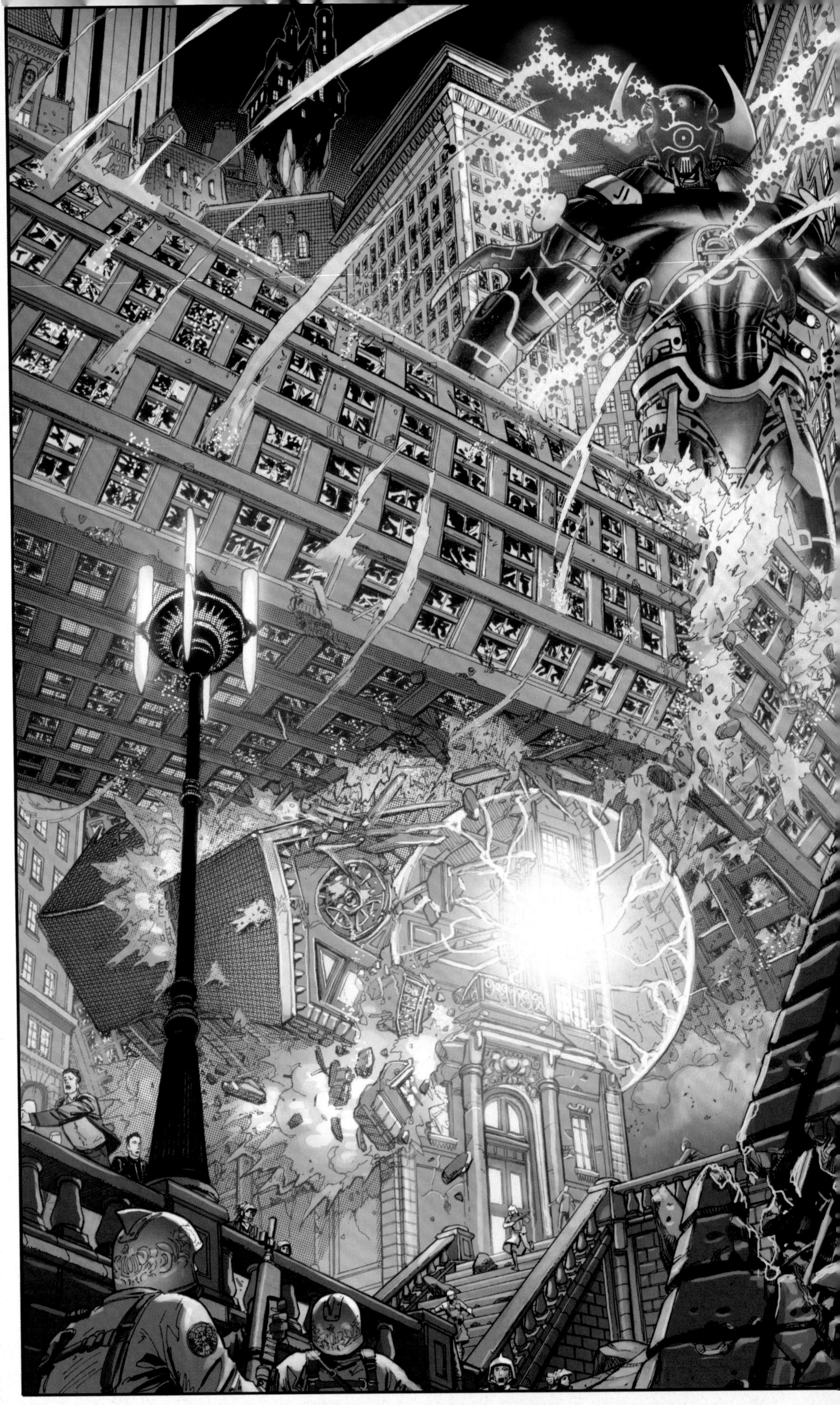

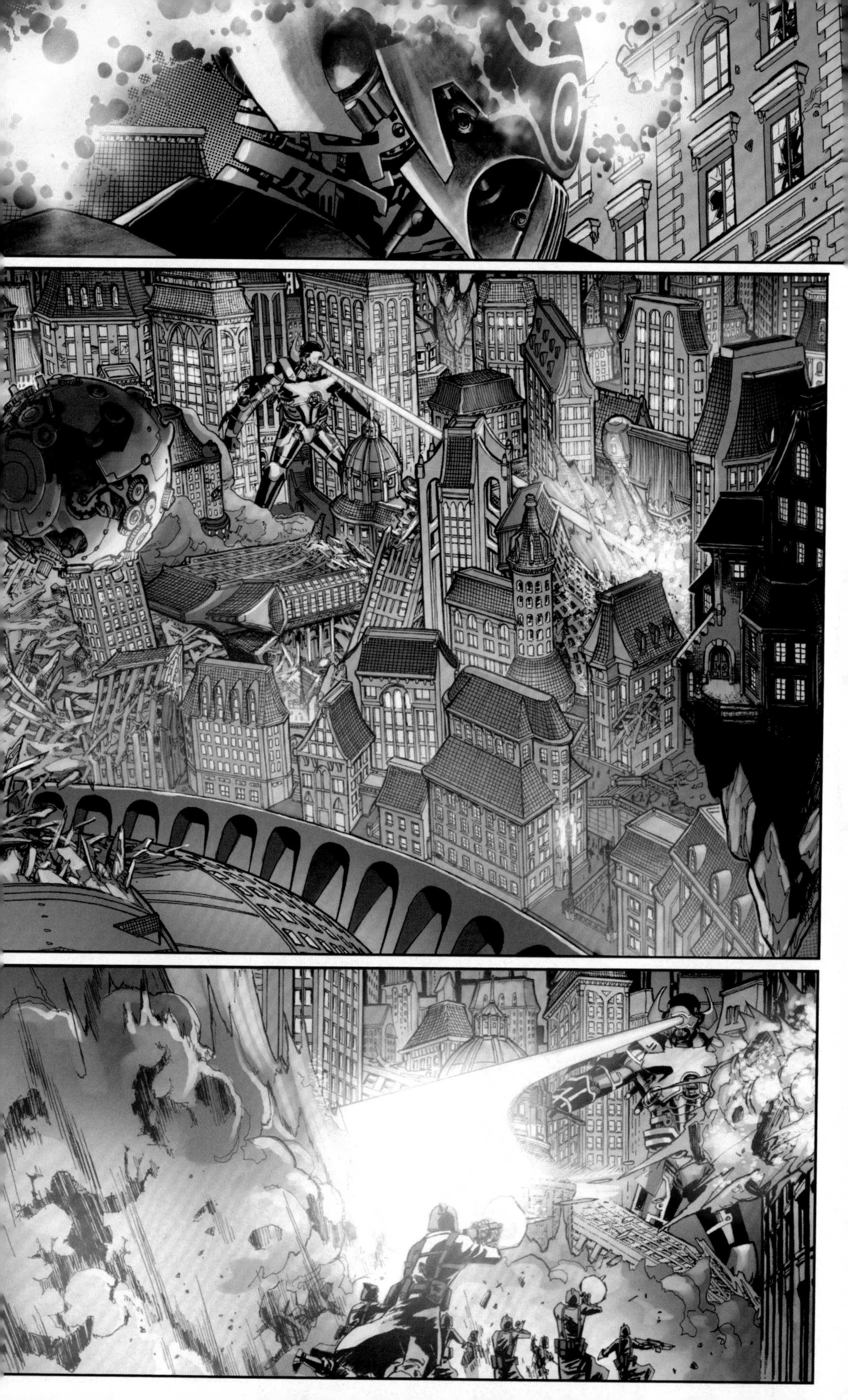

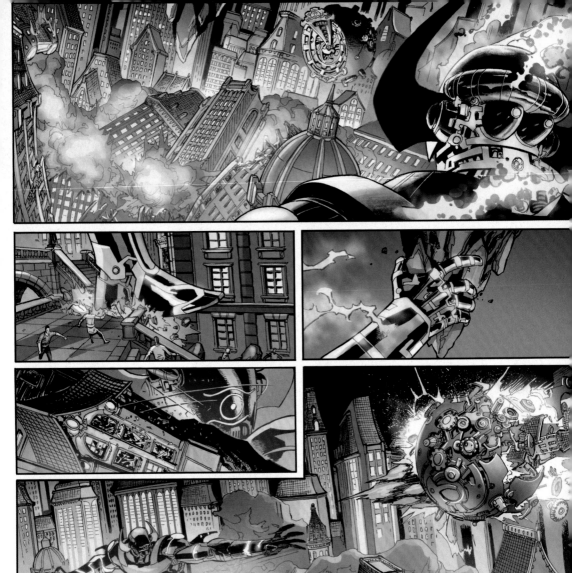

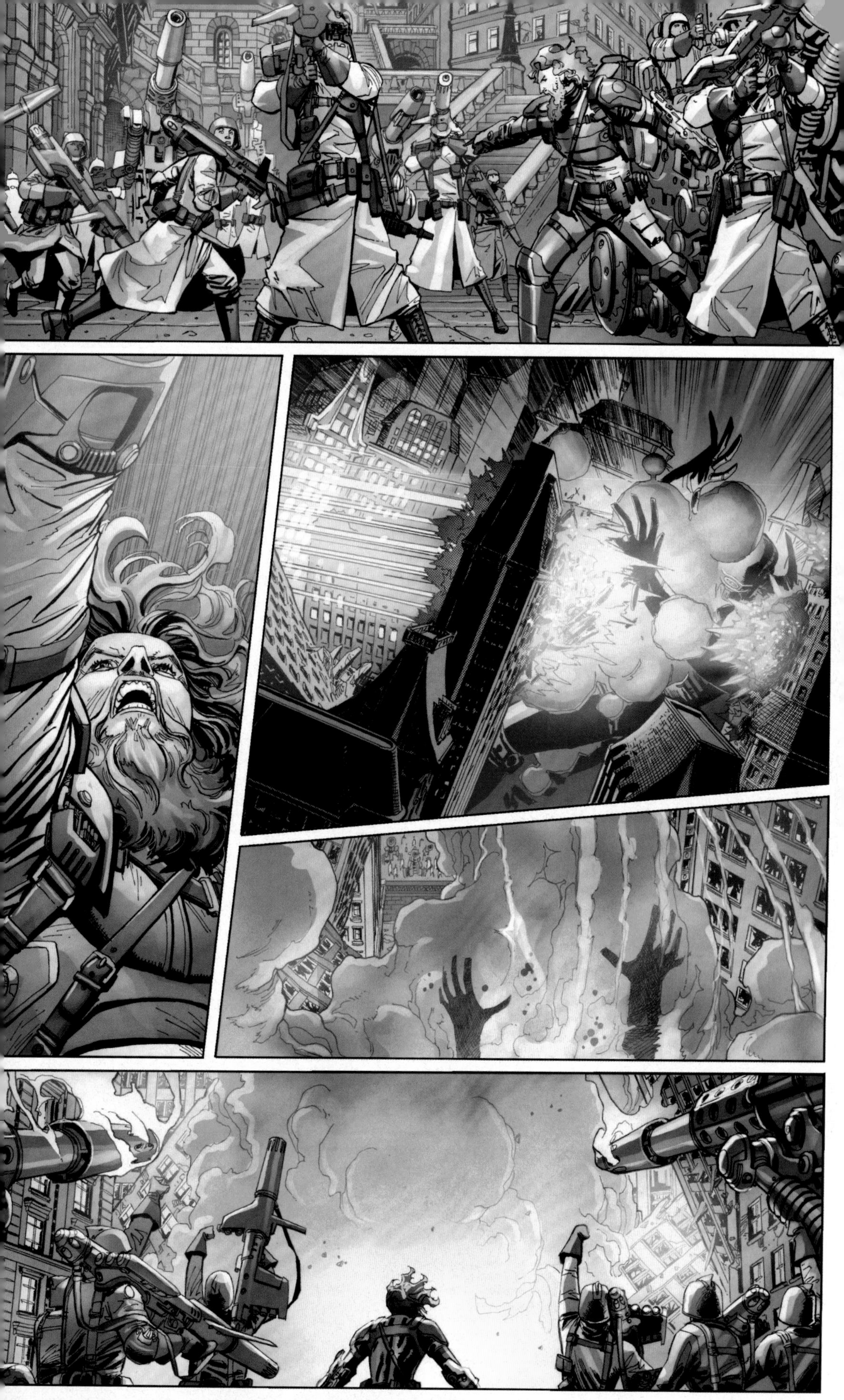

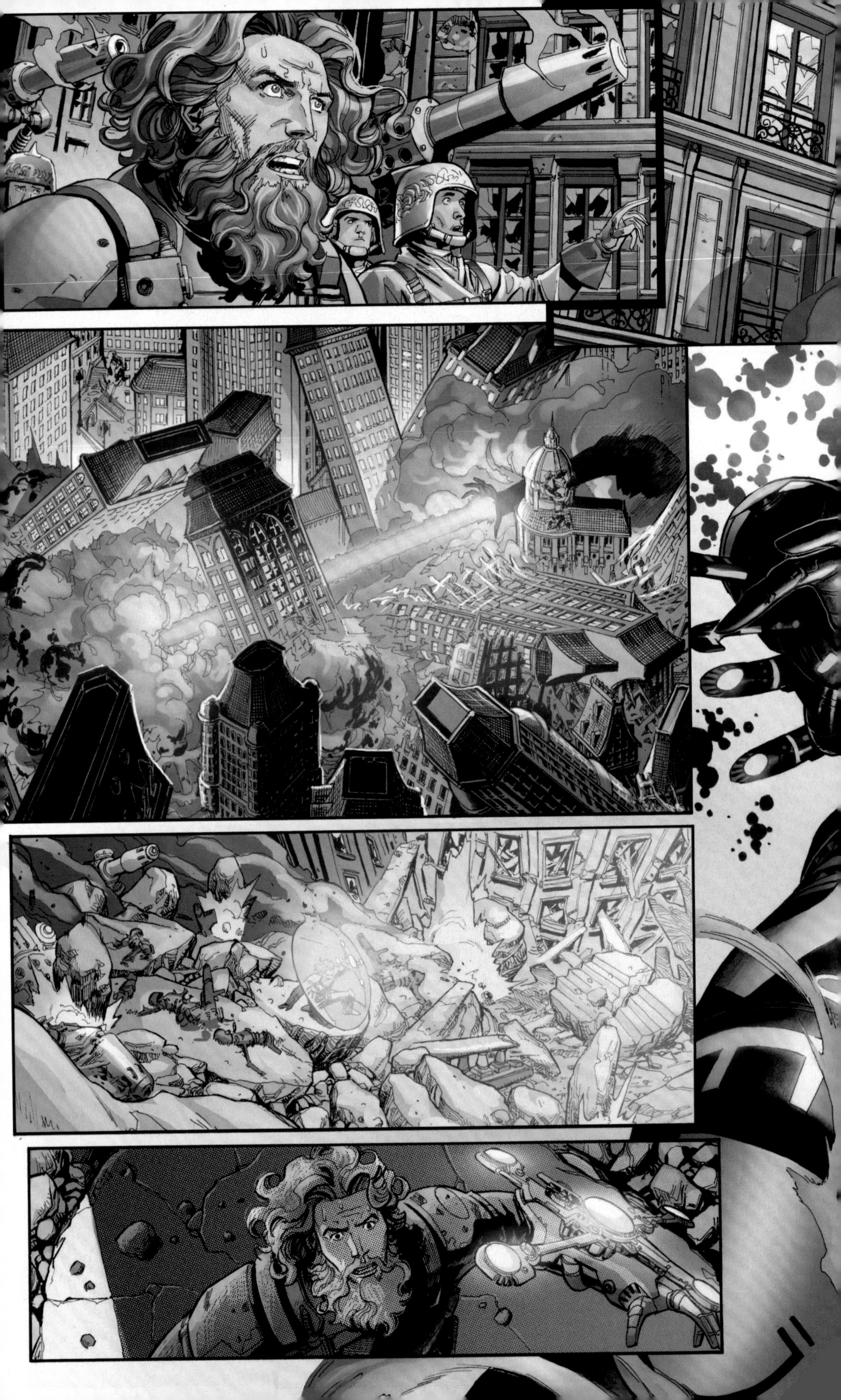

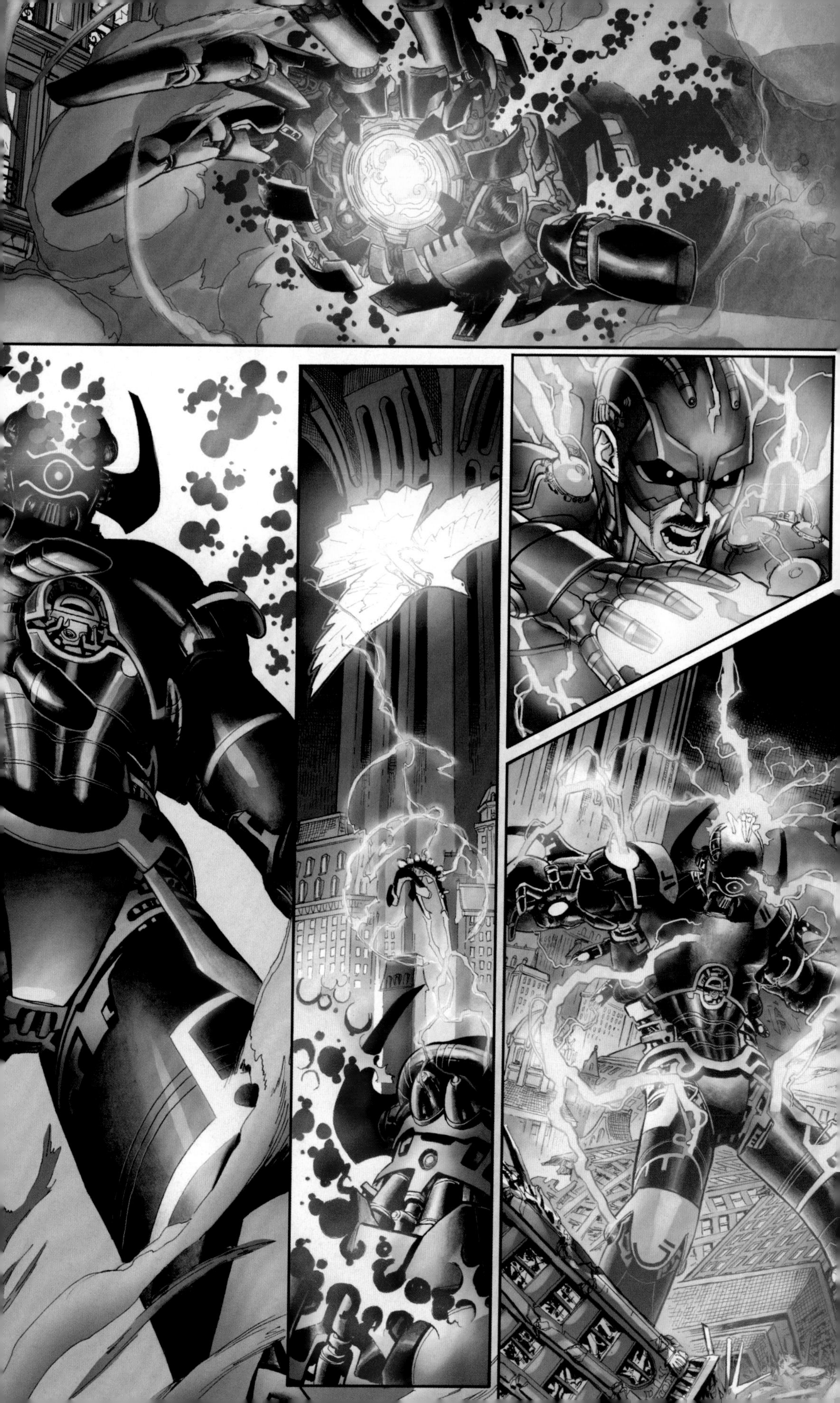

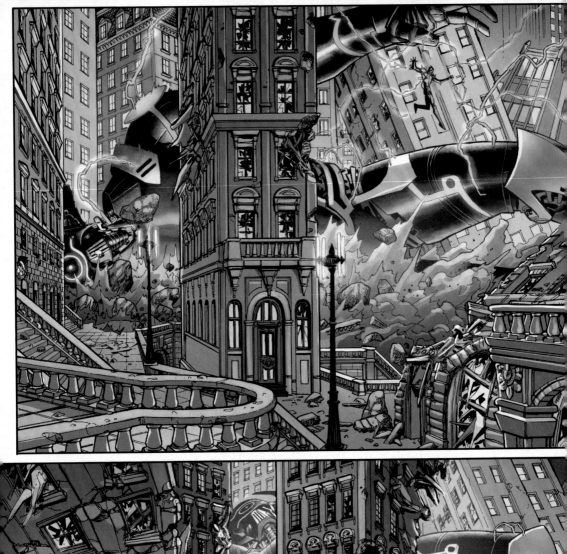

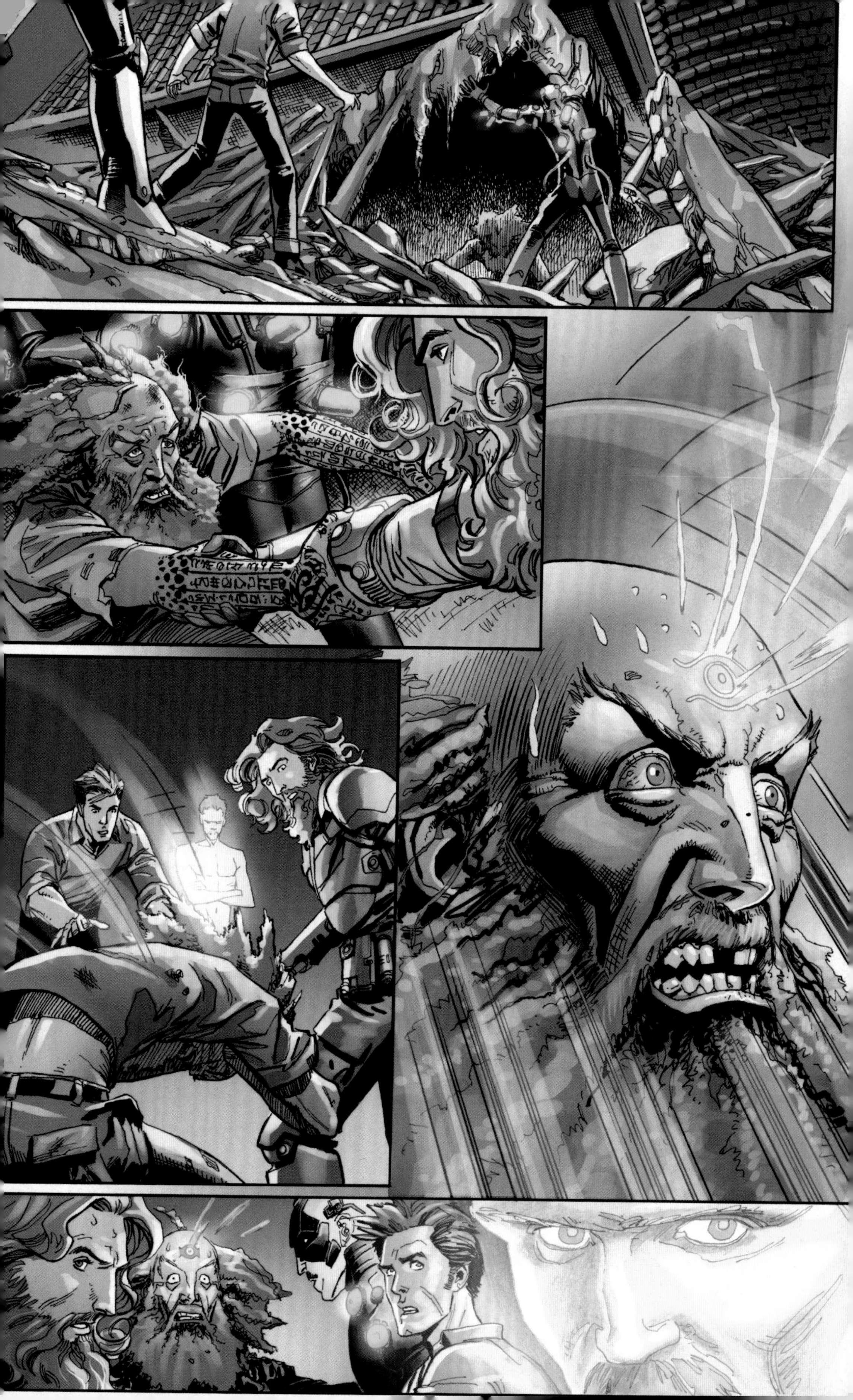

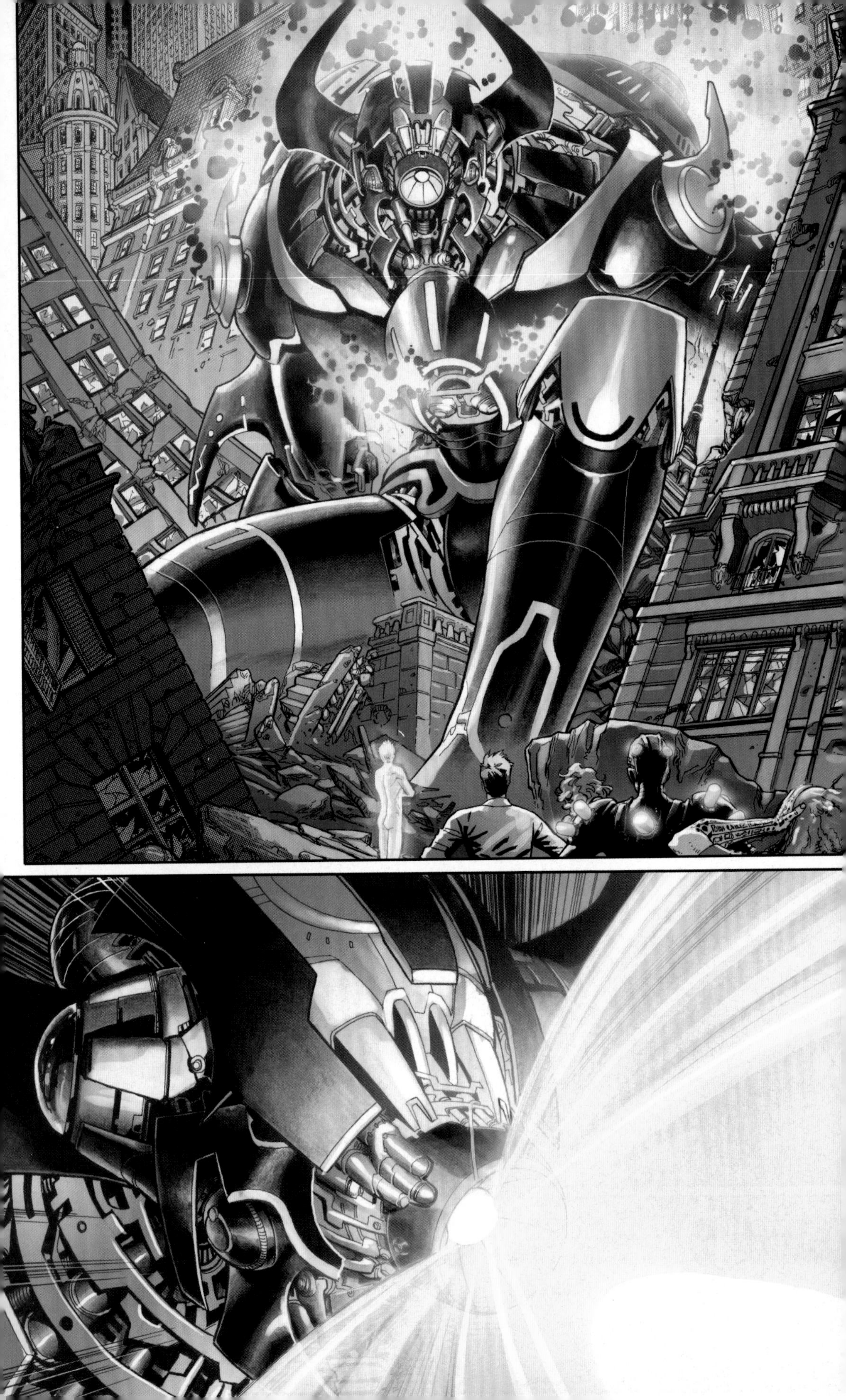

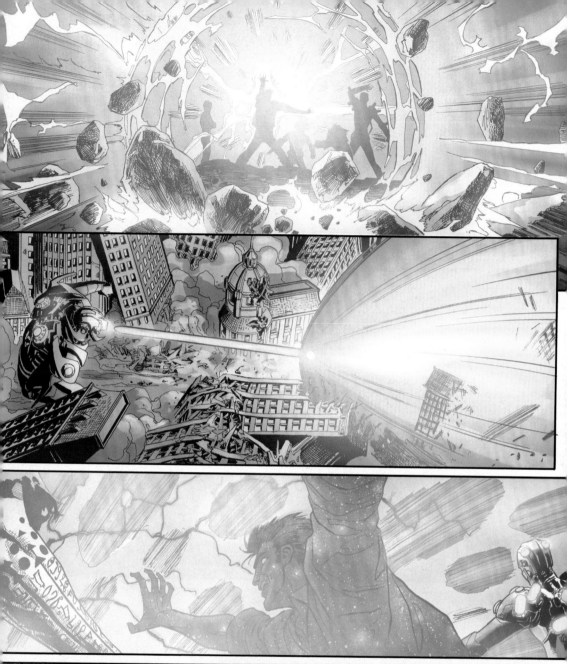

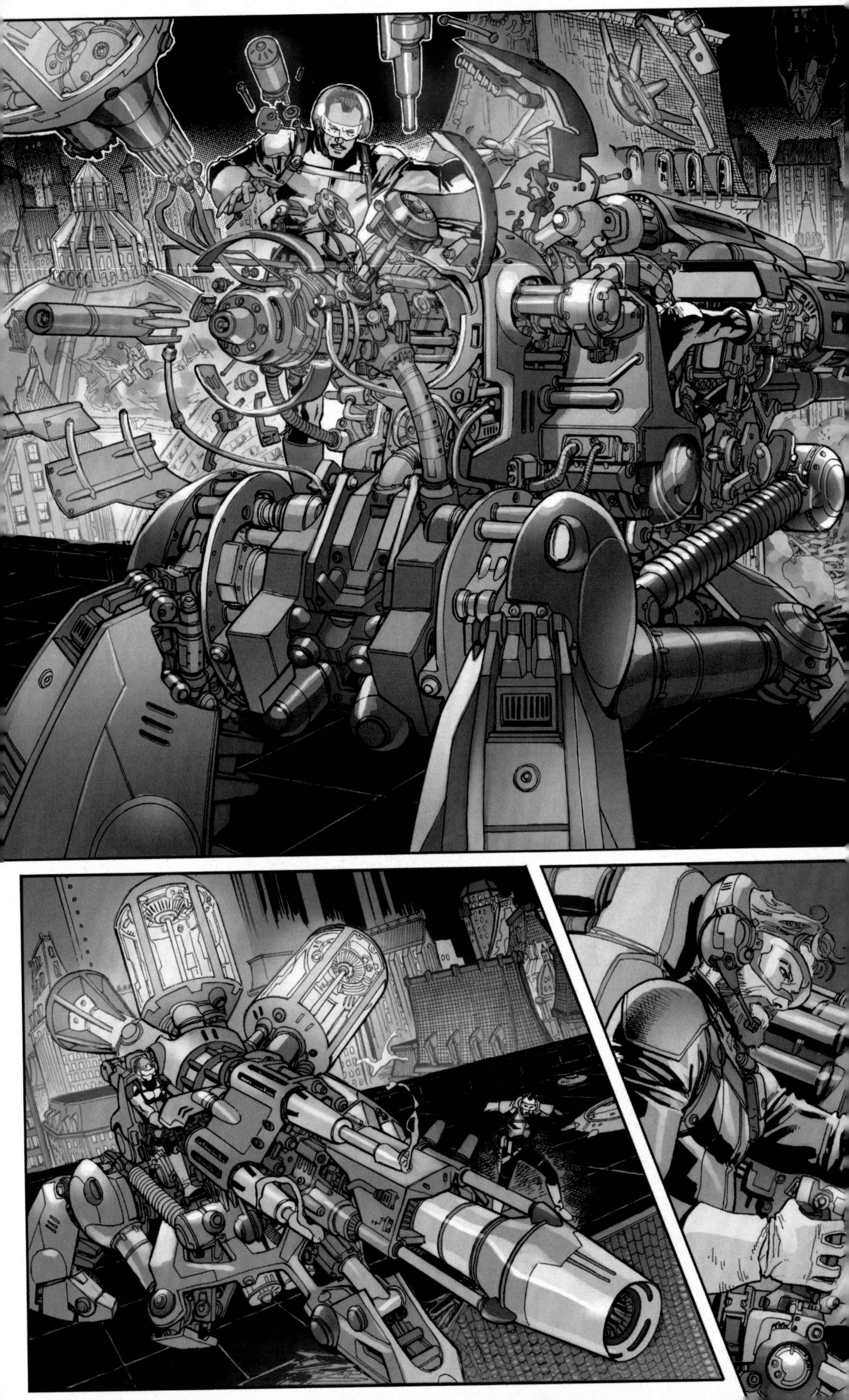

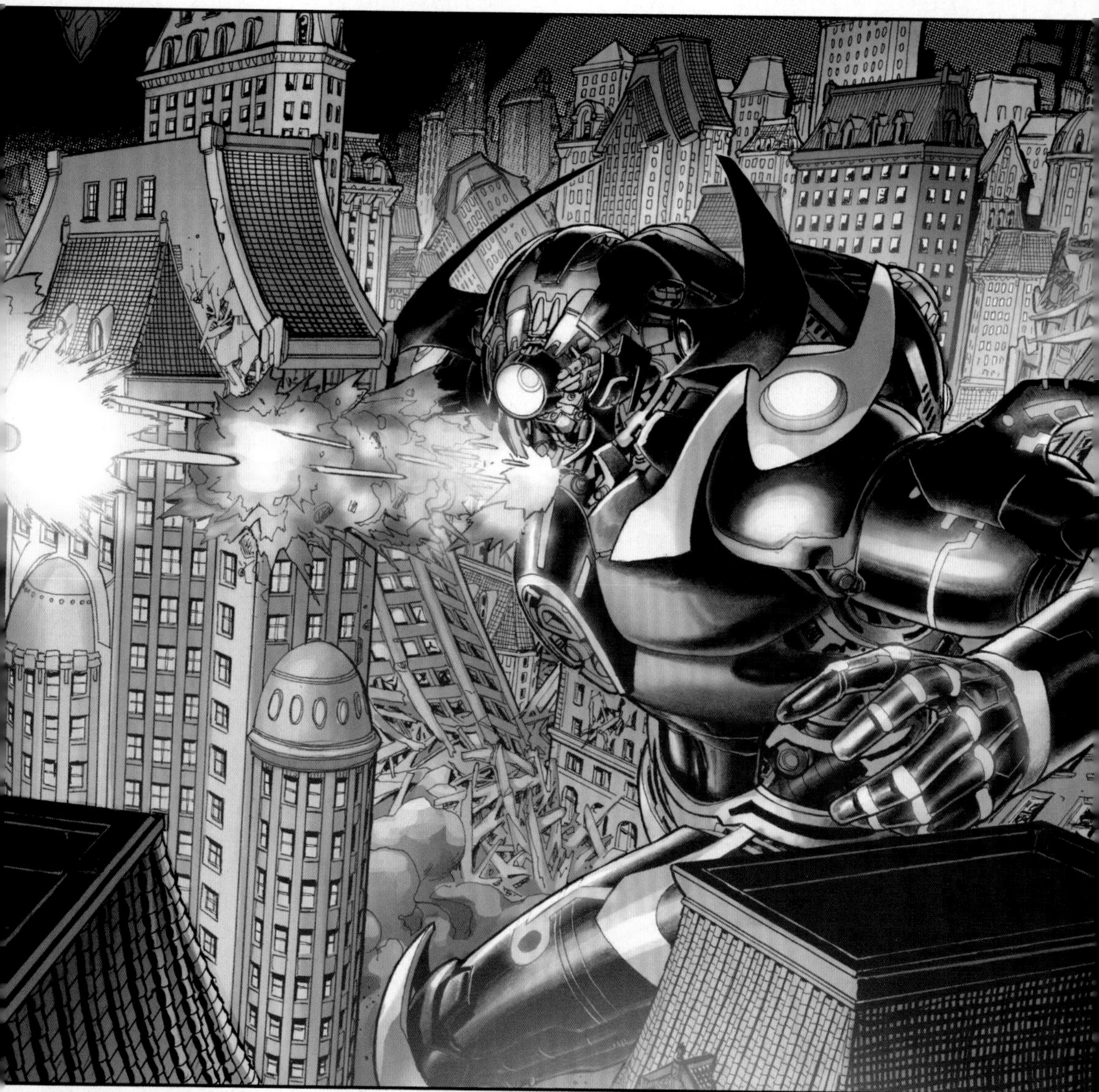
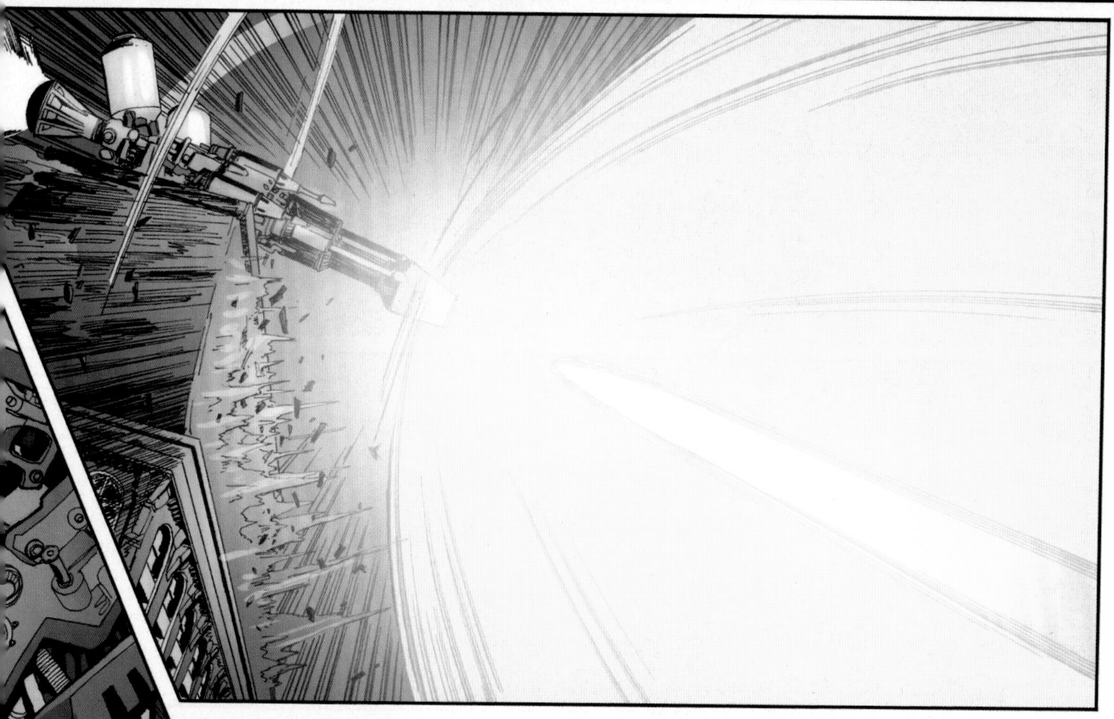

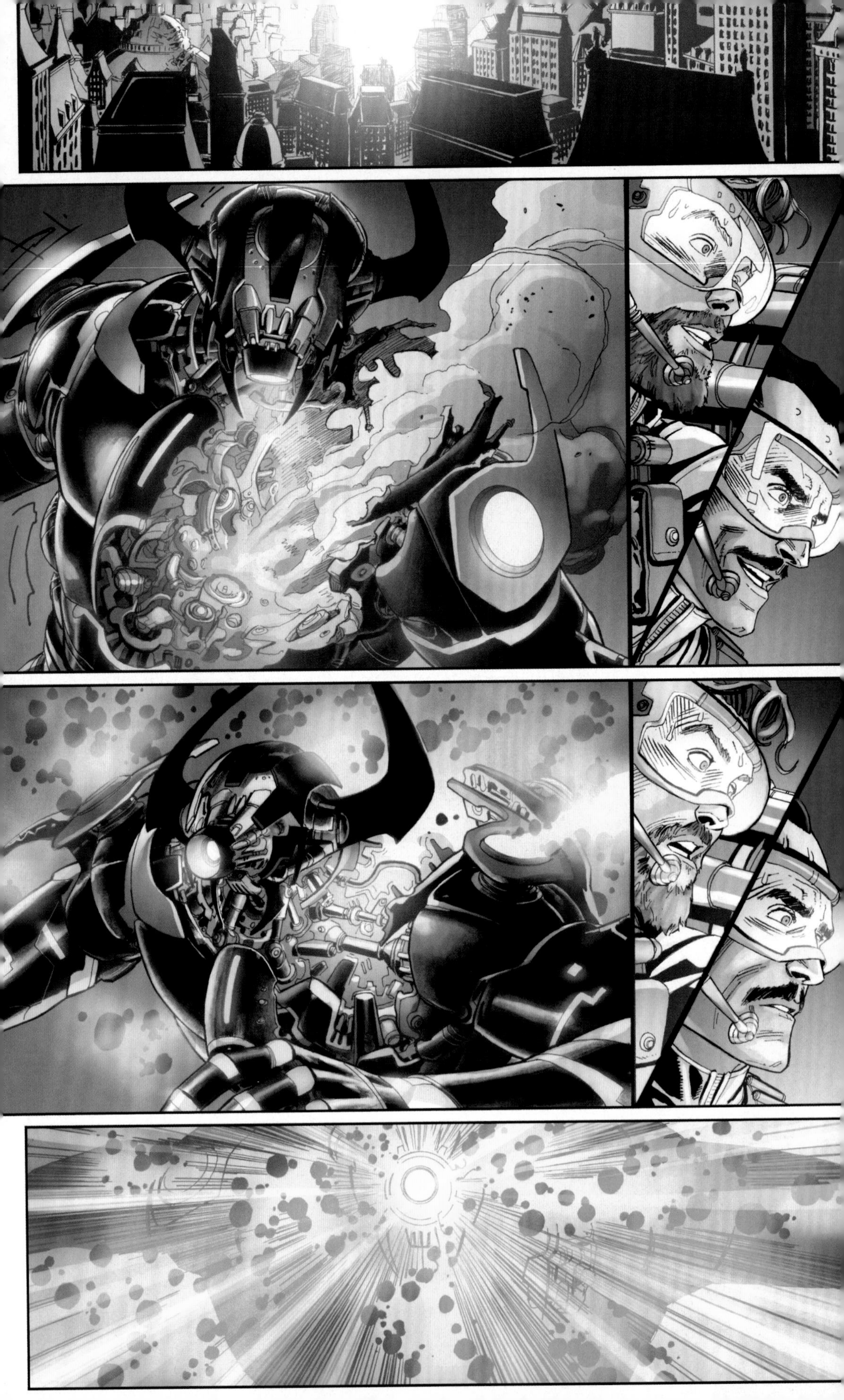

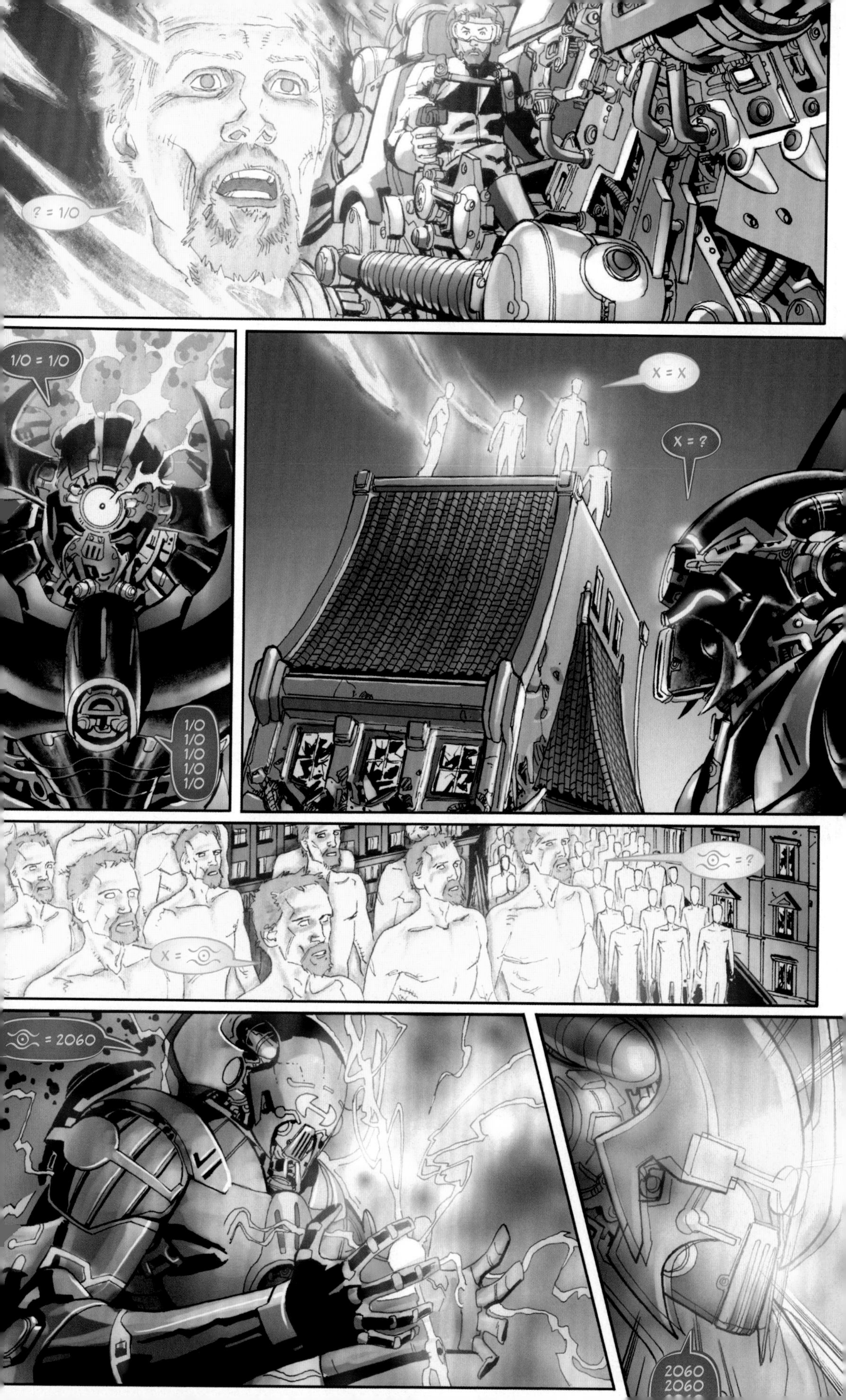
? = 1/0
1/0 = 1/0
1/0
1/0
1/0
1/0
1/0
X = X
X = ?
X =
= ?
= 2060
2060
2060

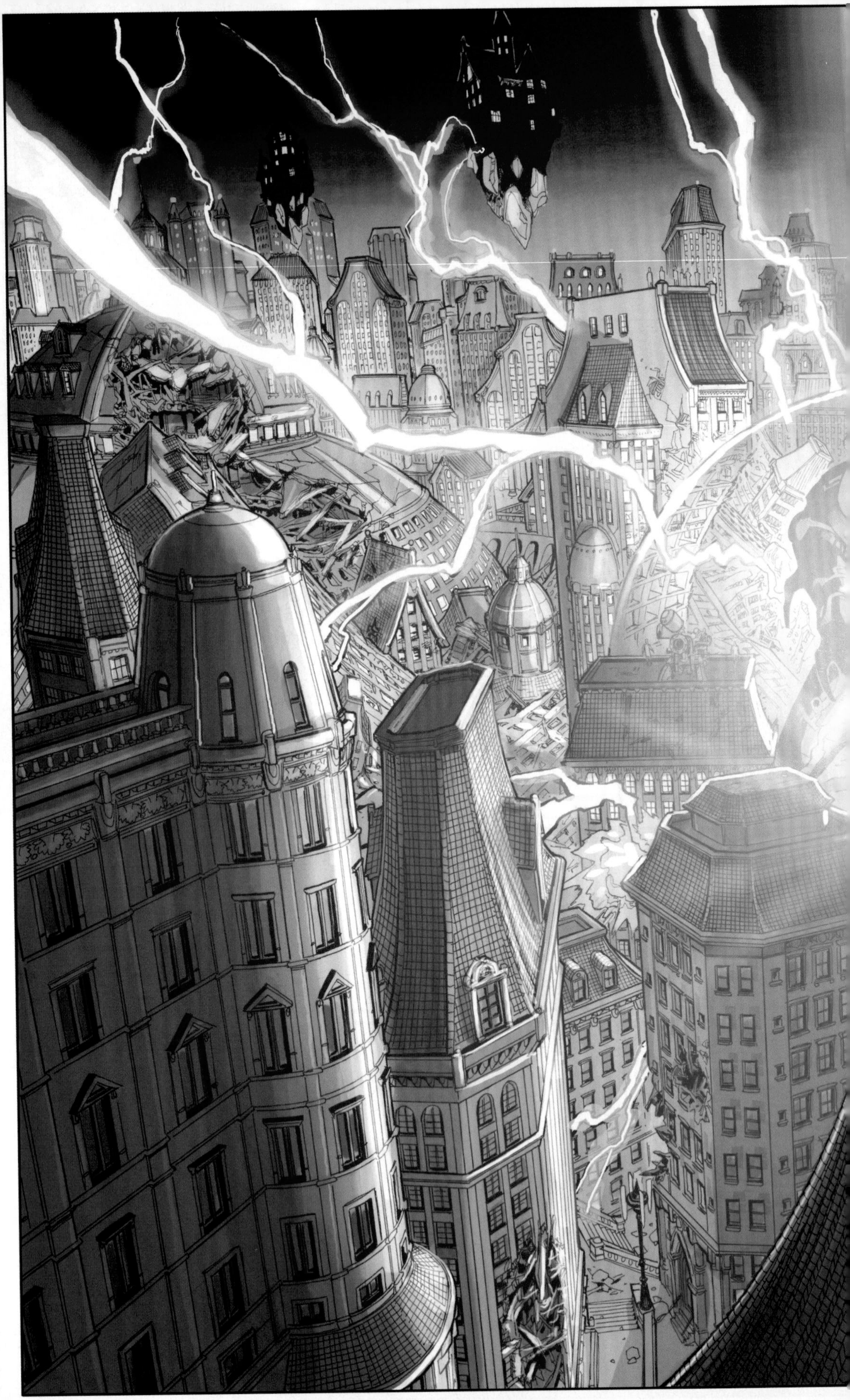

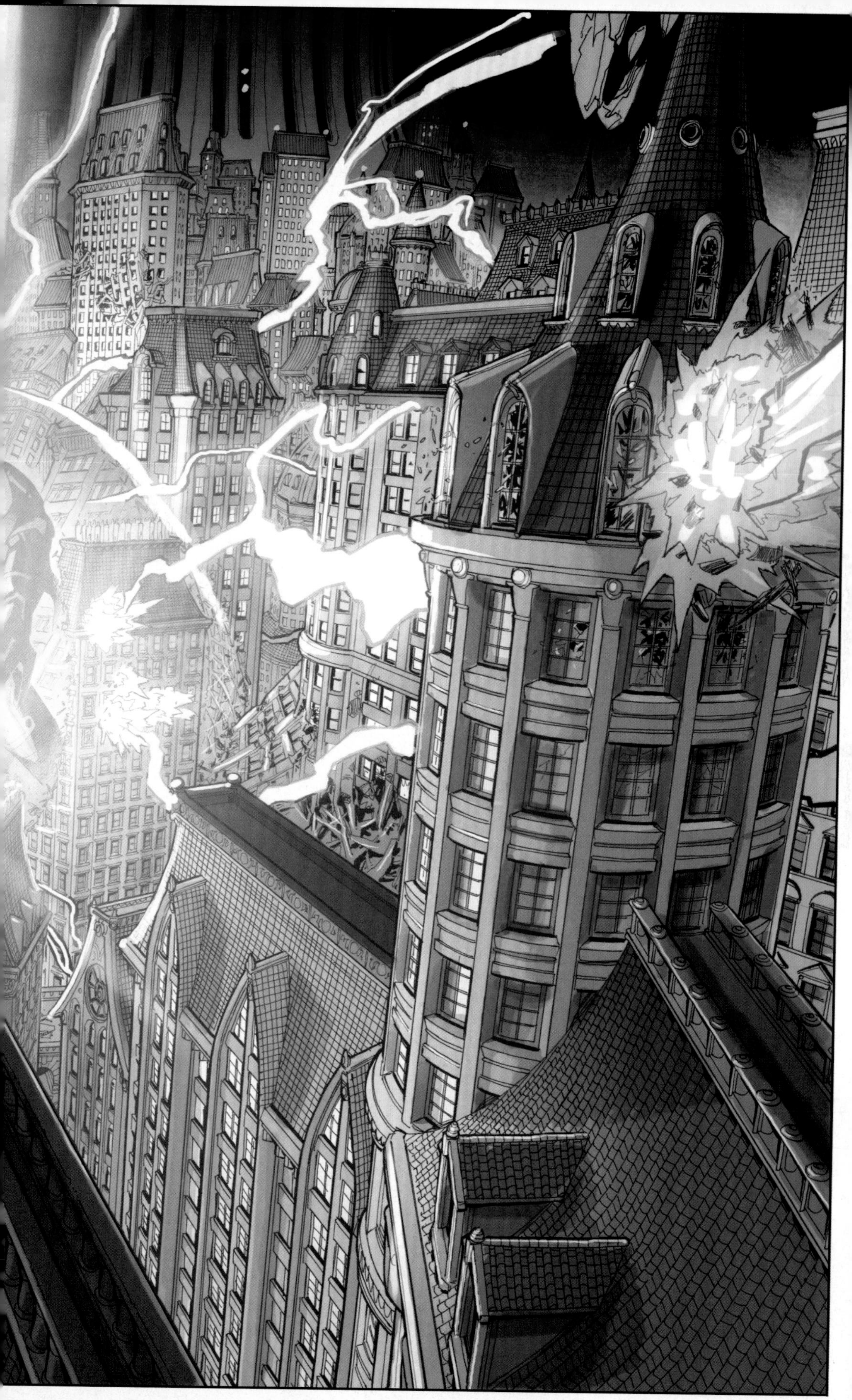

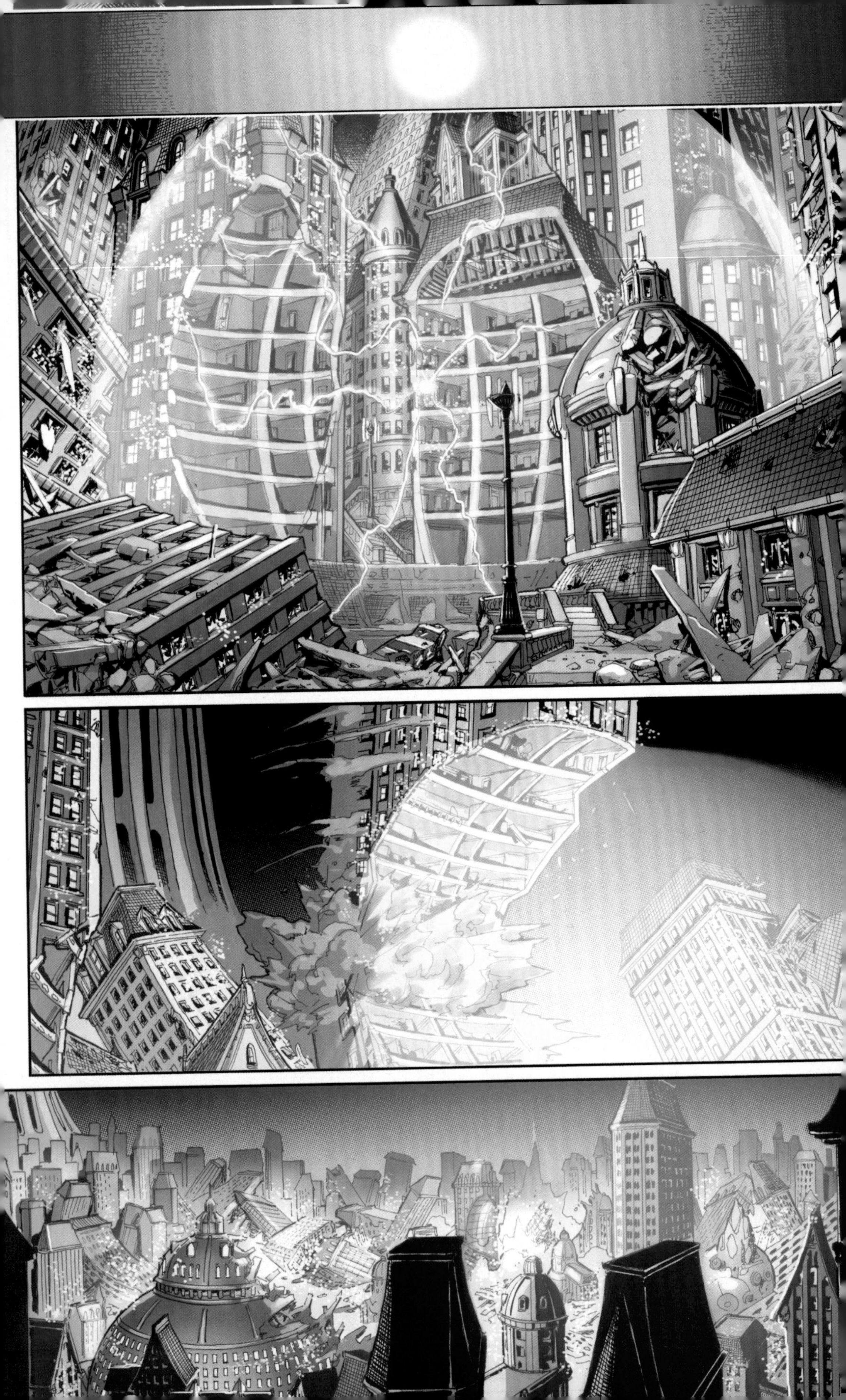

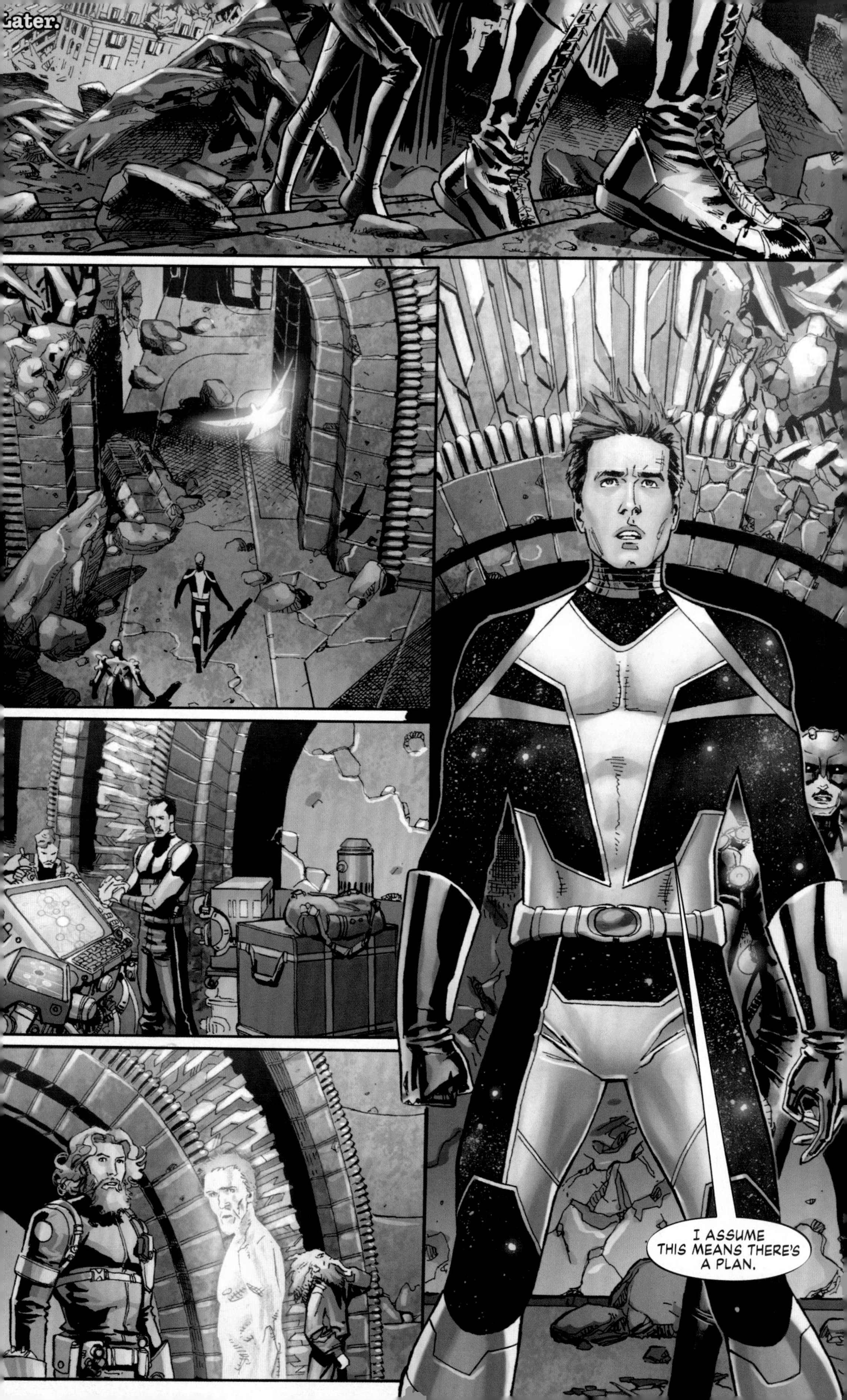
Later.
I ASSUME THIS MEANS THERE'S A PLAN.

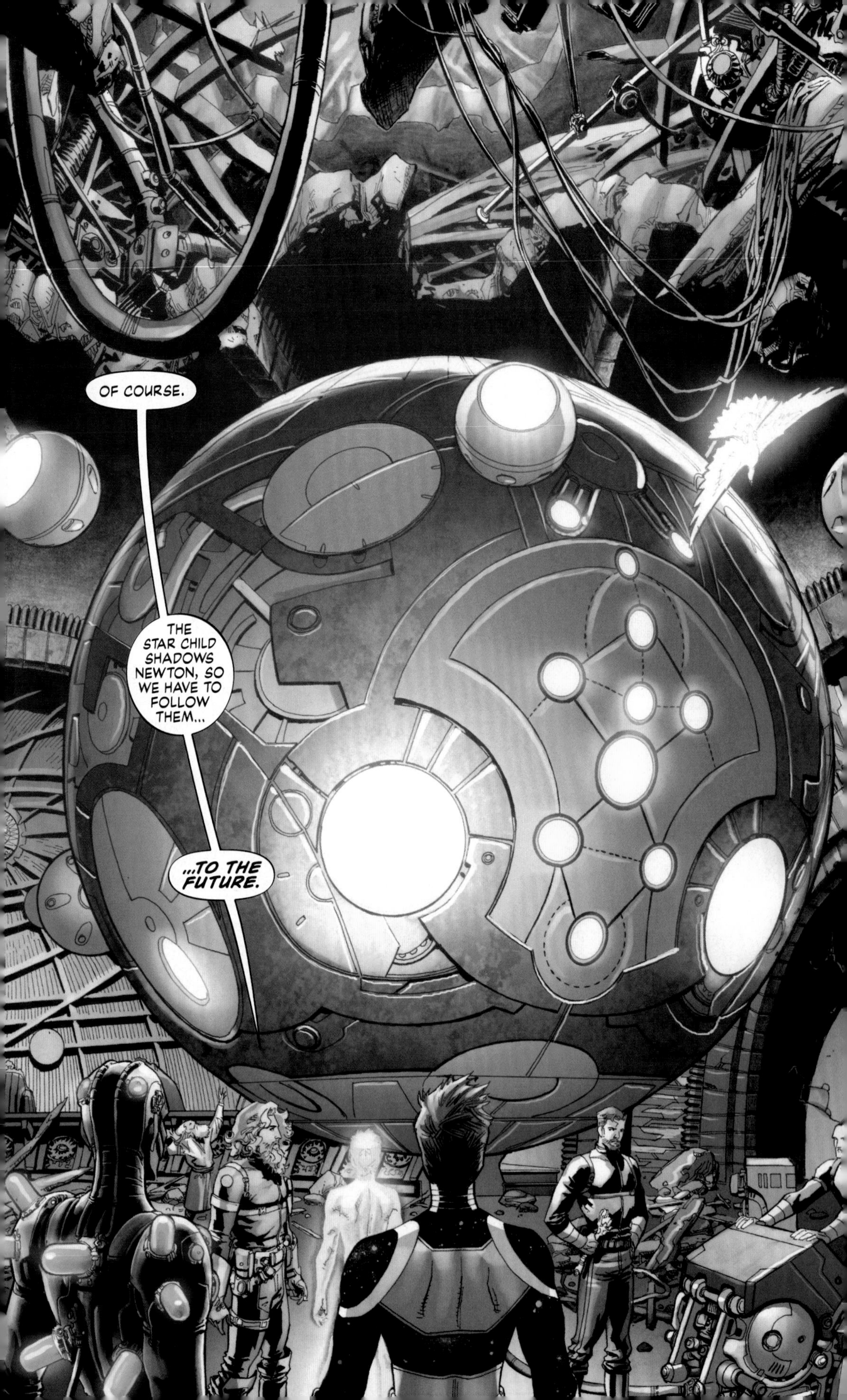
OF COURSE.
THE STAR CHILD SHADOWS NEWTON, SO WE HAVE TO FOLLOW THEM...
...TO THE FUTURE.

Chapter Four
"All Together Now"

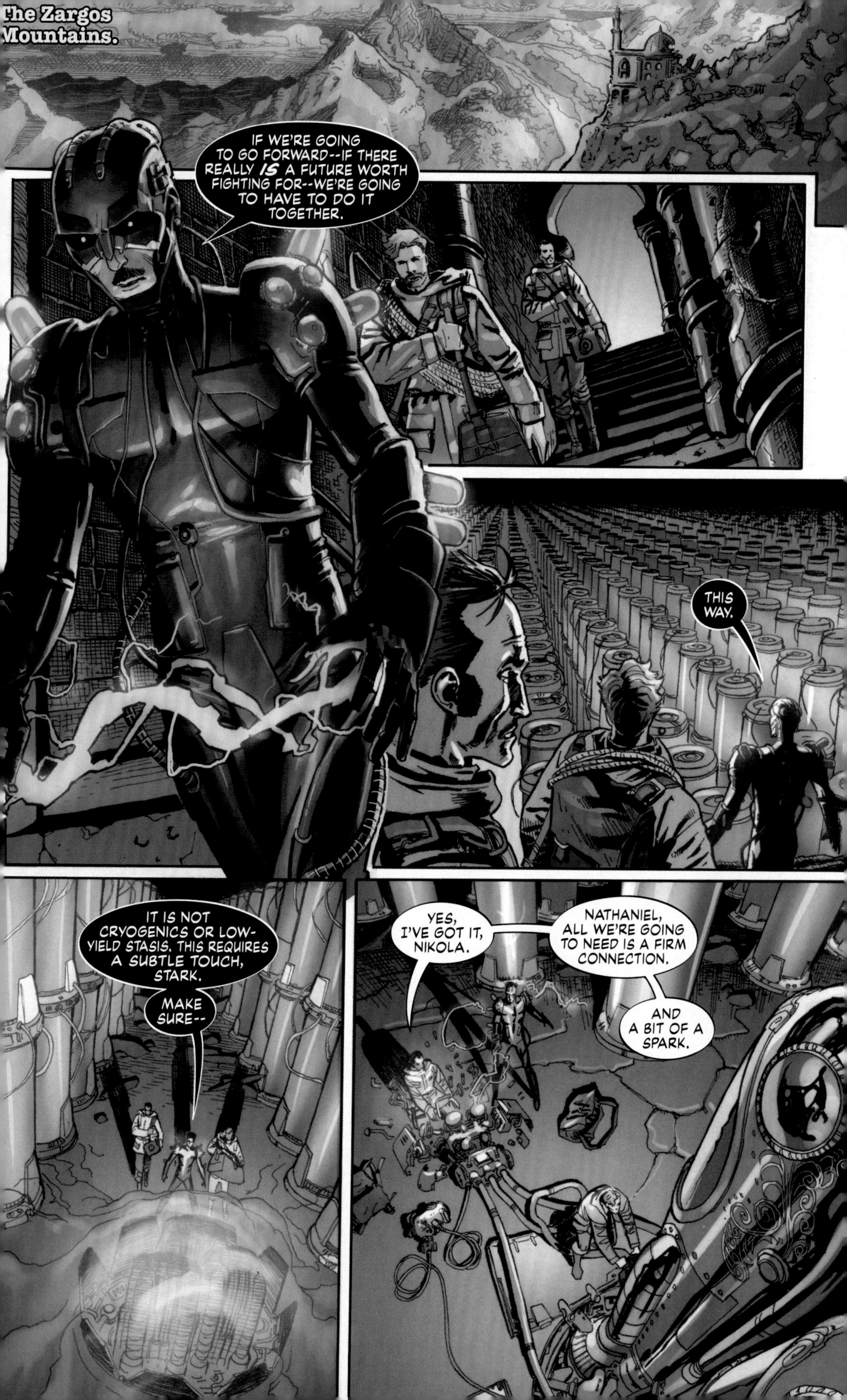
The Zargos Mountains.
IF WE'RE GOING TO GO FORWARD--IF THERE REALLY IS A FUTURE WORTH FIGHTING FOR--WE'RE GOING TO HAVE TO DO IT TOGETHER.
THIS WAY.
IT IS NOT CRYOGENICS OR LOW-YIELD STASIS. THIS REQUIRES A SUBTLE TOUCH, STARK.
MAKE SURE--
YES, I'VE GOT IT, NIKOLA.
NATHANIEL, ALL WE'RE GOING TO NEED IS A FIRM CONNECTION.
AND A BIT OF A SPARK.

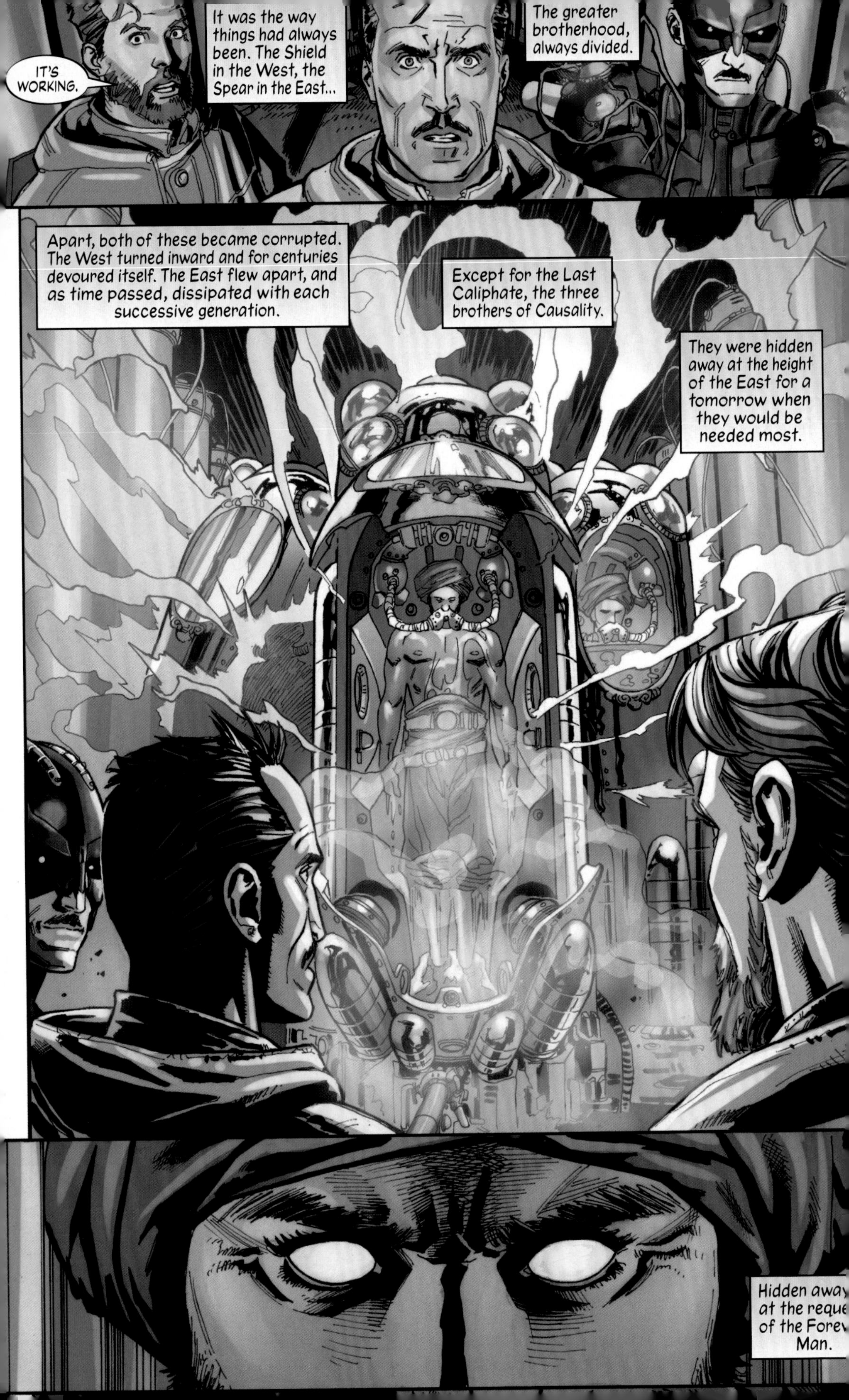

IT'S WORKING.
It was the way things had always been. The Shield in the West, the Spear in the East...
The greater brotherhood, always divided.
Apart, both of these became corrupted. The West turned inward and for centuries devoured itself. The East flew apart, and as time passed, dissipated with each successive generation.
Except for the Last Caliphate, the three brothers of Causality.
They were hidden away at the height of the East for a tomorrow when they would be needed most.
Hidden away at the reque of the Forev Man.

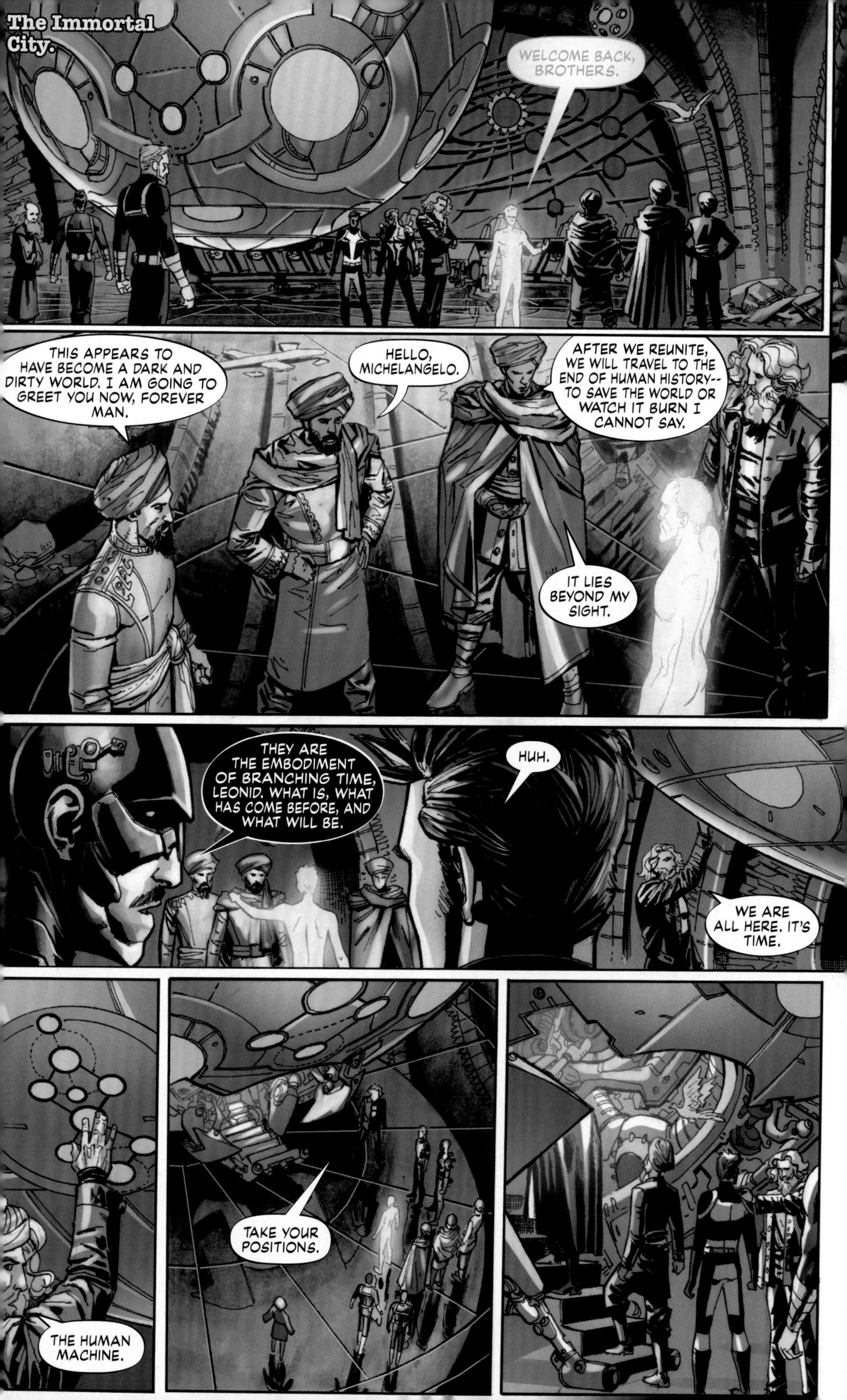
The Immortal City.
WELCOME BACK, BROTHERS.
THIS APPEARS TO HAVE BECOME A DARK AND DIRTY WORLD. I AM GOING TO GREET YOU NOW, FOREVER MAN.
HELLO, MICHELANGELO.
AFTER WE REUNITE, WE WILL TRAVEL TO THE END OF HUMAN HISTORY--TO SAVE THE WORLD OR WATCH IT BURN I CANNOT SAY.
IT LIES BEYOND MY SIGHT.
THEY ARE THE EMBODIMENT OF BRANCHING TIME, LEONID. WHAT IS, WHAT HAS COME BEFORE, AND WHAT WILL BE.
HUH.
WE ARE ALL HERE. IT'S TIME.
THE HUMAN MACHINE.
TAKE YOUR POSITIONS.

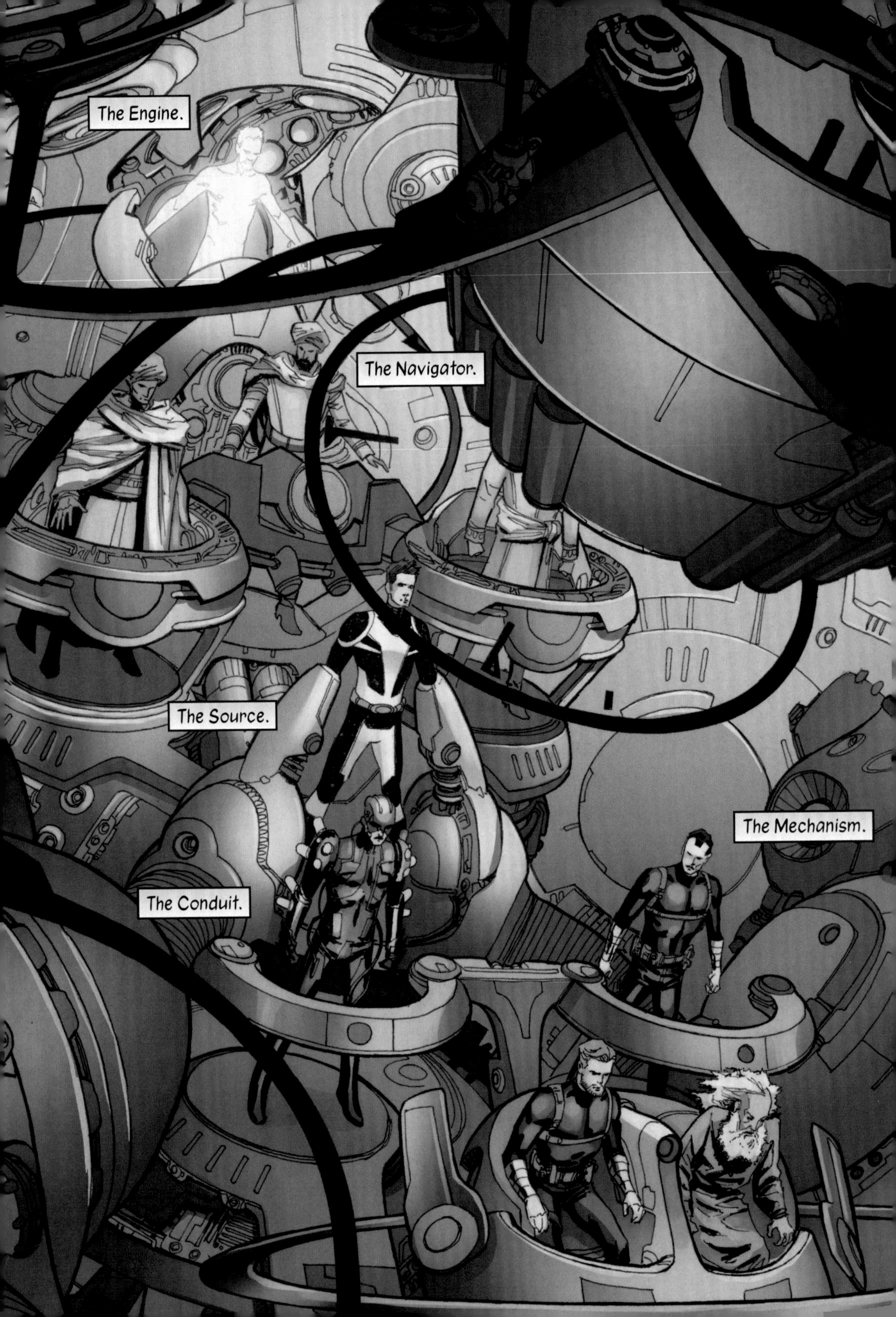
The Engine.
The Navigator.
The Source.
The Mechanism.
The Conduit.

The Anchor.

WHEN YOU ARE READY, LEONID.

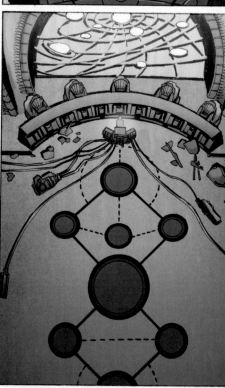

The Sacrifice. The man left behind.

The BUILDER.

SUCCESS... GLORY...AND HOPEFULLY BOTH.

FAREWELL, MY FRIENDS.

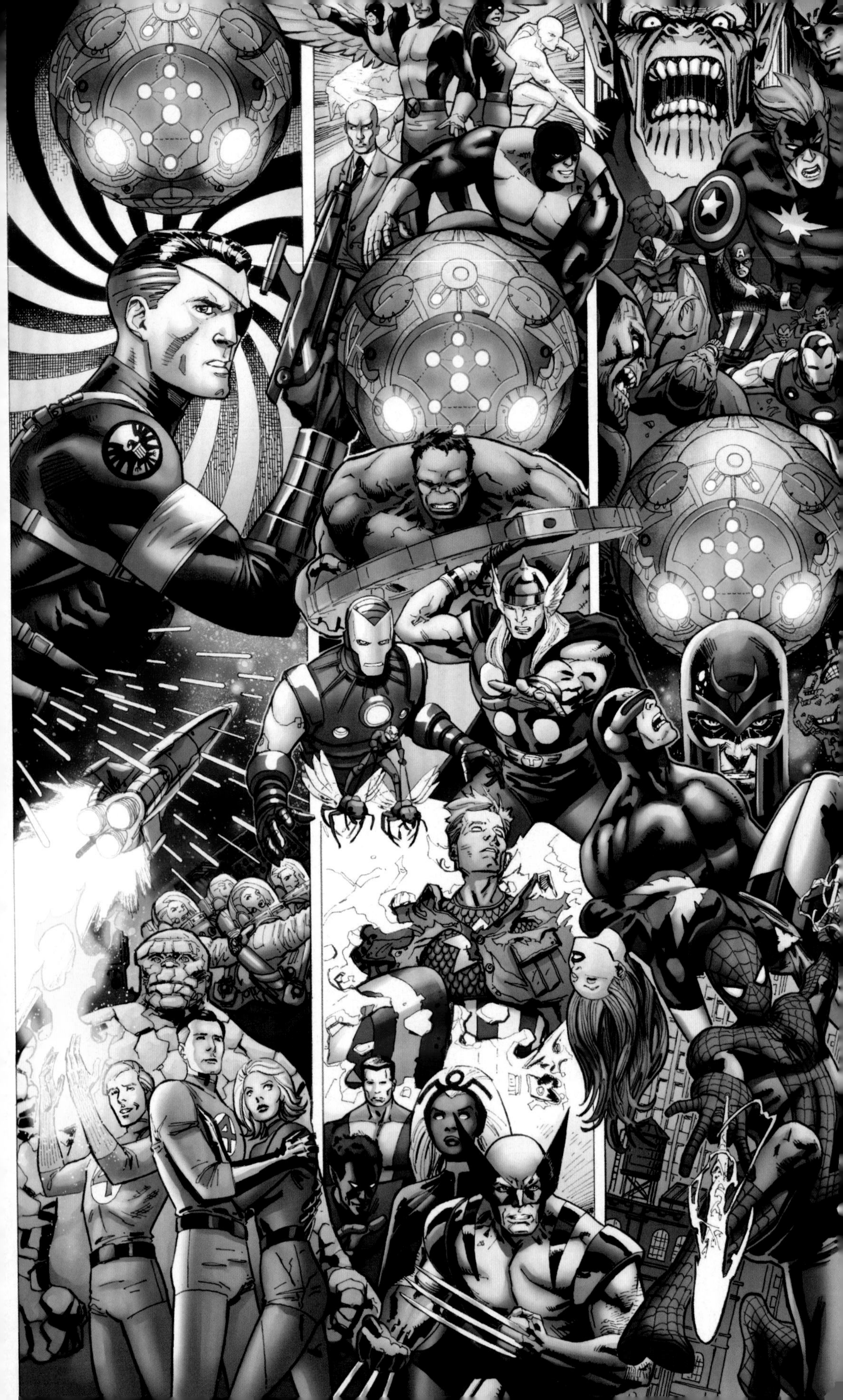

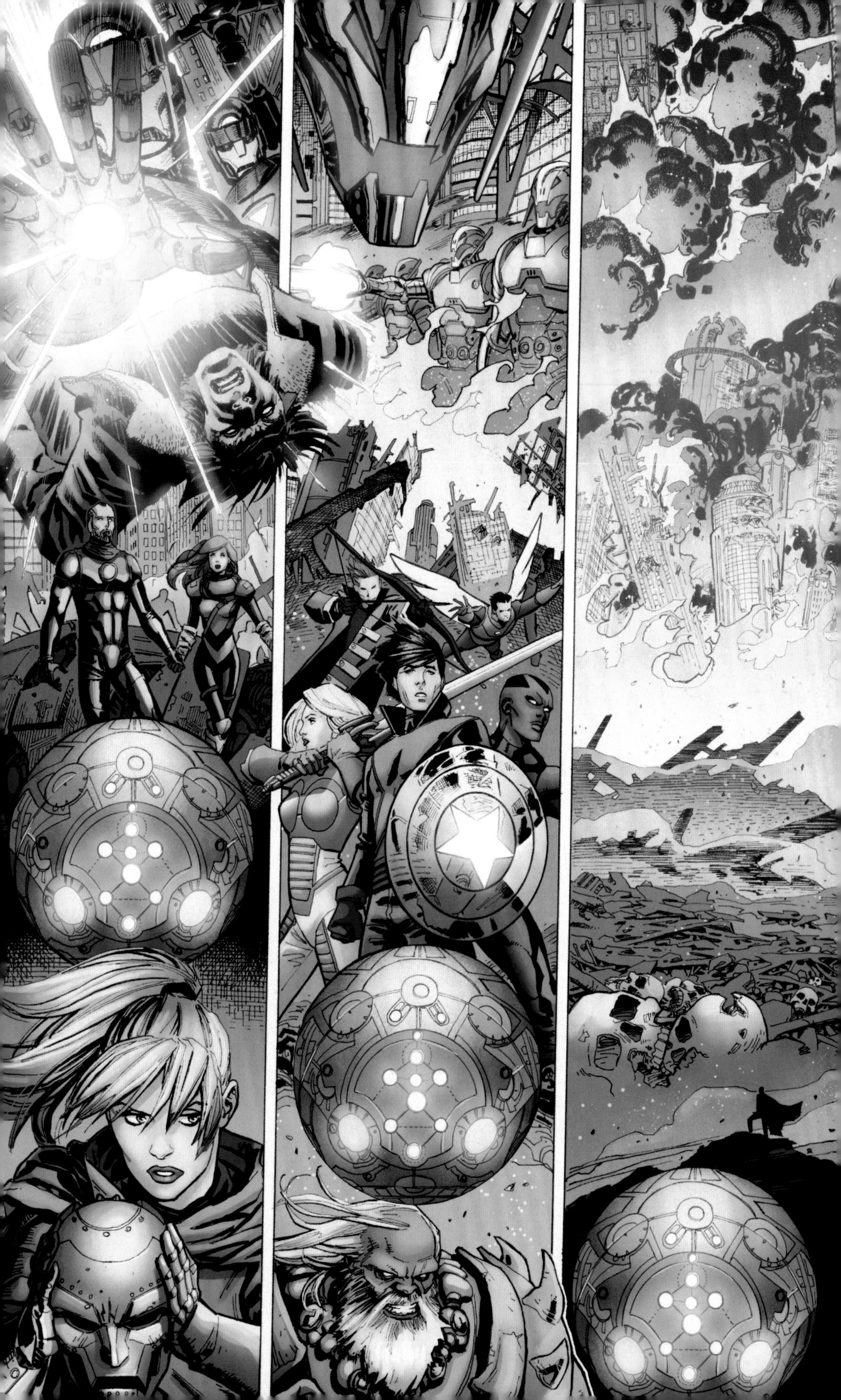

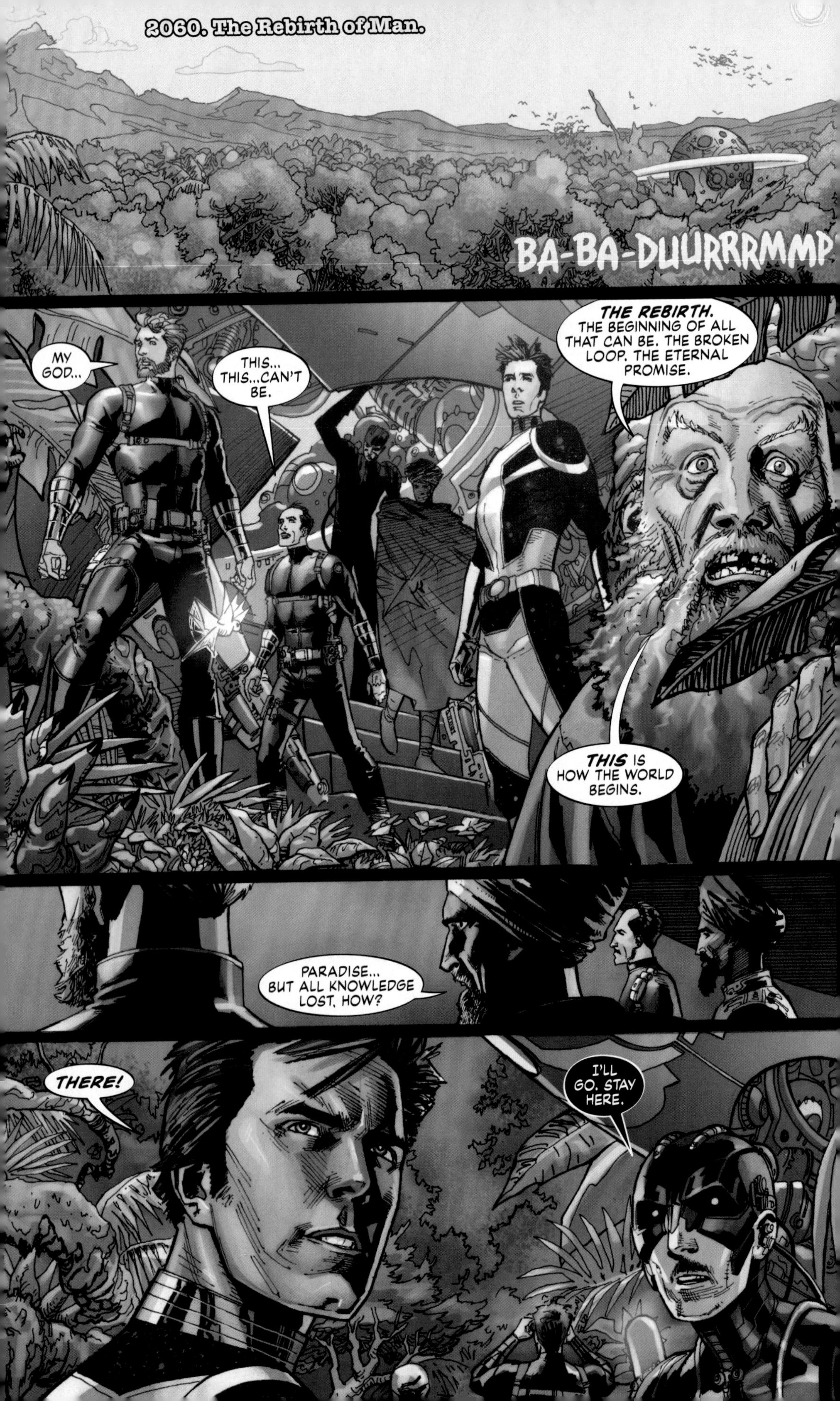

2060. The Rebirth of Man.
BA-BA-DUURRRMMP
MY GOD...
THIS... THIS...CAN'T BE.
THE REBIRTH. THE BEGINNING OF ALL THAT CAN BE. THE BROKEN LOOP. THE ETERNAL PROMISE.
THIS IS HOW THE WORLD BEGINS.
PARADISE... BUT ALL KNOWLEDGE LOST. HOW?
THERE!
I'LL GO. STAY HERE.

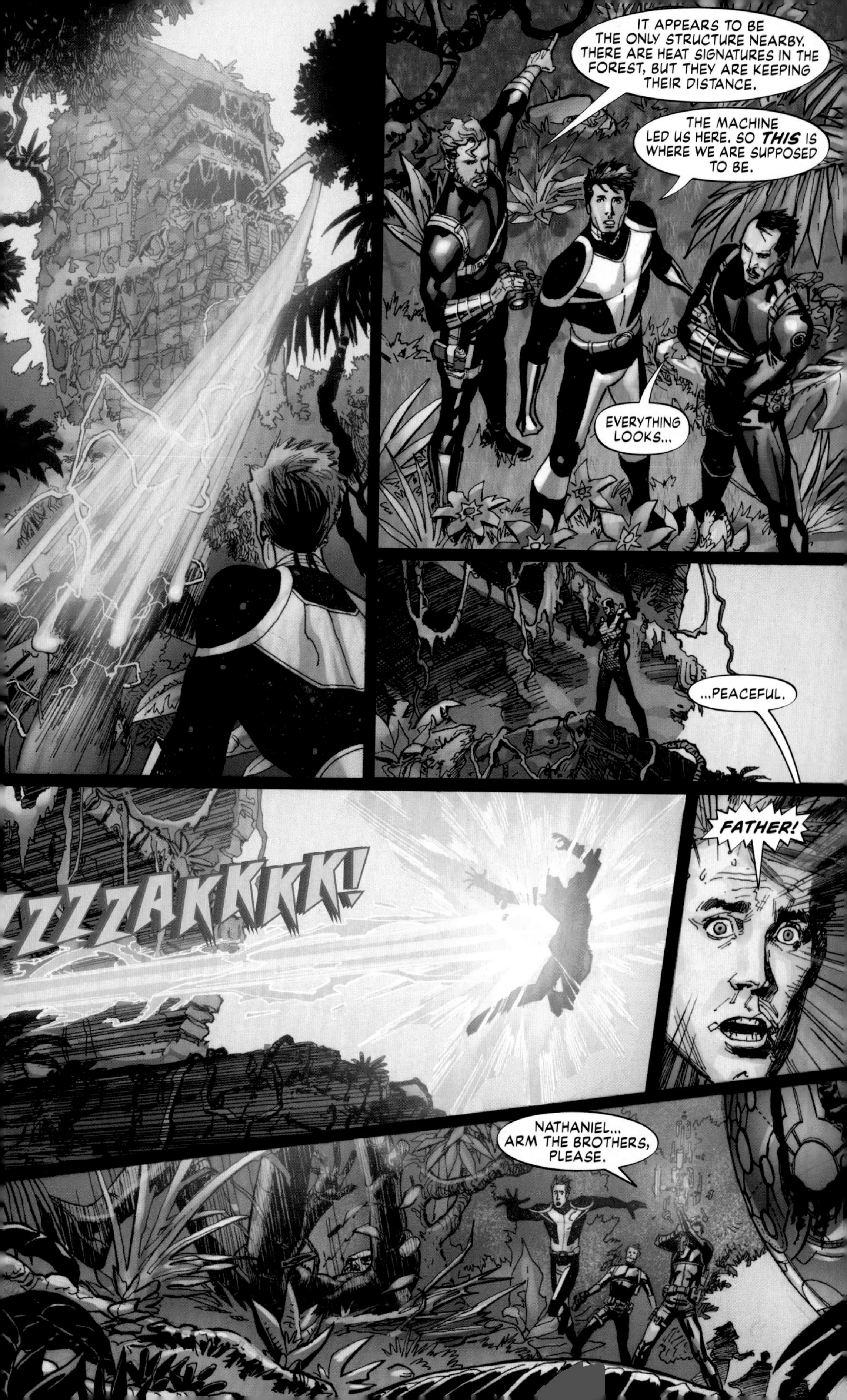
IT APPEARS TO BE THE ONLY STRUCTURE NEARBY. THERE ARE HEAT SIGNATURES IN THE FOREST, BUT THEY ARE KEEPING THEIR DISTANCE.
THE MACHINE LED US HERE. SO *THIS* IS WHERE WE ARE SUPPOSED TO BE.
EVERYTHING LOOKS...
...PEACEFUL.
ZZZZAKKKKK!
FATHER!
NATHANIEL... ARM THE BROTHERS, PLEASE.

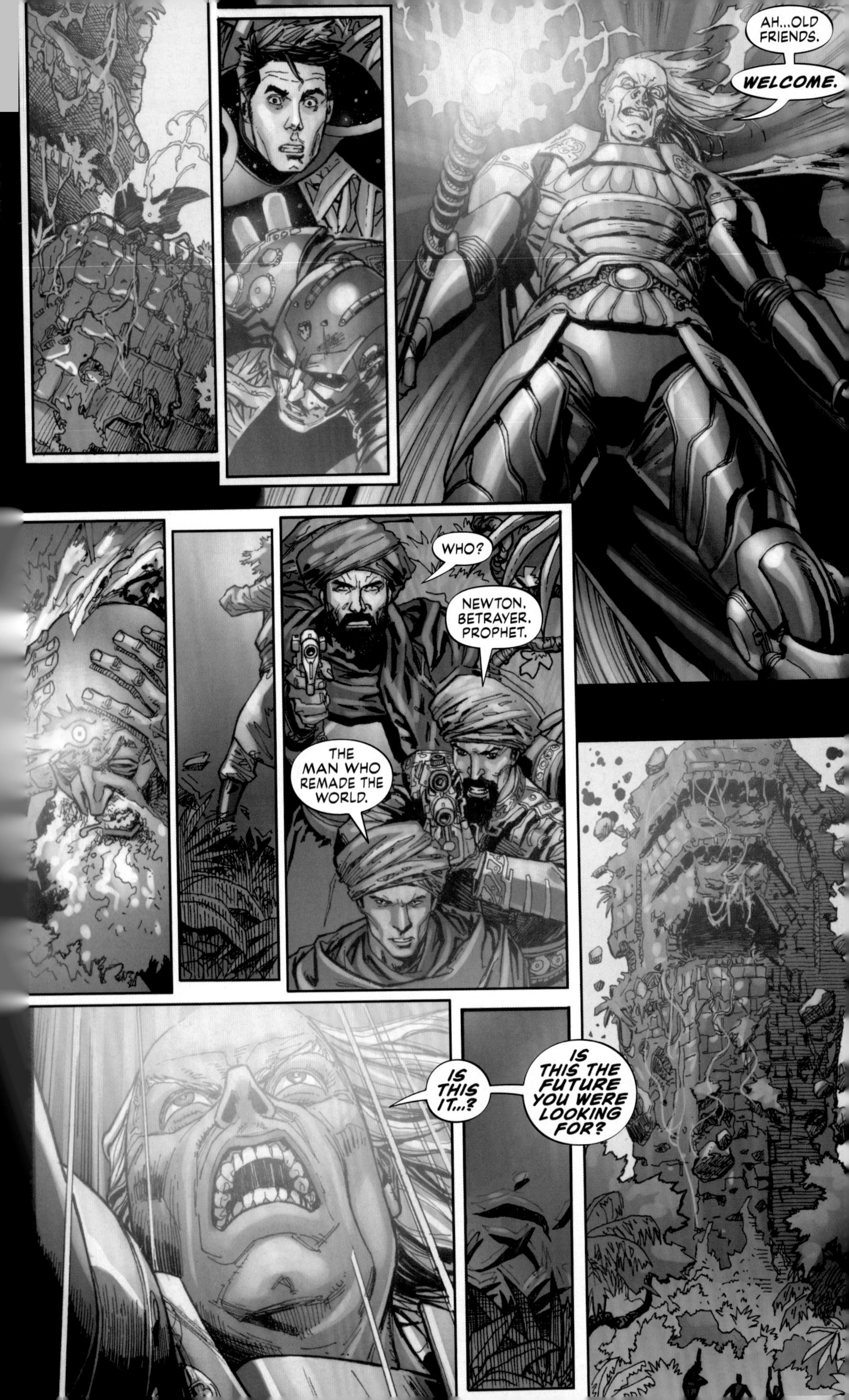
AH...OLD FRIENDS.
WELCOME.
WHO?
NEWTON. BETRAYER. PROPHET.
THE MAN WHO REMADE THE WORLD.
IS THIS IT...?
IS THIS THE FUTURE YOU WERE LOOKING FOR?

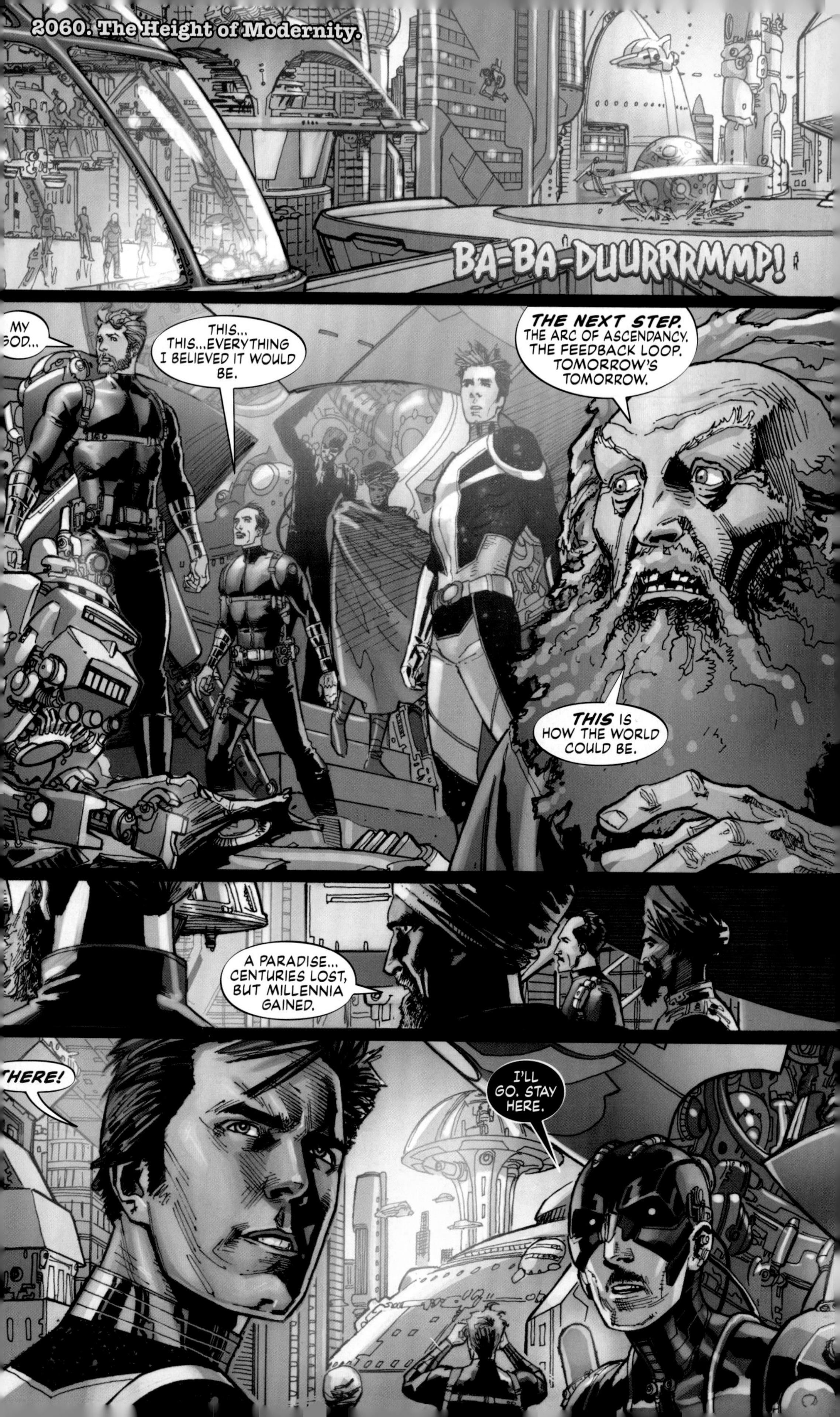

2060. The Height of Modernity.
BA-BA-DUURRRMMP!
MY GOD...
THIS... THIS...EVERYTHING I BELIEVED IT WOULD BE.
THE NEXT STEP. THE ARC OF ASCENDANCY. THE FEEDBACK LOOP. TOMORROW'S TOMORROW.
THIS IS HOW THE WORLD COULD BE.
A PARADISE... CENTURIES LOST, BUT MILLENNIA GAINED.
THERE!
I'LL GO. STAY HERE.

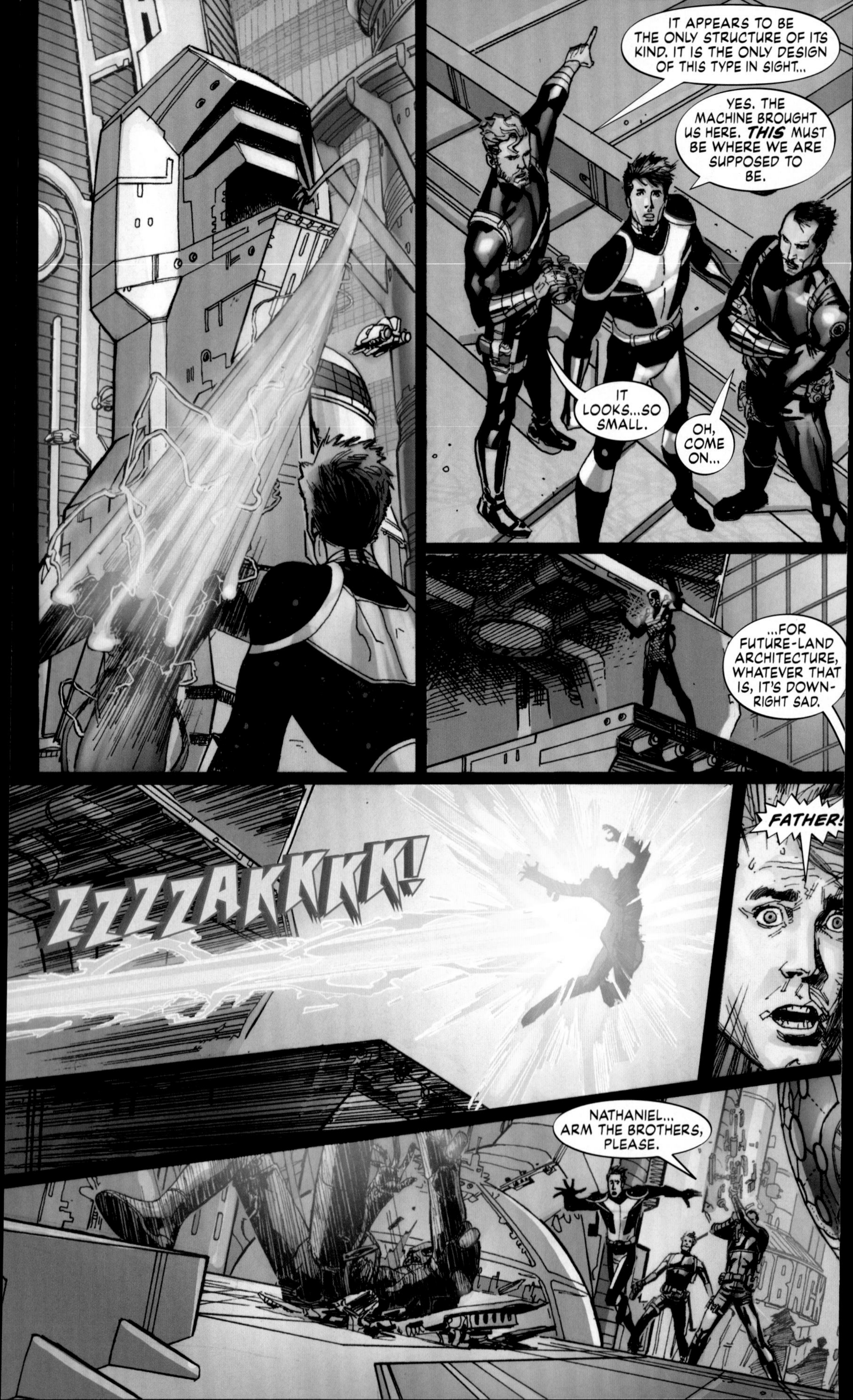
IT APPEARS TO BE THE ONLY STRUCTURE OF ITS KIND. IT IS THE ONLY DESIGN OF THIS TYPE IN SIGHT...
YES. THE MACHINE BROUGHT US HERE. ***THIS*** MUST BE WHERE WE ARE SUPPOSED TO BE.
IT LOOKS...SO SMALL.
OH, COME ON...
...FOR FUTURE-LAND ARCHITECTURE, WHATEVER THAT IS, IT'S DOWN-RIGHT SAD.
ZZZZAKKKK!
FATHER!
NATHANIEL... ARM THE BROTHERS, PLEASE.

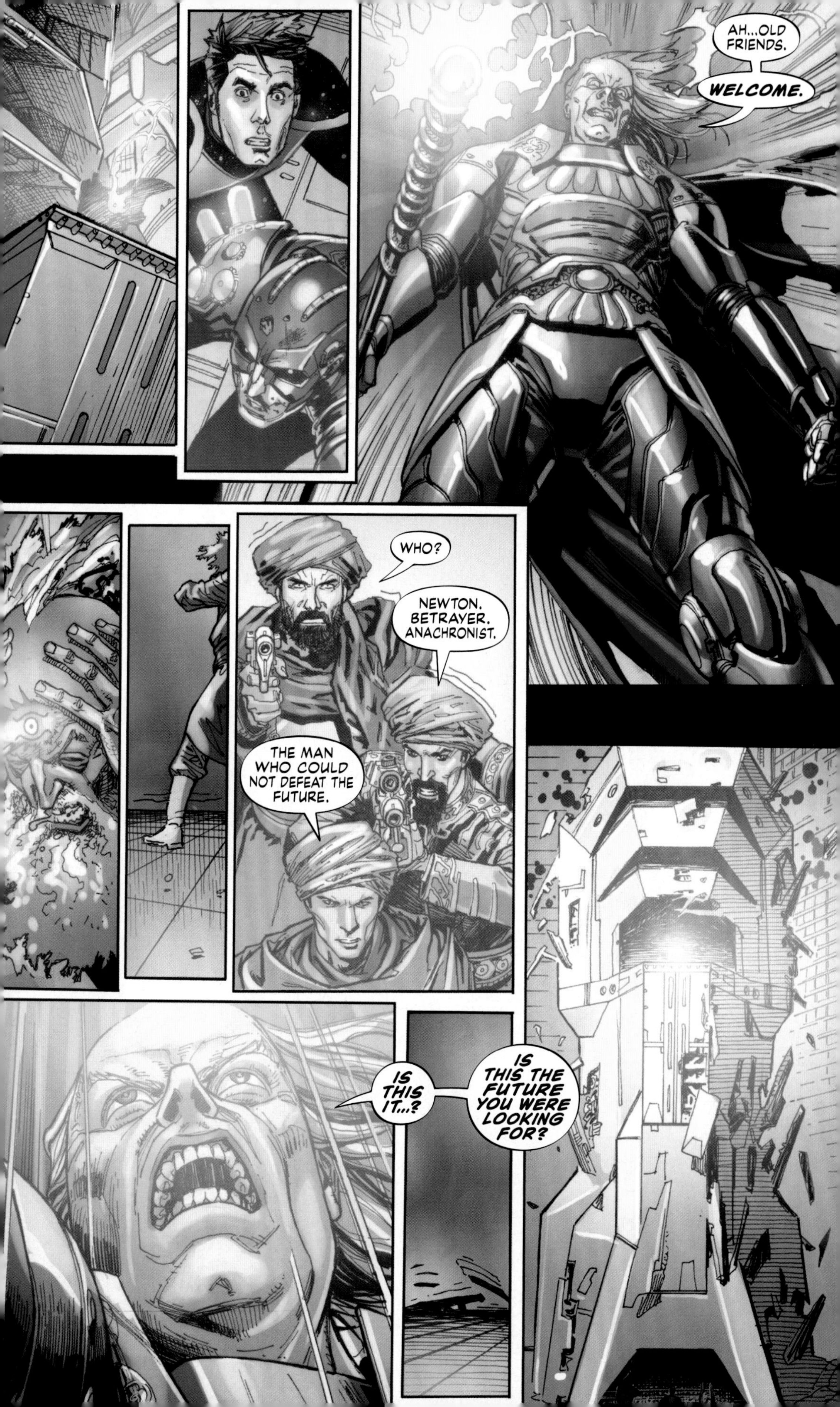

AH...OLD FRIENDS.
WELCOME.
WHO?
NEWTON. BETRAYER. ANACHRONIST.
THE MAN WHO COULD NOT DEFEAT THE FUTURE.
IS THIS IT...?
IS THIS THE FUTURE YOU WERE LOOKING FOR?

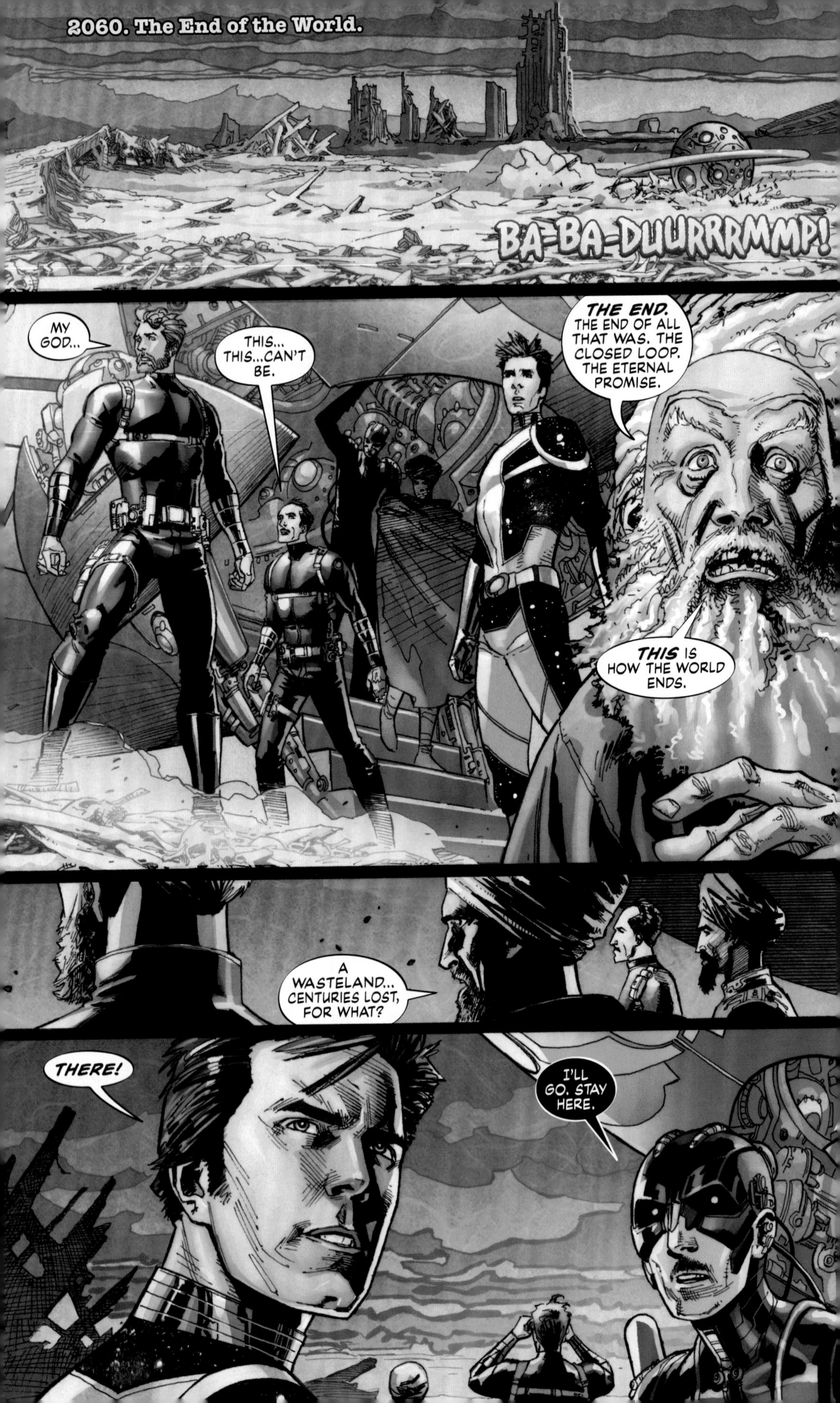

2060. The End of the World.
BA-BA-DUURRRMMP!
MY GOD...
THIS... THIS...CAN'T BE.
THE END. THE END OF ALL THAT WAS. THE CLOSED LOOP. THE ETERNAL PROMISE.
THIS IS HOW THE WORLD ENDS.
A WASTELAND... CENTURIES LOST, FOR WHAT?
THERE!
I'LL GO. STAY HERE.

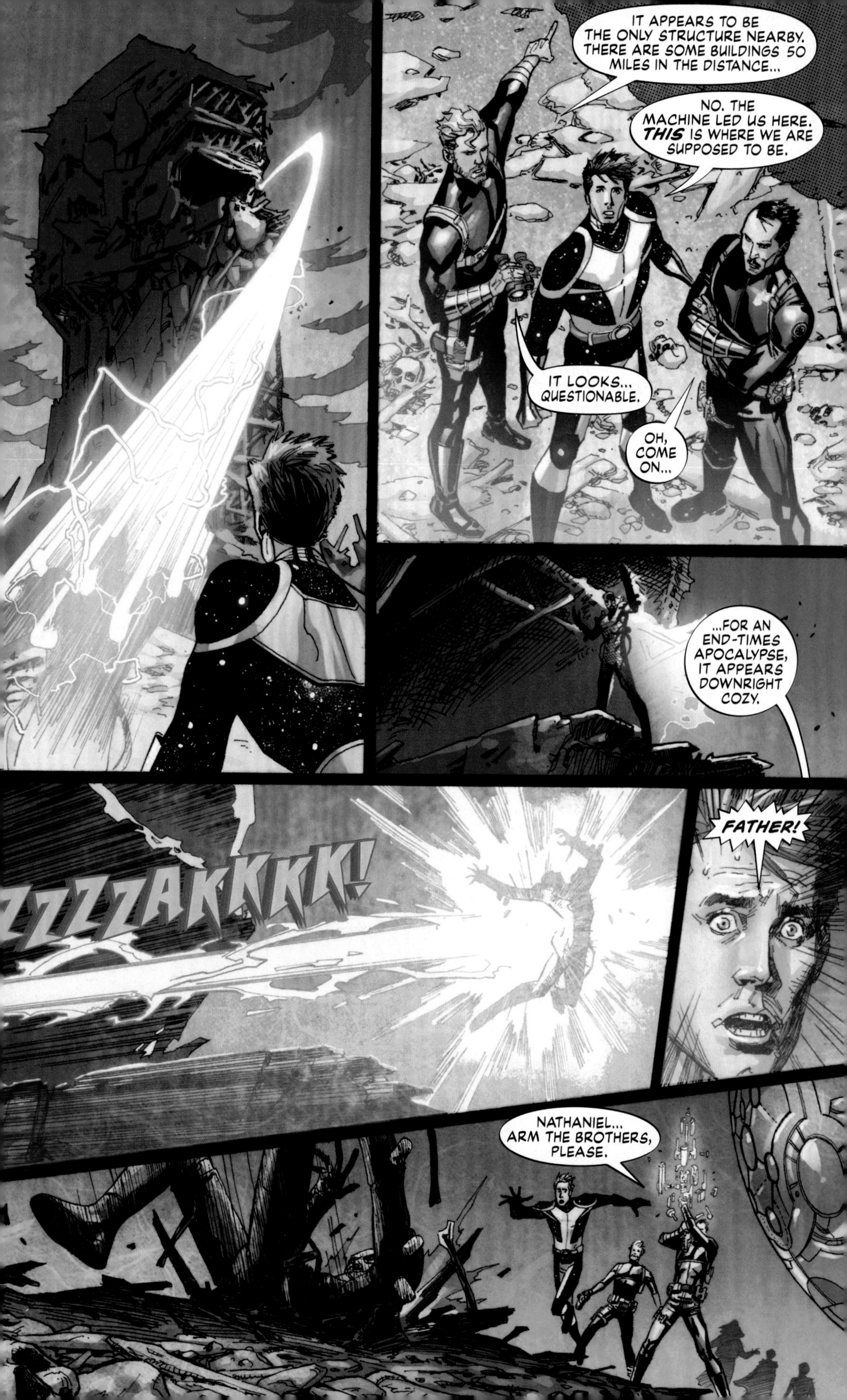
IT APPEARS TO BE THE ONLY STRUCTURE NEARBY. THERE ARE SOME BUILDINGS 50 MILES IN THE DISTANCE...
NO. THE MACHINE LED US HERE. THIS IS WHERE WE ARE SUPPOSED TO BE.
IT LOOKS... QUESTIONABLE.
OH, COME ON...
...FOR AN END-TIMES APOCALYPSE, IT APPEARS DOWNRIGHT COZY.
ZZZZZAKKKKK!
FATHER!
NATHANIEL... ARM THE BROTHERS, PLEASE.

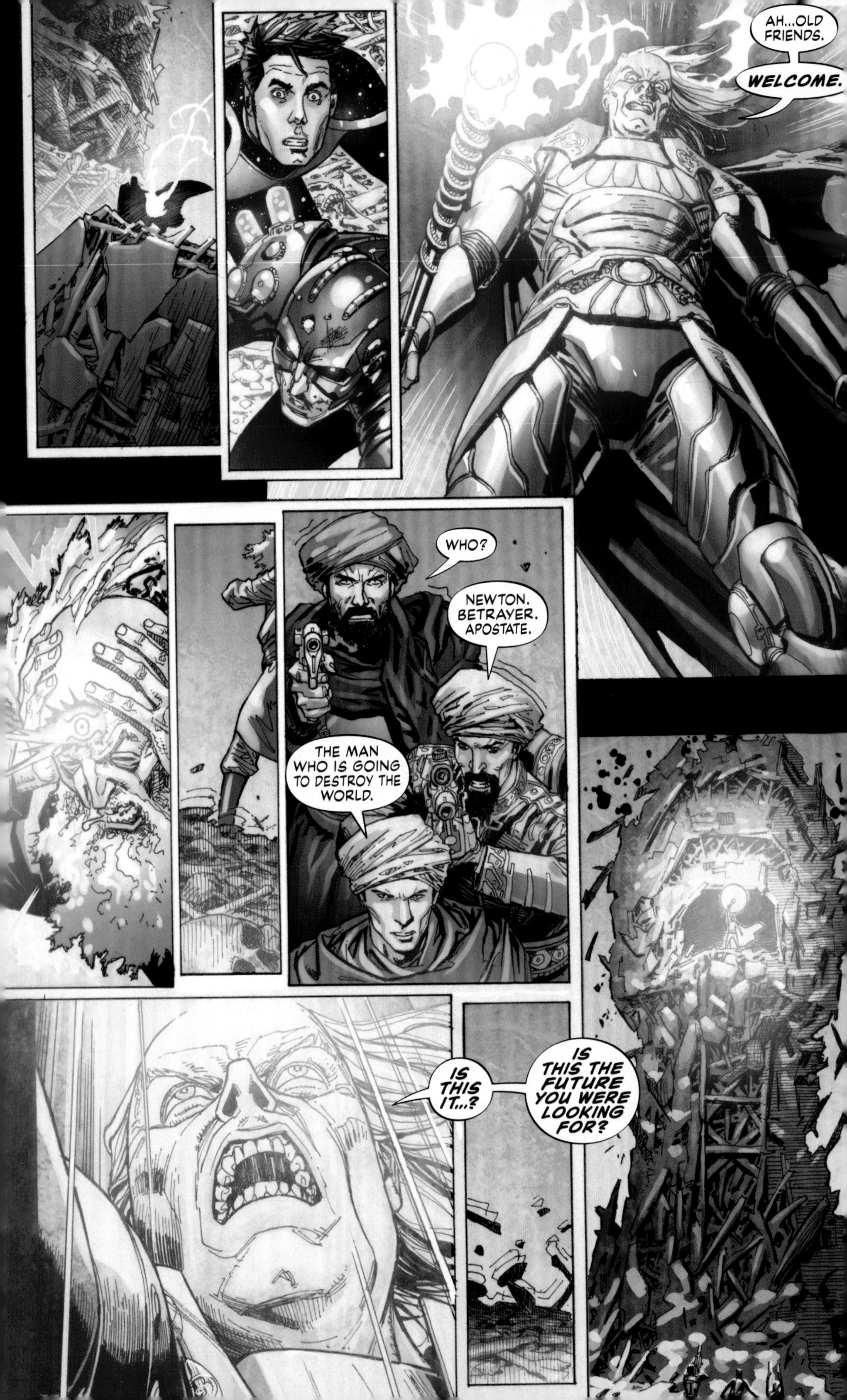
AH...OLD FRIENDS.
WELCOME.
WHO?
NEWTON. BETRAYER. APOSTATE.
THE MAN WHO IS GOING TO DESTROY THE WORLD.
IS THIS IT...?
IS THIS THE FUTURE YOU WERE LOOKING FOR?

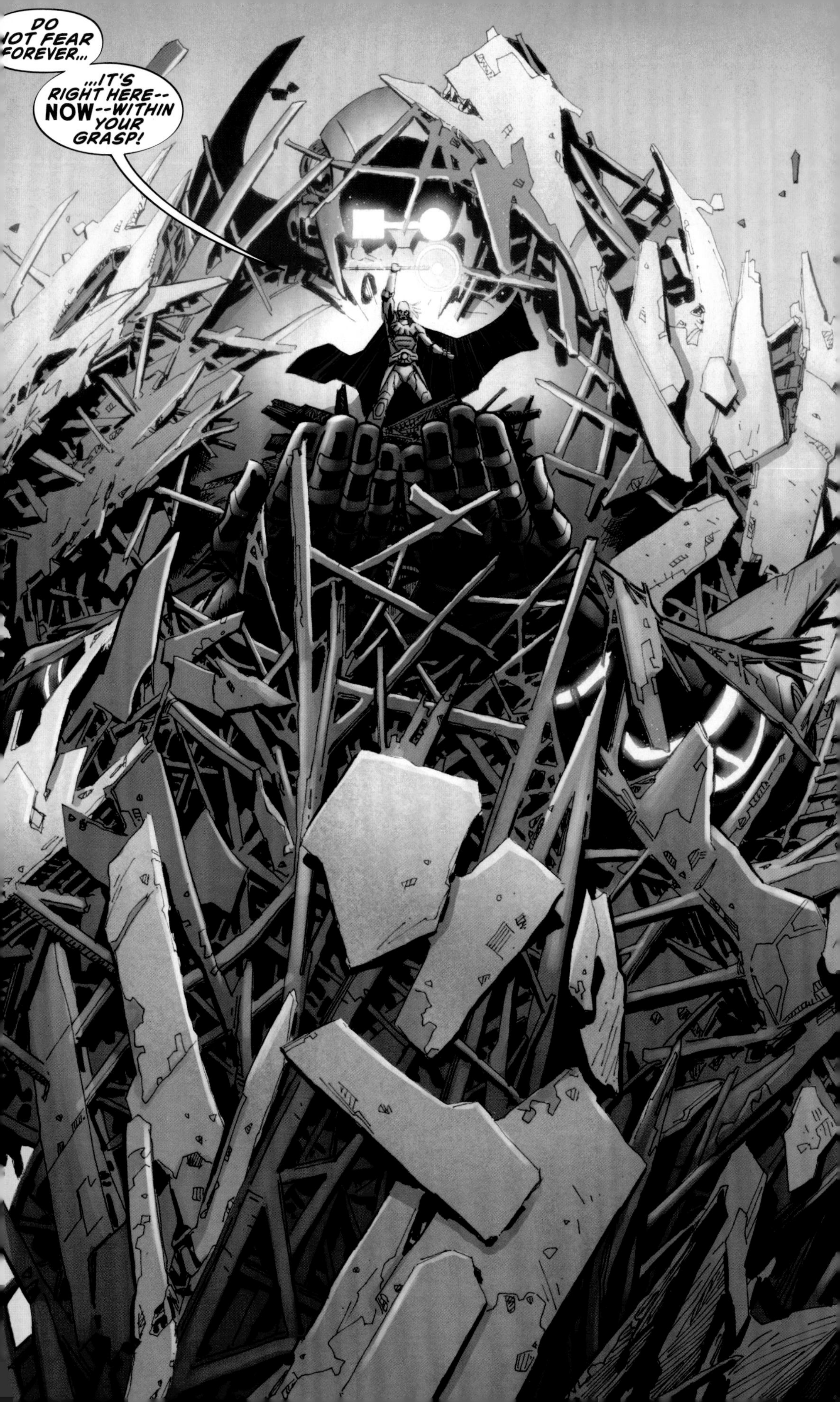
DO NOT FEAR FOREVER...
...IT'S RIGHT HERE-- NOW--WITHIN YOUR GRASP!

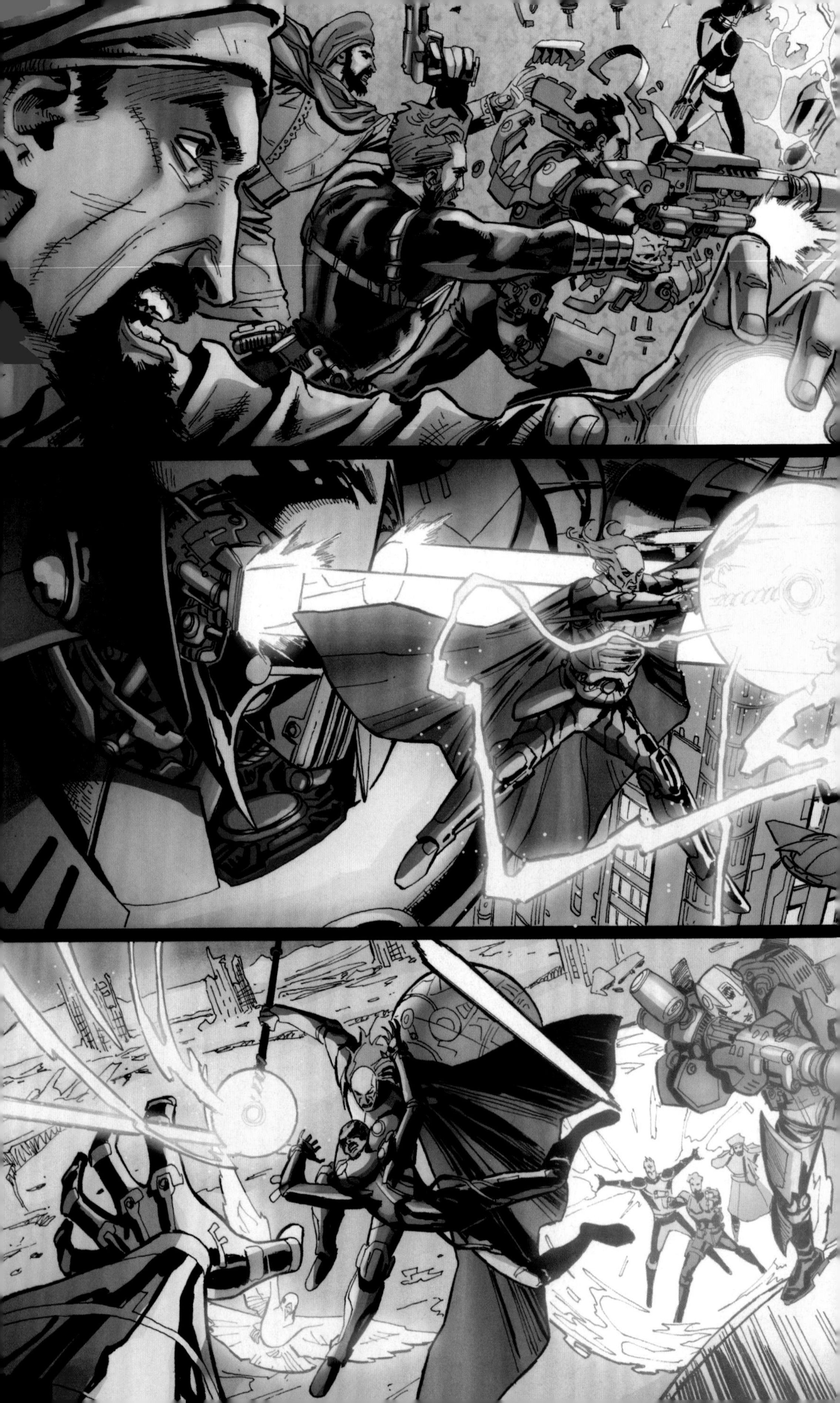

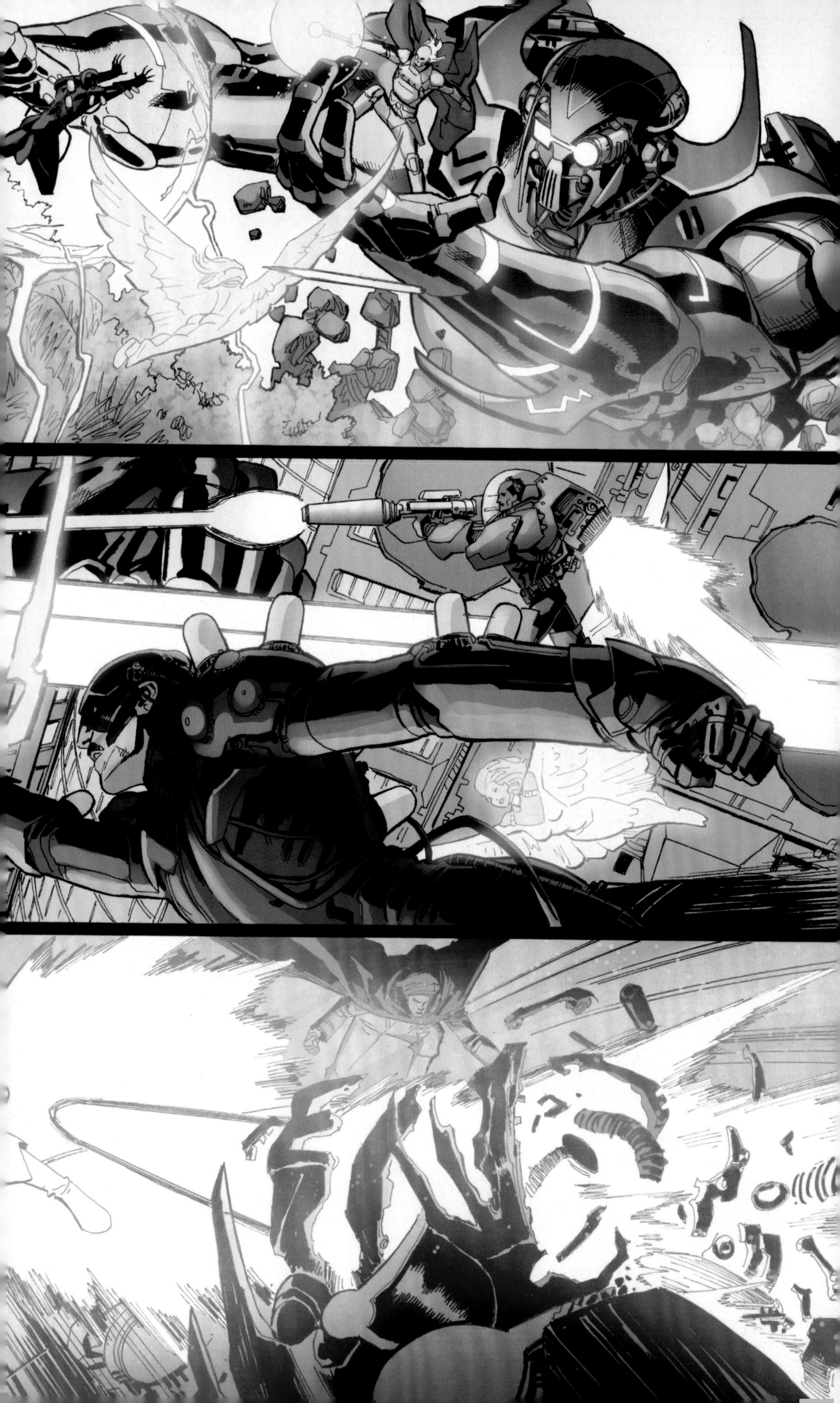

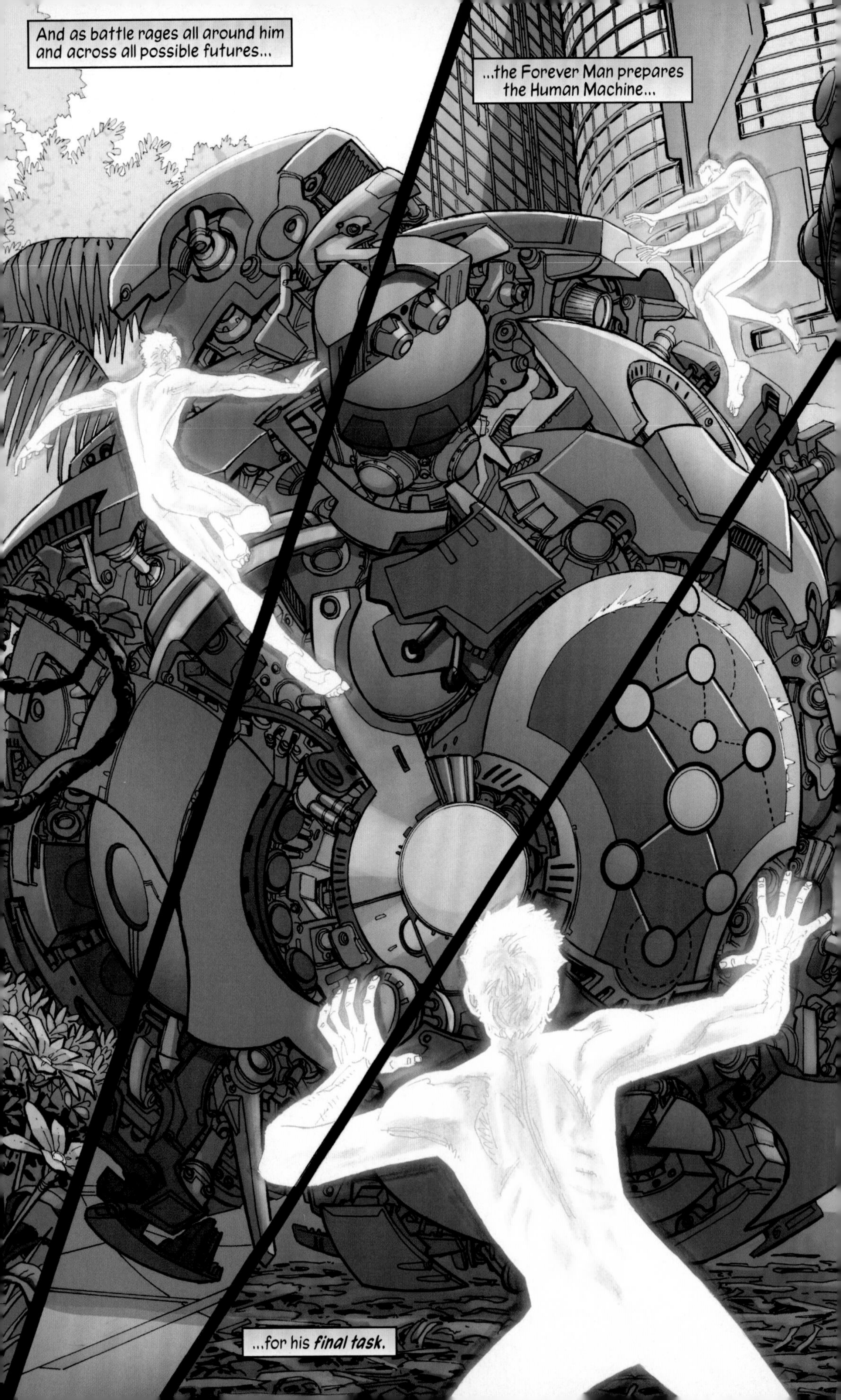
And as battle rages all around him and across all possible futures...
...the Forever Man prepares the Human Machine...
...for his *final task.*

Chapter Five
"Yesterday. Today. Tomorrow."

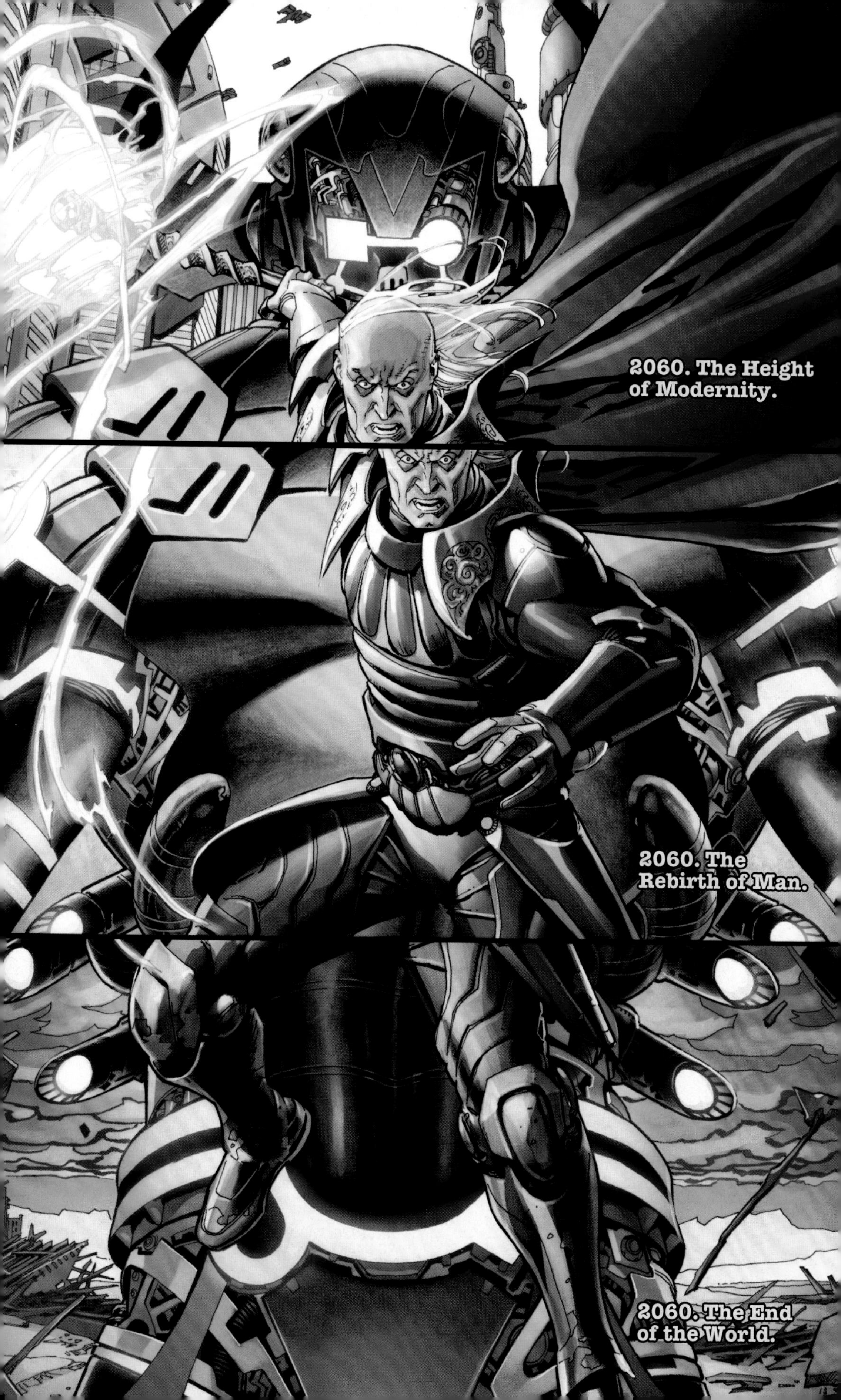
2060. The Height of Modernity.
2060. The Rebirth of Man.
2060. The End of the World.

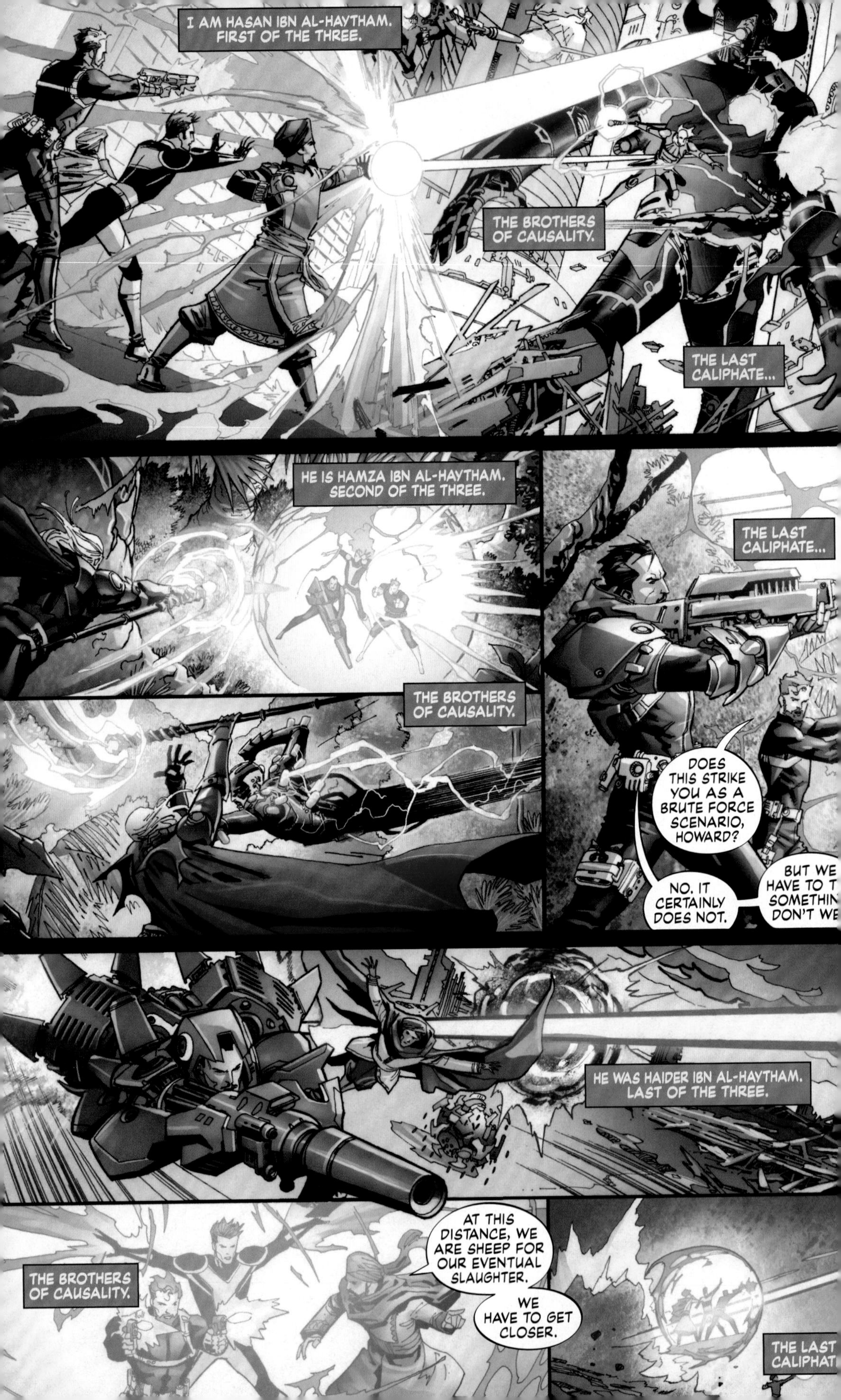
I AM HASAN IBN AL-HAYTHAM. FIRST OF THE THREE.
THE BROTHERS OF CAUSALITY.
THE LAST CALIPHATE...
HE IS HAMZA IBN AL-HAYTHAM. SECOND OF THE THREE.
THE LAST CALIPHATE...
THE BROTHERS OF CAUSALITY.
DOES THIS STRIKE YOU AS A BRUTE FORCE SCENARIO, HOWARD?
NO. IT CERTAINLY DOES NOT.
HE WAS HAIDER IBN AL-HAYTHAM. LAST OF THE THREE.
THE BROTHERS OF CAUSALITY.
AT THIS DISTANCE, WE ARE SHEEP FOR OUR EVENTUAL SLAUGHTER.
WE HAVE TO GET CLOSER.

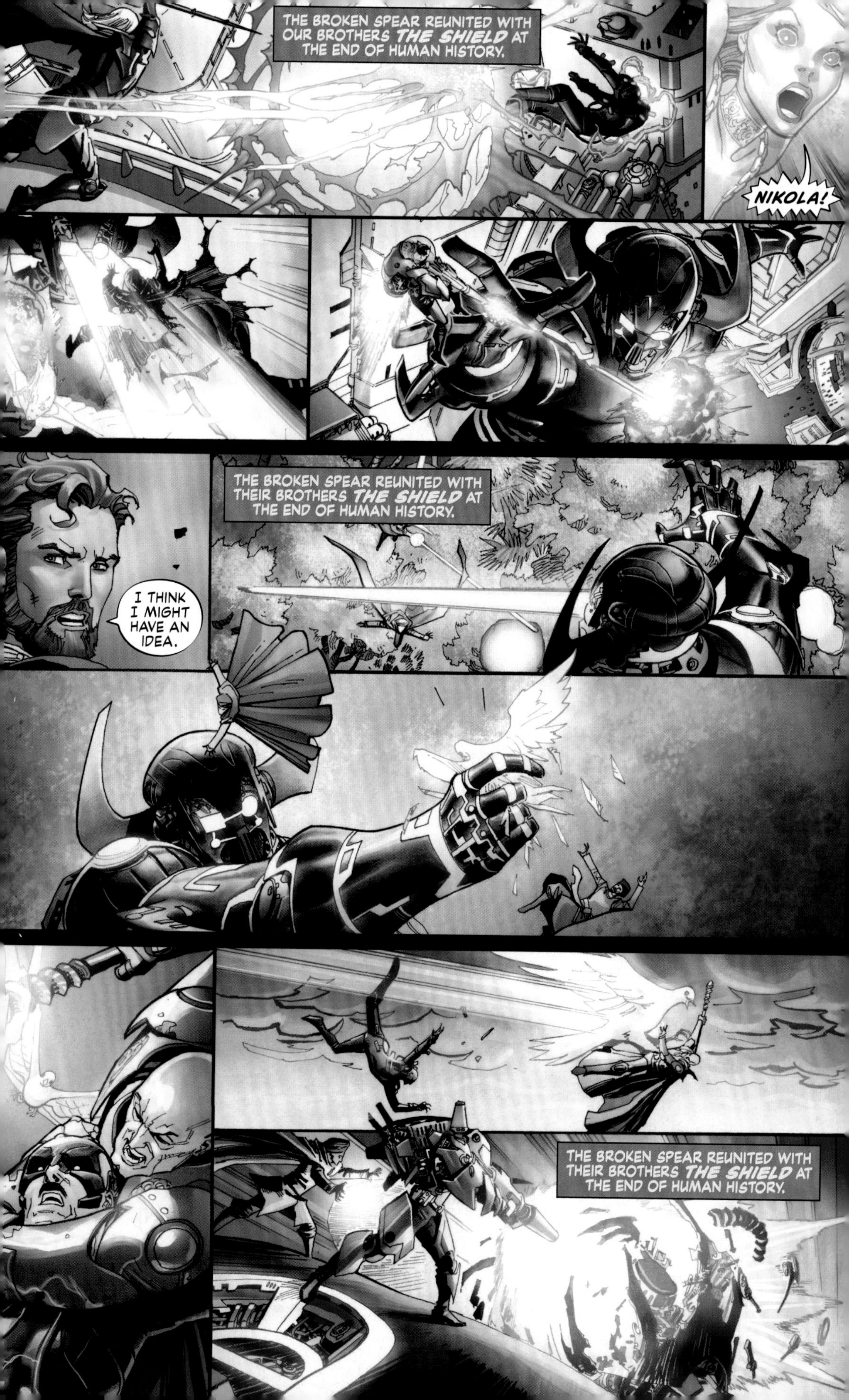
THE BROKEN SPEAR REUNITED WITH OUR BROTHERS THE SHIELD AT THE END OF HUMAN HISTORY.
NIKOLA!
THE BROKEN SPEAR REUNITED WITH THEIR BROTHERS THE SHIELD AT THE END OF HUMAN HISTORY.
I THINK I MIGHT HAVE AN IDEA.
THE BROKEN SPEAR REUNITED WITH THEIR BROTHERS THE SHIELD AT THE END OF HUMAN HISTORY.

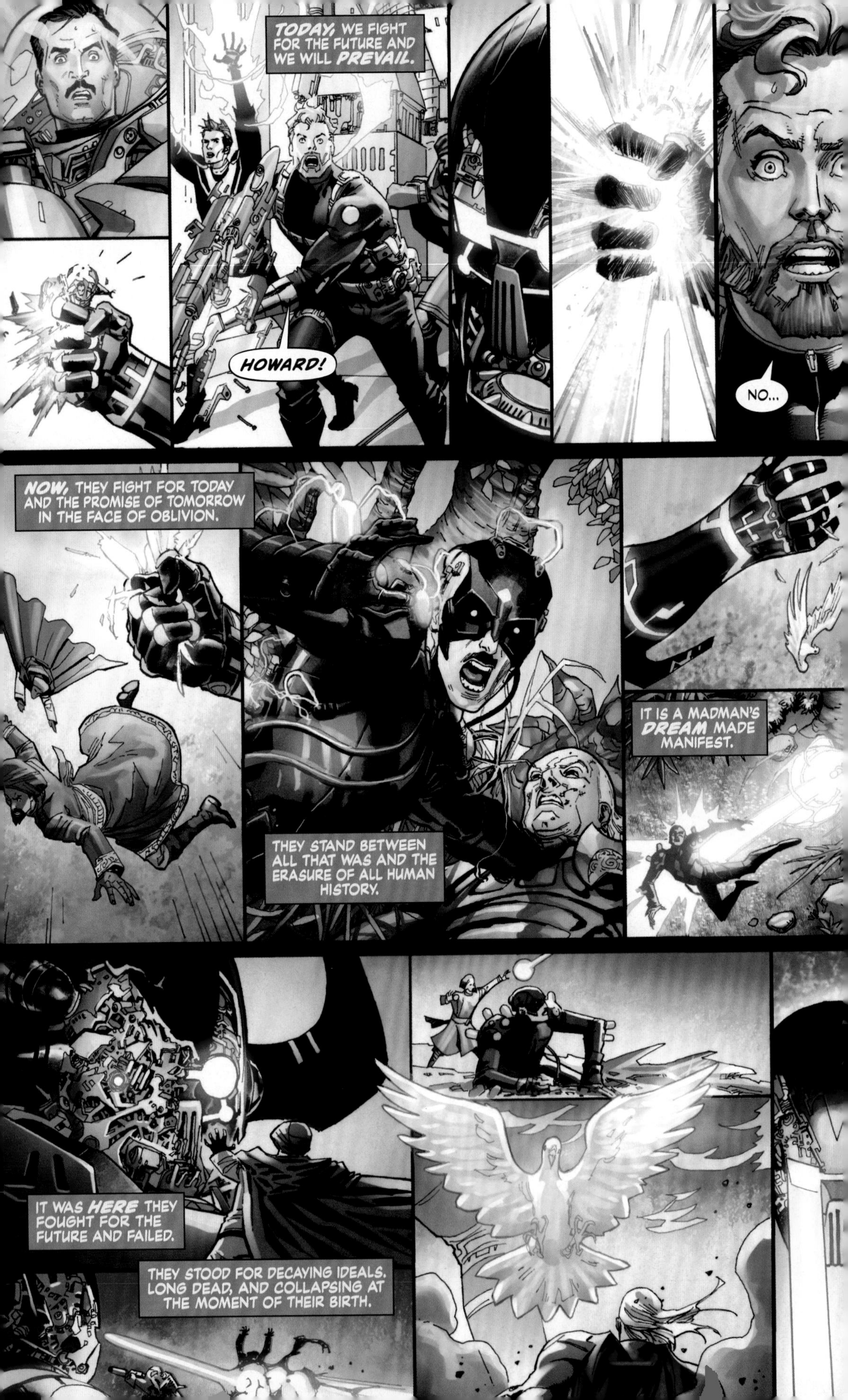
TODAY, WE FIGHT FOR THE FUTURE AND WE WILL PREVAIL.
HOWARD!
NO...
NOW, THEY FIGHT FOR TODAY AND THE PROMISE OF TOMORROW IN THE FACE OF OBLIVION.
THEY STAND BETWEEN ALL THAT WAS AND THE ERASURE OF ALL HUMAN HISTORY.
IT IS A MADMAN'S DREAM MADE MANIFEST.
IT WAS HERE THEY FOUGHT FOR THE FUTURE AND FAILED.
THEY STOOD FOR DECAYING IDEALS. LONG DEAD, AND COLLAPSING AT THE MOMENT OF THEIR BIRTH.

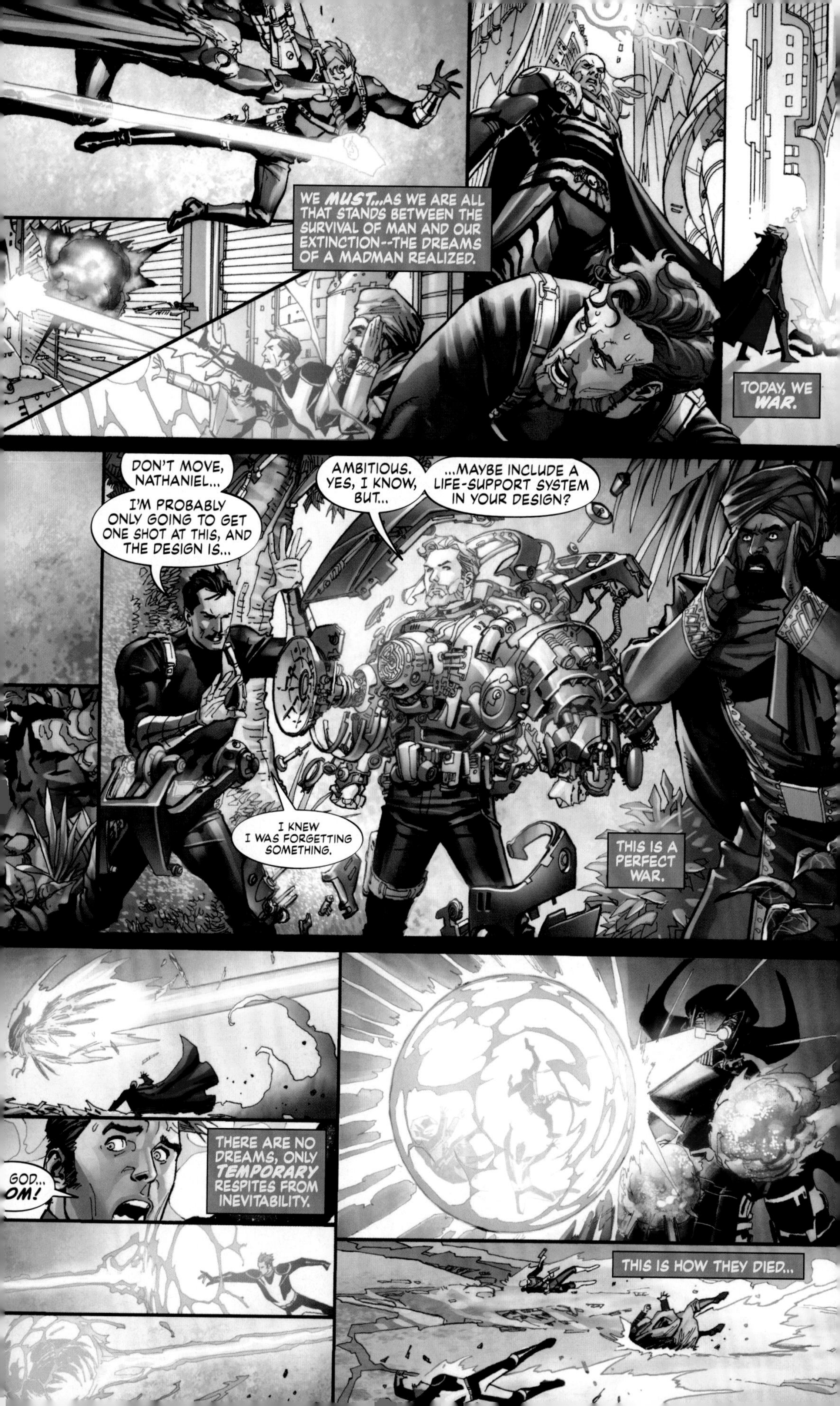

WE MUST...AS WE ARE ALL THAT STANDS BETWEEN THE SURVIVAL OF MAN AND OUR EXTINCTION--THE DREAMS OF A MADMAN REALIZED.
TODAY, WE WAR.
DON'T MOVE, NATHANIEL...
I'M PROBABLY ONLY GOING TO GET ONE SHOT AT THIS, AND THE DESIGN IS...
AMBITIOUS. YES, I KNOW, BUT...
...MAYBE INCLUDE A LIFE-SUPPORT SYSTEM IN YOUR DESIGN?
I KNEW I WAS FORGETTING SOMETHING.
THIS IS A PERFECT WAR.
GOD... OM!
THERE ARE NO DREAMS, ONLY TEMPORARY RESPITES FROM INEVITABILITY.
THIS IS HOW THEY DIED...

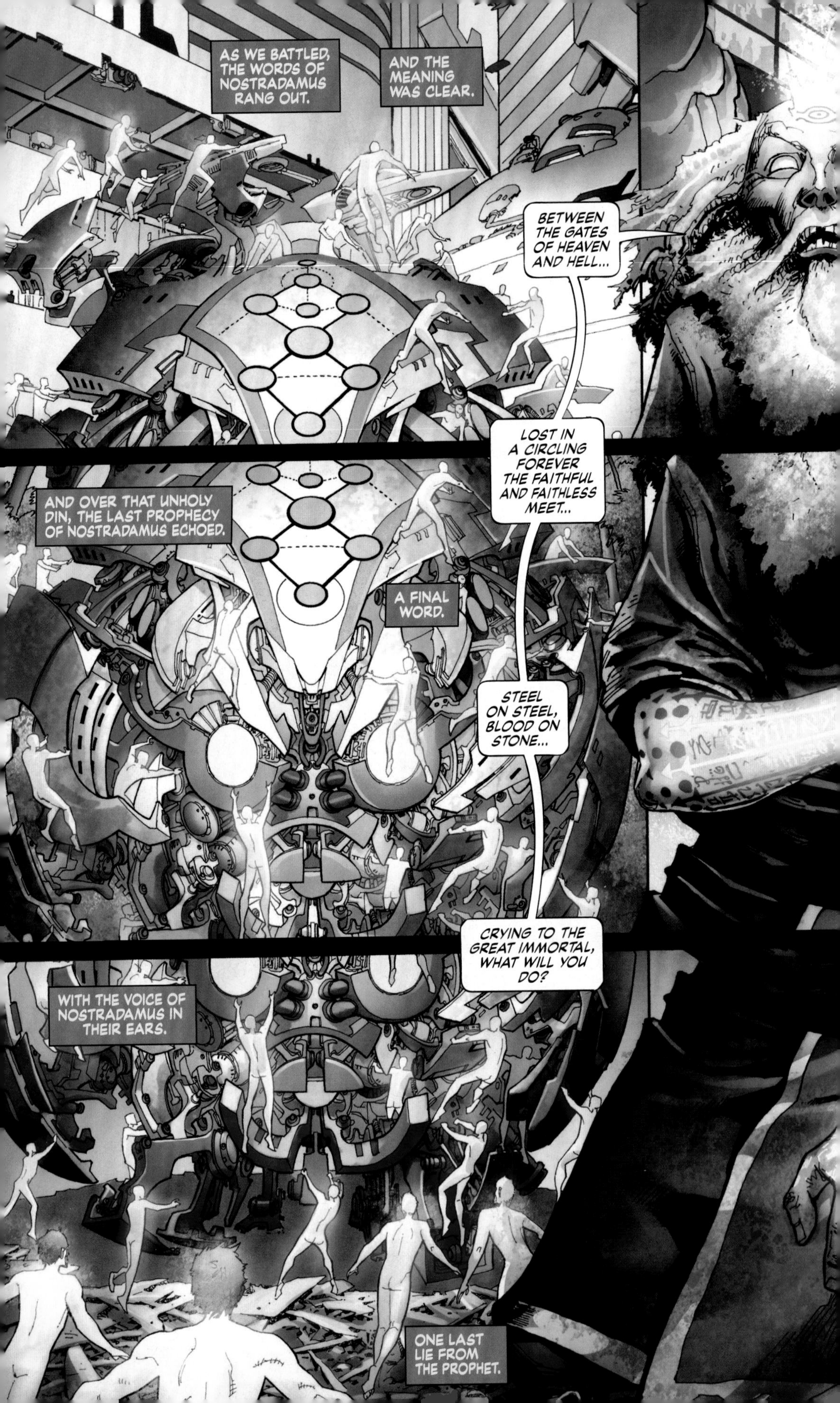
AS WE BATTLED, THE WORDS OF NOSTRADAMUS RANG OUT.
AND THE MEANING WAS CLEAR.
BETWEEN THE GATES OF HEAVEN AND HELL...
LOST IN A CIRCLING FOREVER THE FAITHFUL AND FAITHLESS MEET...
AND OVER THAT UNHOLY DIN, THE LAST PROPHECY OF NOSTRADAMUS ECHOED.
A FINAL WORD.
STEEL ON STEEL, BLOOD ON STONE...
CRYING TO THE GREAT IMMORTAL, WHAT WILL YOU DO?
WITH THE VOICE OF NOSTRADAMUS IN THEIR EARS.
ONE LAST LIE FROM THE PROPHET.

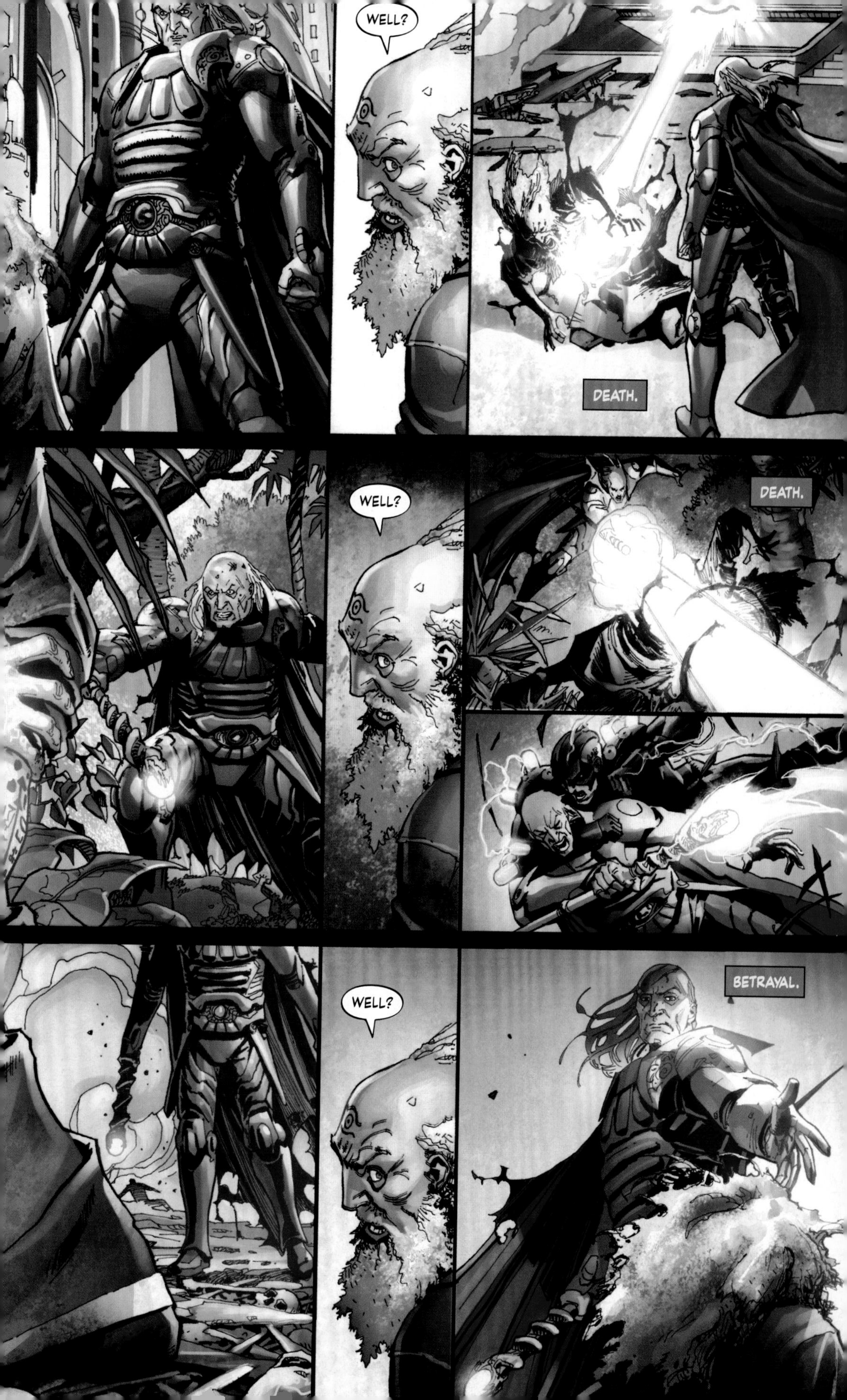
WELL?
DEATH.
WELL?
DEATH.
WELL?
BETRAYAL.

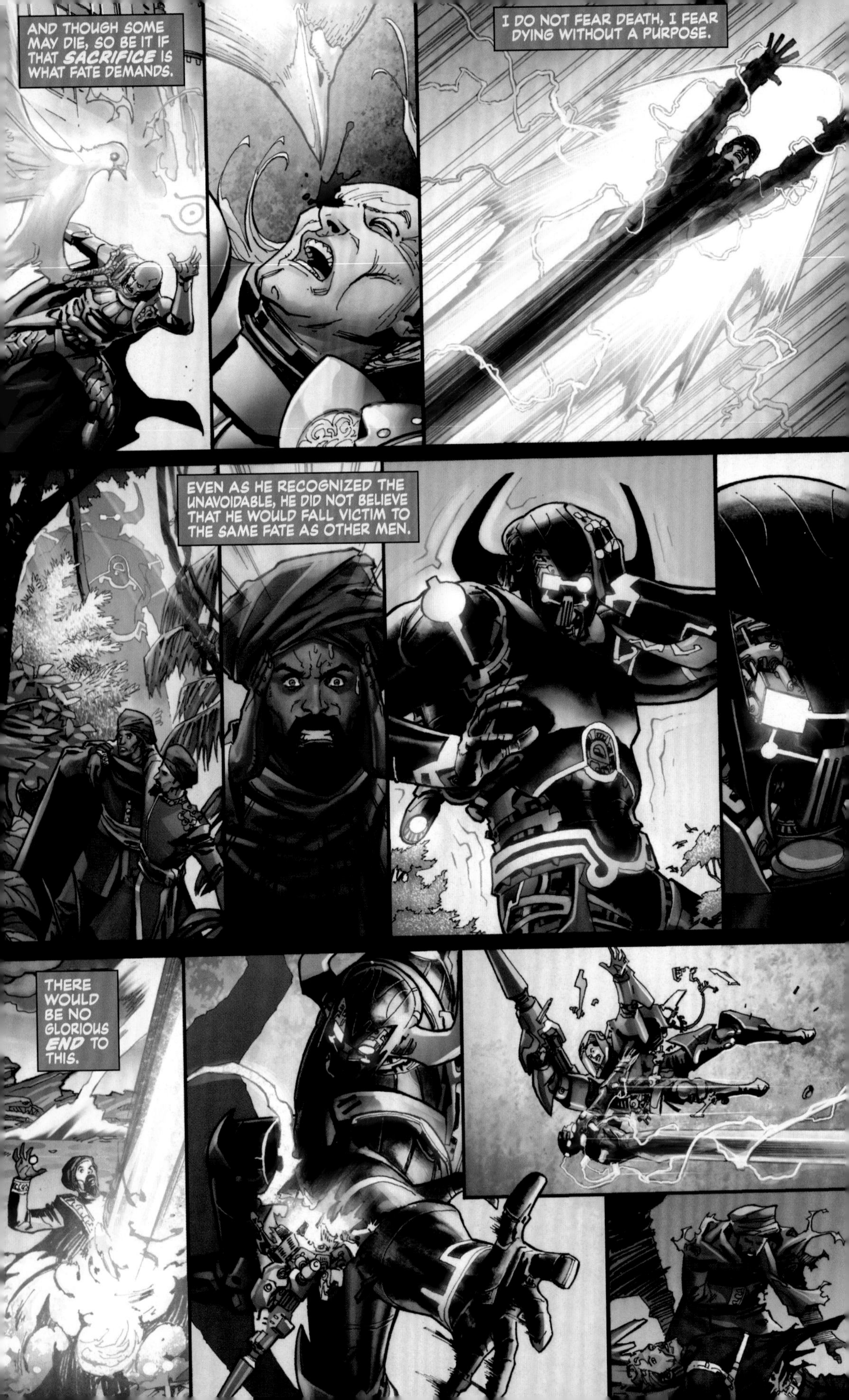
AND THOUGH SOME MAY DIE, SO BE IT IF THAT *SACRIFICE* IS WHAT FATE DEMANDS.
I DO NOT FEAR DEATH, I FEAR DYING WITHOUT A PURPOSE.
EVEN AS HE RECOGNIZED THE UNAVOIDABLE, HE DID NOT BELIEVE THAT HE WOULD FALL VICTIM TO THE SAME FATE AS OTHER MEN.
THERE WOULD BE NO GLORIOUS *END* TO THIS.

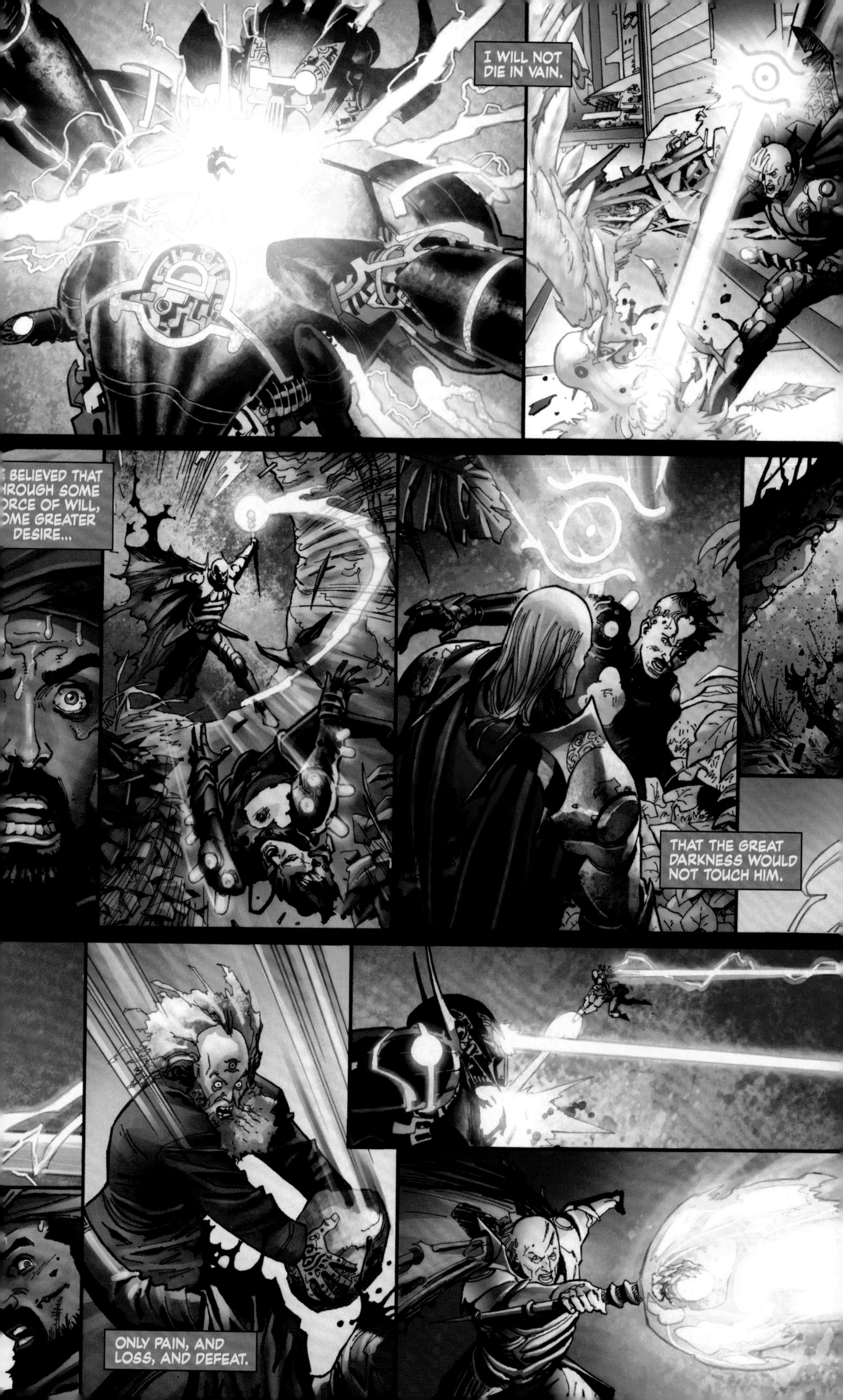
I WILL NOT DIE IN VAIN.
E BELIEVED THAT HROUGH SOME ORCE OF WILL, OME GREATER DESIRE...
THAT THE GREAT DARKNESS WOULD NOT TOUCH HIM.
ONLY PAIN, AND LOSS, AND DEFEAT.

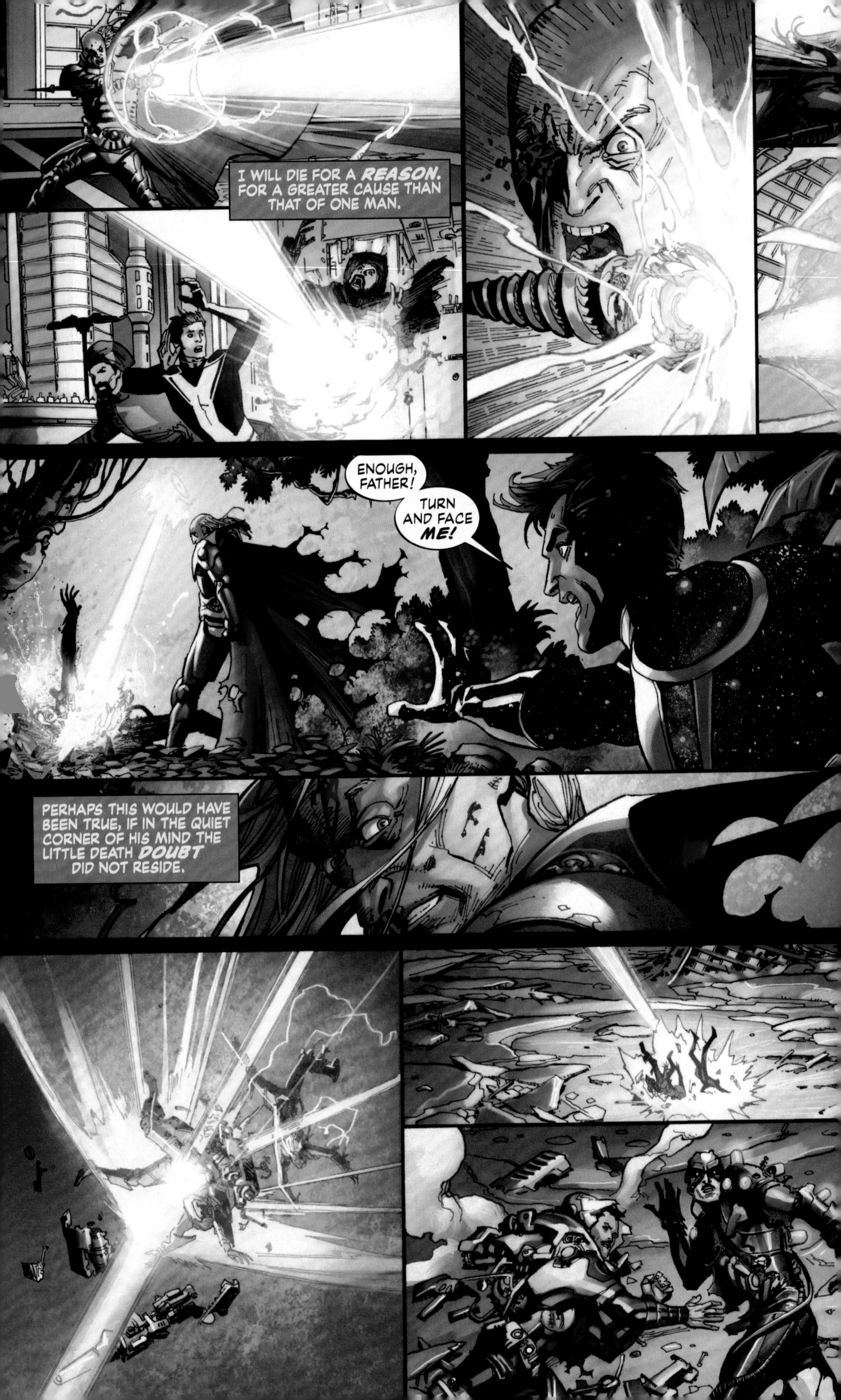
I WILL DIE FOR A REASON. FOR A GREATER CAUSE THAN THAT OF ONE MAN.
ENOUGH, FATHER!
TURN AND FACE ME!
PERHAPS THIS WOULD HAVE BEEN TRUE, IF IN THE QUIET CORNER OF HIS MIND THE LITTLE DEATH DOUBT DID NOT RESIDE.

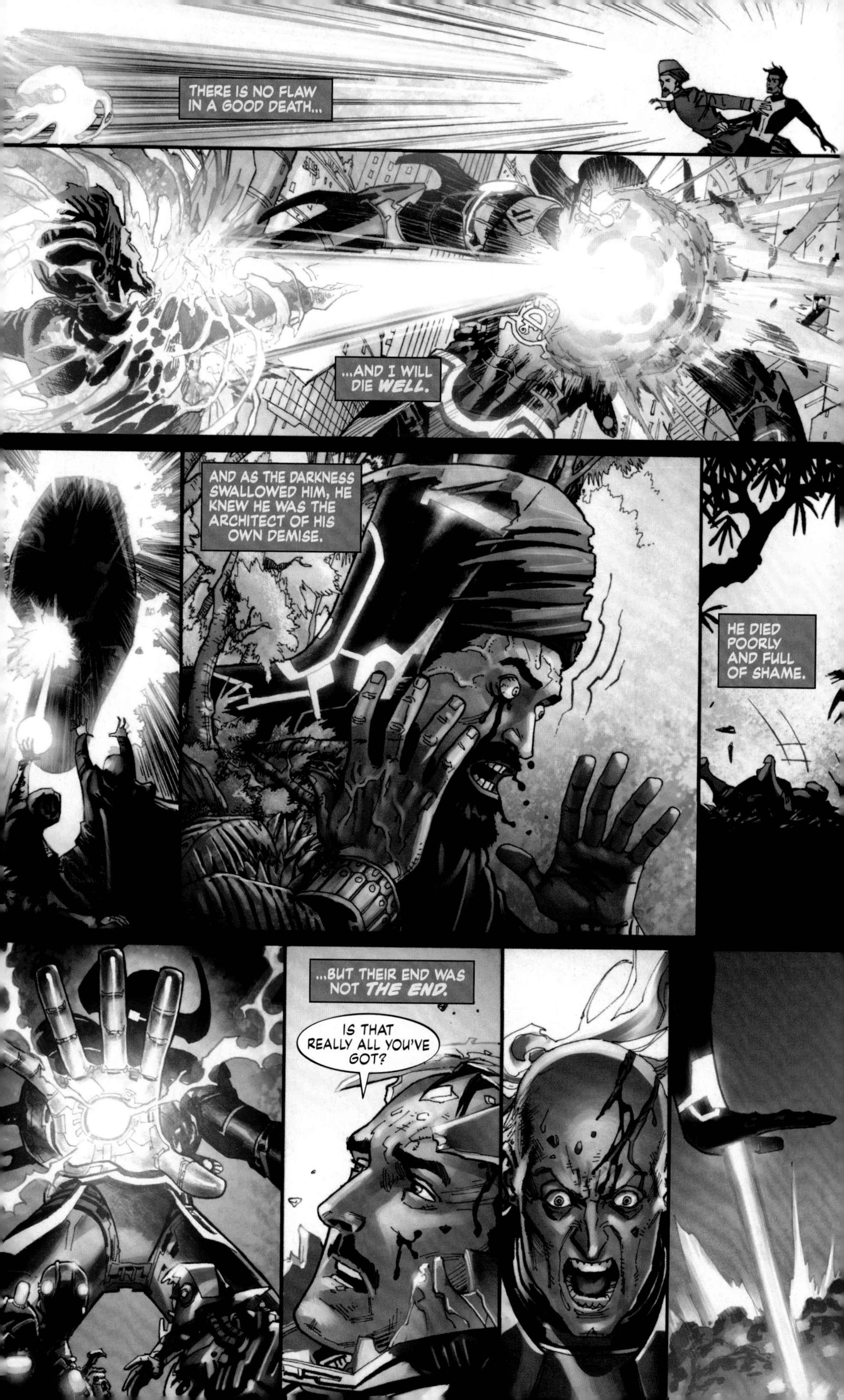
THERE IS NO FLAW IN A GOOD DEATH...
...AND I WILL DIE WELL.
AND AS THE DARKNESS SWALLOWED HIM, HE KNEW HE WAS THE ARCHITECT OF HIS OWN DEMISE.
HE DIED POORLY AND FULL OF SHAME.
...BUT THEIR END WAS NOT THE END.
IS THAT REALLY ALL YOU'VE GOT?

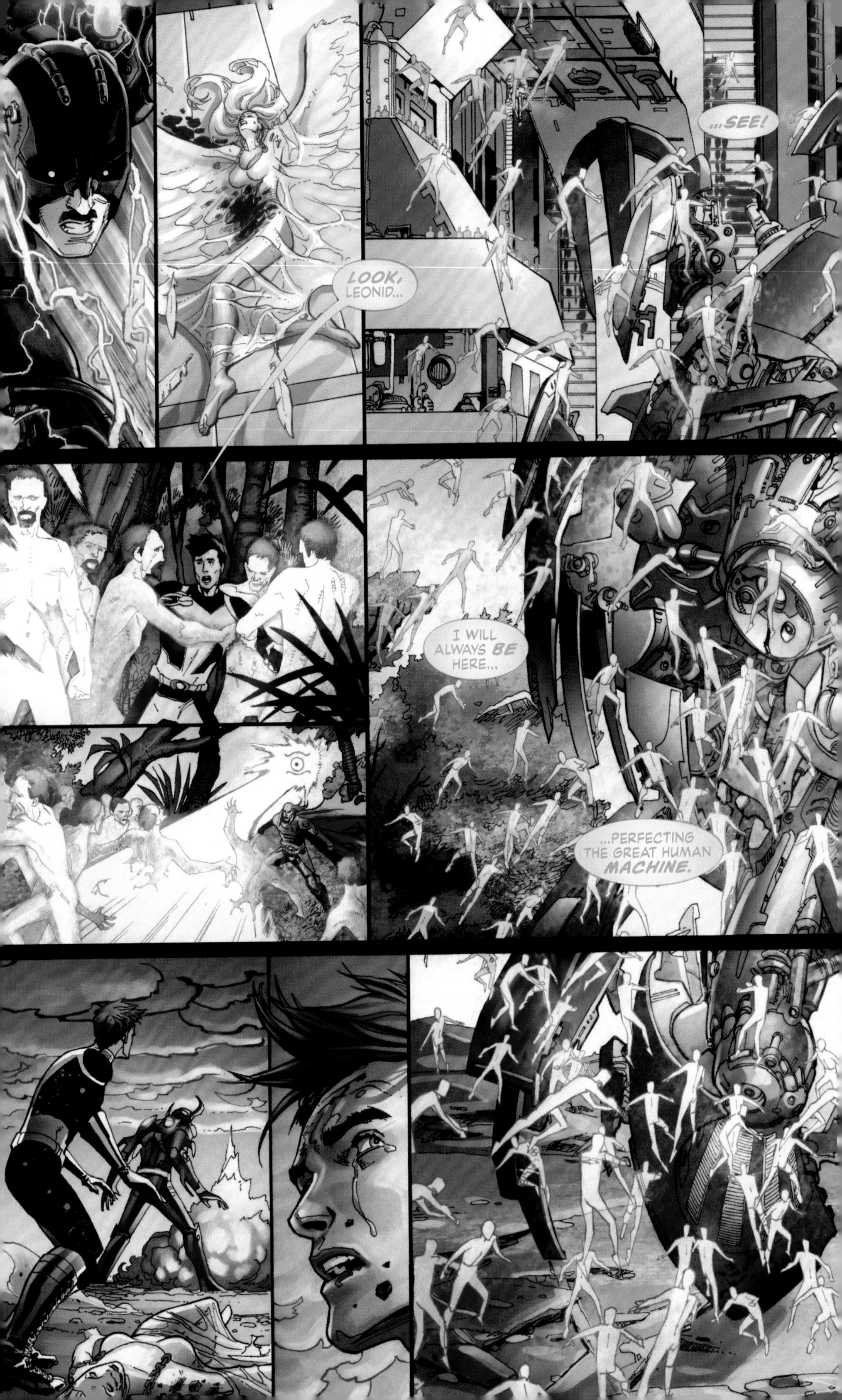
LOOK, LEONID...
...SEE!
I WILL ALWAYS BE HERE...
...PERFECTING THE GREAT HUMAN MACHINE.

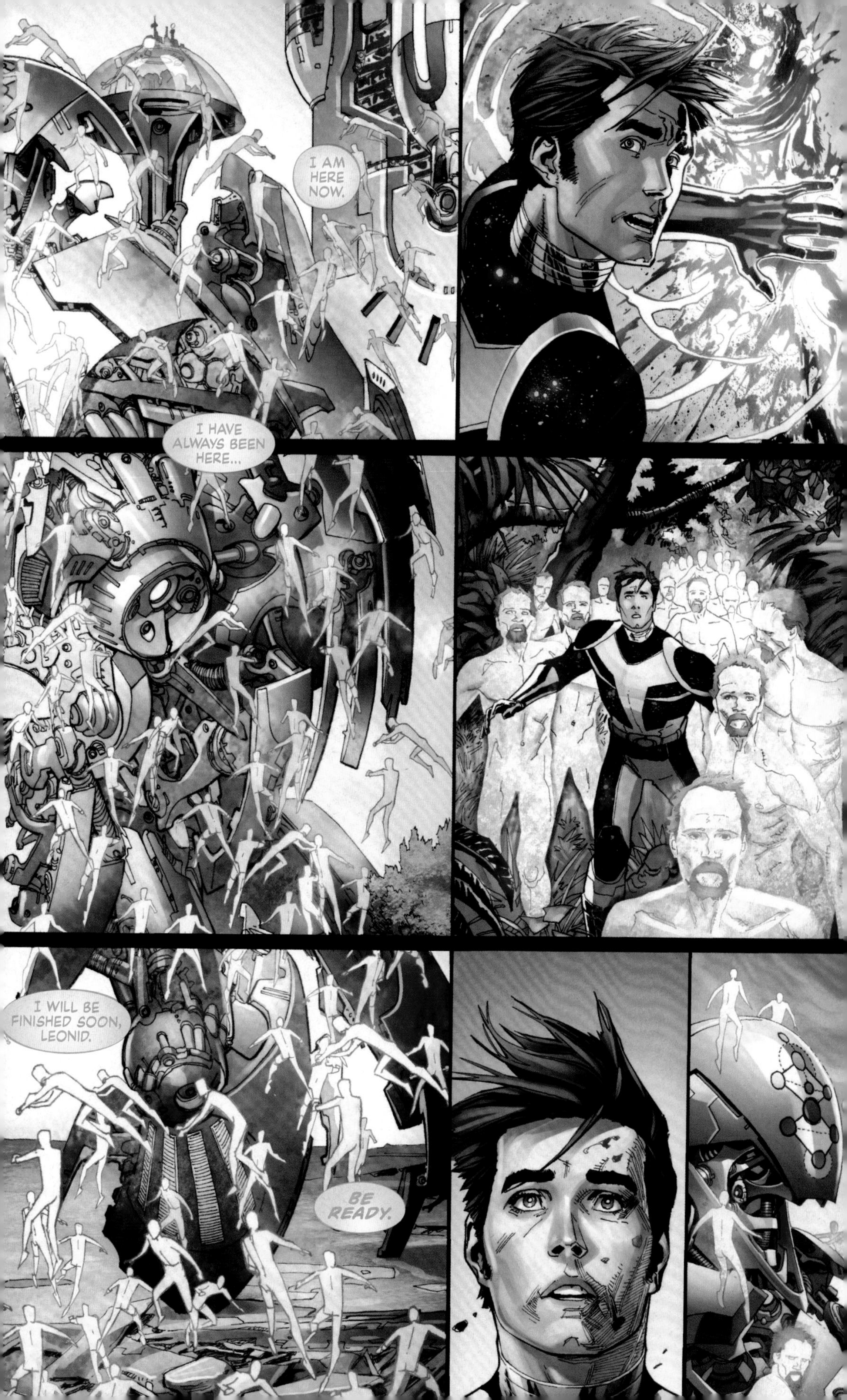
I AM HERE NOW.
I HAVE ALWAYS BEEN HERE...
I WILL BE FINISHED SOON, LEONID.
BE READY.

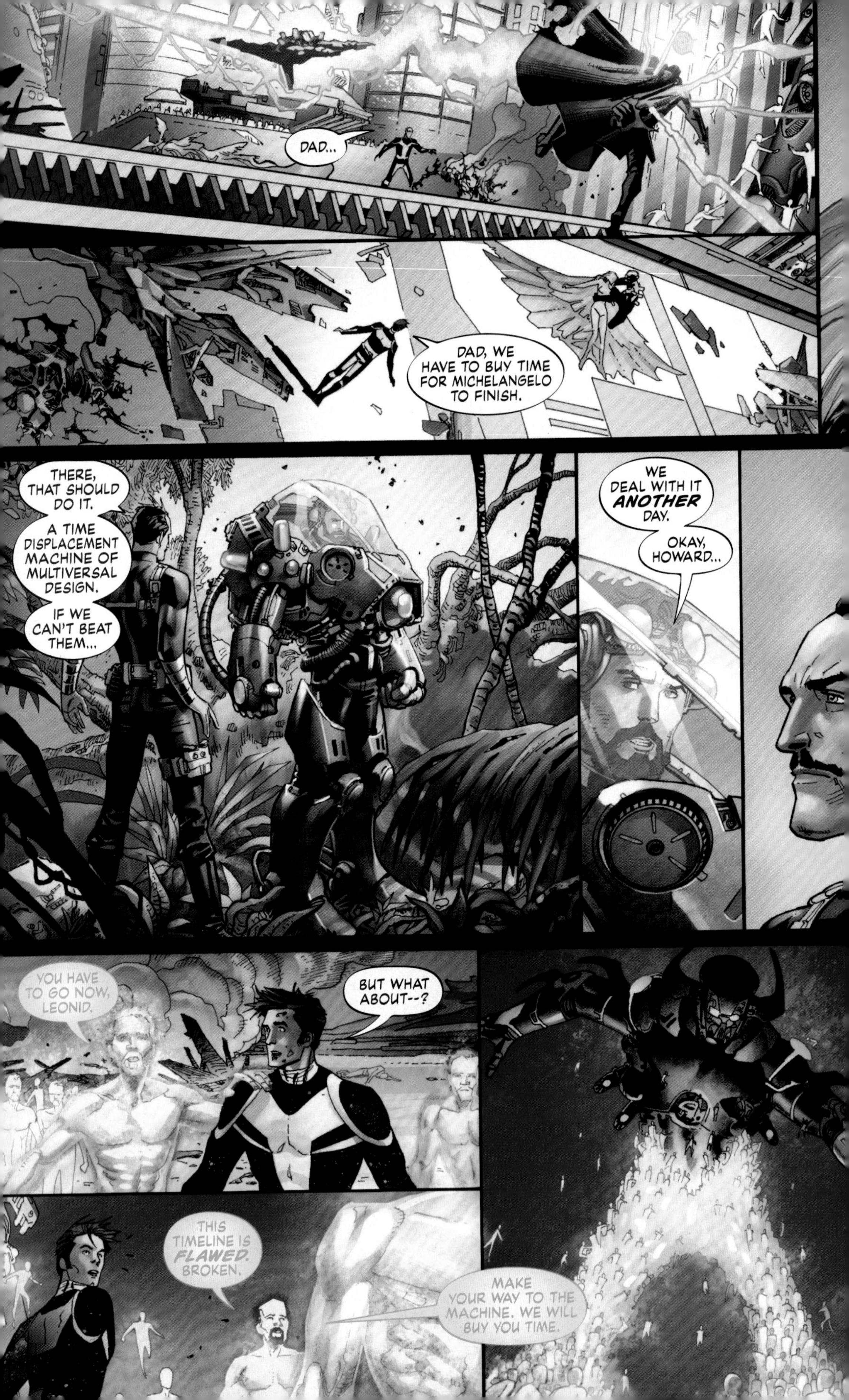
DAD...
DAD, WE HAVE TO BUY TIME FOR MICHELANGELO TO FINISH.
THERE, THAT SHOULD DO IT.
A TIME DISPLACEMENT MACHINE OF MULTIVERSAL DESIGN.
IF WE CAN'T BEAT THEM...
WE DEAL WITH IT ANOTHER DAY.
OKAY, HOWARD...
YOU HAVE TO GO NOW, LEONID.
BUT WHAT ABOUT--?
THIS TIMELINE IS FLAWED. BROKEN.
MAKE YOUR WAY TO THE MACHINE. WE WILL BUY YOU TIME.

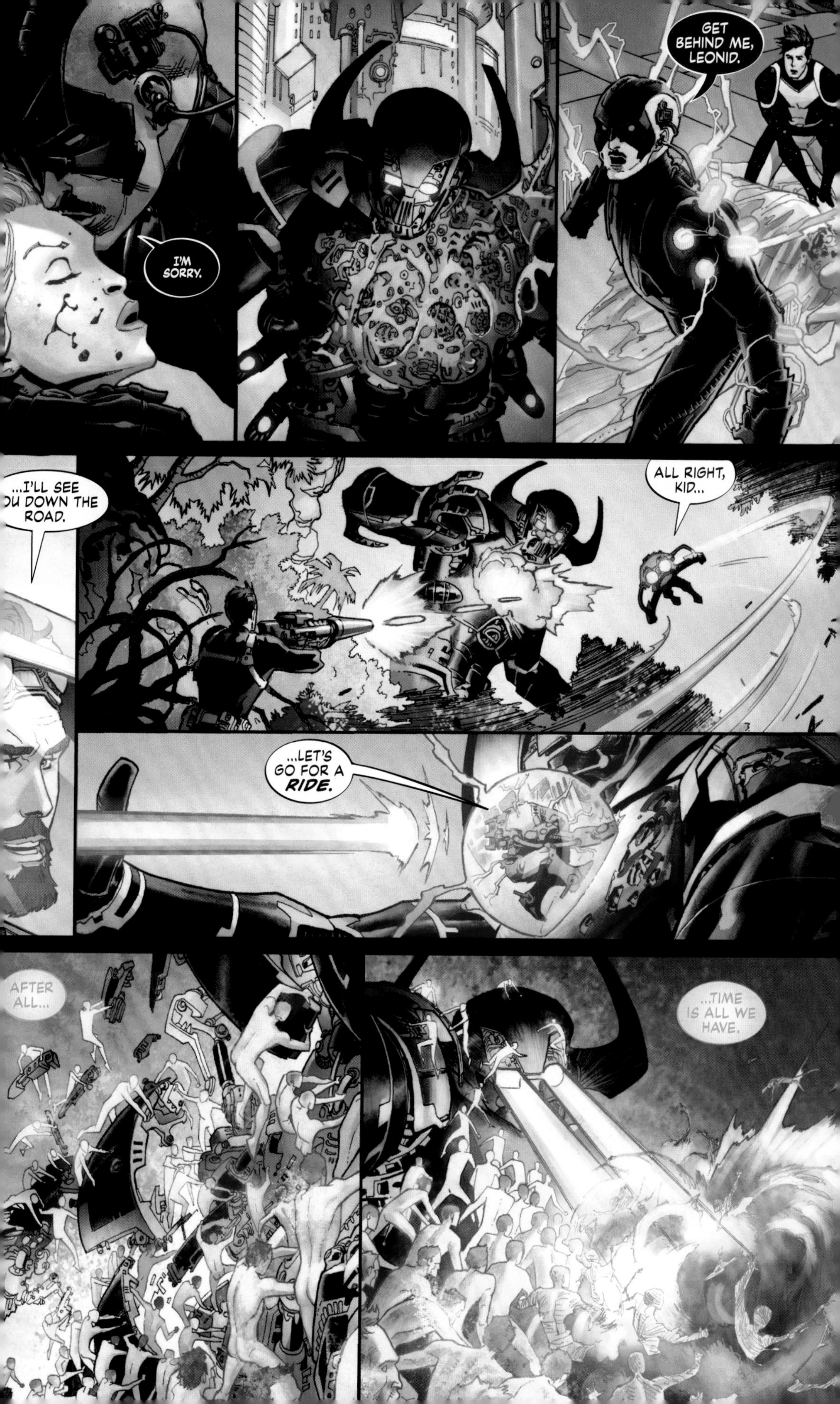
I'M SORRY.
GET BEHIND ME, LEONID.
...I'LL SEE OU DOWN THE ROAD.
ALL RIGHT, KID...
...LET'S GO FOR A ***RIDE.***
AFTER ALL...
...TIME IS ALL WE HAVE.

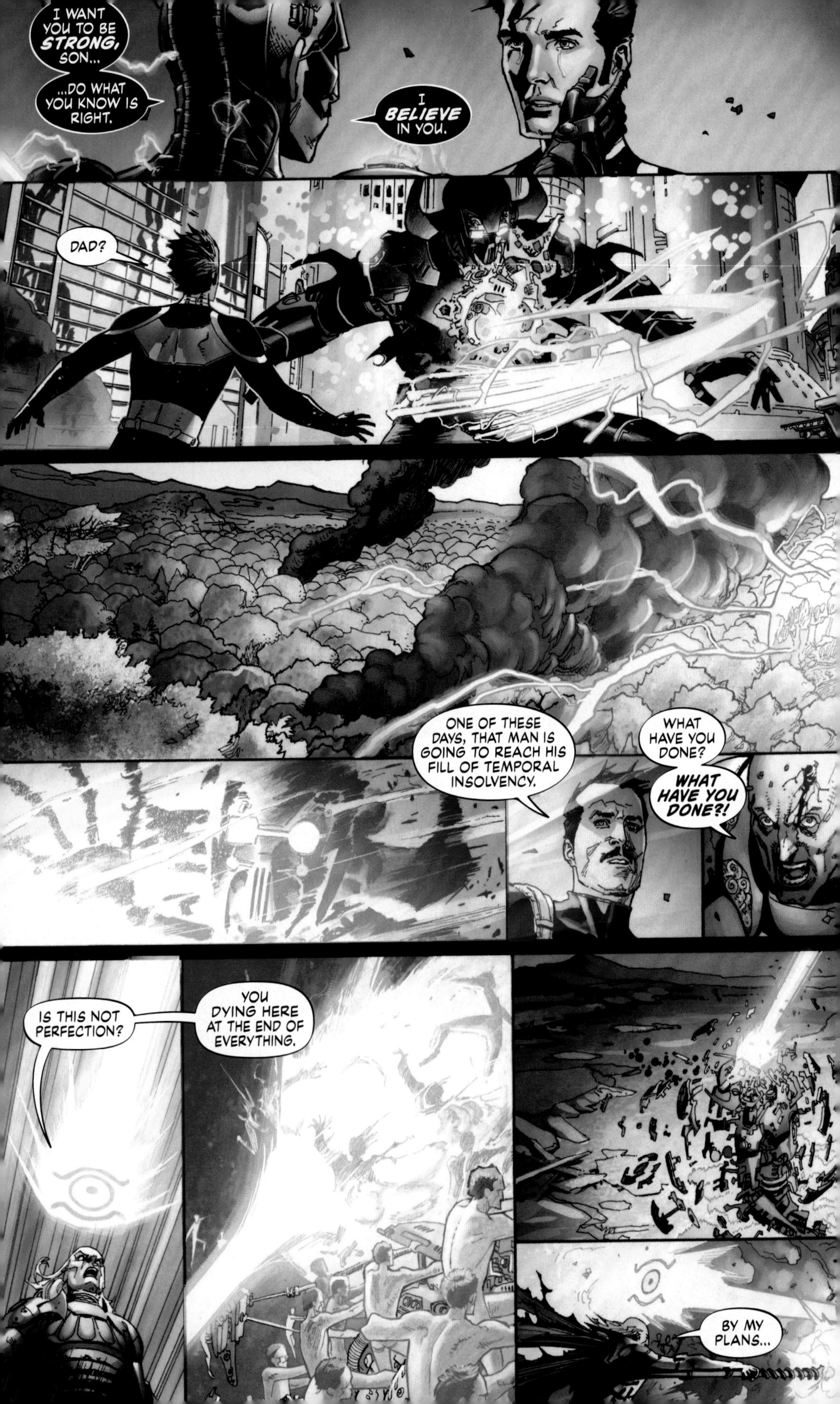
I WANT YOU TO BE STRONG, SON...
...DO WHAT YOU KNOW IS RIGHT.
I BELIEVE IN YOU.
DAD?
ONE OF THESE DAYS, THAT MAN IS GOING TO REACH HIS FILL OF TEMPORAL INSOLVENCY.
WHAT HAVE YOU DONE?
WHAT HAVE YOU DONE?!
IS THIS NOT PERFECTION?
YOU DYING HERE AT THE END OF EVERYTHING.
BY MY PLANS...

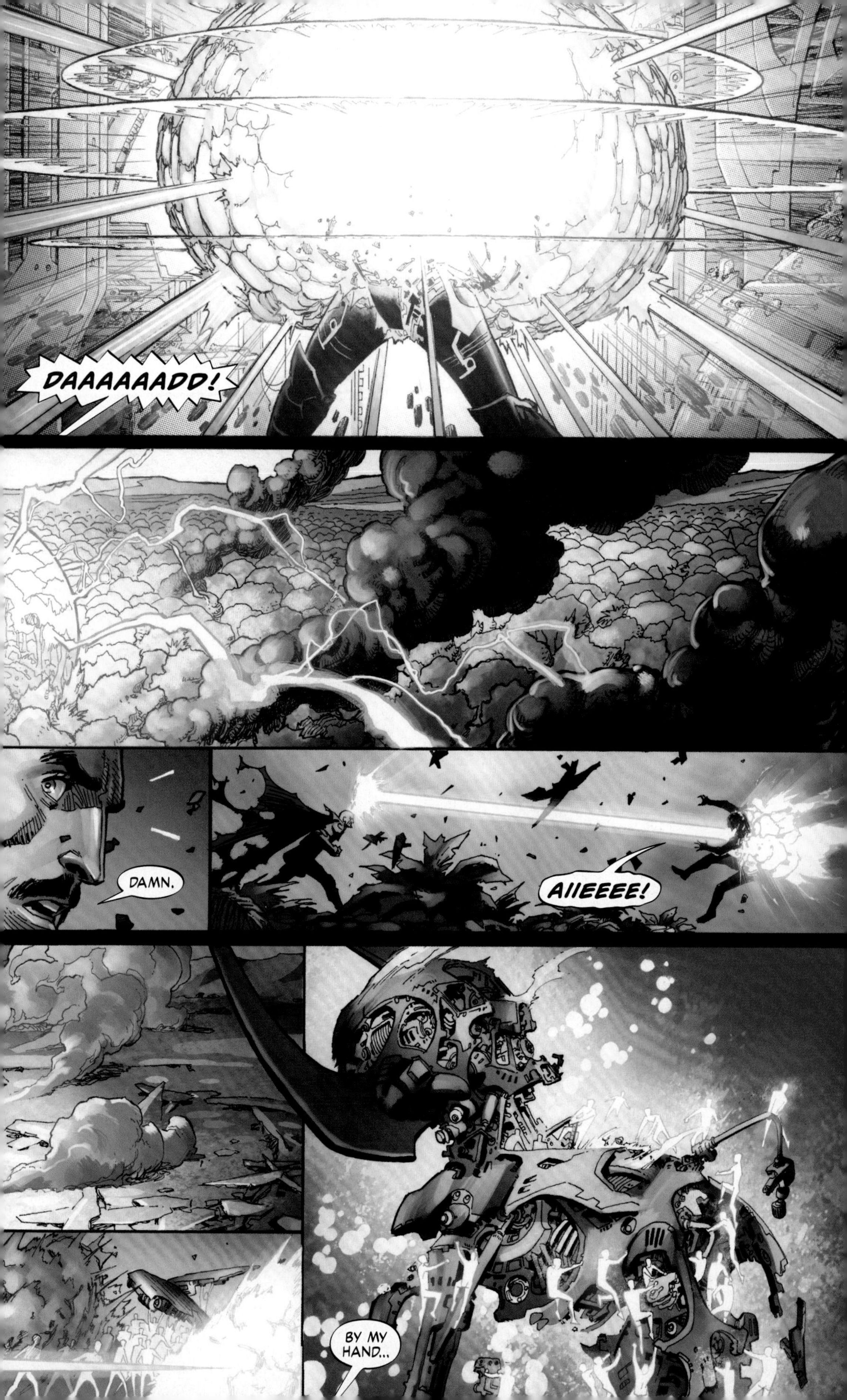
DAAAAAADD!
DAMN.
AIIEEEE!
BY MY HAND...

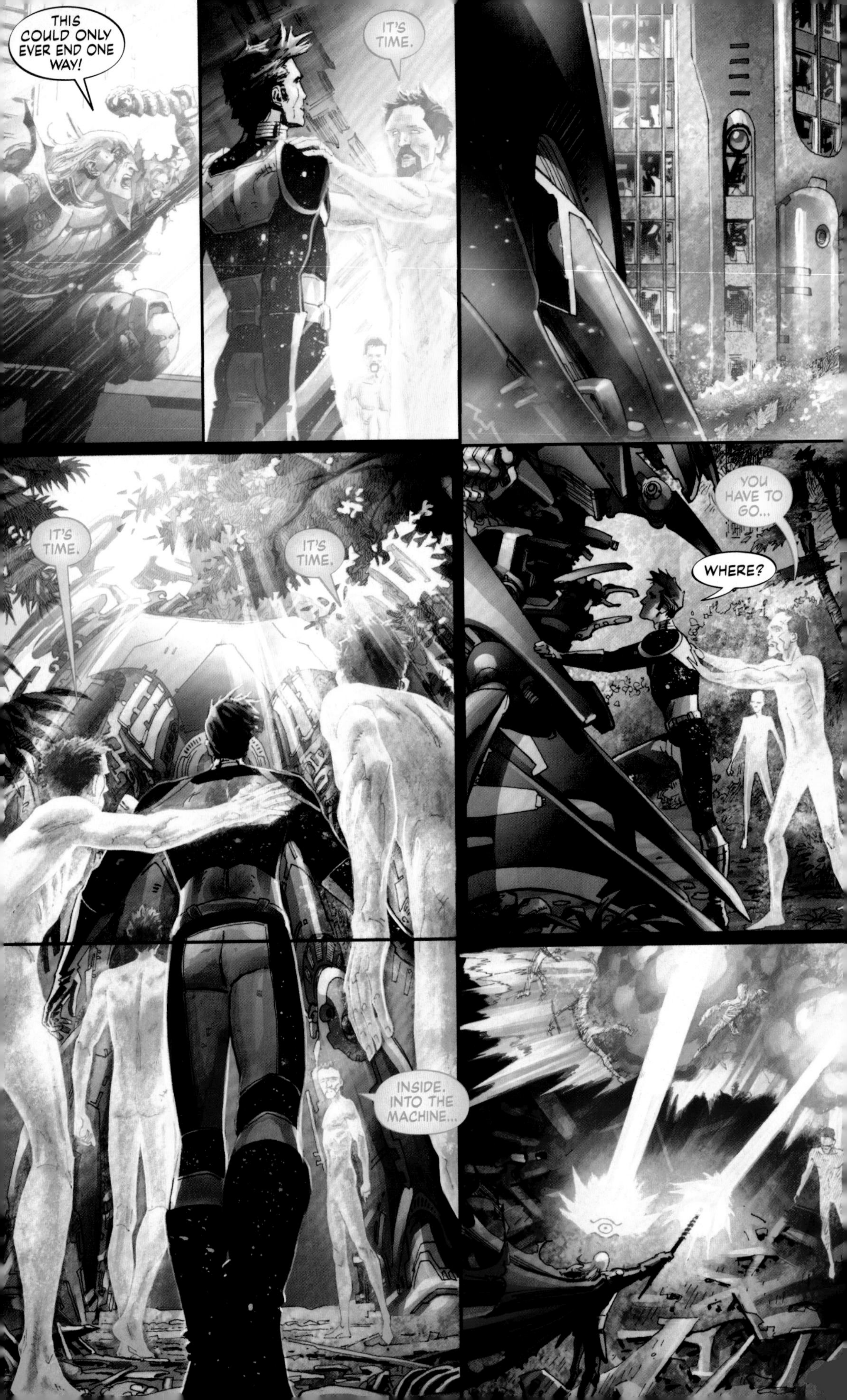
THIS COULD ONLY EVER END ONE WAY!
IT'S TIME.
IT'S TIME.
IT'S TIME.
YOU HAVE TO GO...
WHERE?
INSIDE. INTO THE MACHINE...

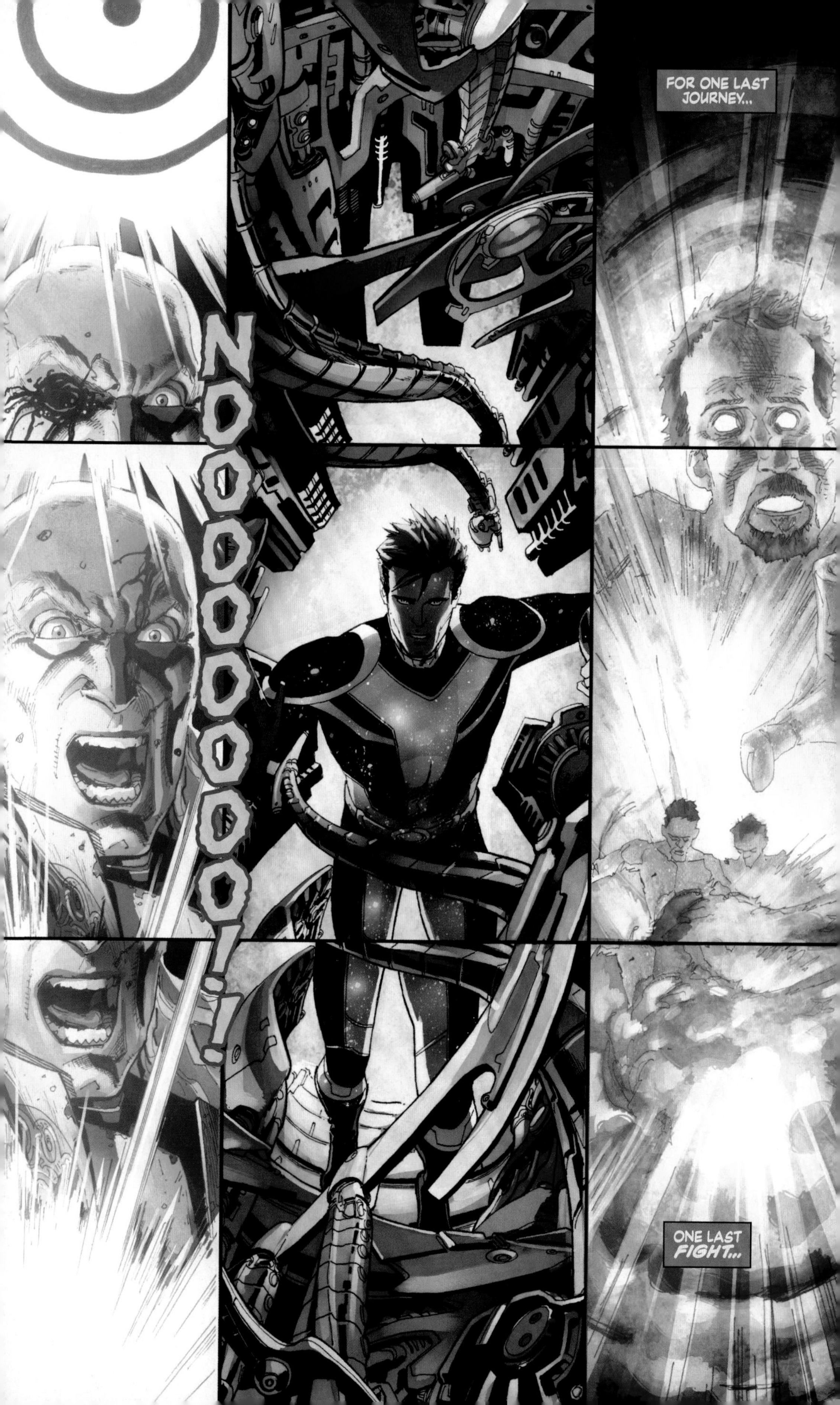
NOOOOOOOO!
FOR ONE LAST JOURNEY...
ONE LAST FIGHT...

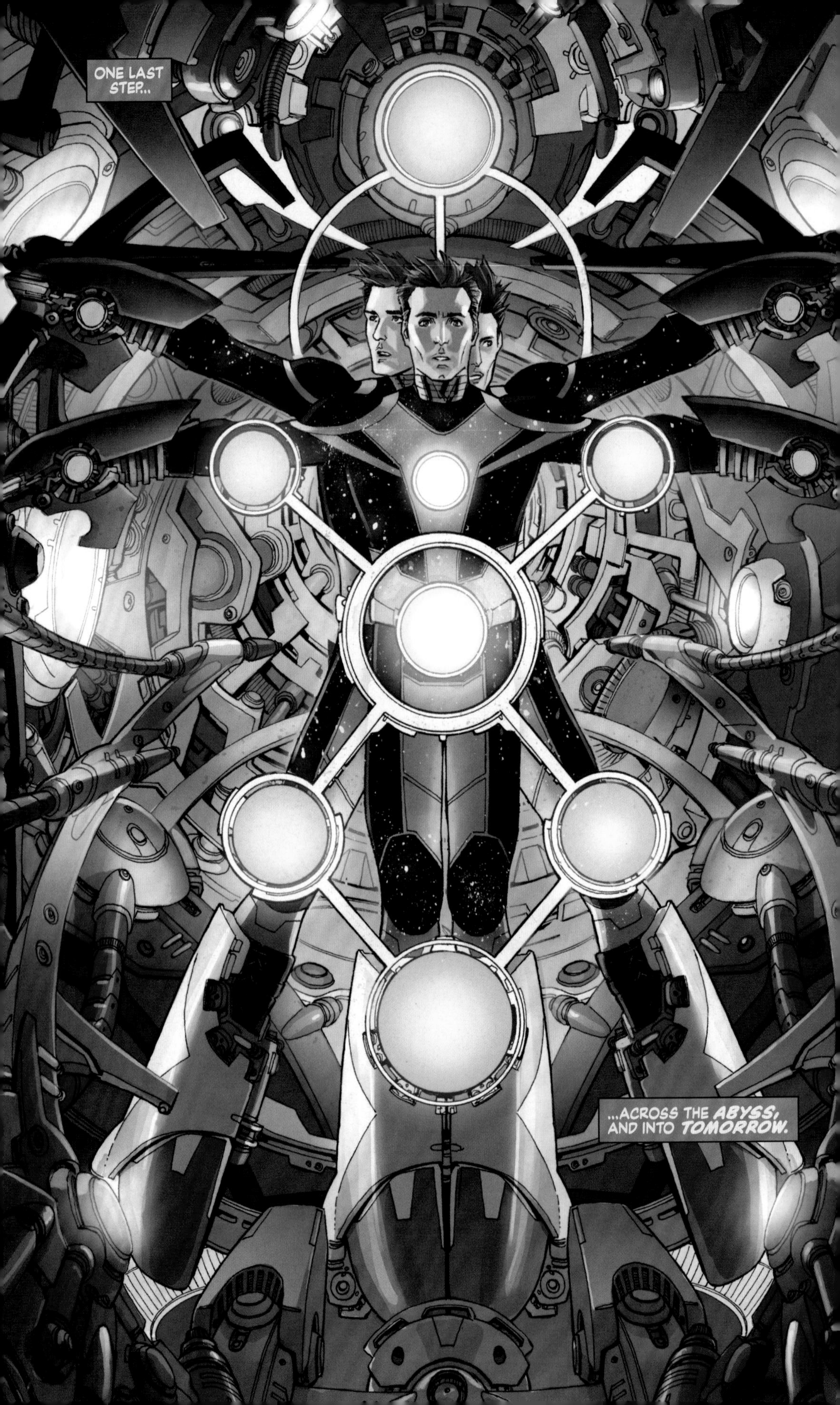
ONE LAST STEP...
...ACROSS THE ABYSS, AND INTO TOMORROW.

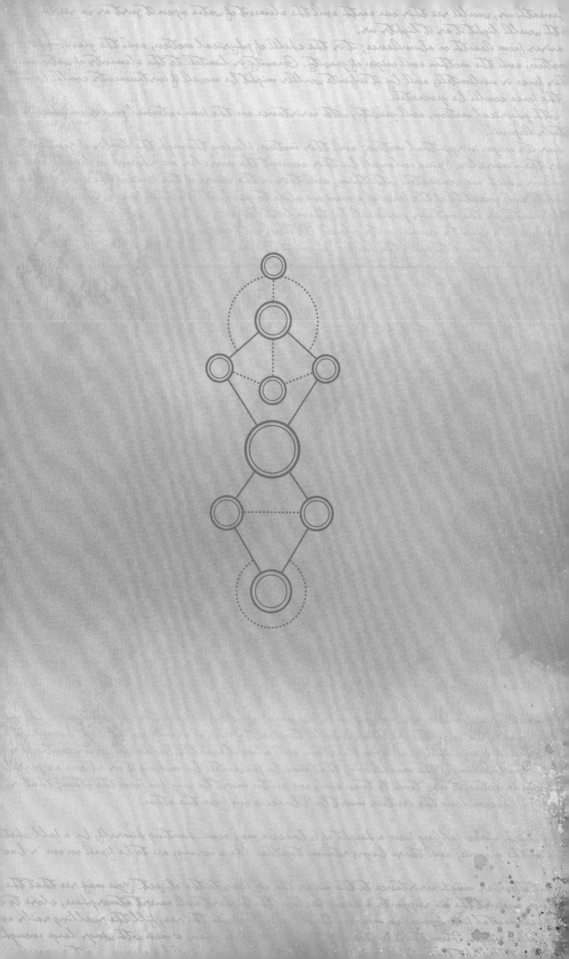

Chapter Six
"I Am the Sun"

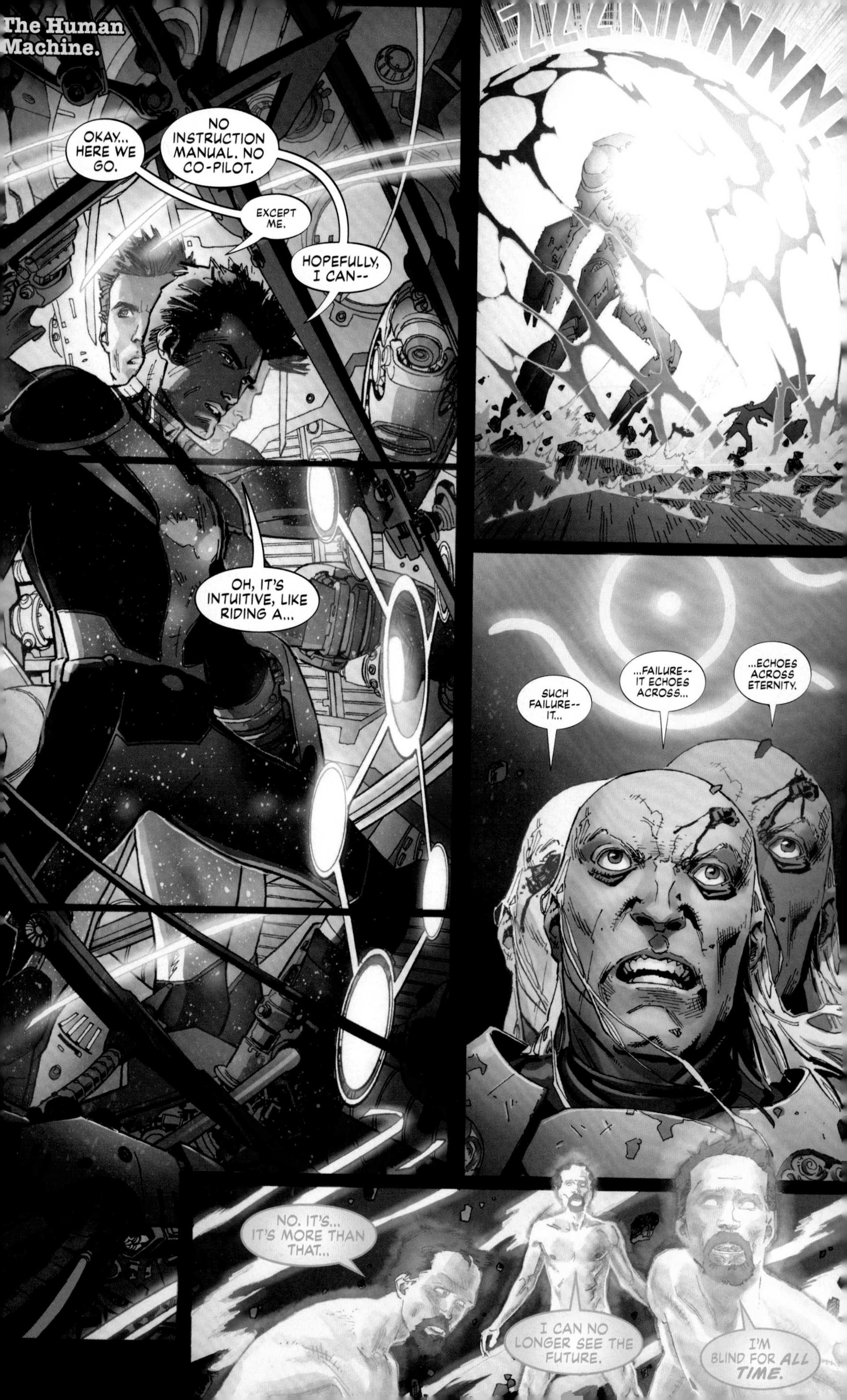
OKAY... HERE WE GO.
NO INSTRUCTION MANUAL. NO CO-PILOT.
EXCEPT ME.
HOPEFULLY, I CAN--
OH, IT'S INTUITIVE, LIKE RIDING A...
ZZZNNNNNN!
SUCH FAILURE-- IT...
...FAILURE-- IT ECHOES ACROSS...
...ECHOES ACROSS ETERNITY.
NO. IT'S... IT'S MORE THAN THAT...
I CAN NO LONGER SEE THE FUTURE.
I'M BLIND FOR ALL TIME.

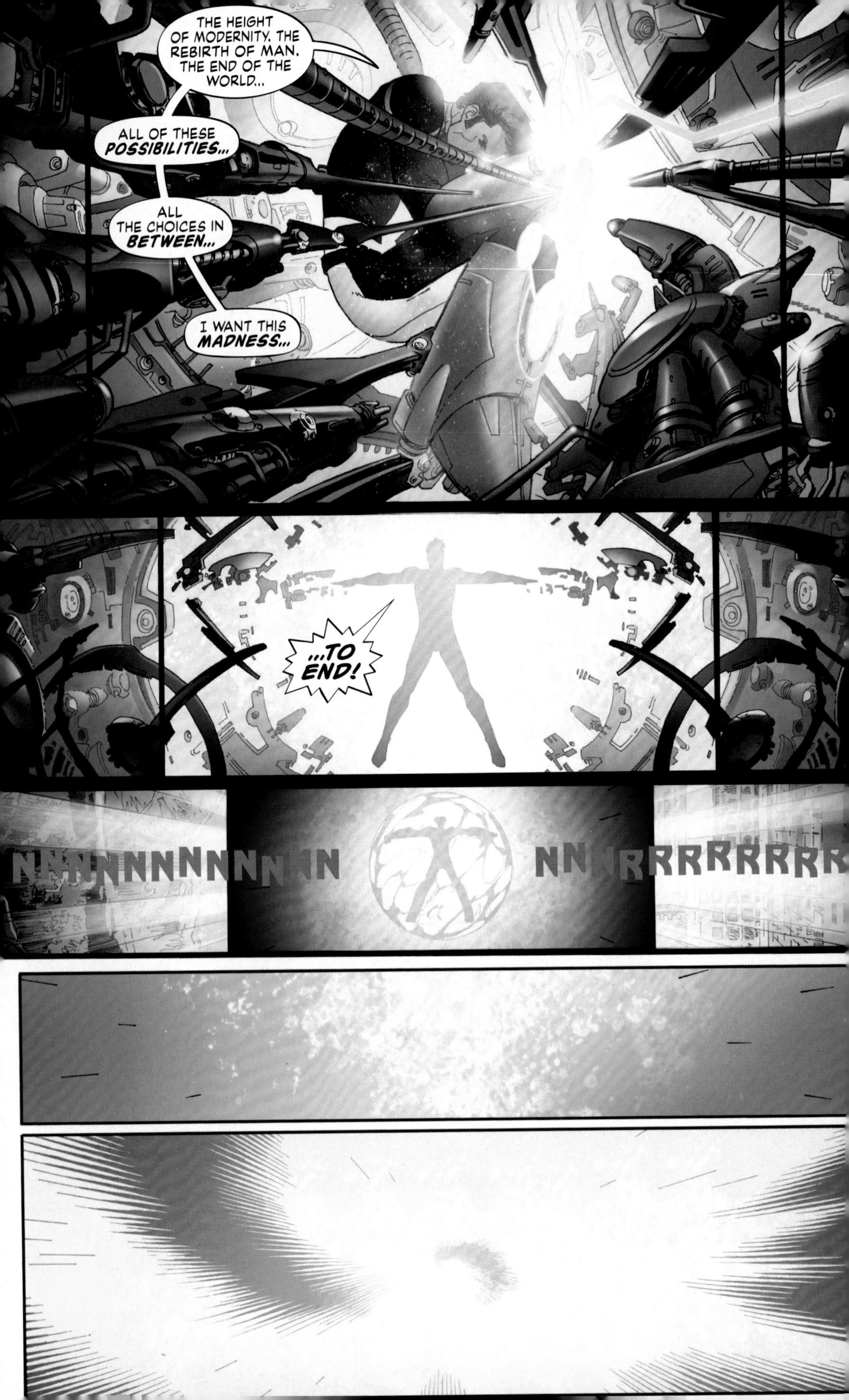
THE HEIGHT OF MODERNITY. THE REBIRTH OF MAN. THE END OF THE WORLD...
ALL OF THESE *POSSIBILITIES...*
ALL THE CHOICES IN *BETWEEN...*
I WANT THIS *MADNESS...*
...TO END!
NNNNNNNNNNNNN
NNNRRRRRRRR

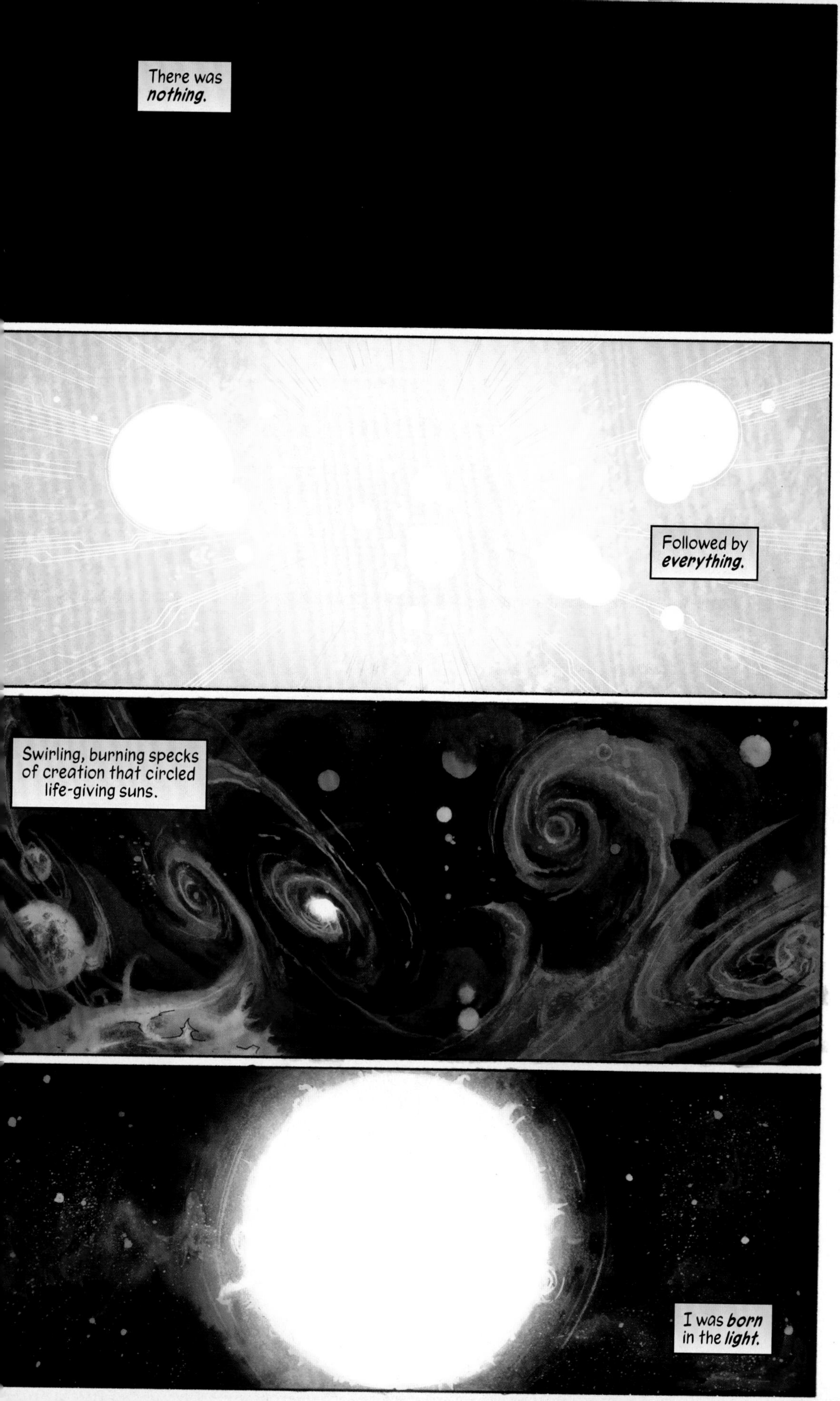
There was nothing.
Followed by everything.
Swirling, burning specks of creation that circled life-giving suns.
I was born in the light.

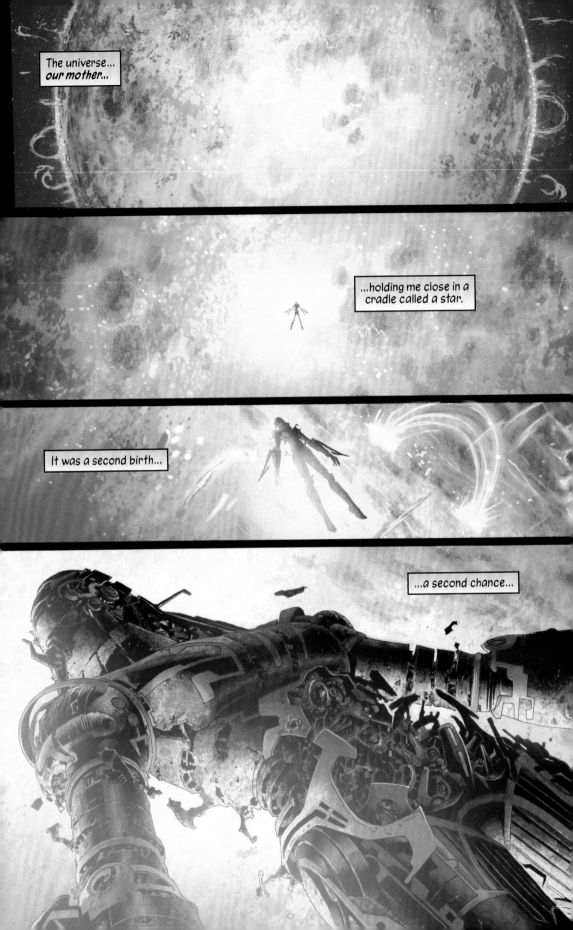

The universe...
our mother...

...holding me close in a
cradle called a star.

It was a second birth...

...a second chance...

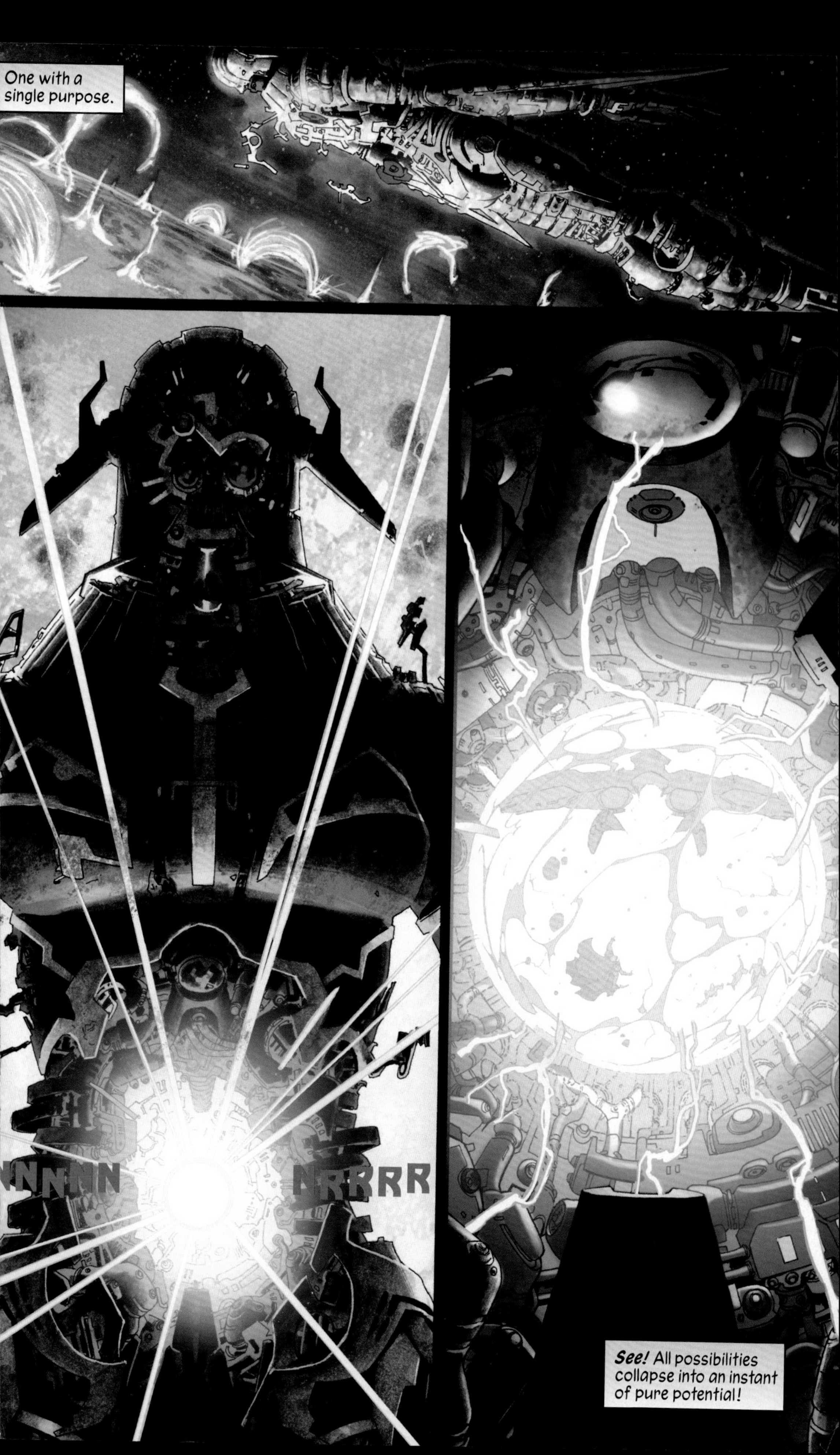
One with a single purpose.
NNNNN
NRRRR
See! All possibilities collapse into an instant of pure potential!

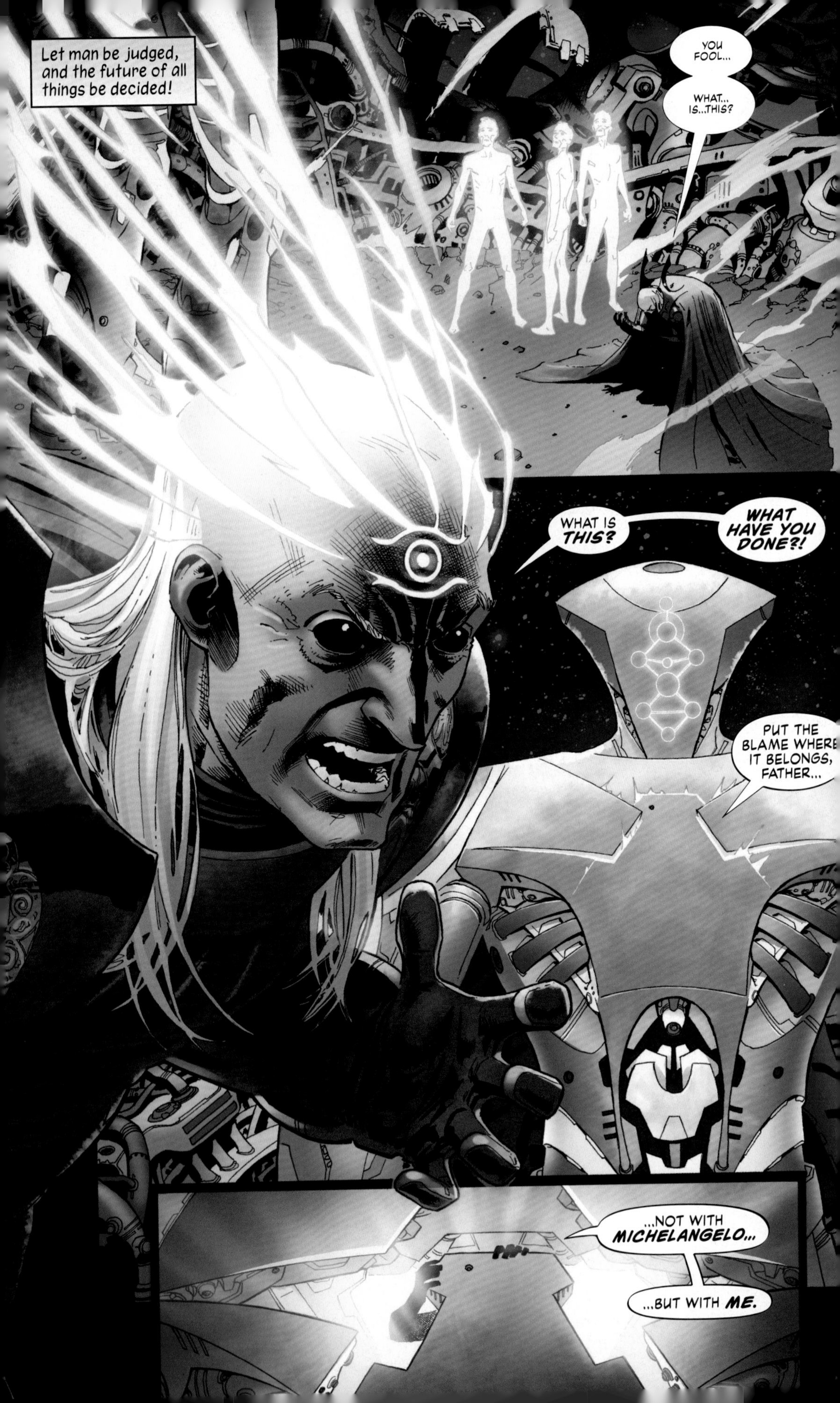
Let man be judged, and the future of all things be decided!
YOU FOOL...
WHAT... IS...THIS?
WHAT IS THIS?
WHAT HAVE YOU DONE?!
PUT THE BLAME WHERE IT BELONGS, FATHER...
...NOT WITH MICHELANGELO...
...BUT WITH ME.

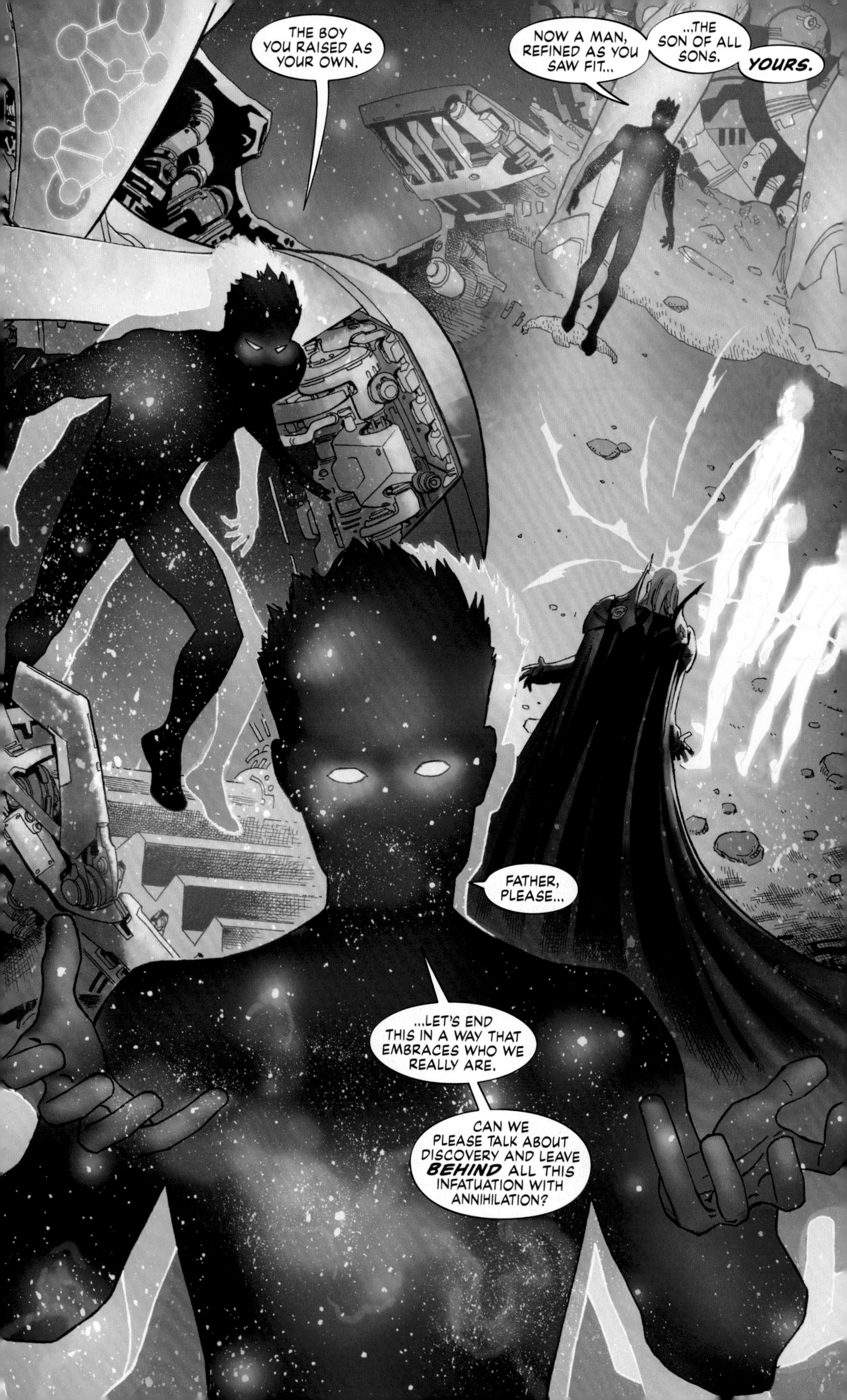
THE BOY YOU RAISED AS YOUR OWN.
NOW A MAN, REFINED AS YOU SAW FIT...
...THE SON OF ALL SONS.
YOURS.
FATHER, PLEASE...
...LET'S END THIS IN A WAY THAT EMBRACES WHO WE REALLY ARE.
CAN WE PLEASE TALK ABOUT DISCOVERY AND LEAVE BEHIND ALL THIS INFATUATION WITH ANNIHILATION?

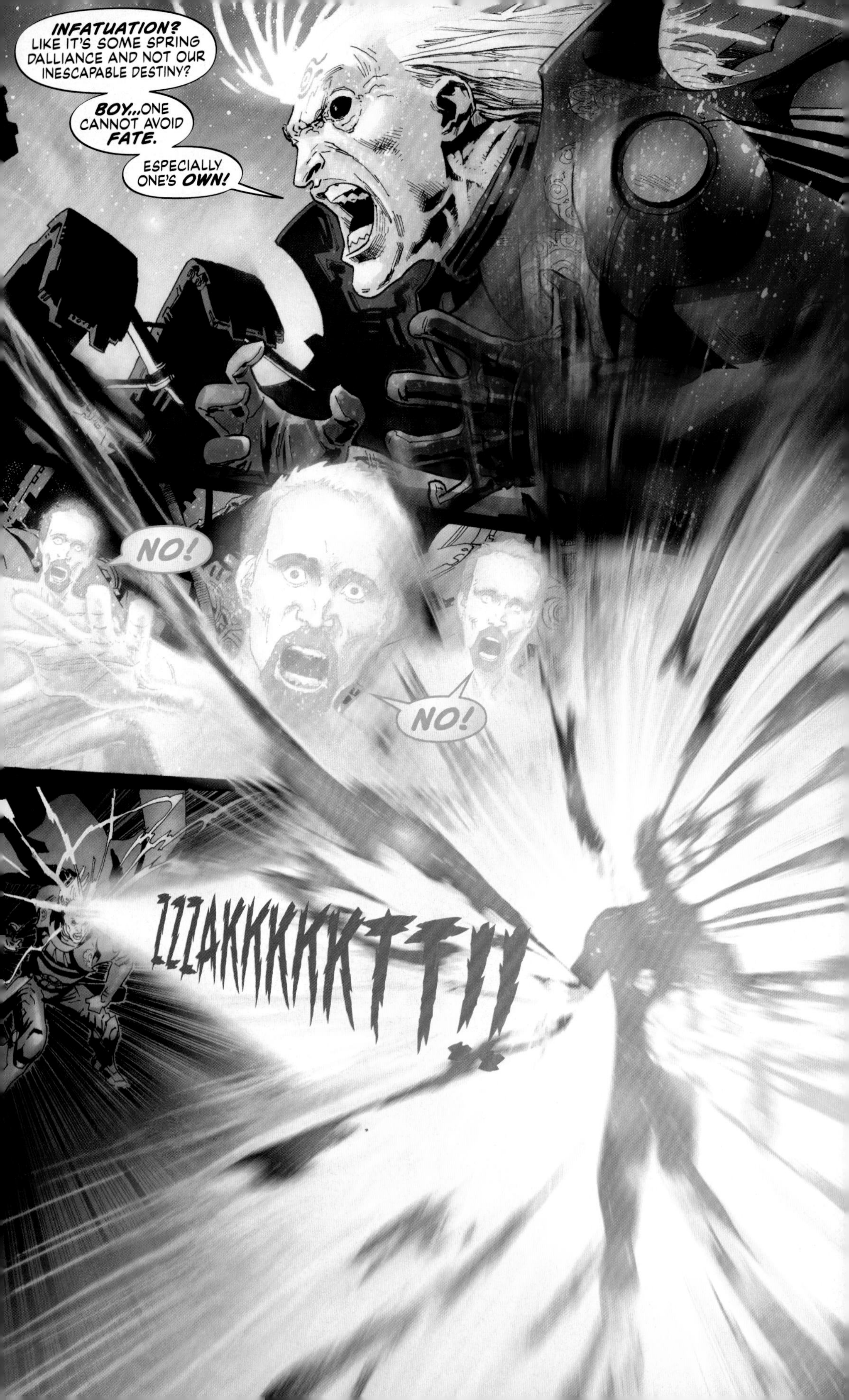
INFATUATION? LIKE IT'S SOME SPRING DALLIANCE AND NOT OUR INESCAPABLE DESTINY?
BOY...ONE CANNOT AVOID FATE.
ESPECIALLY ONE'S OWN!
NO!
NO!
ZZZAKKKKKKTTT!!

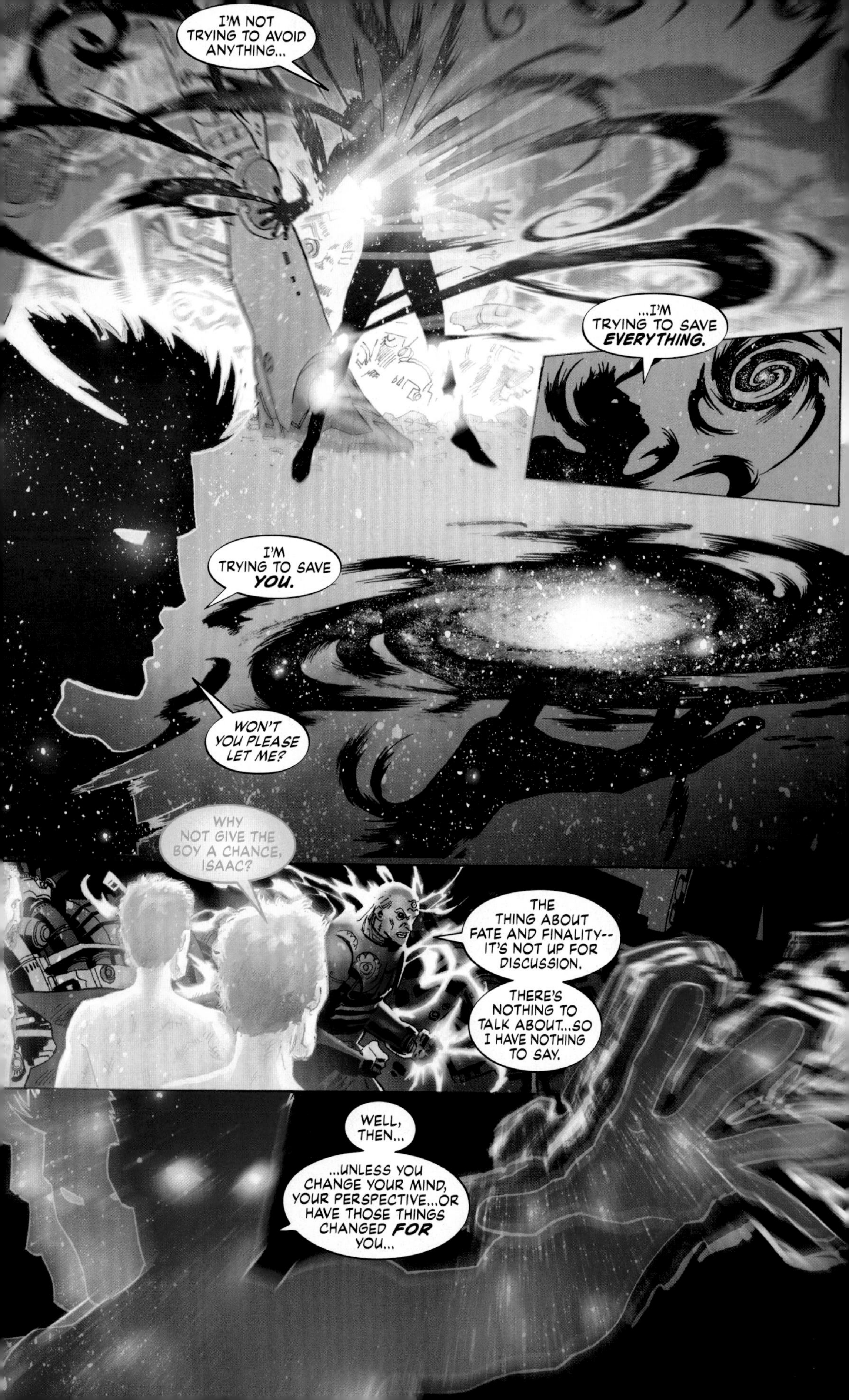
I'M NOT TRYING TO AVOID ANYTHING...
...I'M TRYING TO SAVE EVERYTHING.
I'M TRYING TO SAVE YOU.
WON'T YOU PLEASE LET ME?
WHY NOT GIVE THE BOY A CHANCE, ISAAC?
THE THING ABOUT FATE AND FINALITY-- IT'S NOT UP FOR DISCUSSION.
THERE'S NOTHING TO TALK ABOUT...SO I HAVE NOTHING TO SAY.
WELL, THEN...
...UNLESS YOU CHANGE YOUR MIND, YOUR PERSPECTIVE...OR HAVE THOSE THINGS CHANGED FOR YOU...

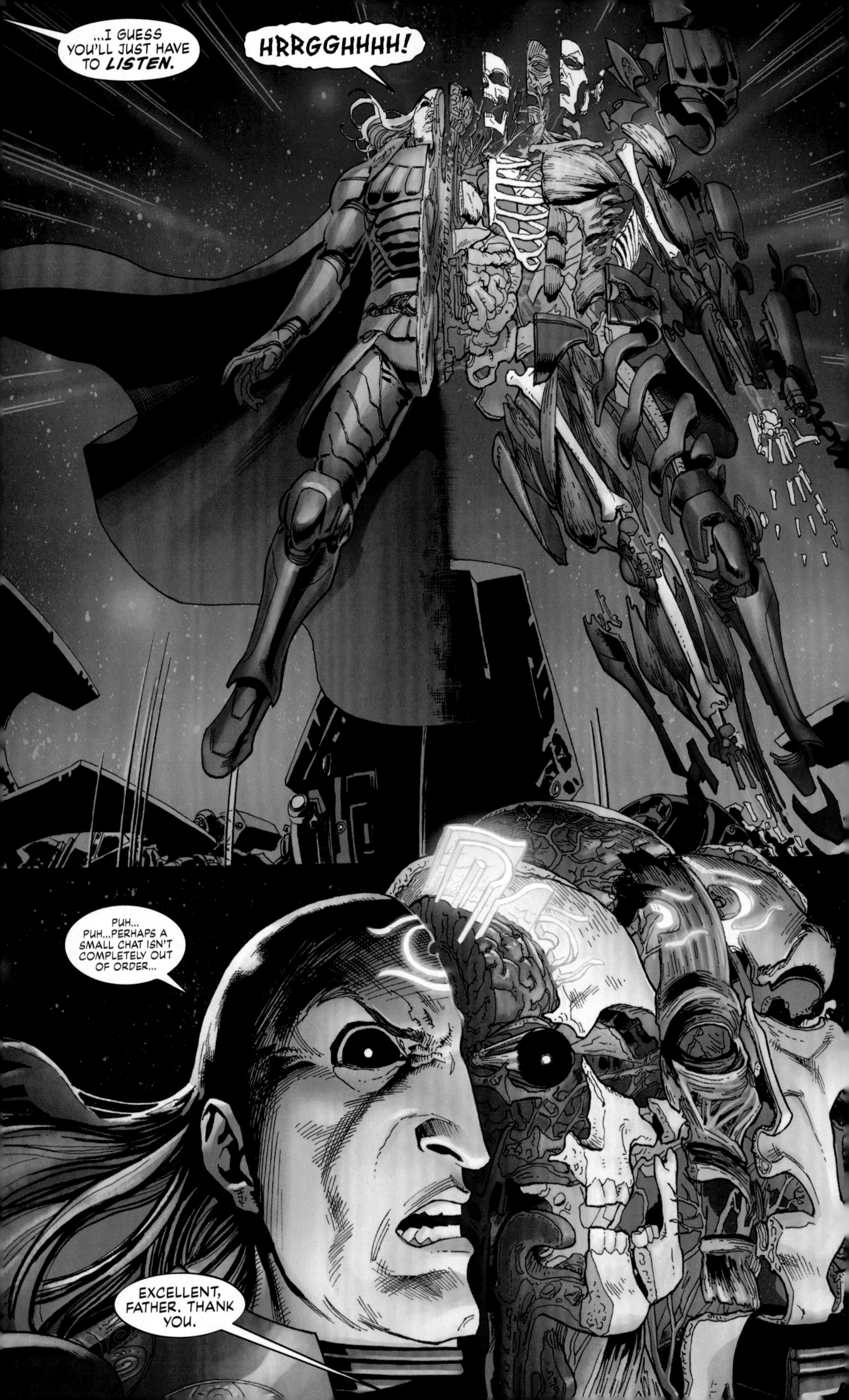
...I GUESS YOU'LL JUST HAVE TO LISTEN.
HRRGGHHHH!
PUH... PUH...PERHAPS A SMALL CHAT ISN'T COMPLETELY OUT OF ORDER...
EXCELLENT, FATHER. THANK YOU.

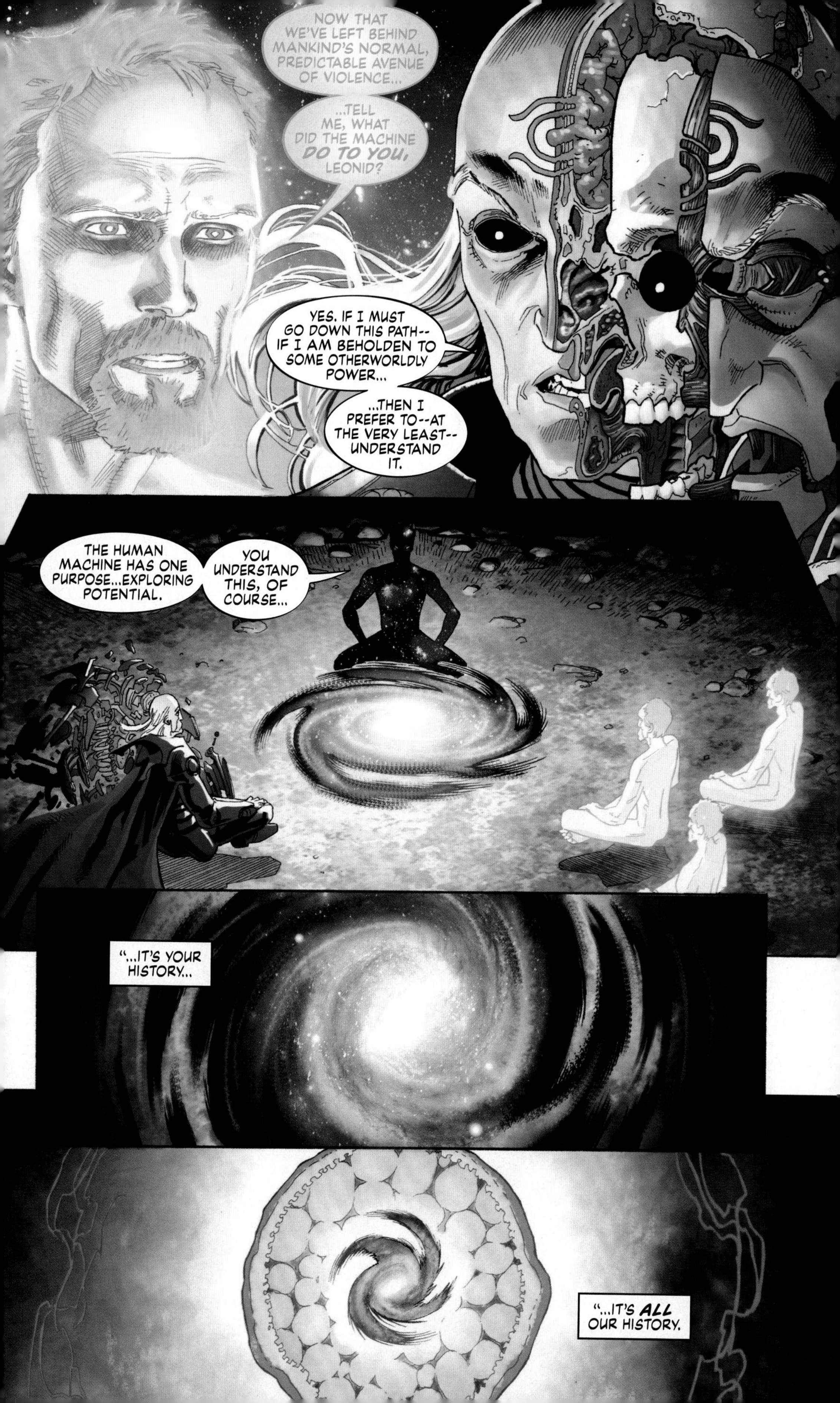

NOW THAT WE'VE LEFT BEHIND MANKIND'S NORMAL, PREDICTABLE AVENUE OF VIOLENCE...
...TELL ME, WHAT DID THE MACHINE DO TO YOU, LEONID?
YES. IF I MUST GO DOWN THIS PATH-- IF I AM BEHOLDEN TO SOME OTHERWORLDLY POWER...
...THEN I PREFER TO--AT THE VERY LEAST-- UNDERSTAND IT.
THE HUMAN MACHINE HAS ONE PURPOSE...EXPLORING POTENTIAL.
YOU UNDERSTAND THIS, OF COURSE...
"...IT'S YOUR HISTORY...
"...IT'S ALL OUR HISTORY.

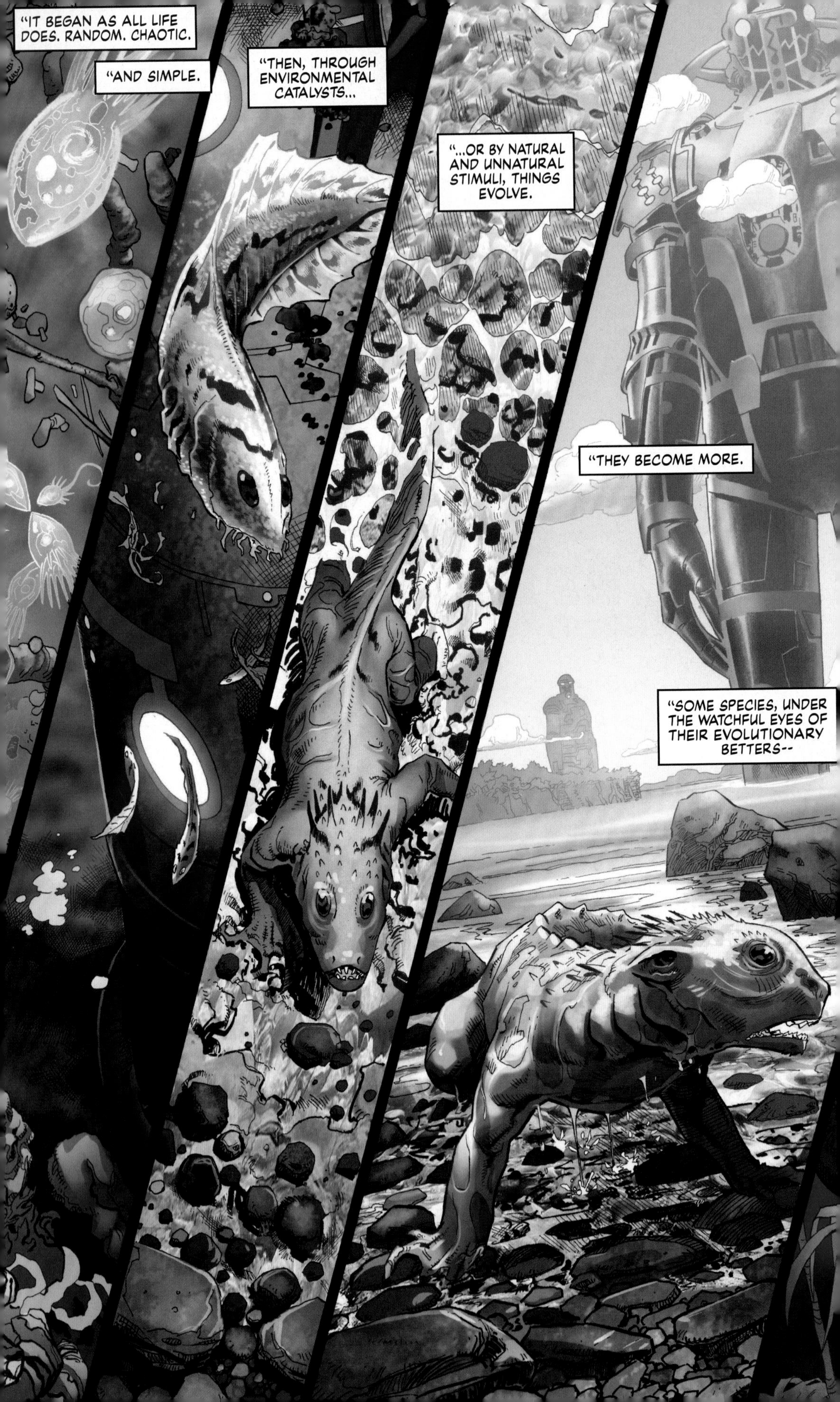
"IT BEGAN AS ALL LIFE DOES. RANDOM. CHAOTIC.
"AND SIMPLE.
"THEN, THROUGH ENVIRONMENTAL CATALYSTS...
"...OR BY NATURAL AND UNNATURAL STIMULI, THINGS EVOLVE.
"THEY BECOME MORE.
"SOME SPECIES, UNDER THE WATCHFUL EYES OF THEIR EVOLUTIONARY BETTERS--

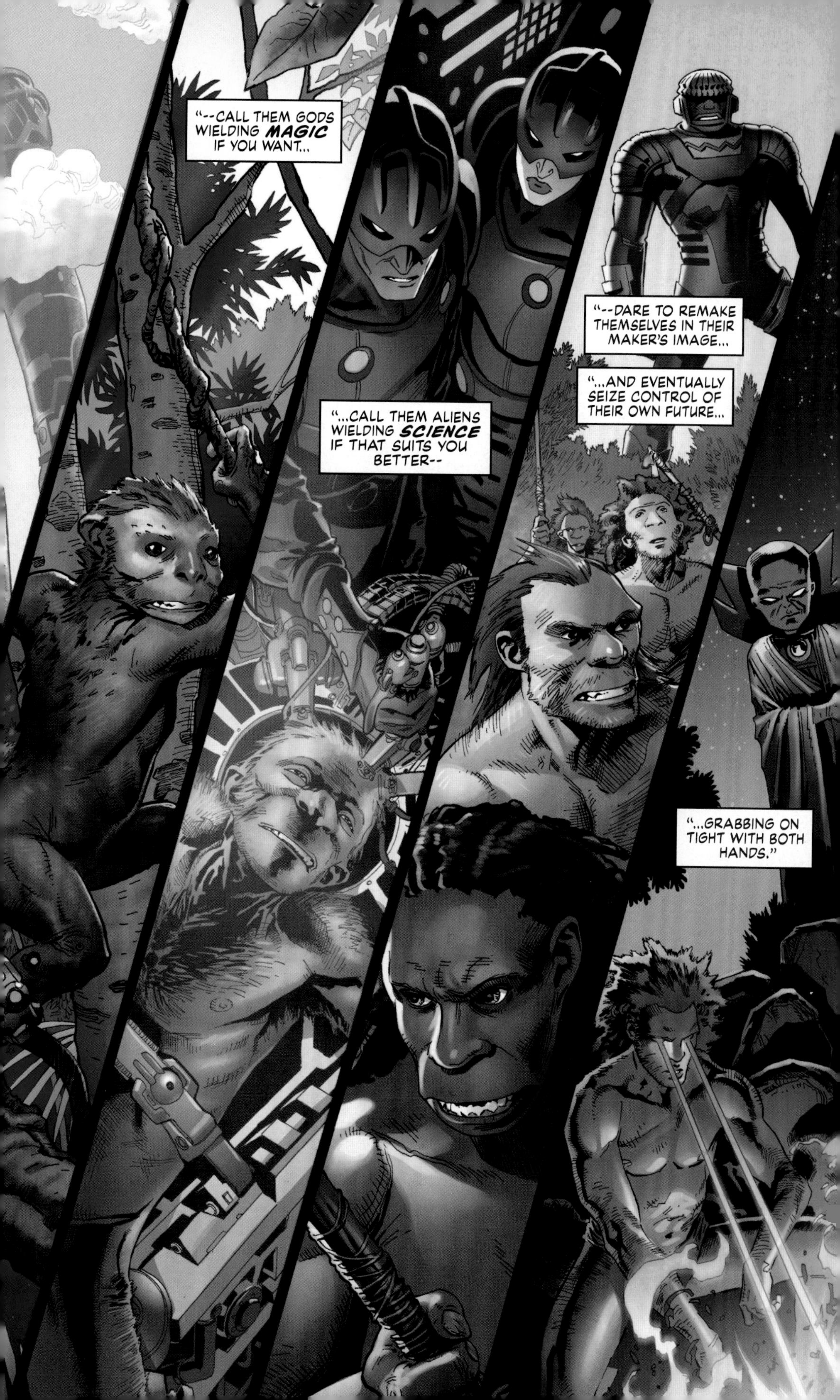
"--CALL THEM GODS WIELDING MAGIC IF YOU WANT...
"...CALL THEM ALIENS WIELDING SCIENCE IF THAT SUITS YOU BETTER--
"--DARE TO REMAKE THEMSELVES IN THEIR MAKER'S IMAGE...
"...AND EVENTUALLY SEIZE CONTROL OF THEIR OWN FUTURE...
"...GRABBING ON TIGHT WITH BOTH HANDS."

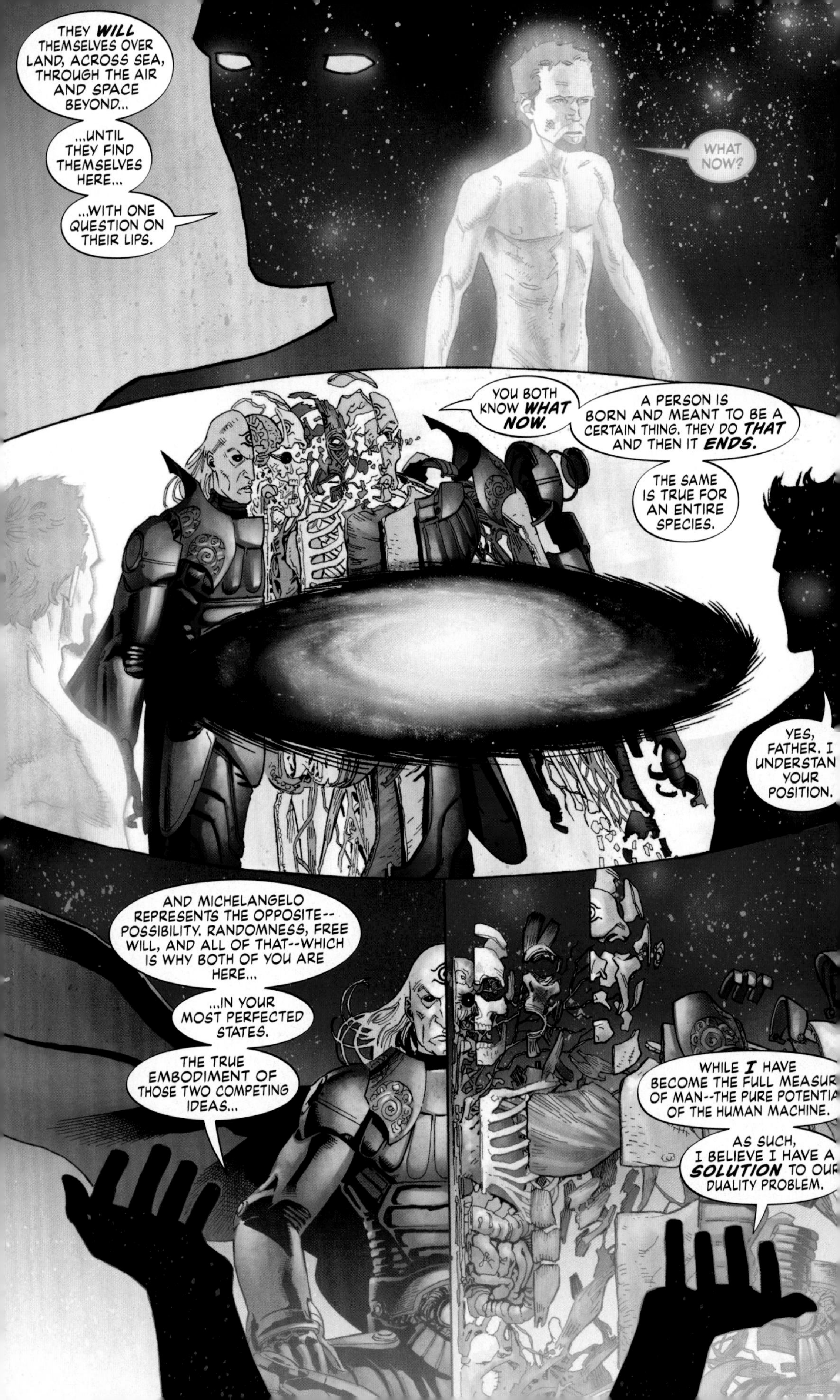
THEY WILL THEMSELVES OVER LAND, ACROSS SEA, THROUGH THE AIR AND SPACE BEYOND...
...UNTIL THEY FIND THEMSELVES HERE...
...WITH ONE QUESTION ON THEIR LIPS.
WHAT NOW?
YOU BOTH KNOW WHAT NOW.
A PERSON IS BORN AND MEANT TO BE A CERTAIN THING. THEY DO THAT AND THEN IT ENDS.
THE SAME IS TRUE FOR AN ENTIRE SPECIES.
YES, FATHER. I UNDERSTAN YOUR POSITION.
AND MICHELANGELO REPRESENTS THE OPPOSITE--POSSIBILITY. RANDOMNESS, FREE WILL, AND ALL OF THAT--WHICH IS WHY BOTH OF YOU ARE HERE...
...IN YOUR MOST PERFECTED STATES.
THE TRUE EMBODIMENT OF THOSE TWO COMPETING IDEAS...
WHILE I HAVE BECOME THE FULL MEASUR OF MAN--THE PURE POTENTIA OF THE HUMAN MACHINE.
AS SUCH, I BELIEVE I HAVE A SOLUTION TO OUR DUALITY PROBLEM.

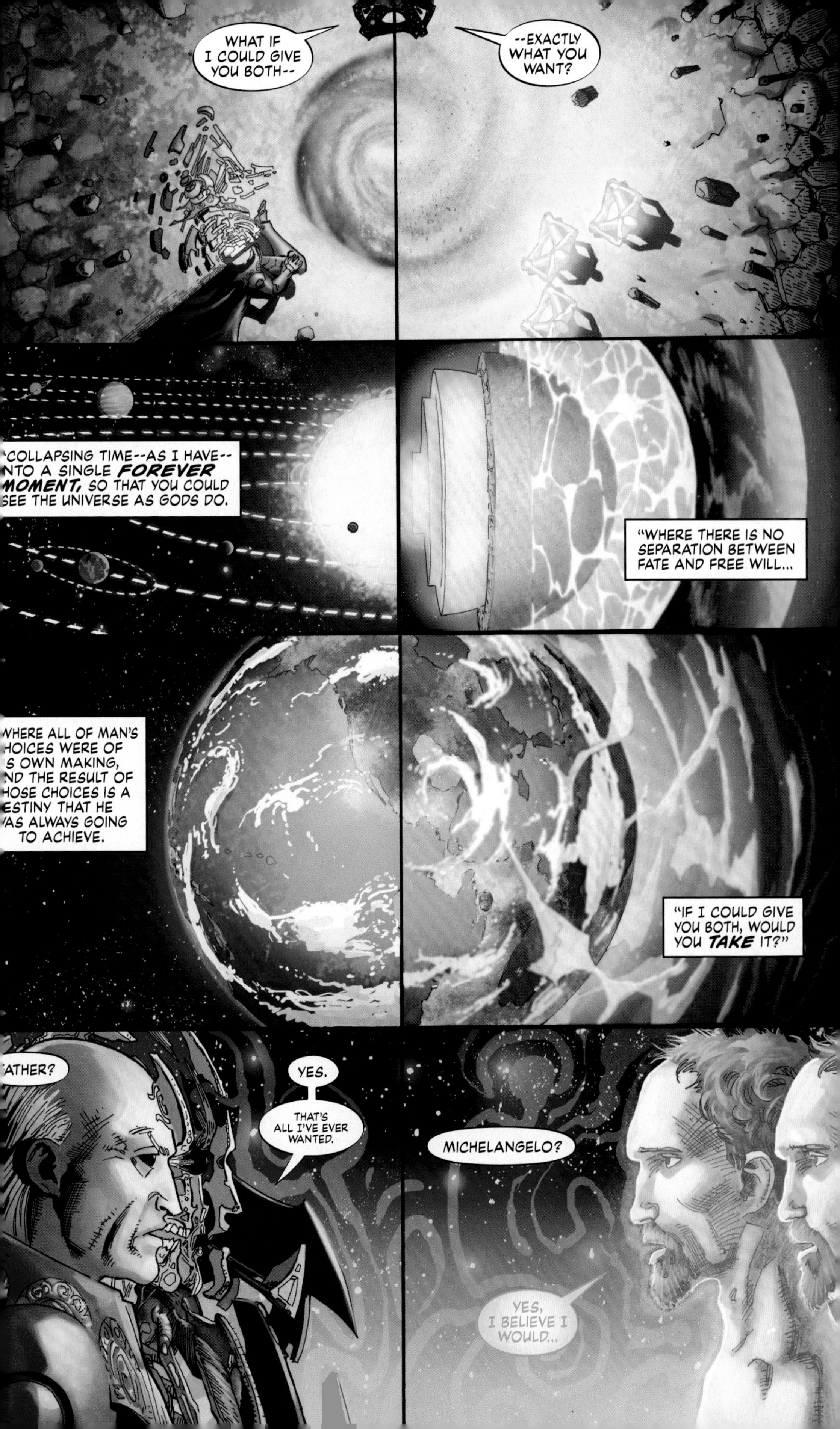
WHAT IF I COULD GIVE YOU BOTH--
--EXACTLY WHAT YOU WANT?
"COLLAPSING TIME--AS I HAVE--NTO A SINGLE *FOREVER MOMENT,* SO THAT YOU COULD SEE THE UNIVERSE AS GODS DO.
"WHERE THERE IS NO SEPARATION BETWEEN FATE AND FREE WILL...
WHERE ALL OF MAN'S HOICES WERE OF S OWN MAKING, ND THE RESULT OF HOSE CHOICES IS A ESTINY THAT HE VAS ALWAYS GOING TO ACHIEVE.
"IF I COULD GIVE YOU BOTH, WOULD YOU *TAKE* IT?"
ATHER?
YES.
THAT'S ALL I'VE EVER WANTED.
MICHELANGELO?
YES, I BELIEVE I WOULD...

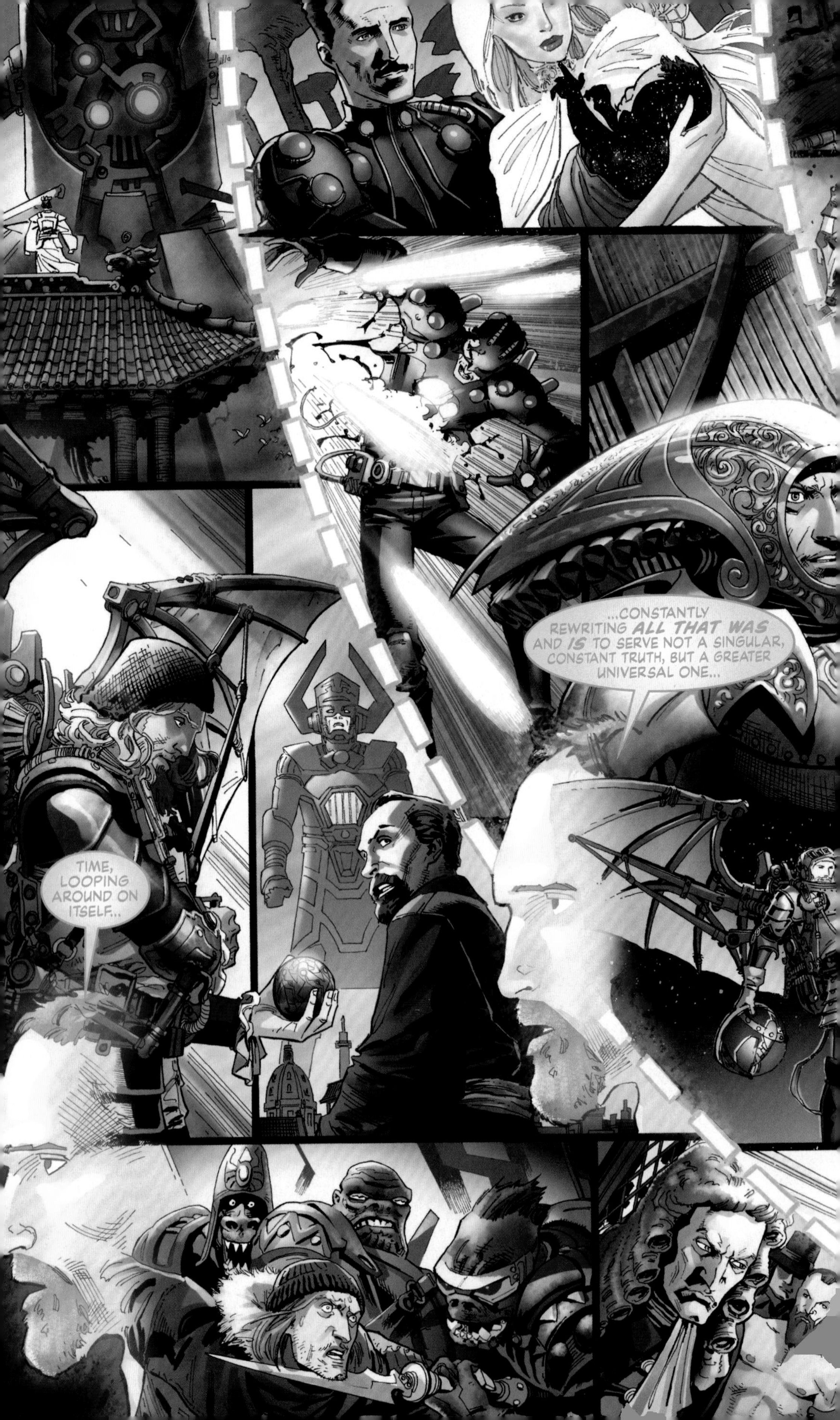
...CONSTANTLY REWRITING ALL THAT WAS AND IS TO SERVE NOT A SINGULAR, CONSTANT TRUTH, BUT A GREATER UNIVERSAL ONE...
TIME, LOOPING AROUND ON ITSELF...

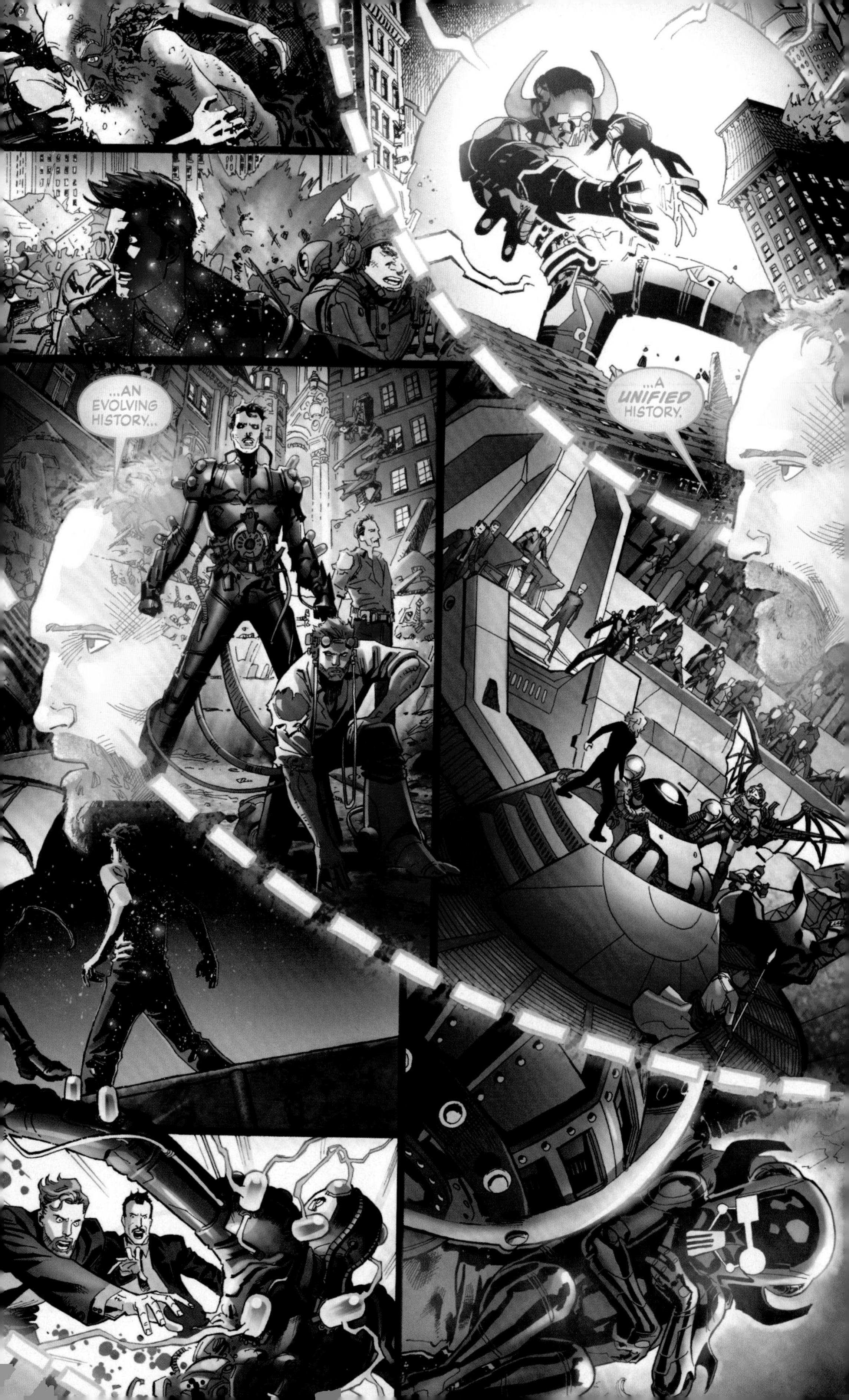
...AN EVOLVING HISTORY...
...A UNIFIED HISTORY.

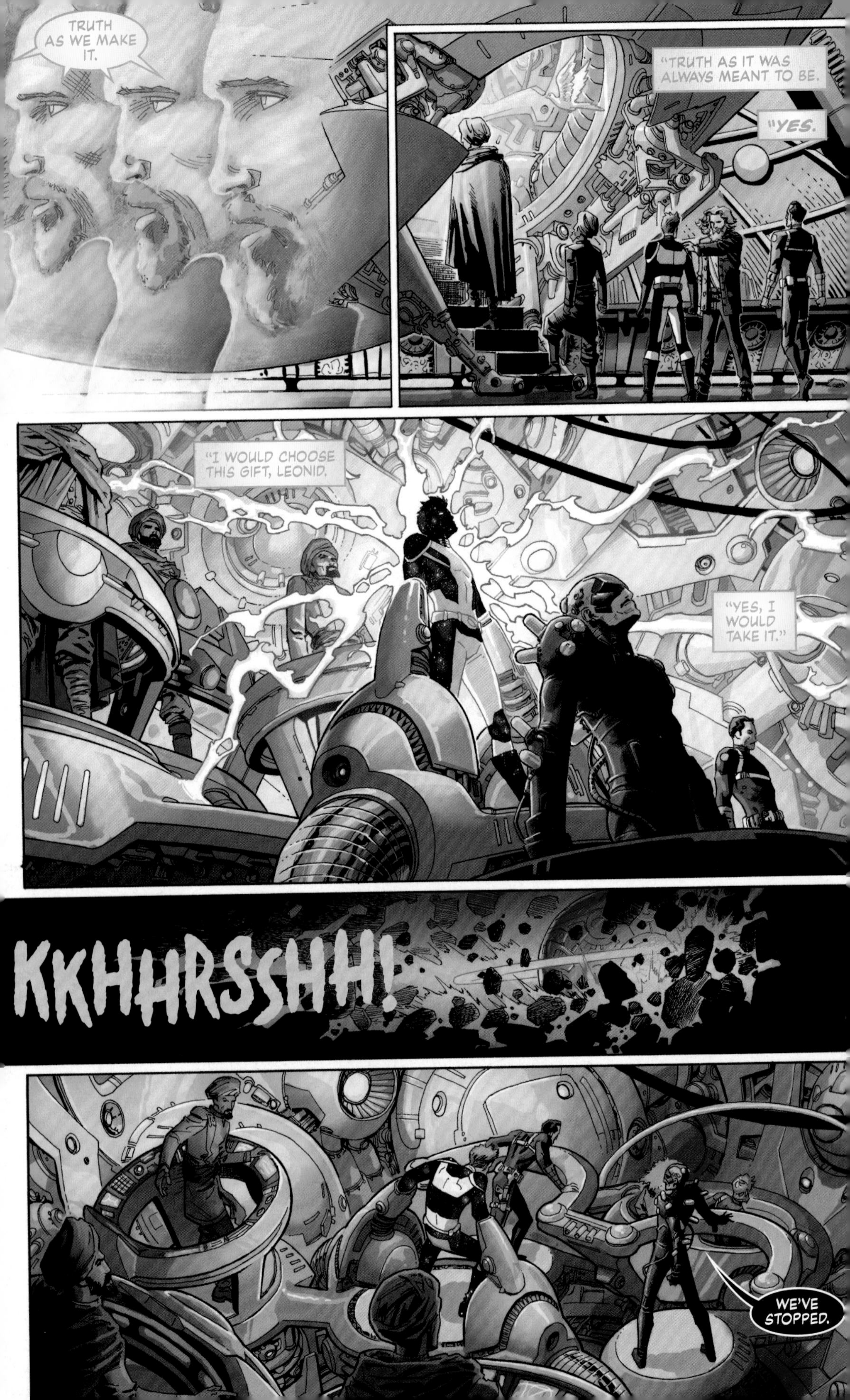
TRUTH AS WE MAKE IT.
"TRUTH AS IT WAS ALWAYS MEANT TO BE.
"YES.
"I WOULD CHOOSE THIS GIFT, LEONID.
"YES, I WOULD TAKE IT."
KKHHRSSHH!
WE'VE STOPPED.

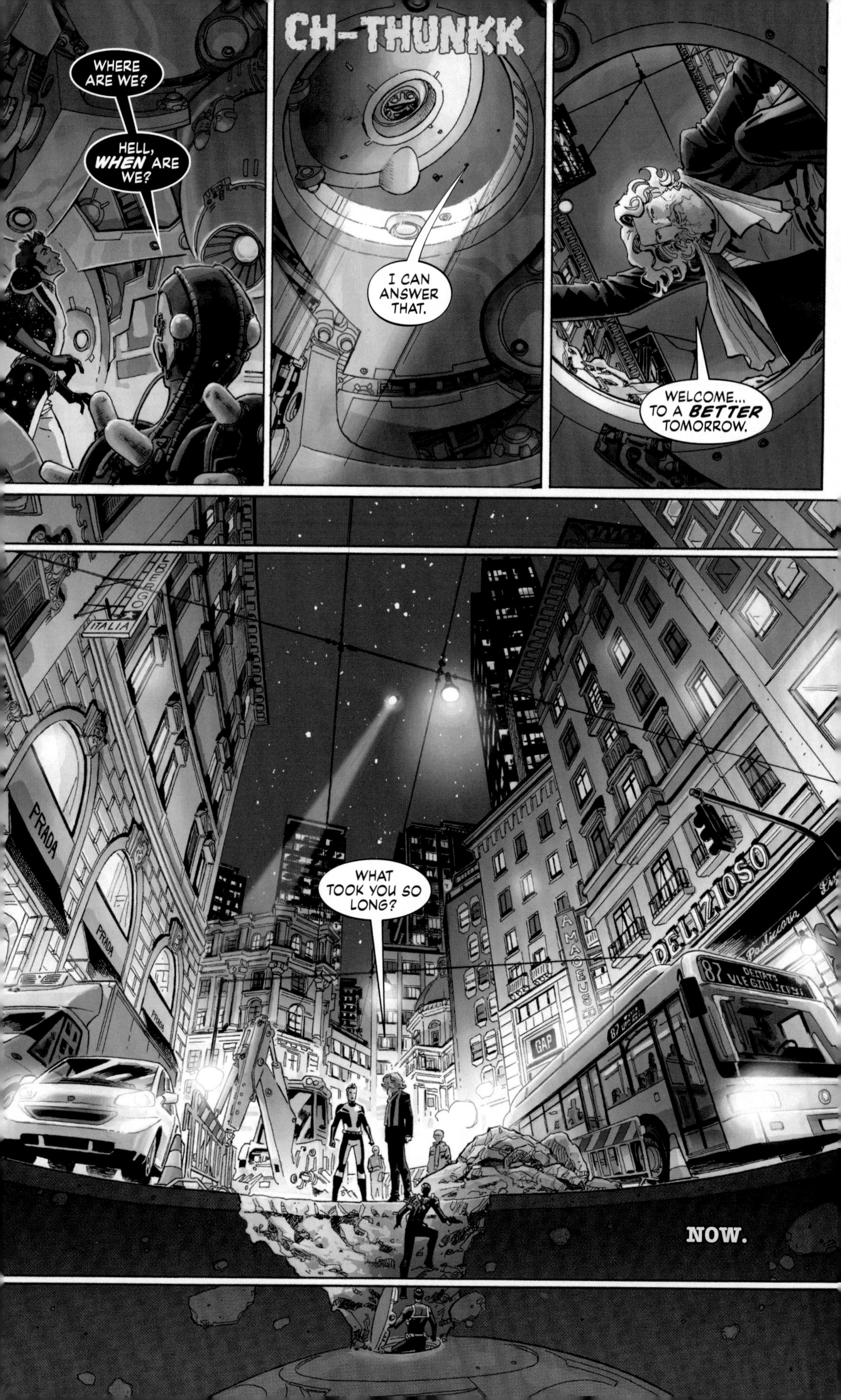

WHERE ARE WE?
HELL, WHEN ARE WE?
CH-THUNKK
I CAN ANSWER THAT.
WELCOME... TO A BETTER TOMORROW.
ITALIA
PRADA
DELIZIOSO
AMADEUS
GAP
WHAT TOOK YOU SO LONG?
NOW.

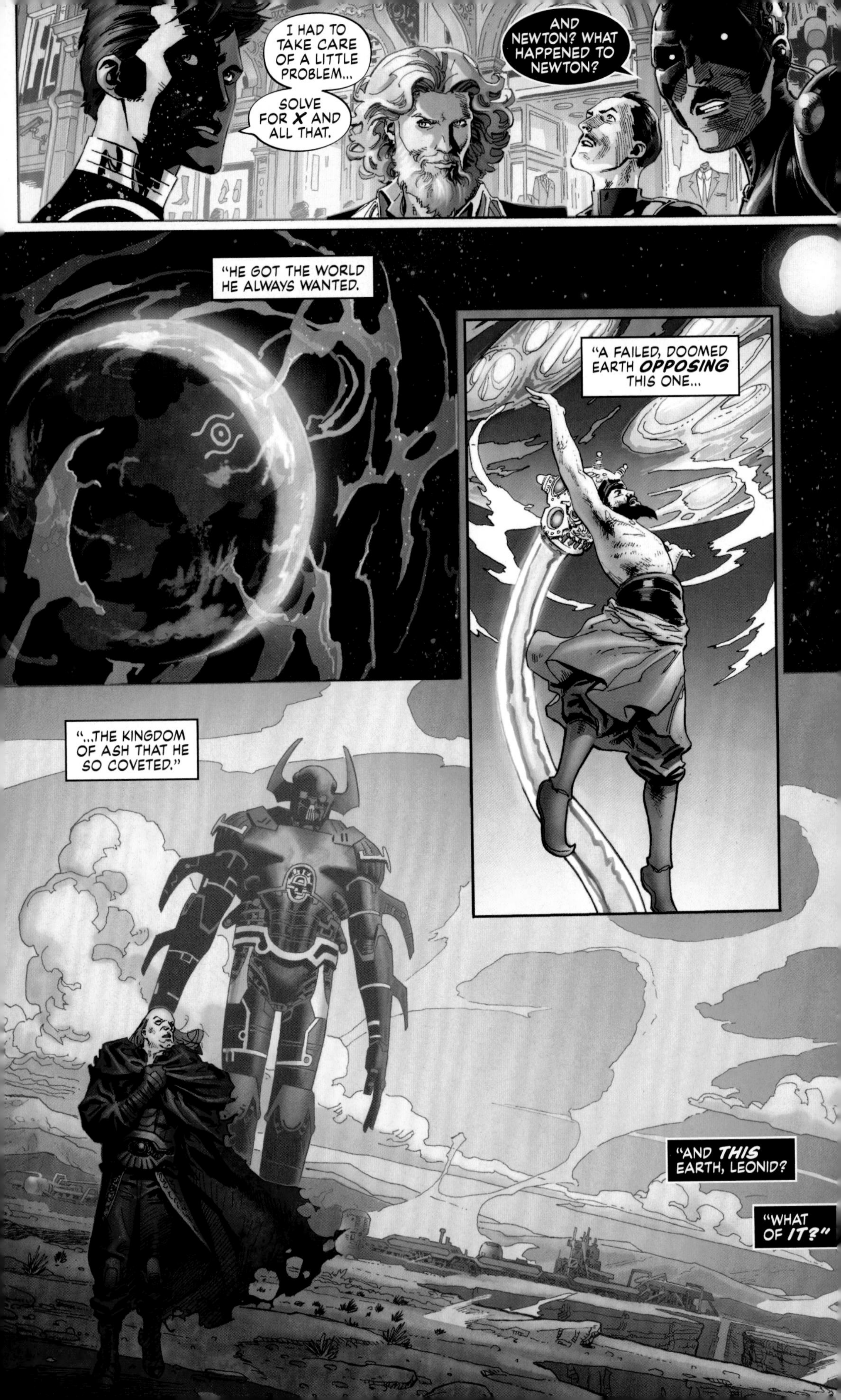
I HAD TO TAKE CARE OF A LITTLE PROBLEM...
SOLVE FOR X AND ALL THAT.
AND NEWTON? WHAT HAPPENED TO NEWTON?
"HE GOT THE WORLD HE ALWAYS WANTED.
"A FAILED, DOOMED EARTH OPPOSING THIS ONE...
"...THE KINGDOM OF ASH THAT HE SO COVETED."
"AND THIS EARTH, LEONID?
"WHAT OF IT?"

My dearest Anthony,

This machine contains a full record of all the things I believe to matter.

A codex of what little wisdom I have.

I leave it all to you in the hopes that it will both inform and inspire you to be something better than the man I was, and eventually, the man I became.

I want you to understand that this is a simple world made complex by the most mediocre of men.

IF I LEAVE YOU WITH ONE THING...IF THERE IS ONE SINGLE THOUGHT THAT YOU SHOULD CARRY WITH YOU FOR ALL YOUR LIFE, LET IT BE THIS:

SEE THINGS CLEARLY.

You must be able to recognize what this world is lacking--diagnose it--and then find an elegant solution to make it better.

My dearest Ant

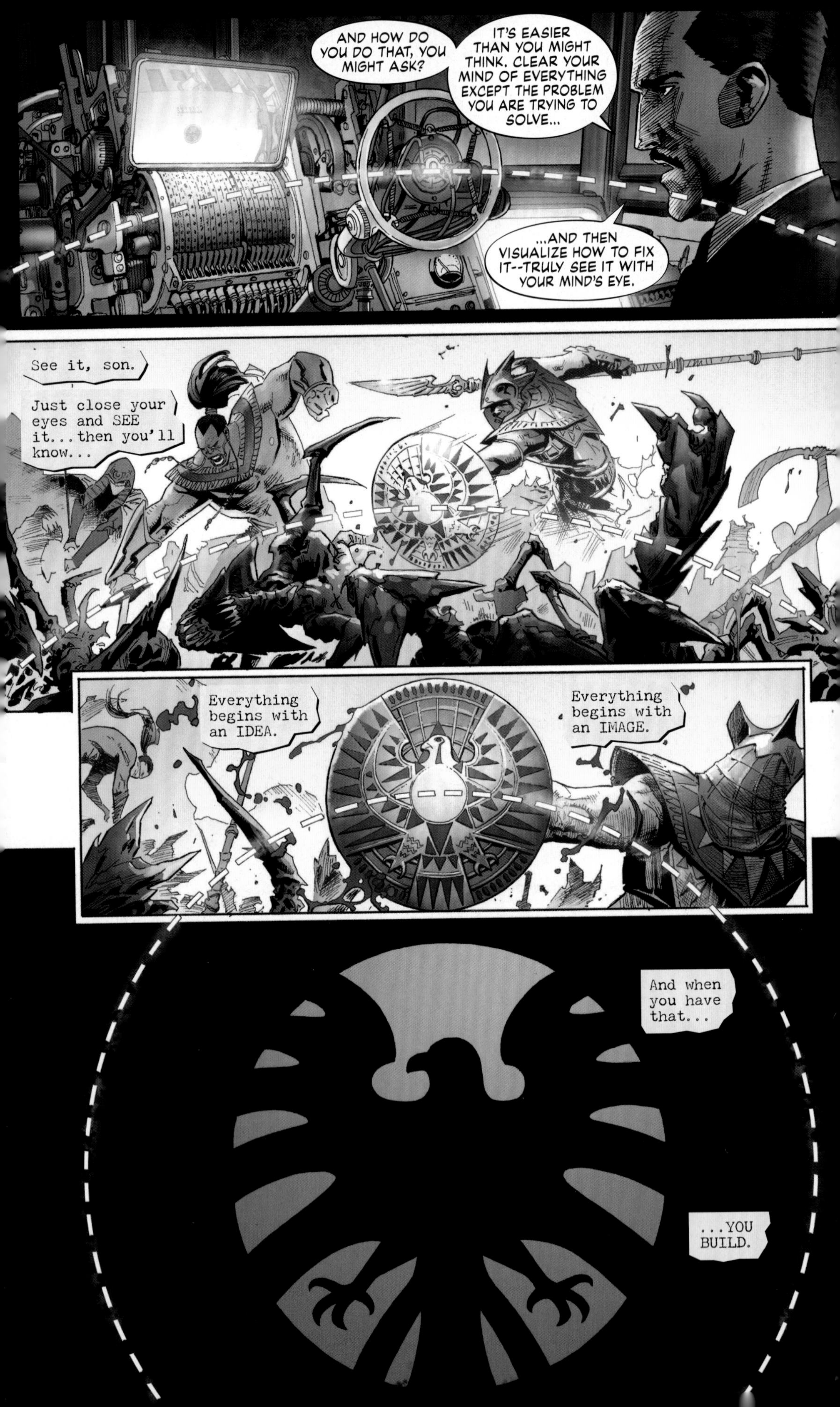
AND HOW DO YOU DO THAT, YOU MIGHT ASK?
IT'S EASIER THAN YOU MIGHT THINK. CLEAR YOUR MIND OF EVERYTHING EXCEPT THE PROBLEM YOU ARE TRYING TO SOLVE...
...AND THEN VISUALIZE HOW TO FIX IT--TRULY SEE IT WITH YOUR MIND'S EYE.
See it, son.
Just close your eyes and SEE it...then you'll know...
Everything begins with an IDEA.
Everything begins with an IMAGE.
And when you have that...
...YOU BUILD.

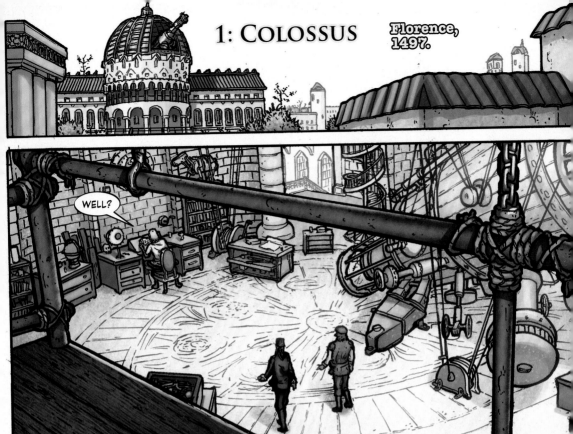

WELL?

WE HAVE FAILED, MASTER.

THE MAN WILL NOT LISTEN TO REASON...

...I SAY THIS IS A WASTE OF TIME. HE LACKS THE VISION TO BE ONE OF THE BROTHERHOOD.

OH, I THINK YOU'RE VERY WRONG THERE, PIETRO... PERHAPS YOUNG MICHAELANGELO SIMPLY HAS INTERESTS THAT DIVERGE FROM OUR OWN.

PERHAPS ONE DAY I WILL CALL ON HIM MYSELF AND STATE THE CASE...*MORE CLEARLY.*

REGARDLESS, FOR NOW, PLEASE MONITOR MY EXPERIMENTS WHILE I AM ABSENT.

WHERE ARE YOU GOING, MASTER?

TO FILL YOUNG MINDS WITH WONDER, LORENZO...

IT'S TIME FOR CLASS.

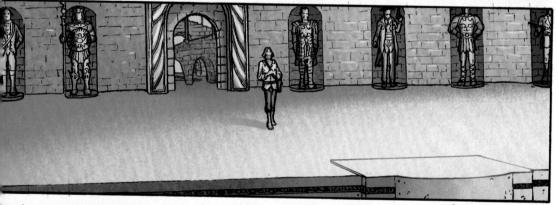

SO...WHO WANTS TO HEAR A STORY?

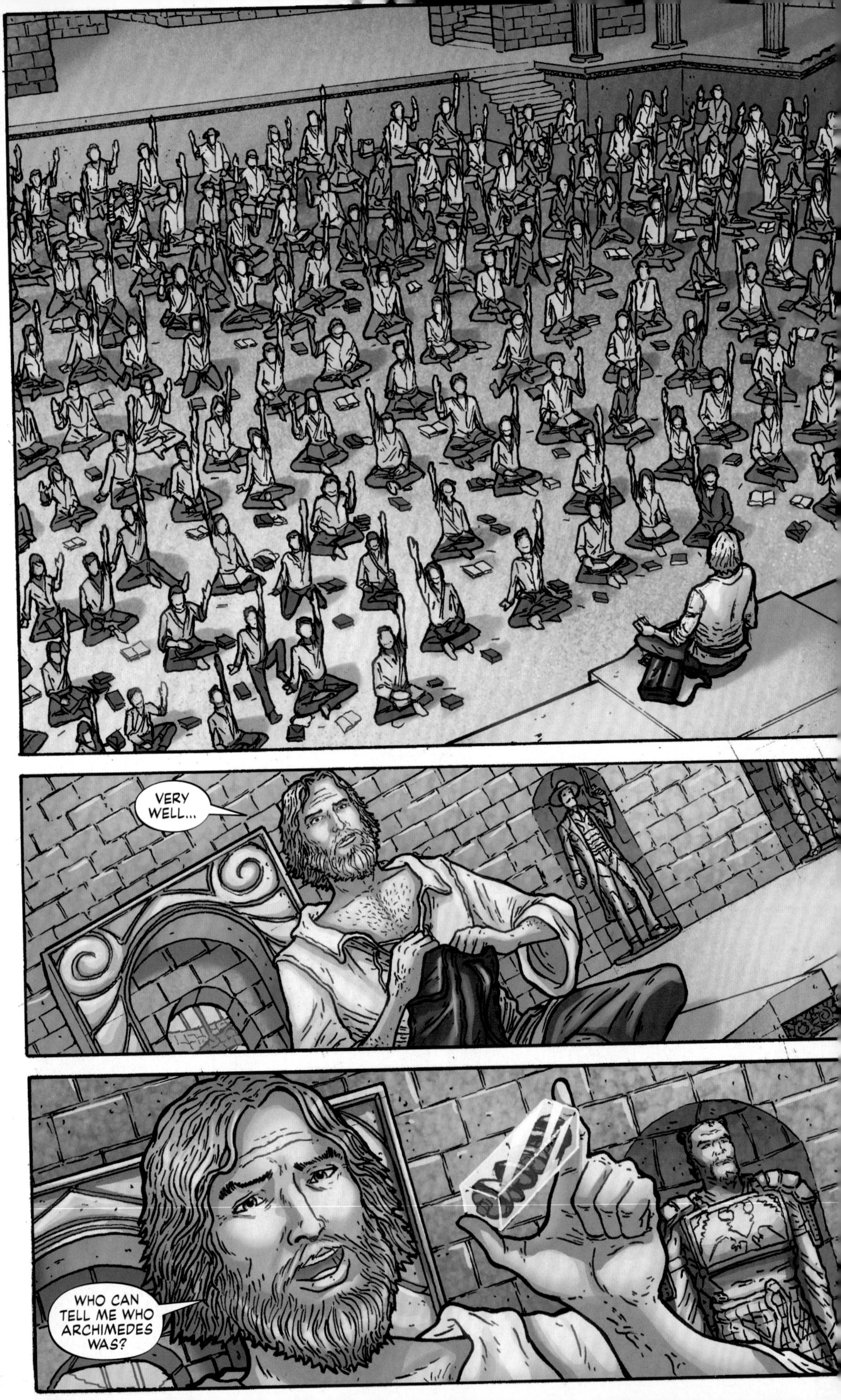
VERY WELL...
WHO CAN TELL ME WHO ARCHIMEDES WAS?

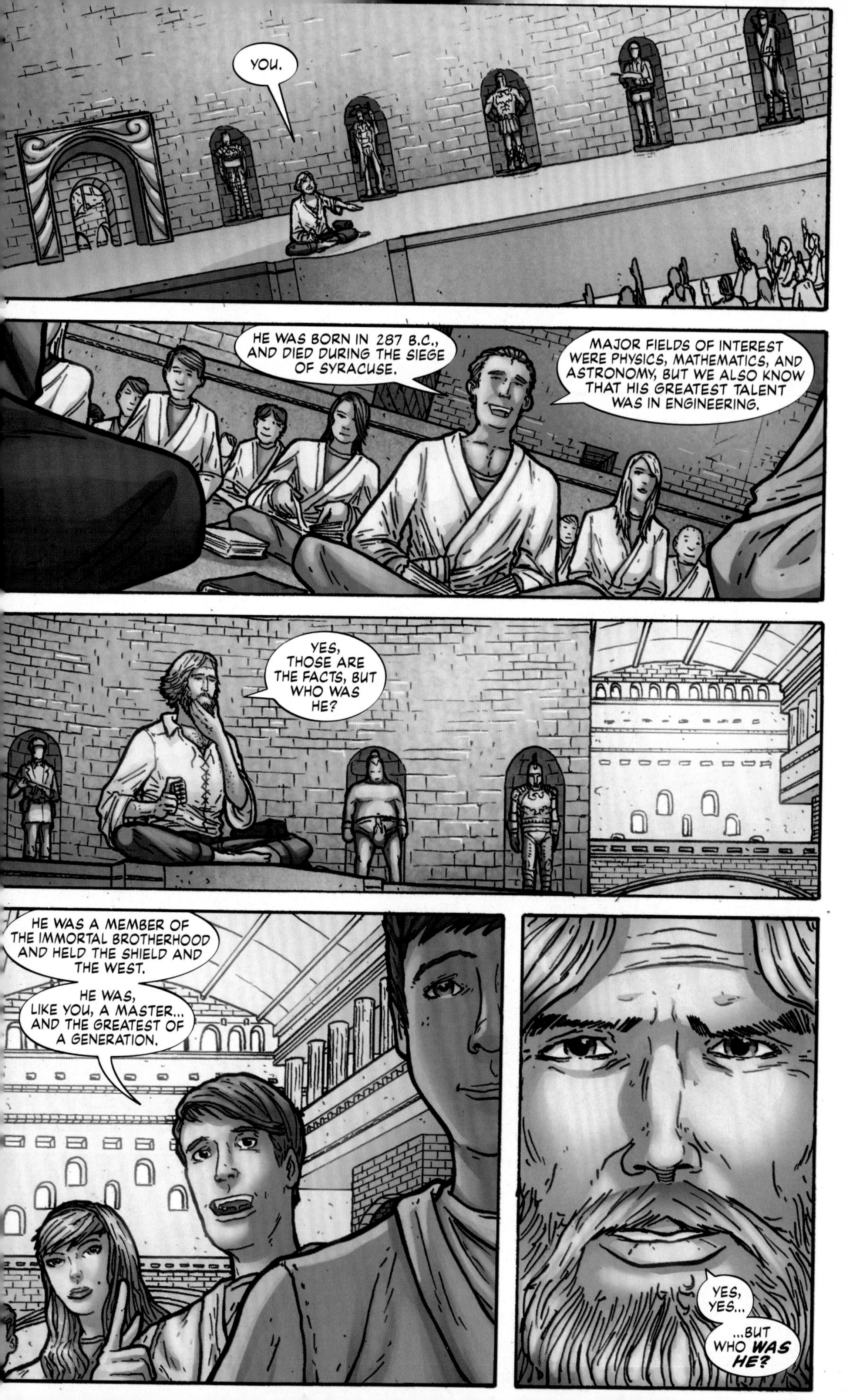
YOU.
HE WAS BORN IN 287 B.C., AND DIED DURING THE SIEGE OF SYRACUSE.
MAJOR FIELDS OF INTEREST WERE PHYSICS, MATHEMATICS, AND ASTRONOMY, BUT WE ALSO KNOW THAT HIS GREATEST TALENT WAS IN ENGINEERING.
YES, THOSE ARE THE FACTS, BUT WHO WAS HE?
HE WAS A MEMBER OF THE IMMORTAL BROTHERHOOD AND HELD THE SHIELD AND THE WEST.
HE WAS, LIKE YOU, A MASTER... AND THE GREATEST OF A GENERATION.
YES, YES...
...BUT WHO ***WAS HE?***

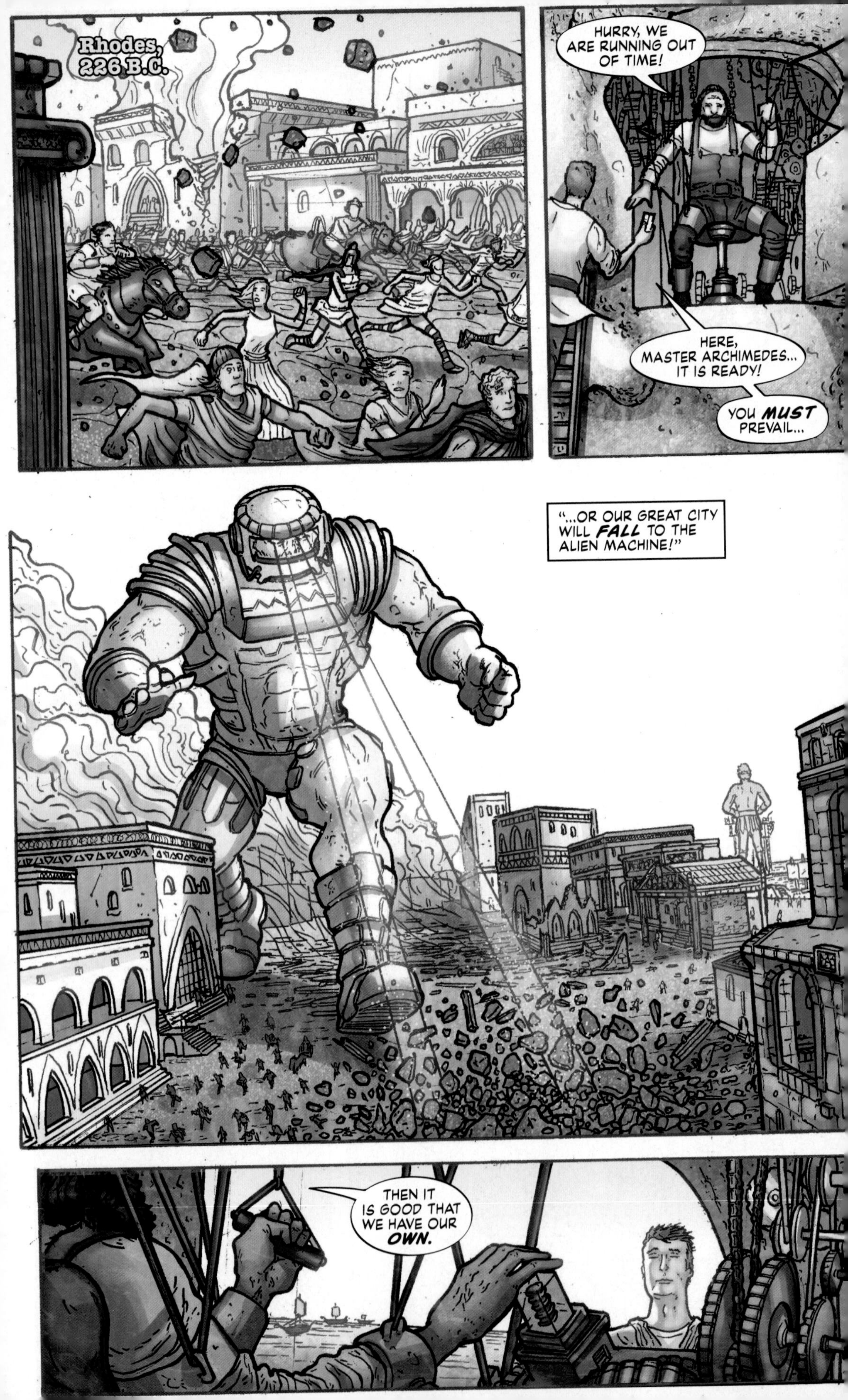
Rhodes, 226 B.C.
HURRY, WE ARE RUNNING OUT OF TIME!
HERE, MASTER ARCHIMEDES... IT IS READY!
YOU MUST PREVAIL...
"...OR OUR GREAT CITY WILL FALL TO THE ALIEN MACHINE!"
THEN IT IS GOOD THAT WE HAVE OUR OWN.

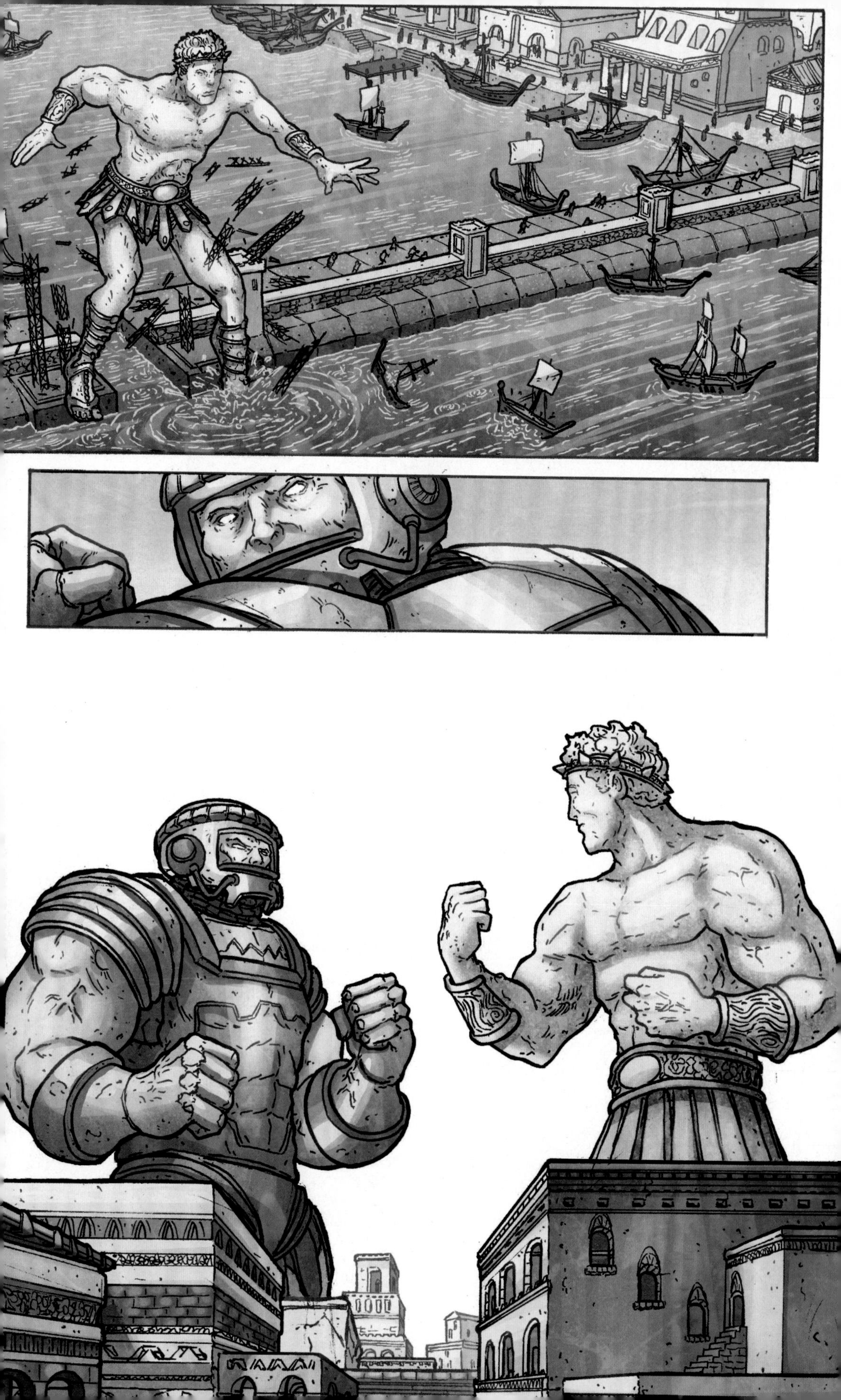

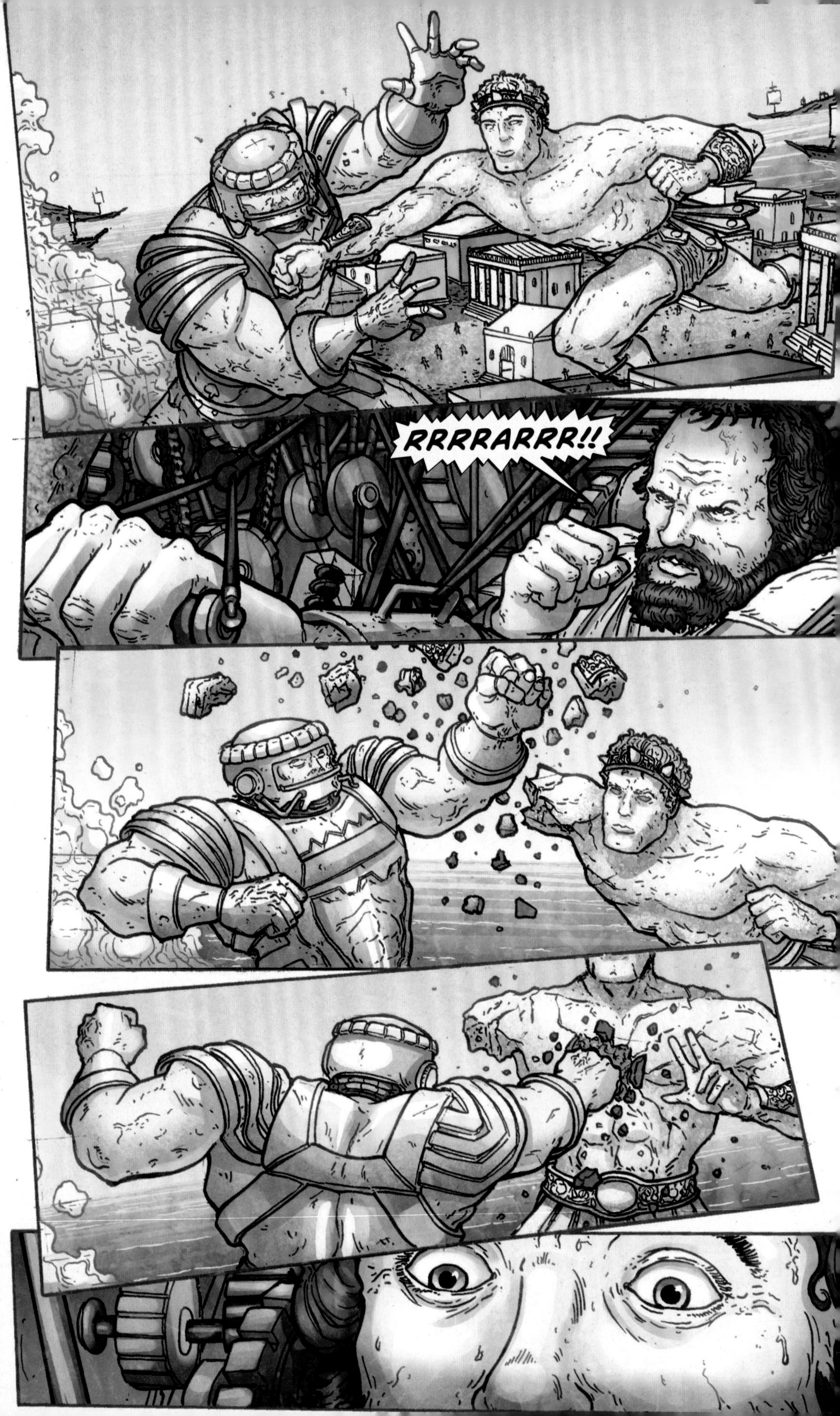
RRRRARRR!!

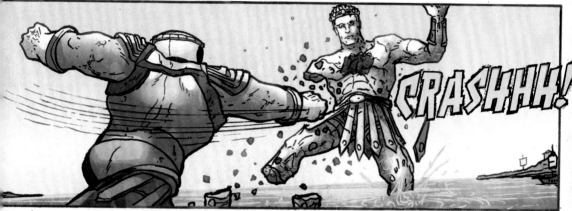

CRASHHH!

NO...

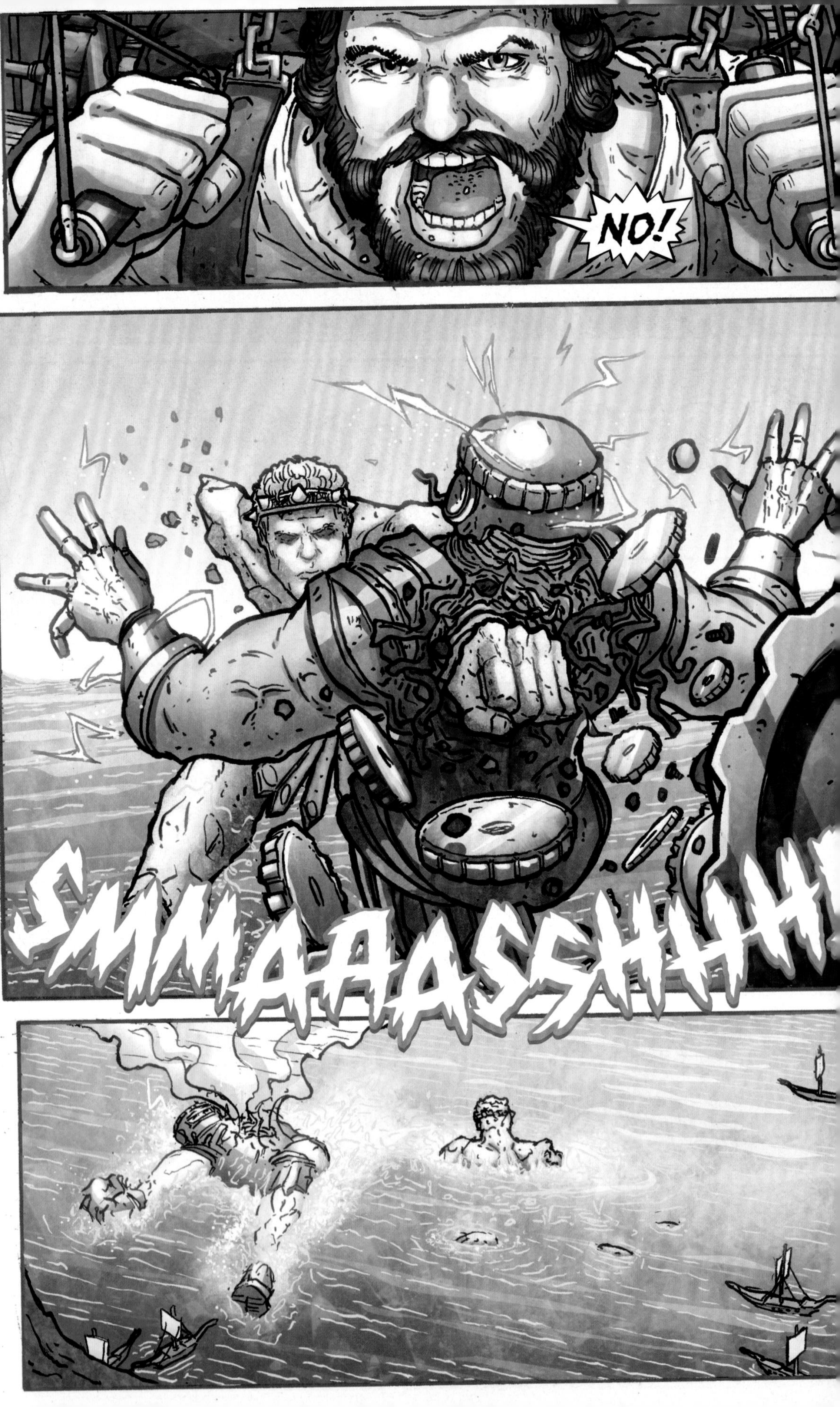
NO!
SMMAAASSHHH

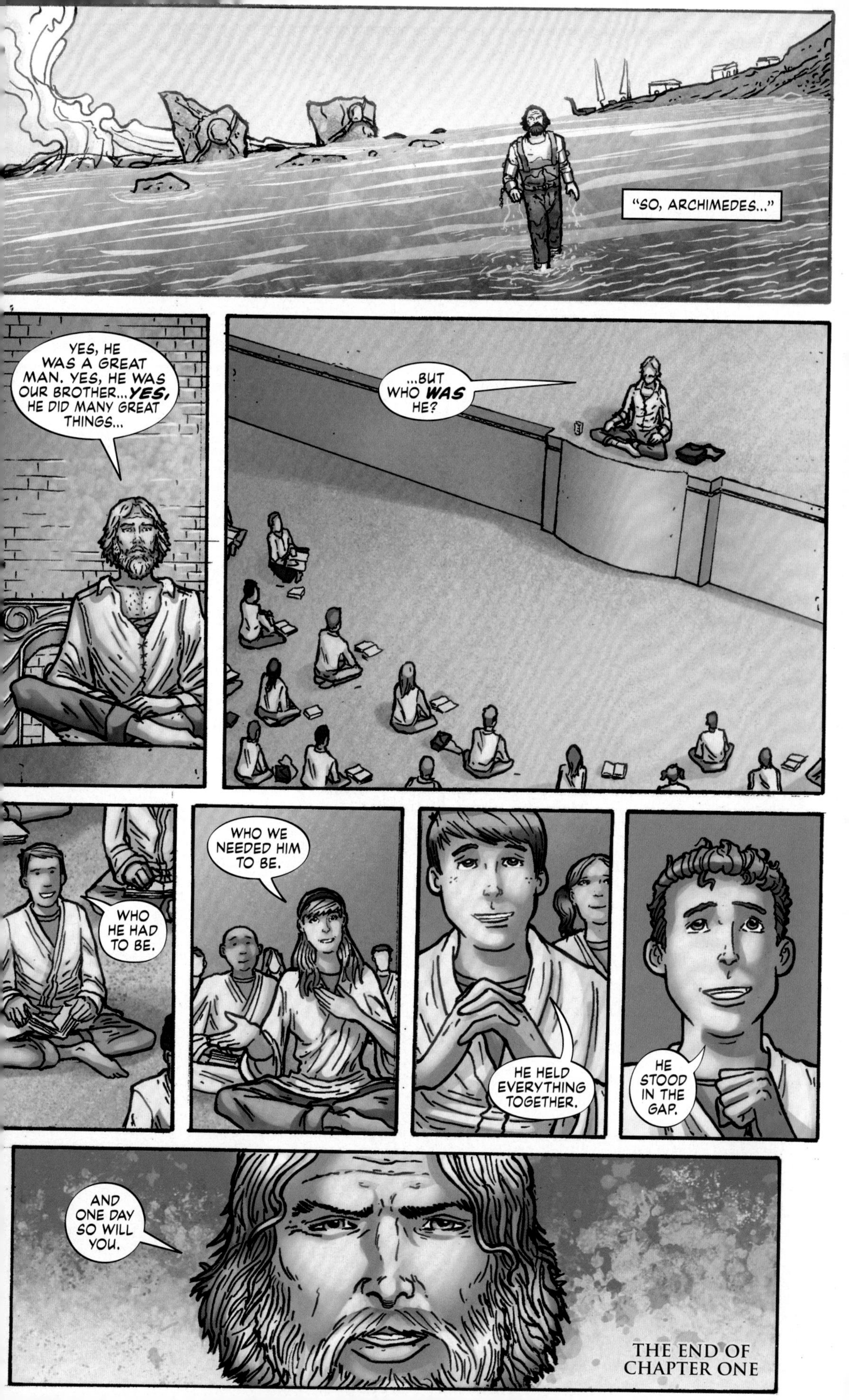
"SO, ARCHIMEDES..."
YES, HE WAS A GREAT MAN. YES, HE WAS OUR BROTHER... YES, HE DID MANY GREAT THINGS...
...BUT WHO WAS HE?
WHO HE HAD TO BE.
WHO WE NEEDED HIM TO BE.
HE HELD EVERYTHING TOGETHER.
HE STOOD IN THE GAP.
AND ONE DAY SO WILL YOU.
THE END OF CHAPTER ONE

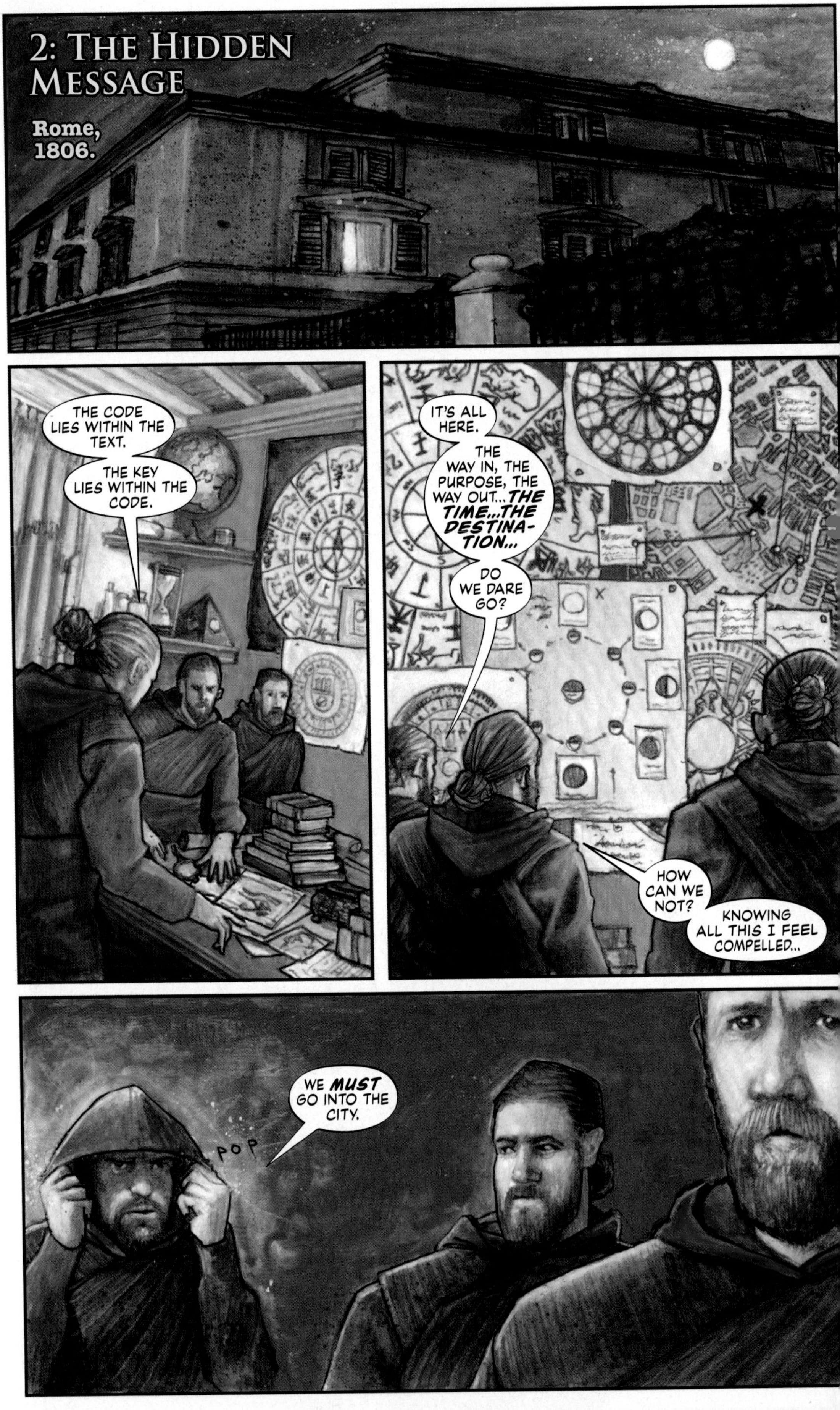
2: The Hidden Message
Rome, 1806.
THE CODE LIES WITHIN THE TEXT.
THE KEY LIES WITHIN THE CODE.
IT'S ALL HERE.
THE WAY IN, THE PURPOSE, THE WAY OUT... THE TIME...THE DESTINATION...
DO WE DARE GO?
HOW CAN WE NOT?
KNOWING ALL THIS I FEEL COMPELLED...
WE MUST GO INTO THE CITY.
POP

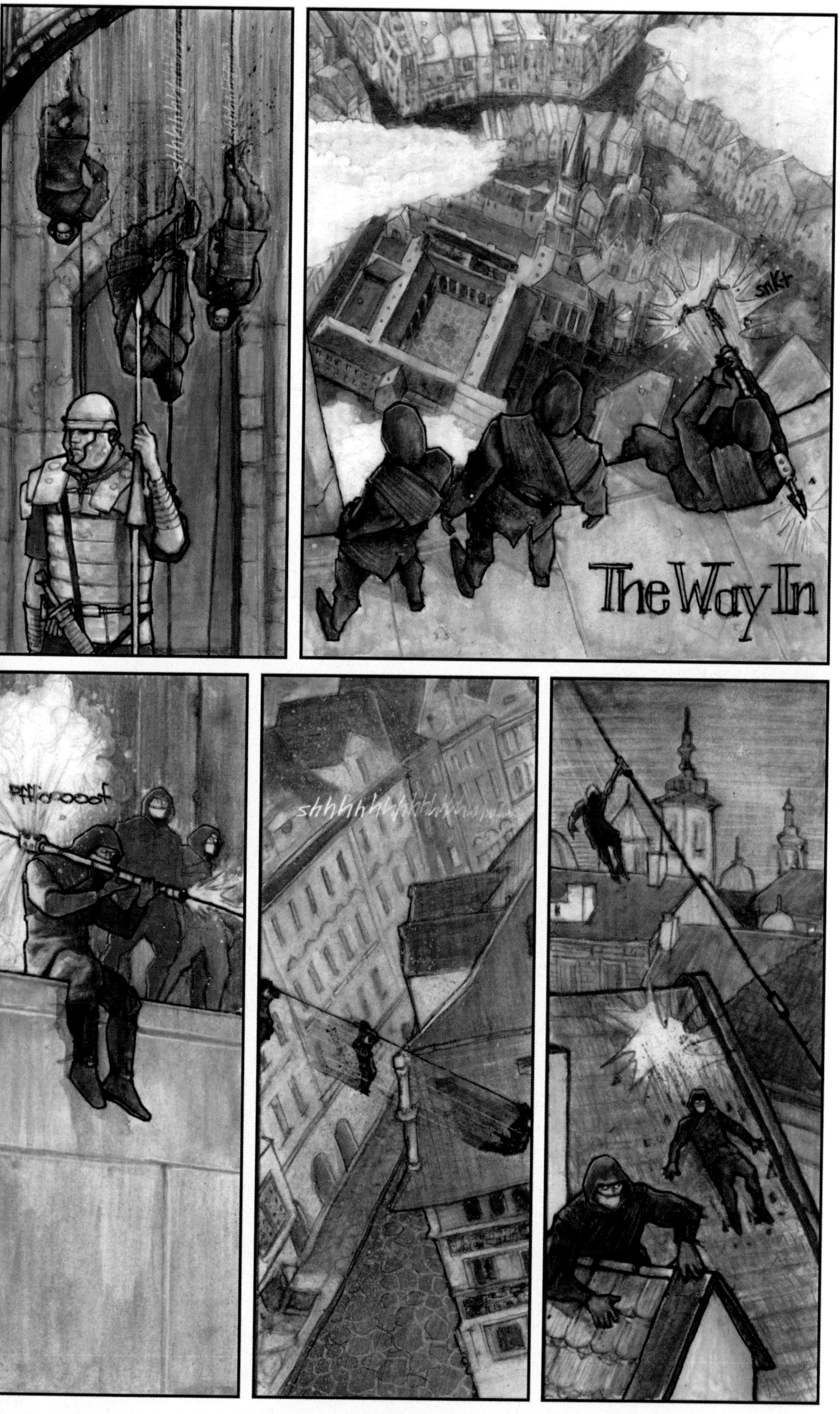
snkt
The Way In

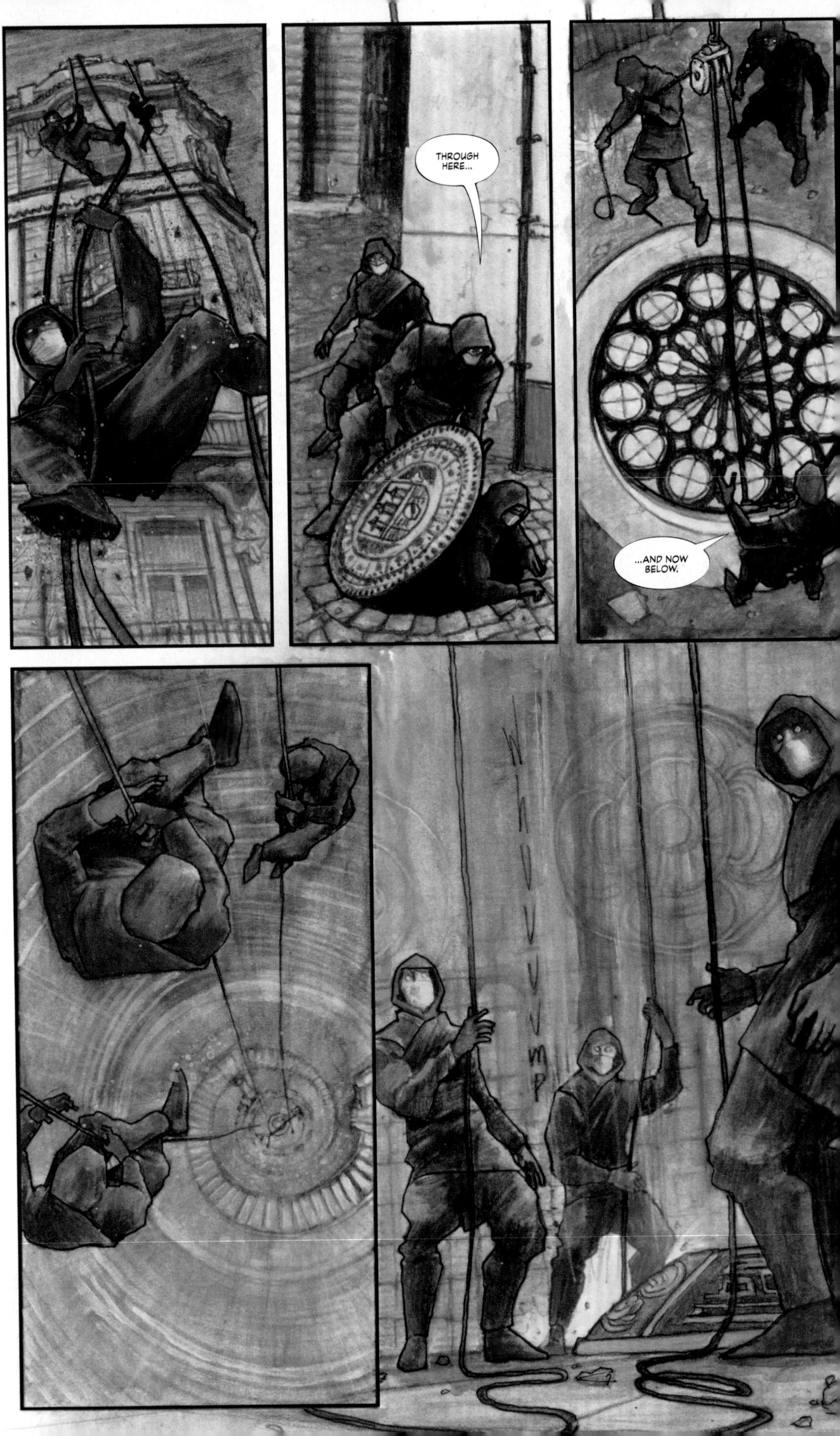
THROUGH HERE...
...AND NOW BELOW.
WHUMP

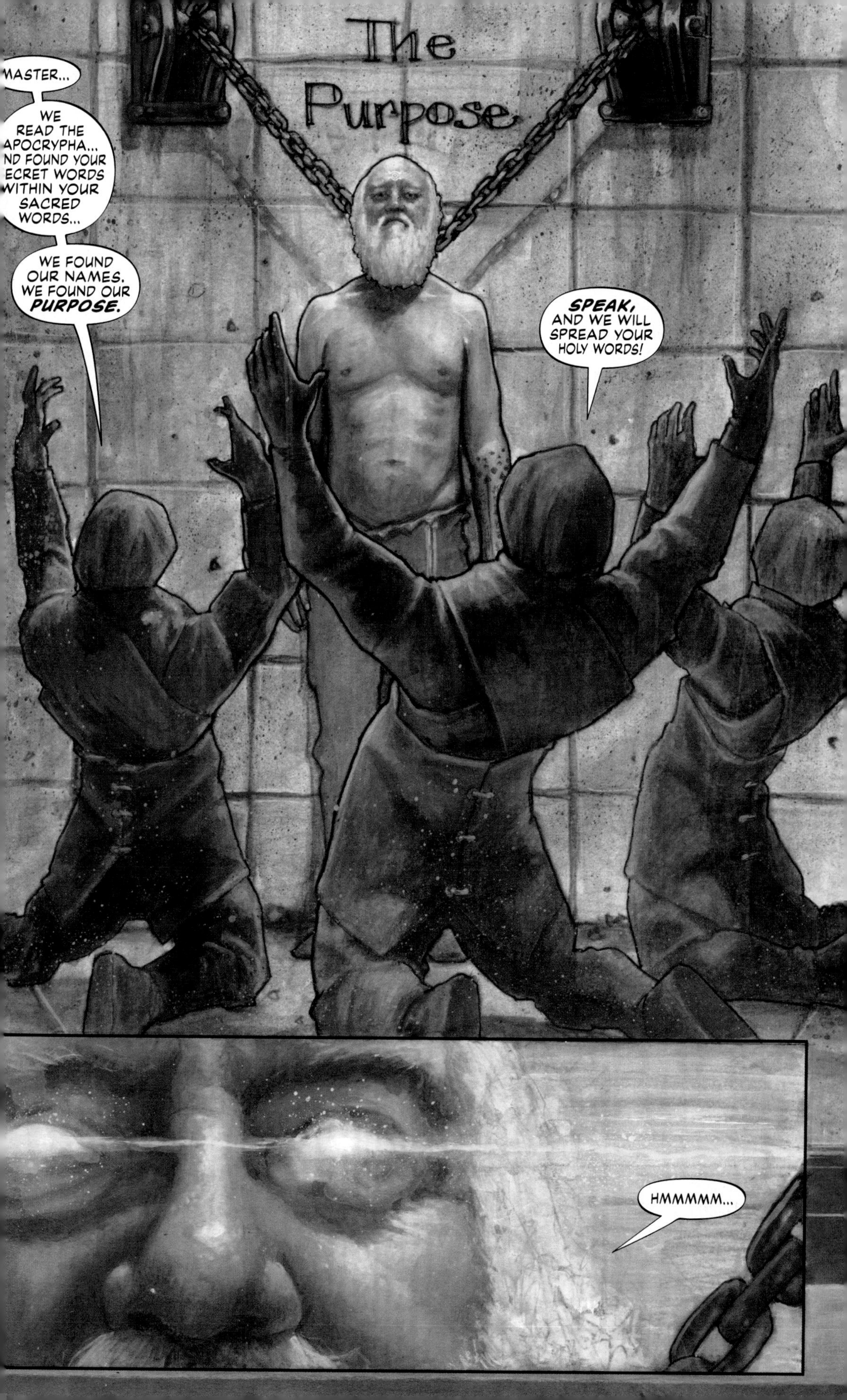
The Purpose
MASTER...
WE READ THE APOCRYPHA... ND FOUND YOUR ECRET WORDS WITHIN YOUR SACRED WORDS...
WE FOUND OUR NAMES. WE FOUND OUR **PURPOSE.**
SPEAK, AND WE WILL SPREAD YOUR HOLY WORDS!
HMMMMM...

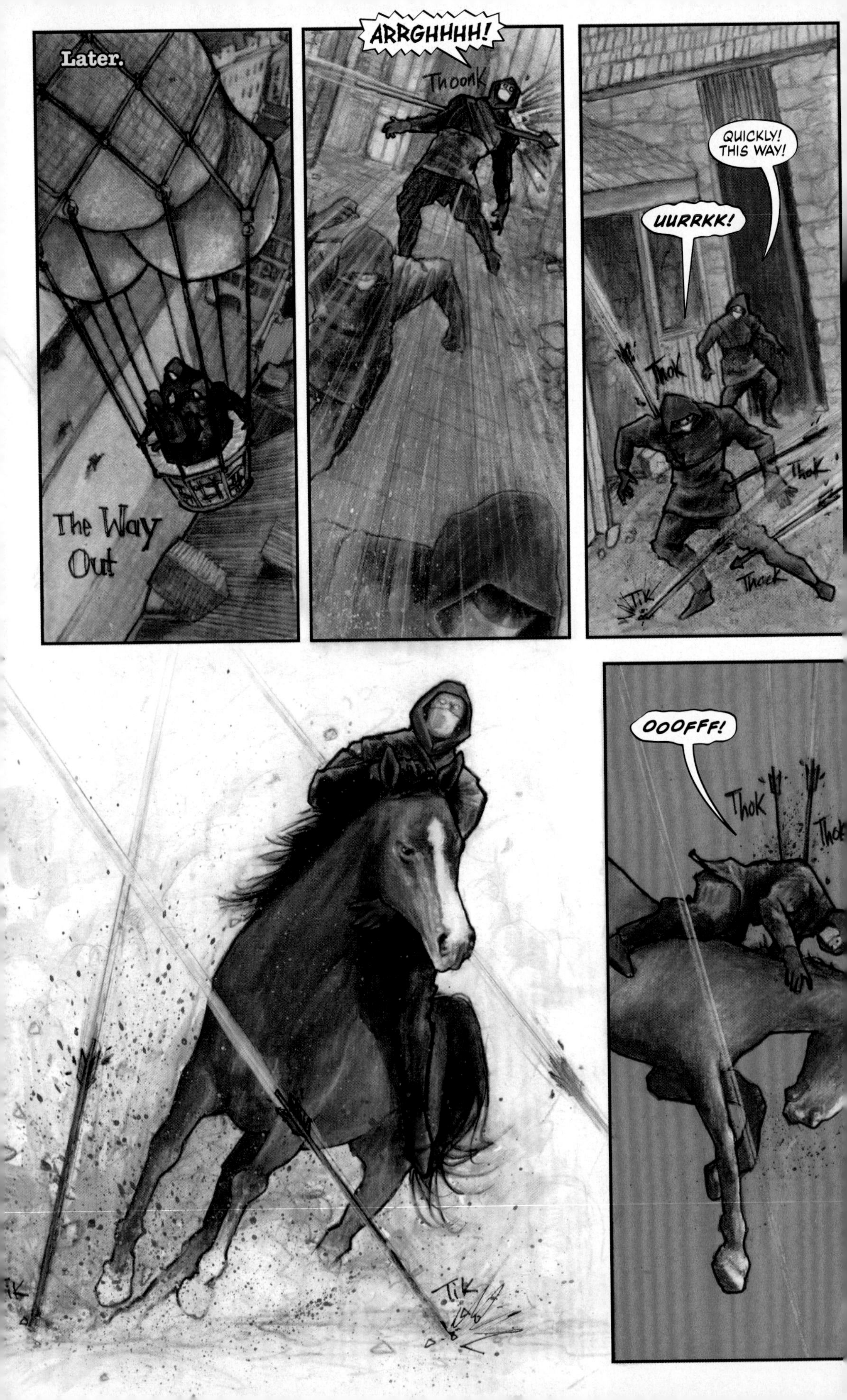
Later.
The Way Out
ARRGHHHH!
Thoonk
QUICKLY! THIS WAY!
UURRKK!
Thok
Thok
Thock
Tik
OOOFFF!
Thok
Thok
Tik

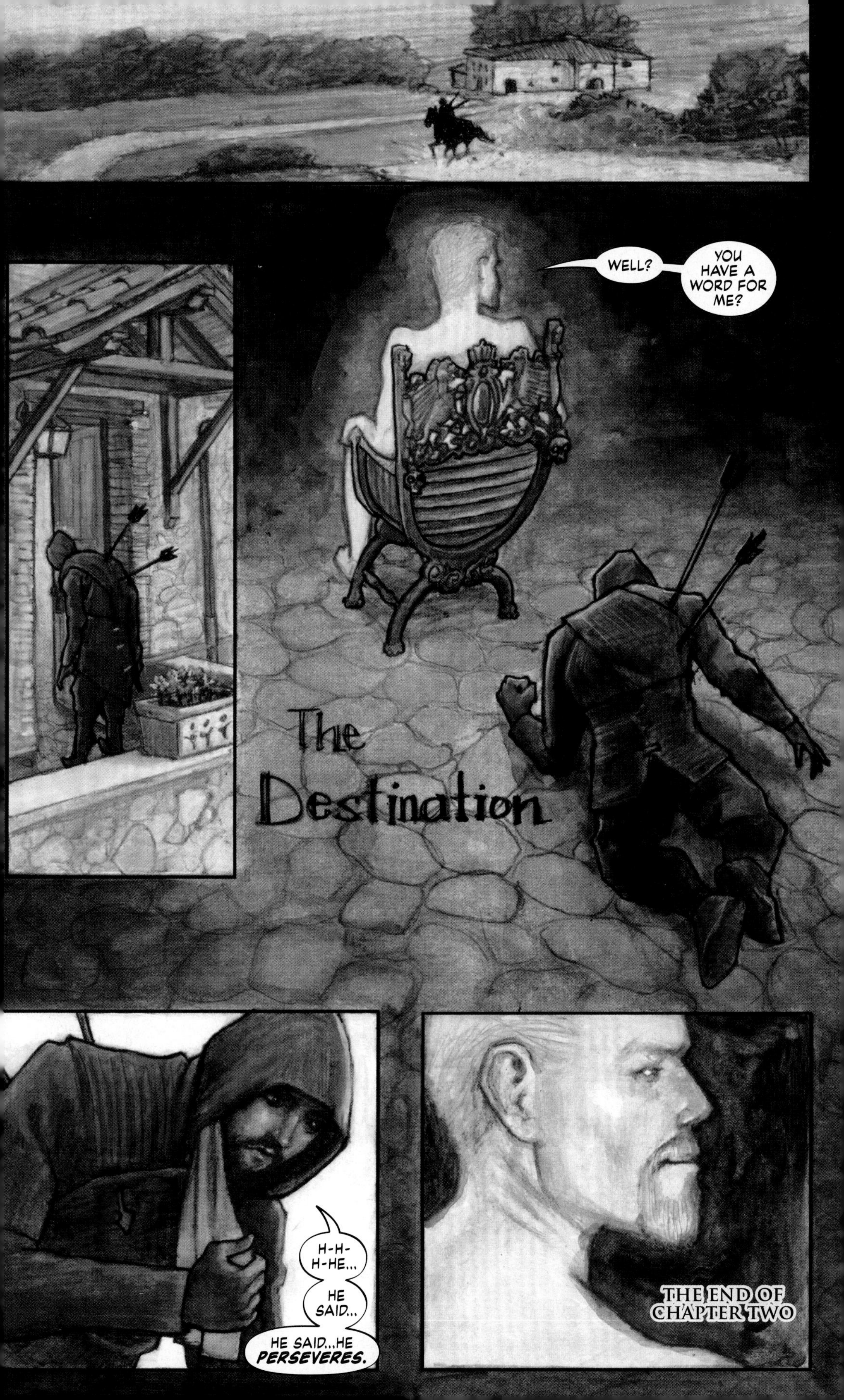
WELL?
YOU HAVE A WORD FOR ME?
The Destination
H-H-H-HE...
HE SAID...
HE SAID...HE PERSEVERES.
THE END OF CHAPTER TWO

3: Life, The End of the World, and the Key

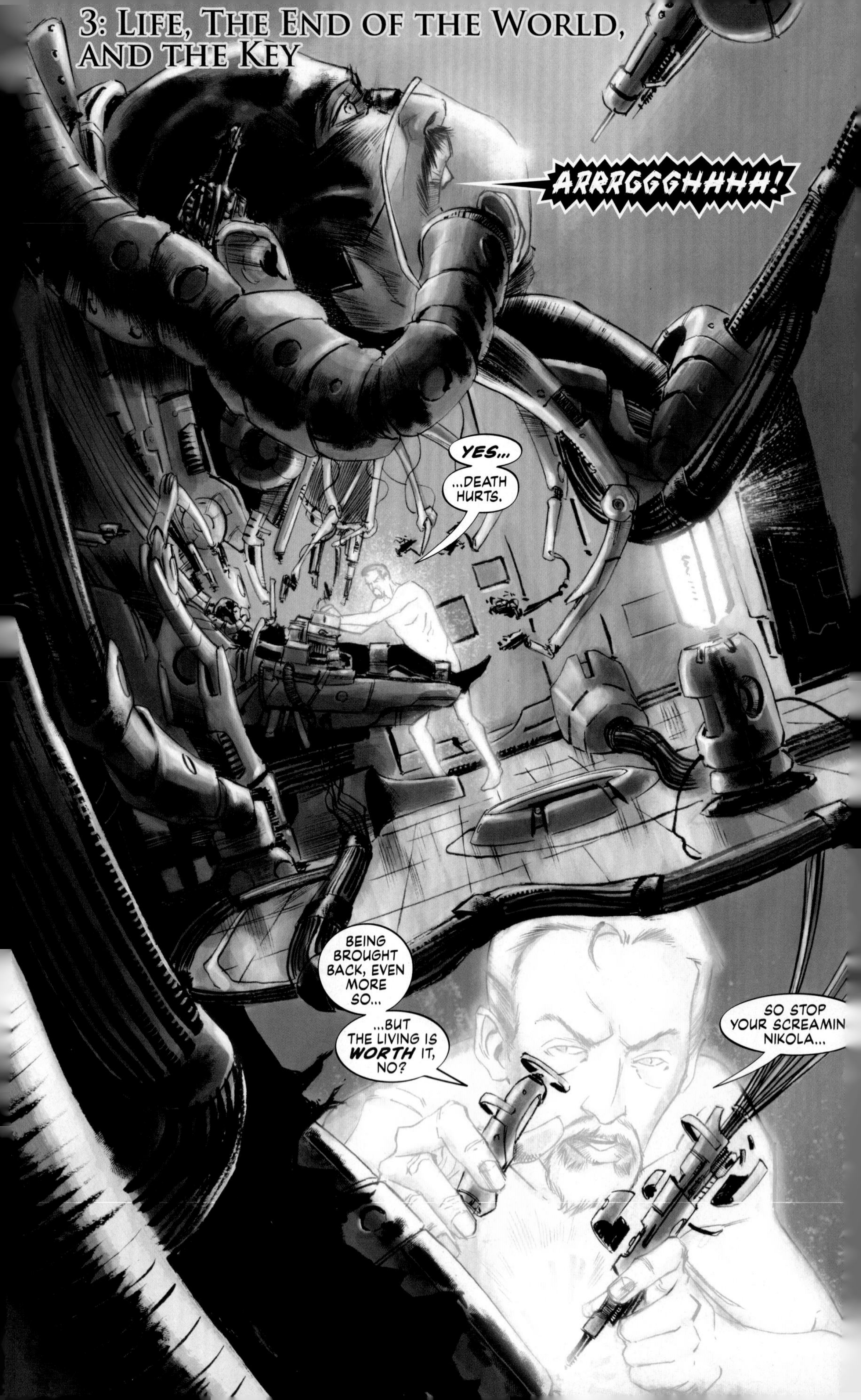
ARRRGGGHHHH!
YES...
...DEATH HURTS.
BEING BROUGHT BACK, EVEN MORE SO...
...BUT THE LIVING IS WORTH IT, NO?
SO STOP YOUR SCREAMIN NIKOLA...

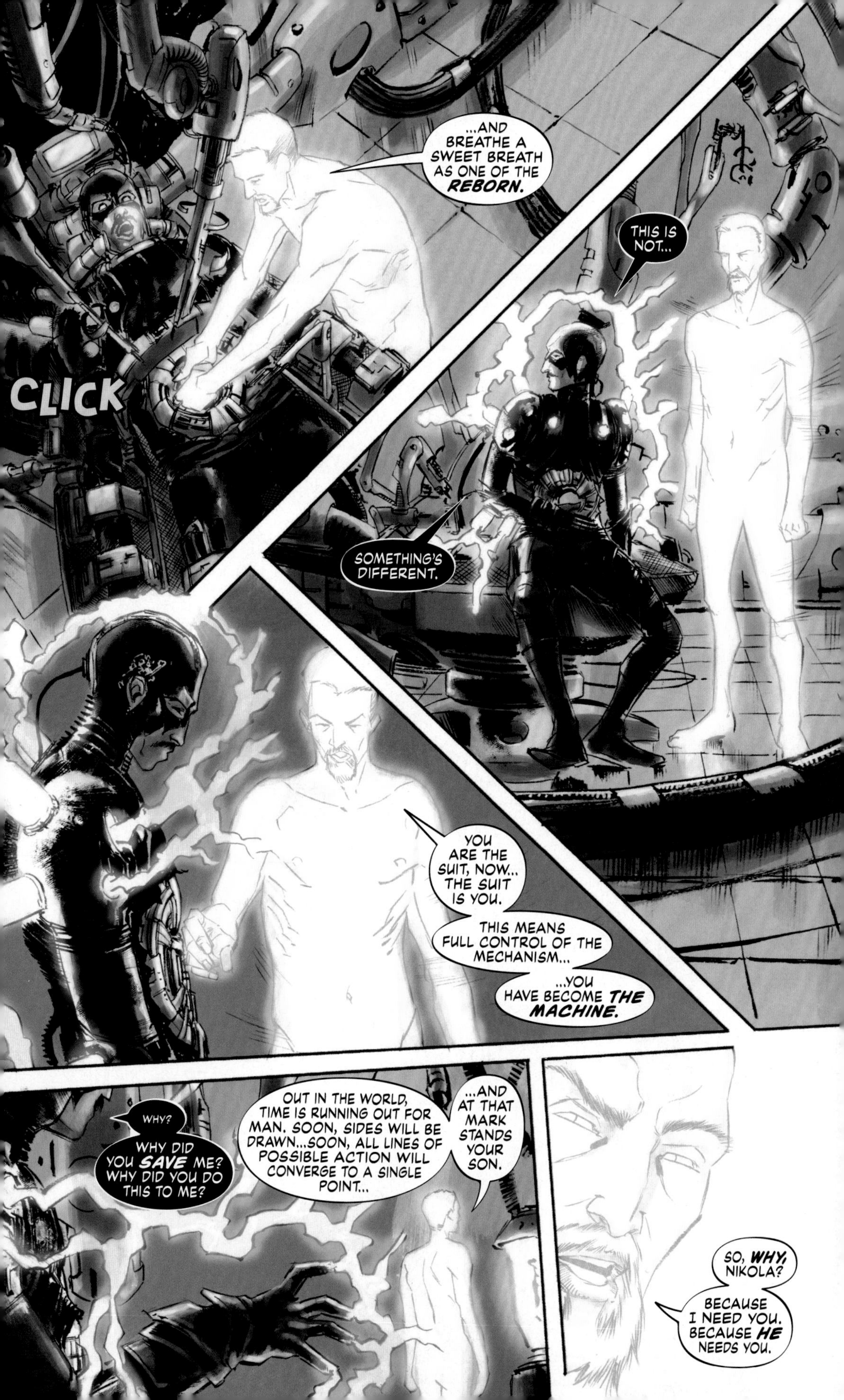
...AND BREATHE A SWEET BREATH AS ONE OF THE REBORN.
CLICK
THIS IS NOT...
SOMETHING'S DIFFERENT.
YOU ARE THE SUIT, NOW... THE SUIT IS YOU.
THIS MEANS FULL CONTROL OF THE MECHANISM...
...YOU HAVE BECOME THE MACHINE.
WHY?
WHY DID YOU SAVE ME? WHY DID YOU DO THIS TO ME?
OUT IN THE WORLD, TIME IS RUNNING OUT FOR MAN. SOON, SIDES WILL BE DRAWN...SOON, ALL LINES OF POSSIBLE ACTION WILL CONVERGE TO A SINGLE POINT...
...AND AT THAT MARK STANDS YOUR SON.
SO, WHY, NIKOLA?
BECAUSE I NEED YOU. BECAUSE HE NEEDS YOU.

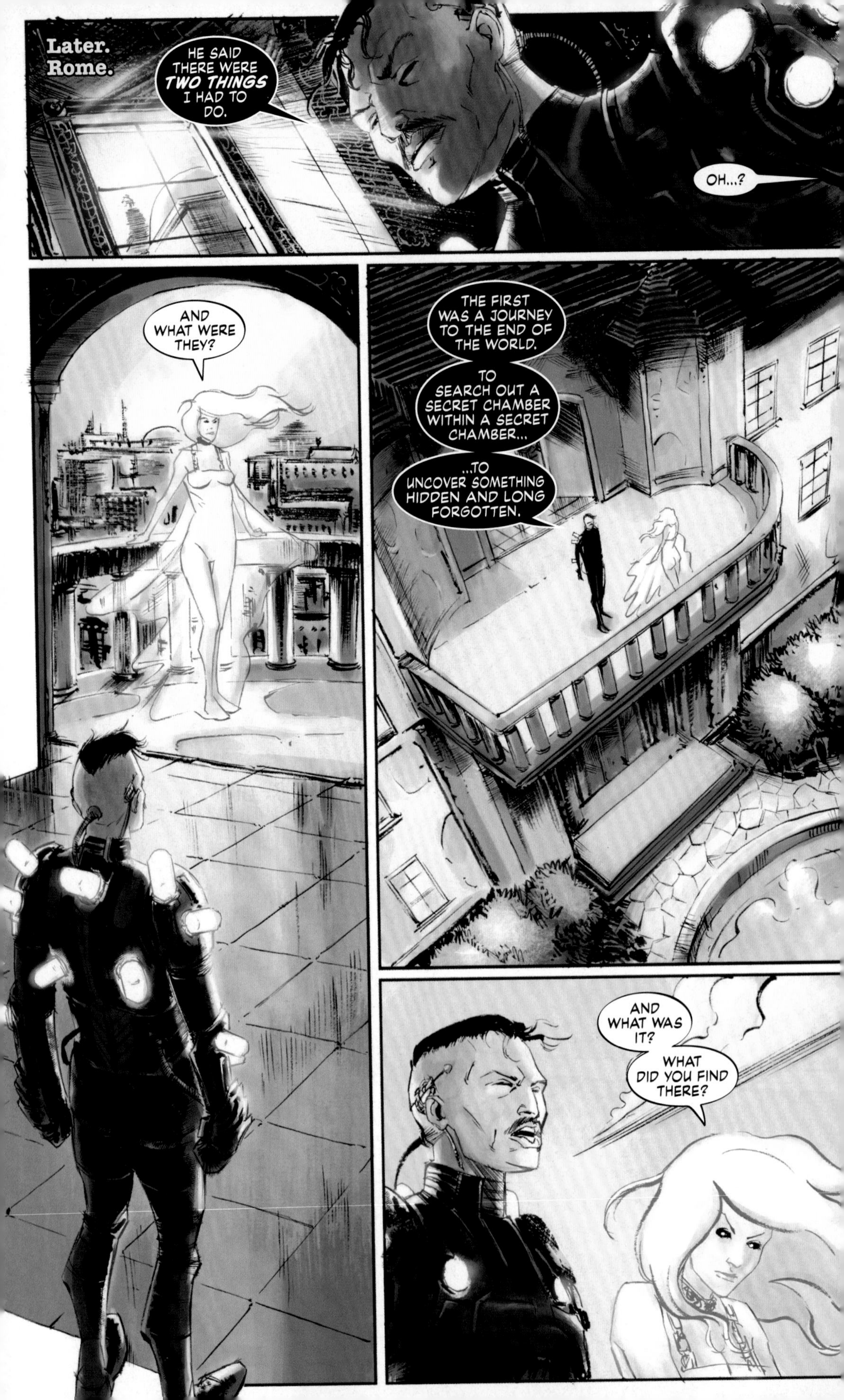
Later. Rome.
HE SAID THERE WERE TWO THINGS I HAD TO DO.
OH...?
AND WHAT WERE THEY?
THE FIRST WAS A JOURNEY TO THE END OF THE WORLD.
TO SEARCH OUT A SECRET CHAMBER WITHIN A SECRET CHAMBER...
...TO UNCOVER SOMETHING HIDDEN AND LONG FORGOTTEN.
AND WHAT WAS IT?
WHAT DID YOU FIND THERE?

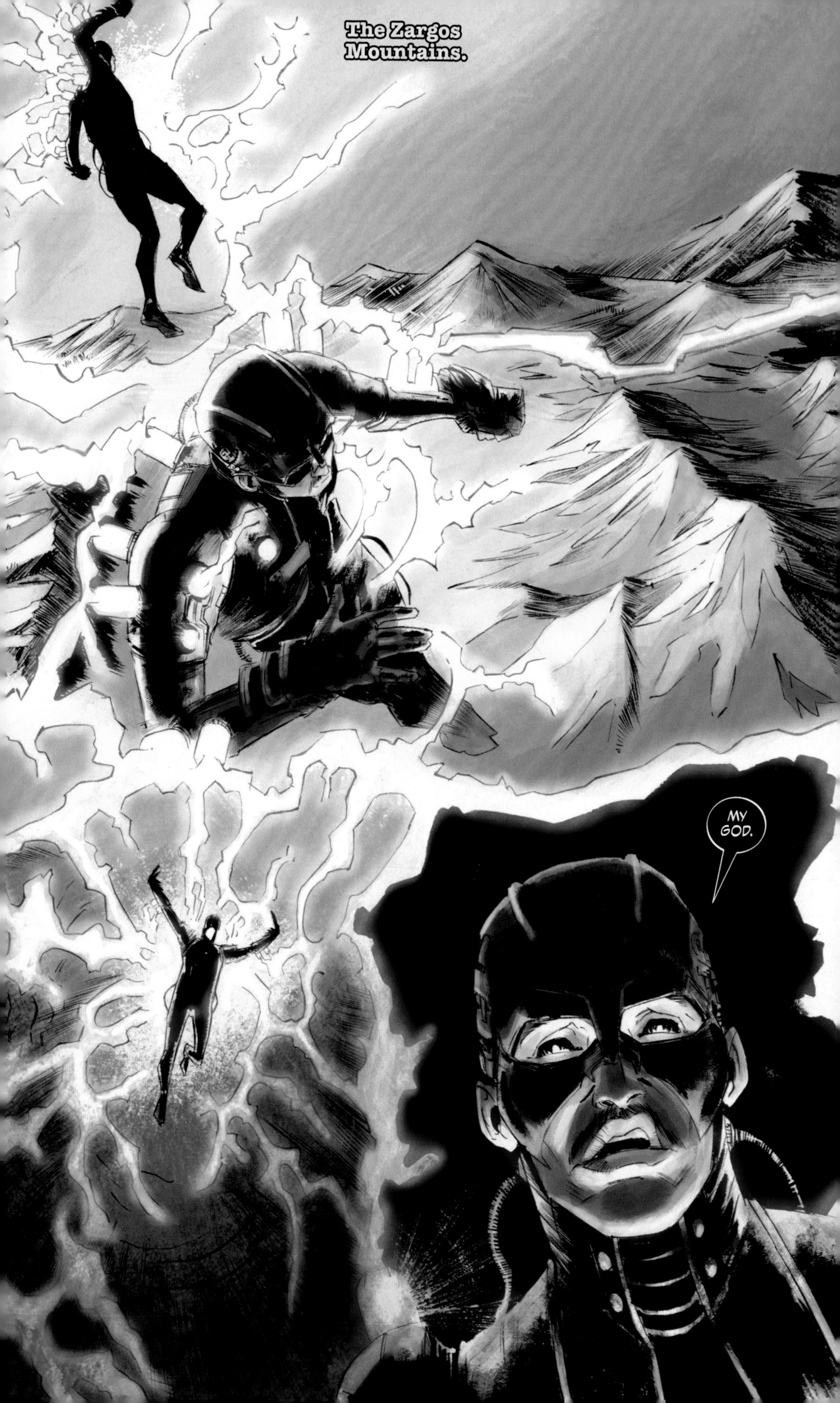
The Zargos Mountains.
MY GOD.

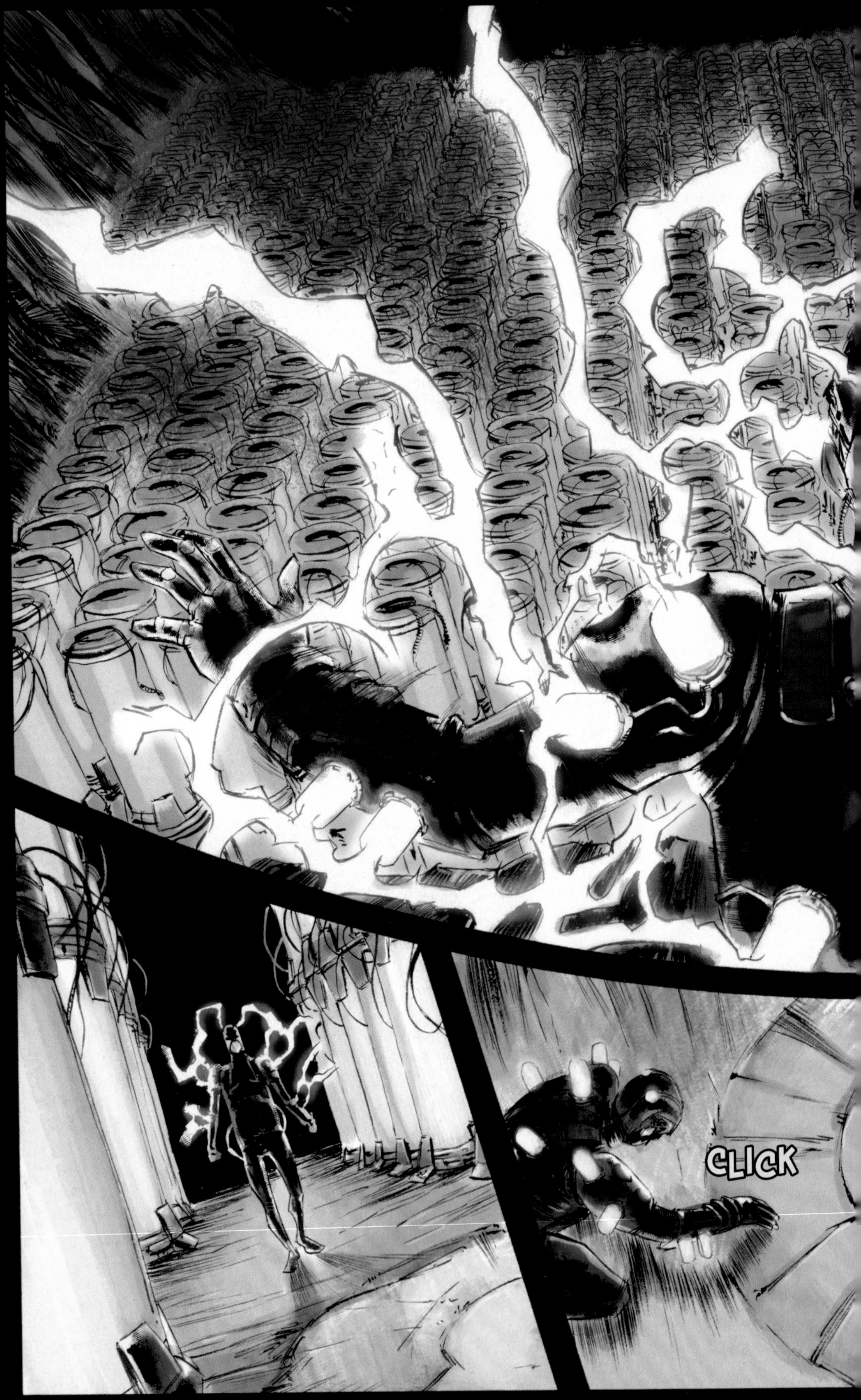
CLICK

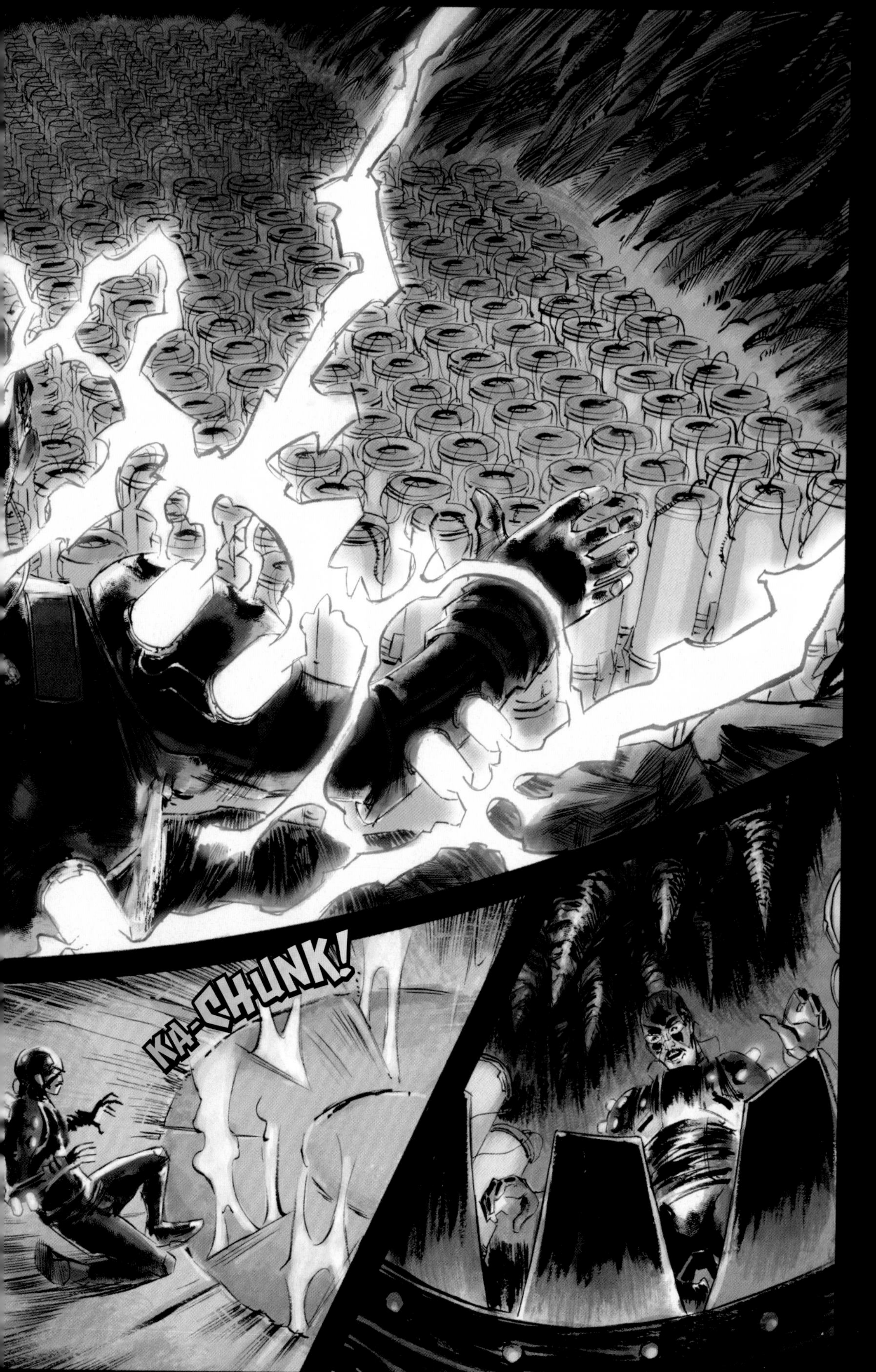
KA-CHUNK!

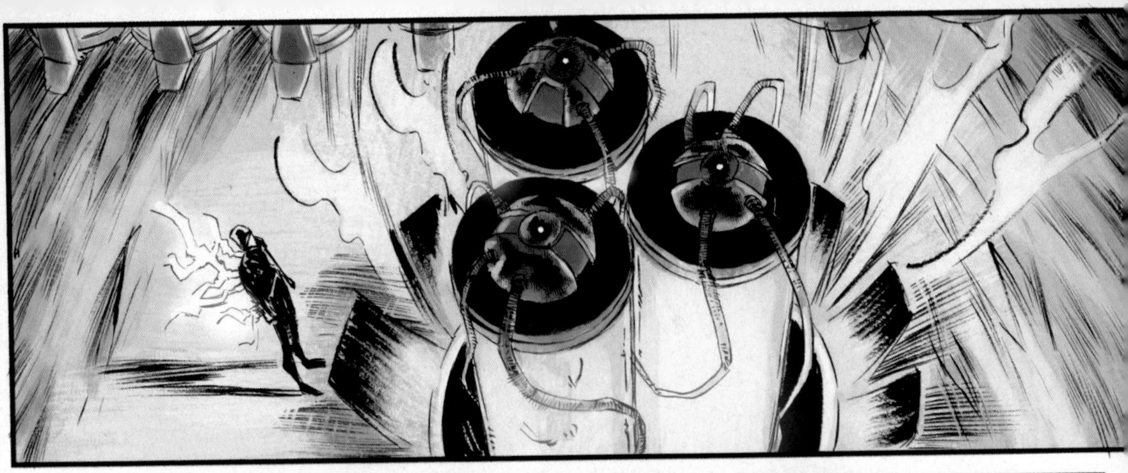

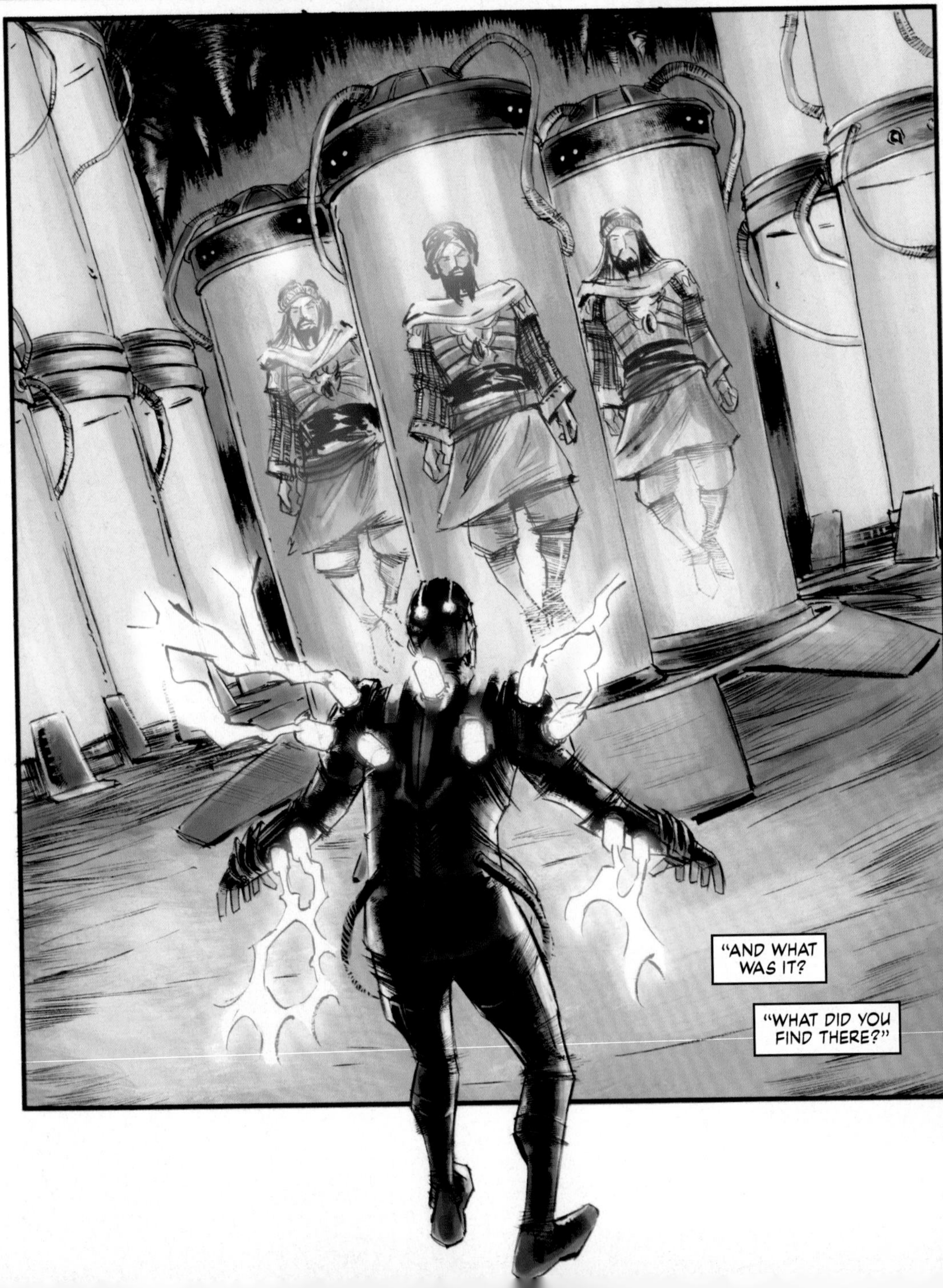
"AND WHAT WAS IT?
"WHAT DID YOU FIND THERE?"

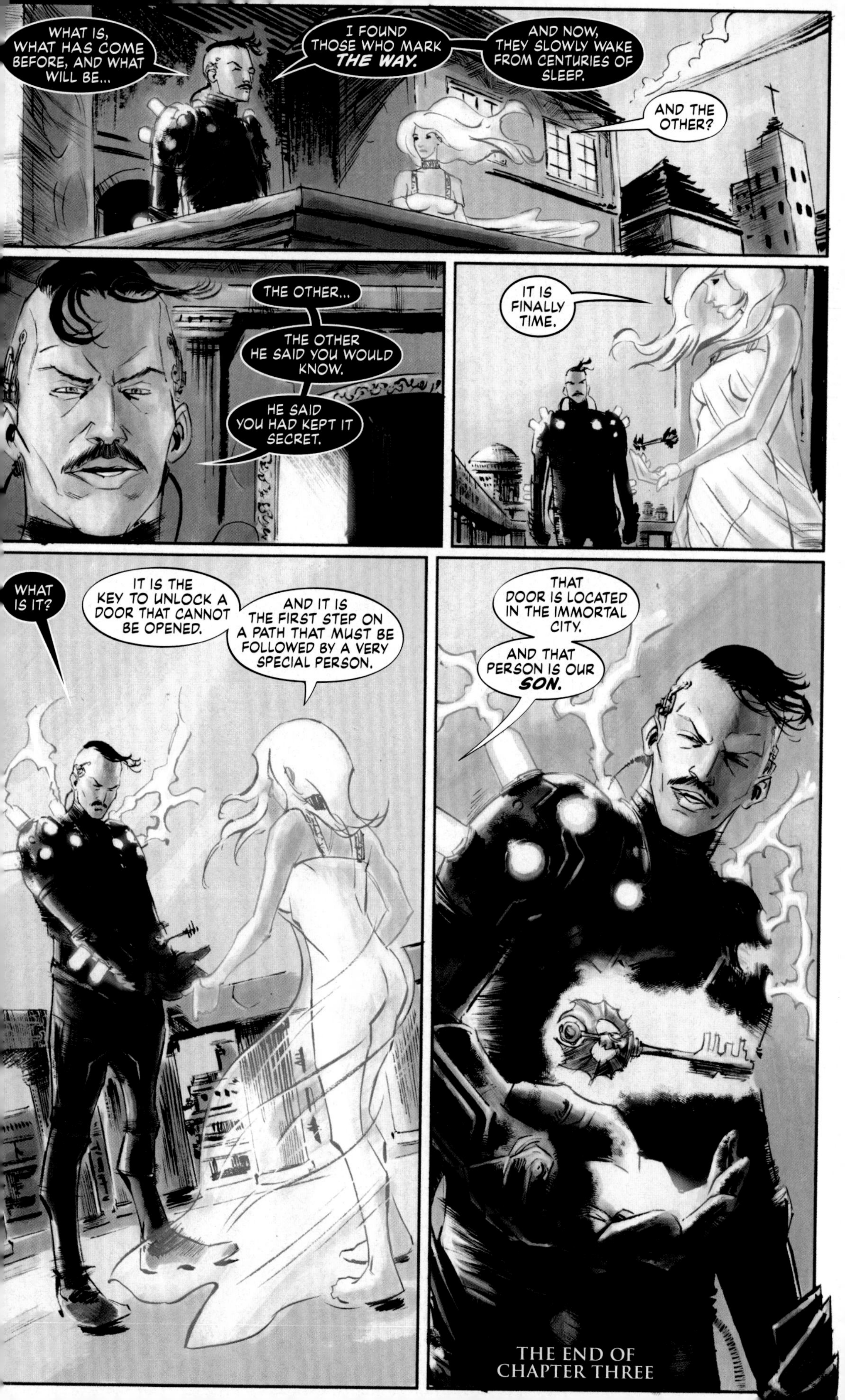
WHAT IS, WHAT HAS COME BEFORE, AND WHAT WILL BE...
I FOUND THOSE WHO MARK **THE WAY.**
AND NOW, THEY SLOWLY WAKE FROM CENTURIES OF SLEEP.
AND THE OTHER?
THE OTHER...
THE OTHER HE SAID YOU WOULD KNOW.
HE SAID YOU HAD KEPT IT SECRET.
IT IS FINALLY TIME.
WHAT IS IT?
IT IS THE KEY TO UNLOCK A DOOR THAT CANNOT BE OPENED.
AND IT IS THE FIRST STEP ON A PATH THAT MUST BE FOLLOWED BY A VERY SPECIAL PERSON.
THAT DOOR IS LOCATED IN THE IMMORTAL CITY.
AND THAT PERSON IS OUR **SON.**
THE END OF CHAPTER THREE

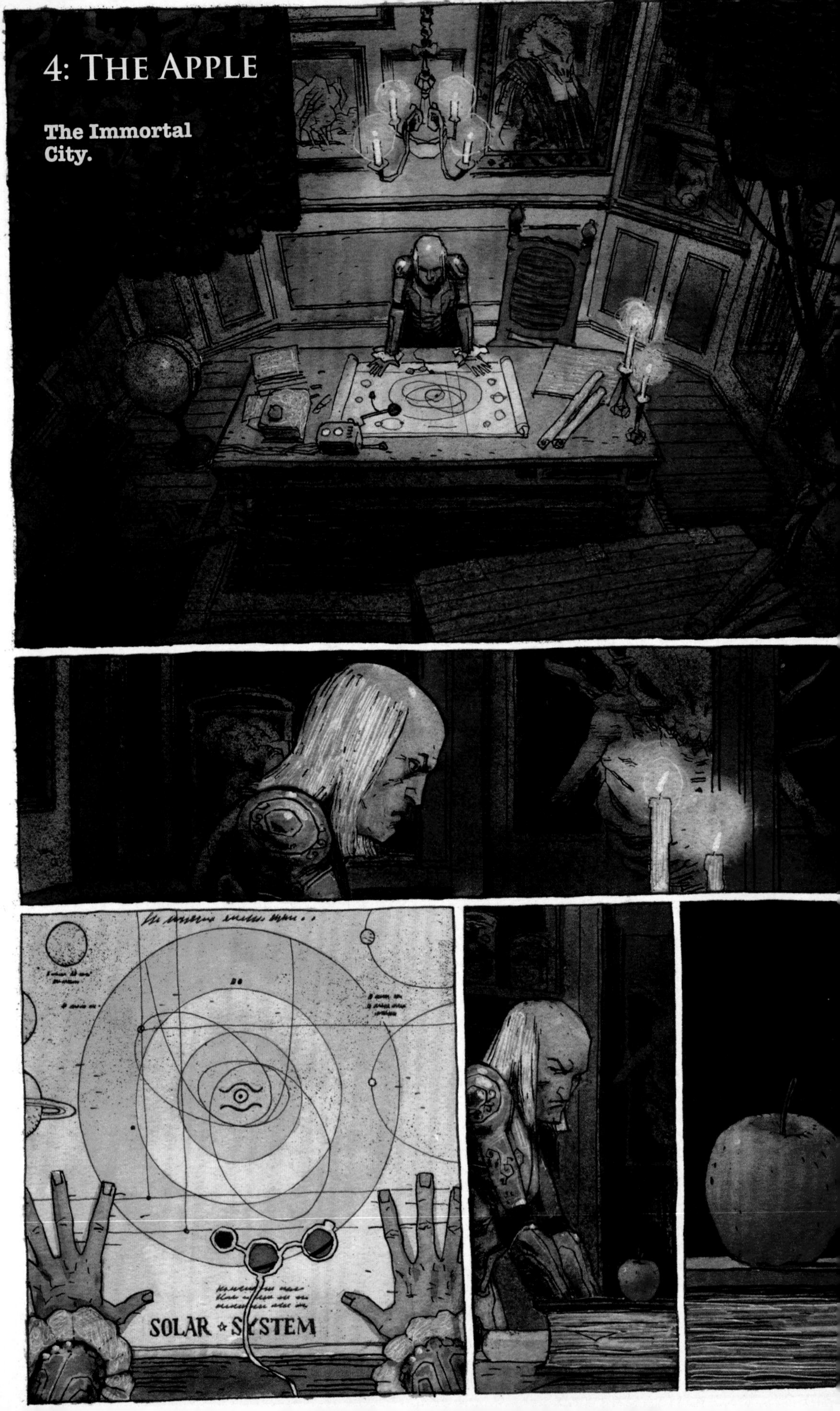
4: The Apple
The Immortal City.
SOLAR SYSTEM

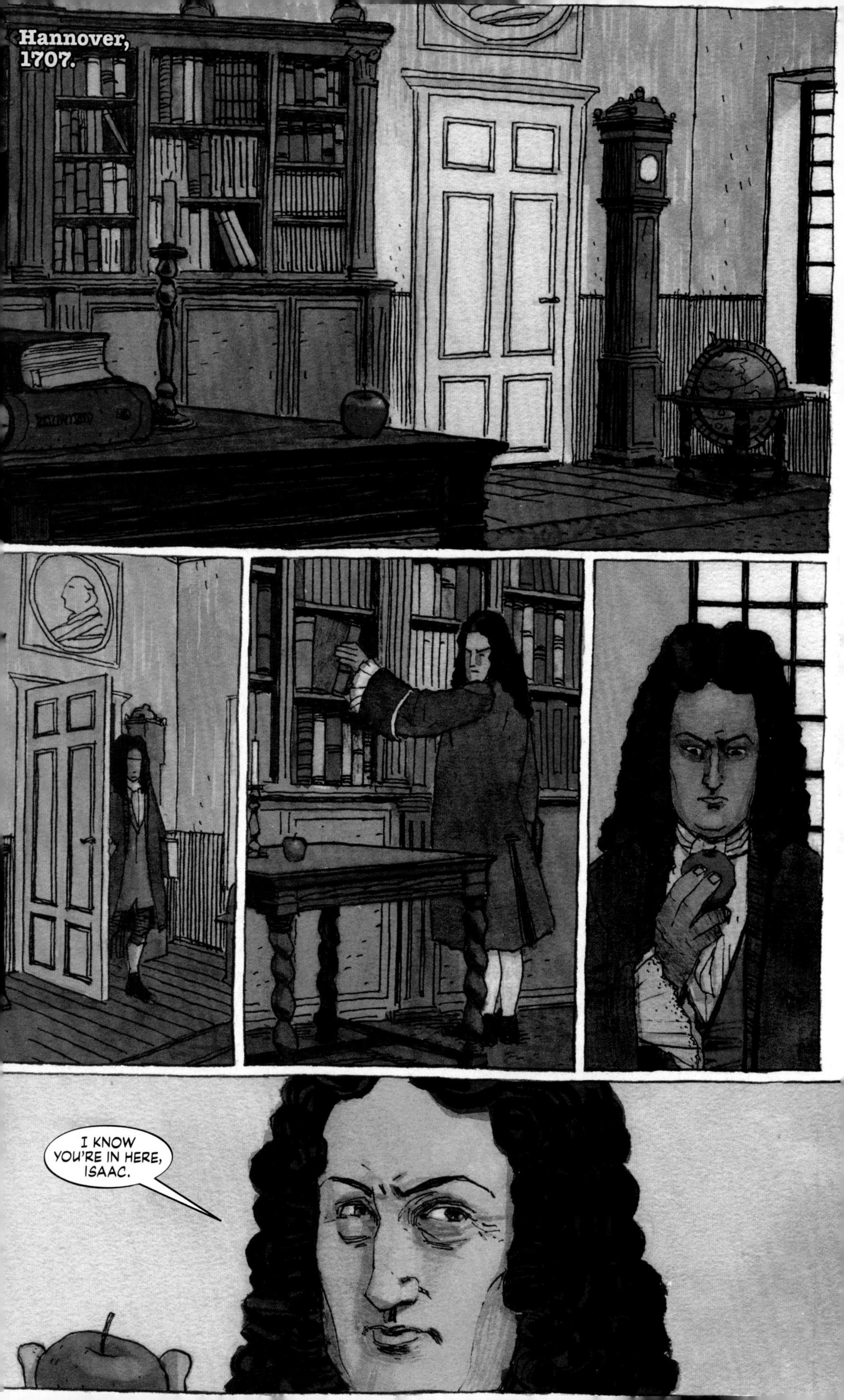
Hannover, 1707.
I KNOW YOU'RE IN HERE, ISAAC.

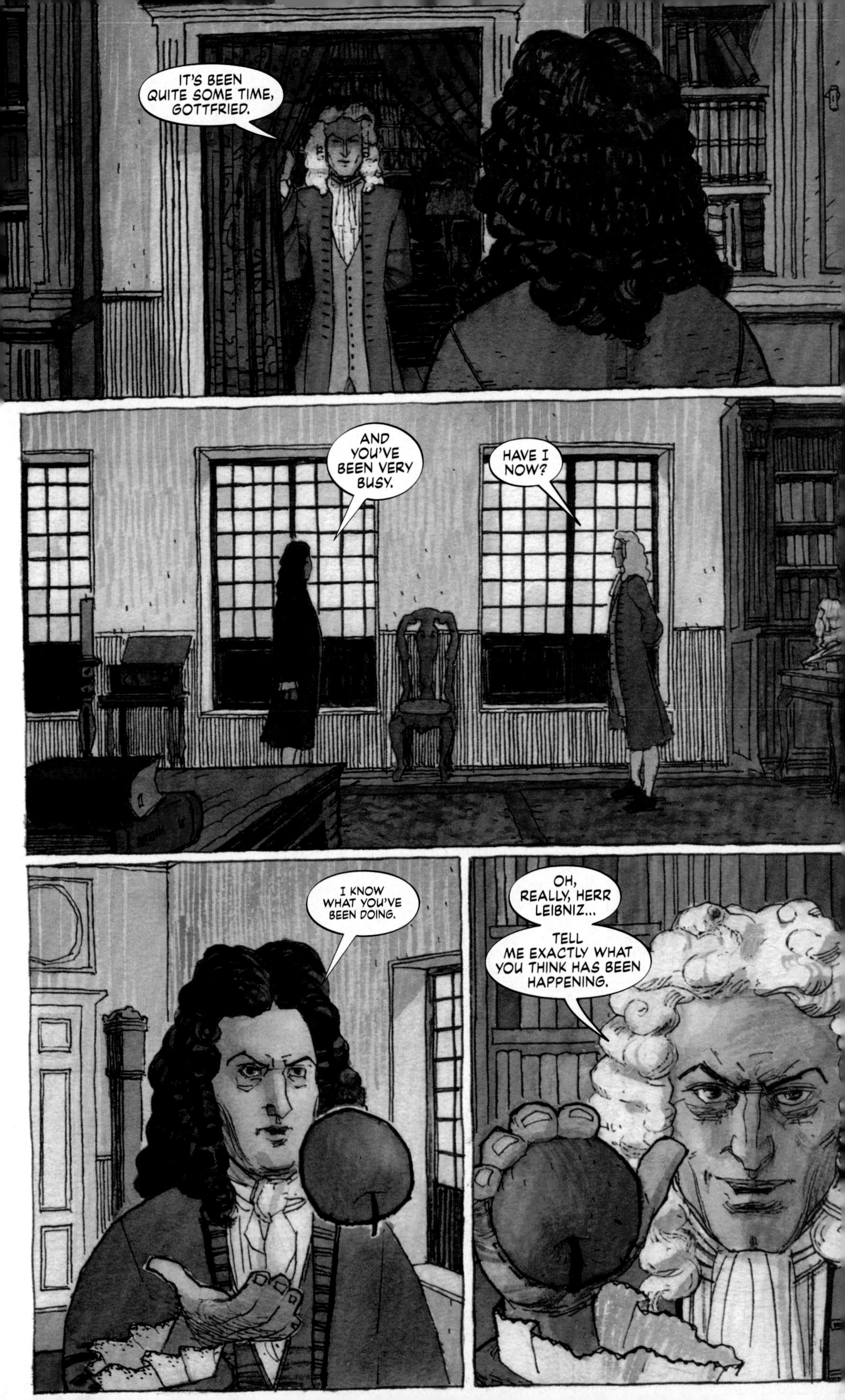
IT'S BEEN QUITE SOME TIME, GOTTFRIED.
AND YOU'VE BEEN VERY BUSY.
HAVE I NOW?
I KNOW WHAT YOU'VE BEEN DOING.
OH, REALLY, HERR LEIBNIZ...
TELL ME EXACTLY WHAT YOU THINK HAS BEEN HAPPENING.

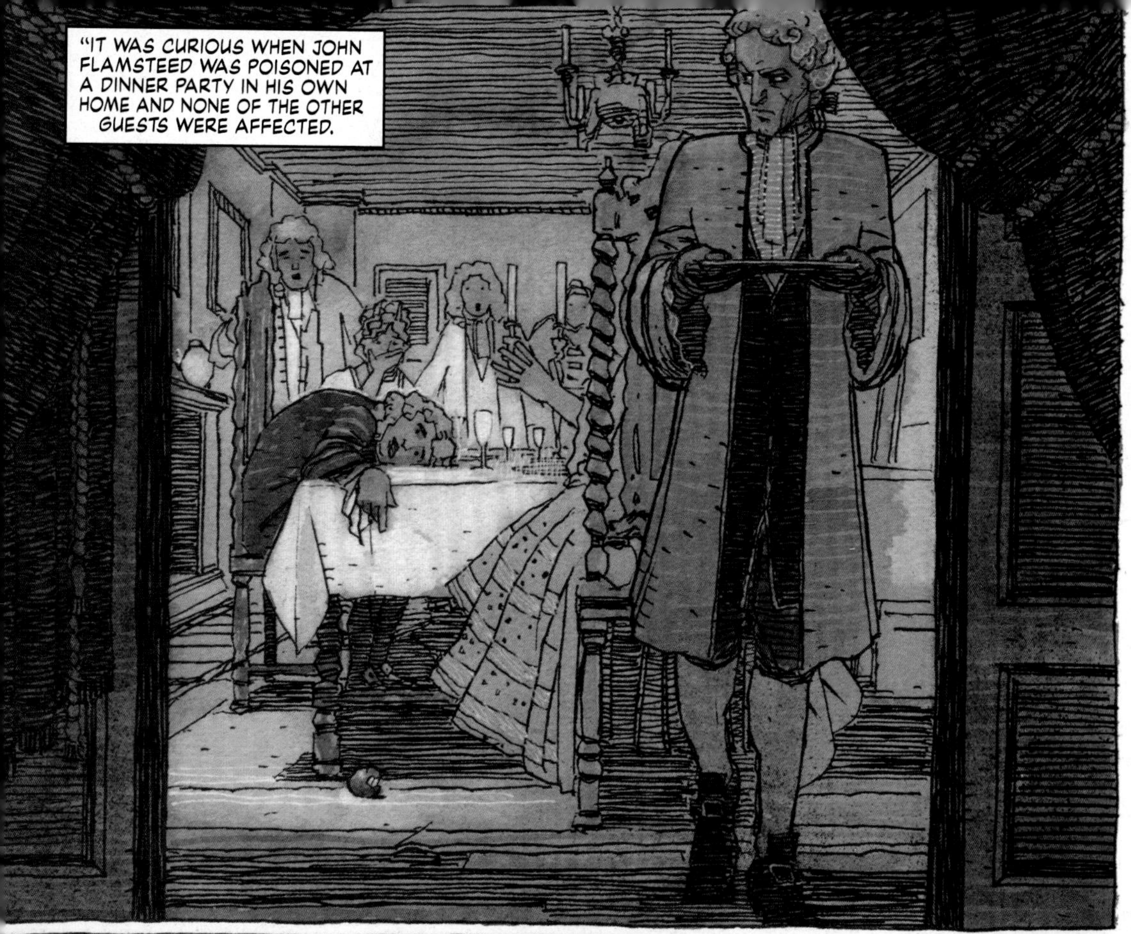
"IT WAS CURIOUS WHEN JOHN FLAMSTEED WAS POISONED AT A DINNER PARTY IN HIS OWN HOME AND NONE OF THE OTHER GUESTS WERE AFFECTED.

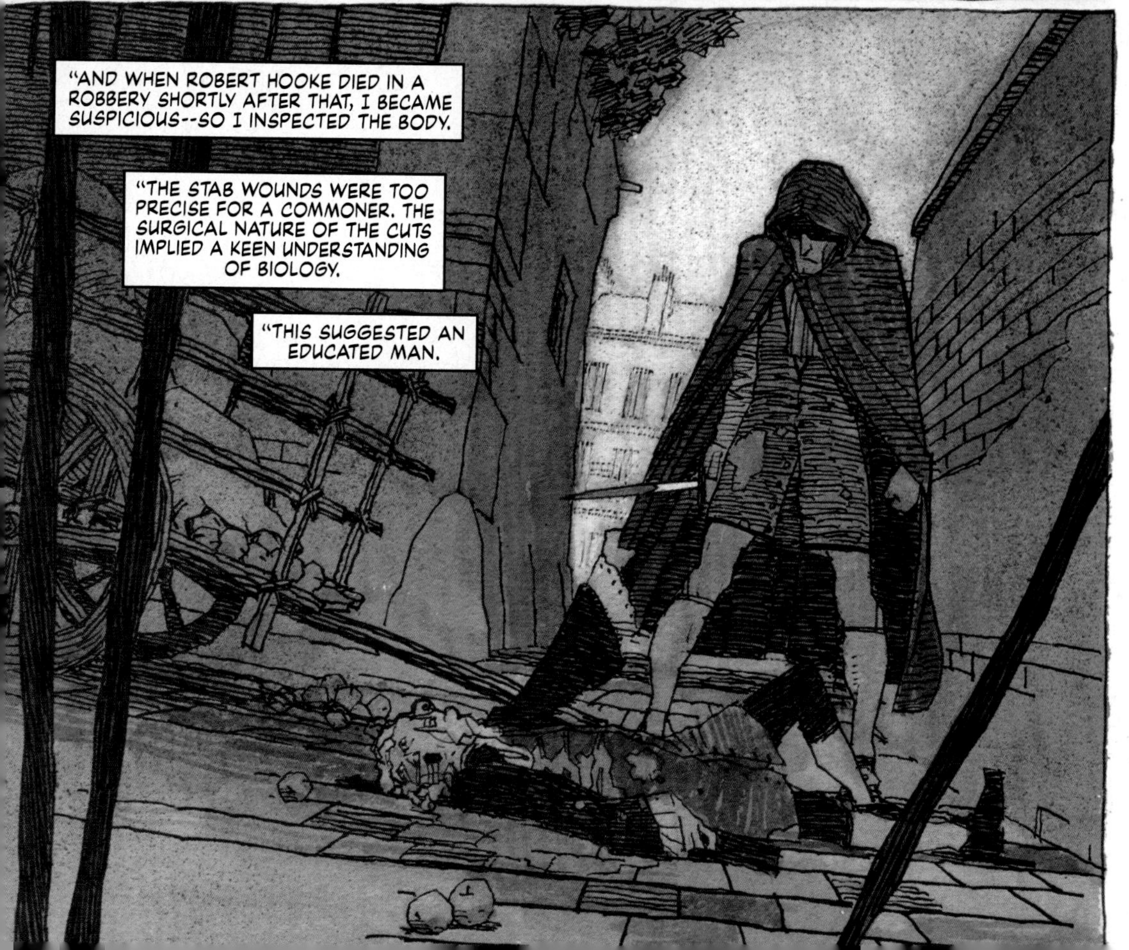
"AND WHEN ROBERT HOOKE DIED IN A ROBBERY SHORTLY AFTER THAT, I BECAME SUSPICIOUS--SO I INSPECTED THE BODY.
"THE STAB WOUNDS WERE TOO PRECISE FOR A COMMONER. THE SURGICAL NATURE OF THE CUTS IMPLIED A KEEN UNDERSTANDING OF BIOLOGY.
"THIS SUGGESTED AN EDUCATED MAN.

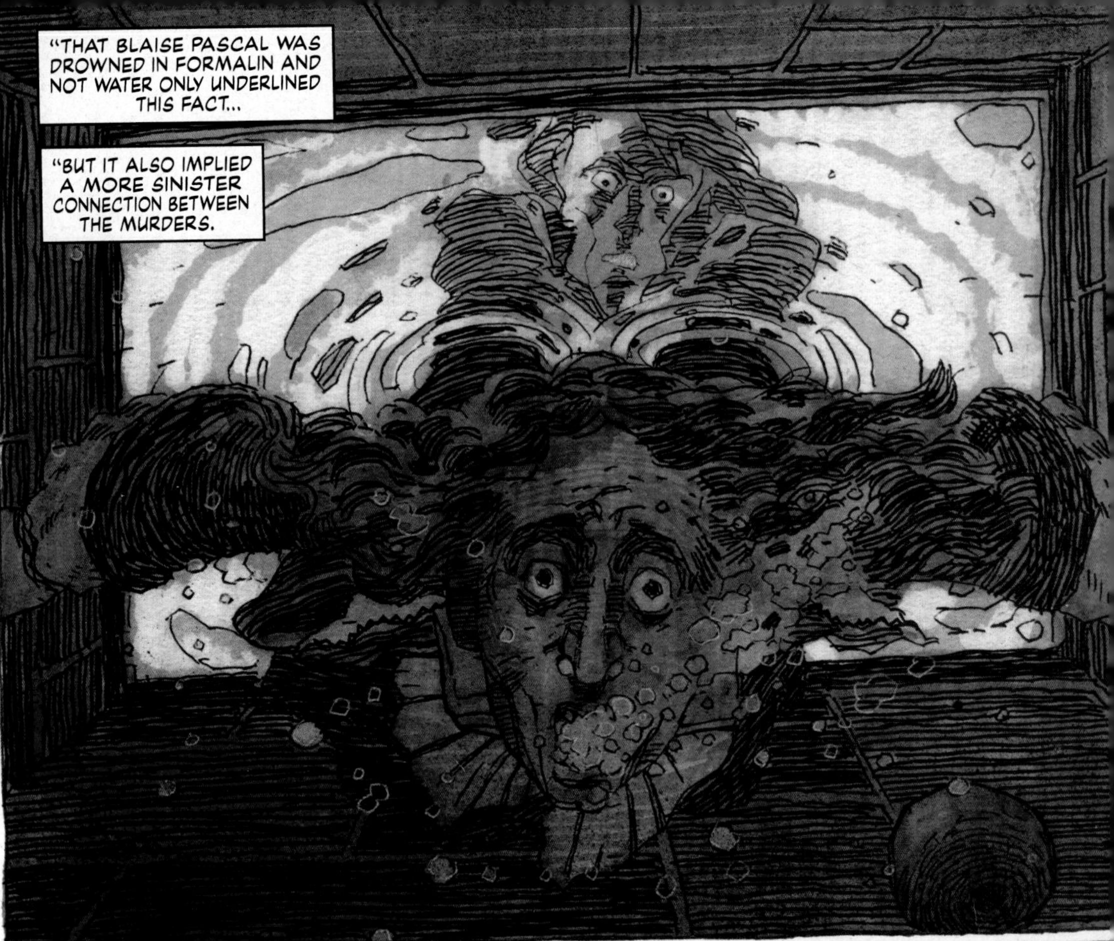
"THAT BLAISE PASCAL WAS DROWNED IN FORMALIN AND NOT WATER ONLY UNDERLINED THIS FACT...
"BUT IT ALSO IMPLIED A MORE SINISTER CONNECTION BETWEEN THE MURDERS.

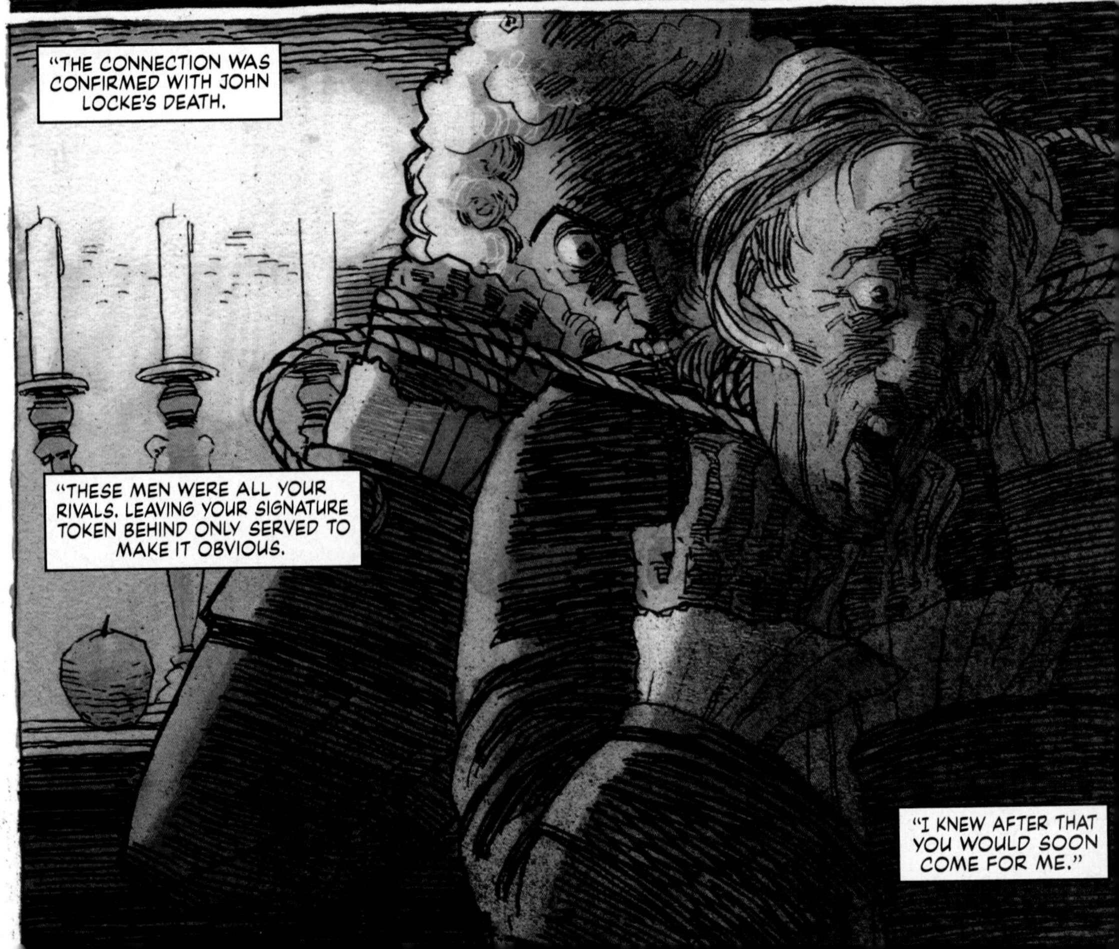
"THE CONNECTION WAS CONFIRMED WITH JOHN LOCKE'S DEATH.
"THESE MEN WERE ALL YOUR RIVALS. LEAVING YOUR SIGNATURE TOKEN BEHIND ONLY SERVED TO MAKE IT OBVIOUS.
"I KNEW AFTER THAT YOU WOULD SOON COME FOR ME."

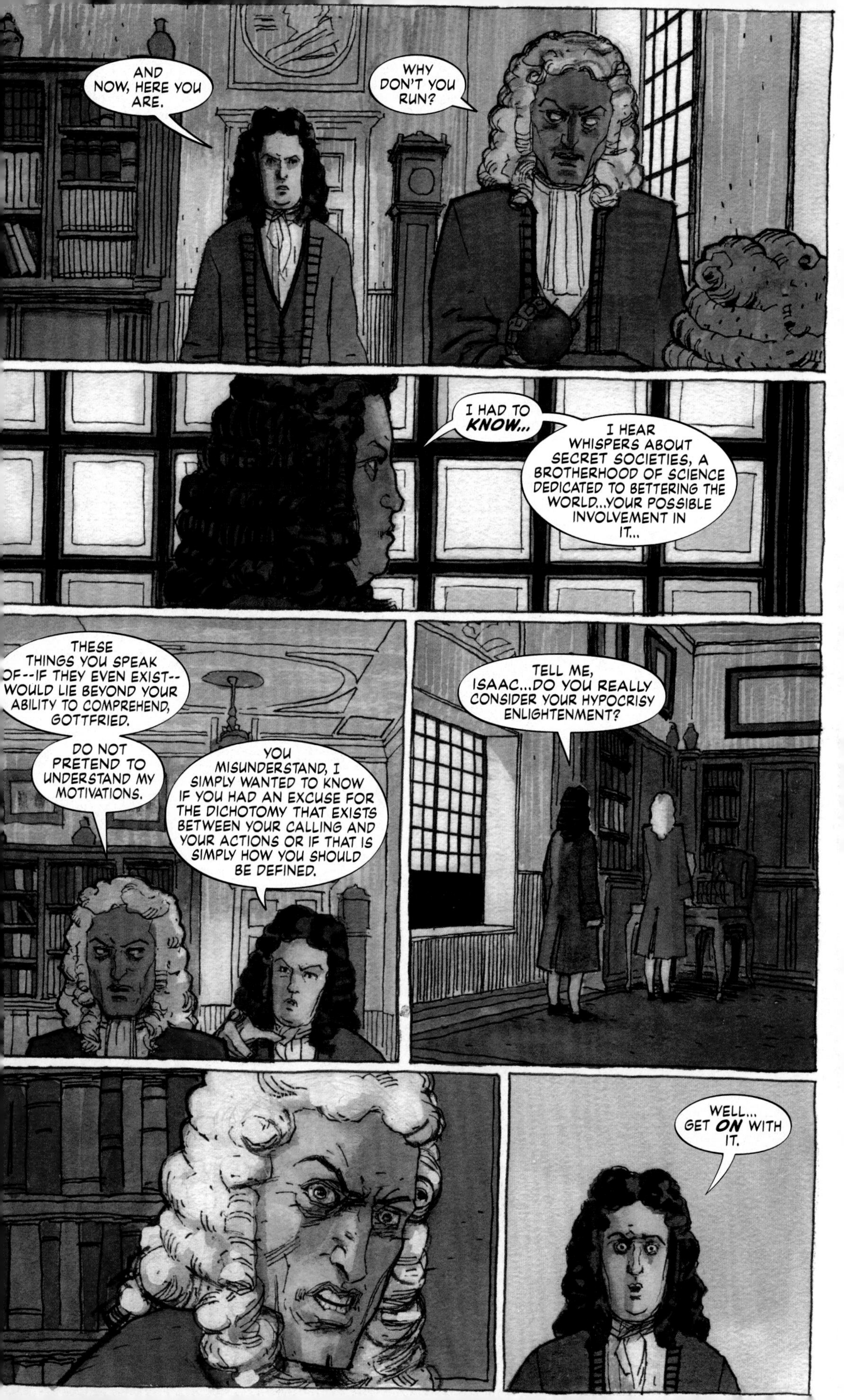
AND NOW, HERE YOU ARE.
WHY DON'T YOU RUN?
I HAD TO **KNOW...**
I HEAR WHISPERS ABOUT SECRET SOCIETIES, A BROTHERHOOD OF SCIENCE DEDICATED TO BETTERING THE WORLD...YOUR POSSIBLE INVOLVEMENT IN IT...
THESE THINGS YOU SPEAK OF--IF THEY EVEN EXIST--WOULD LIE BEYOND YOUR ABILITY TO COMPREHEND, GOTTFRIED.
DO NOT PRETEND TO UNDERSTAND MY MOTIVATIONS.
YOU MISUNDERSTAND, I SIMPLY WANTED TO KNOW IF YOU HAD AN EXCUSE FOR THE DICHOTOMY THAT EXISTS BETWEEN YOUR CALLING AND YOUR ACTIONS OR IF THAT IS SIMPLY HOW YOU SHOULD BE DEFINED.
TELL ME, ISAAC...DO YOU REALLY CONSIDER YOUR HYPOCRISY ENLIGHTENMENT?
WELL... GET **ON** WITH IT.

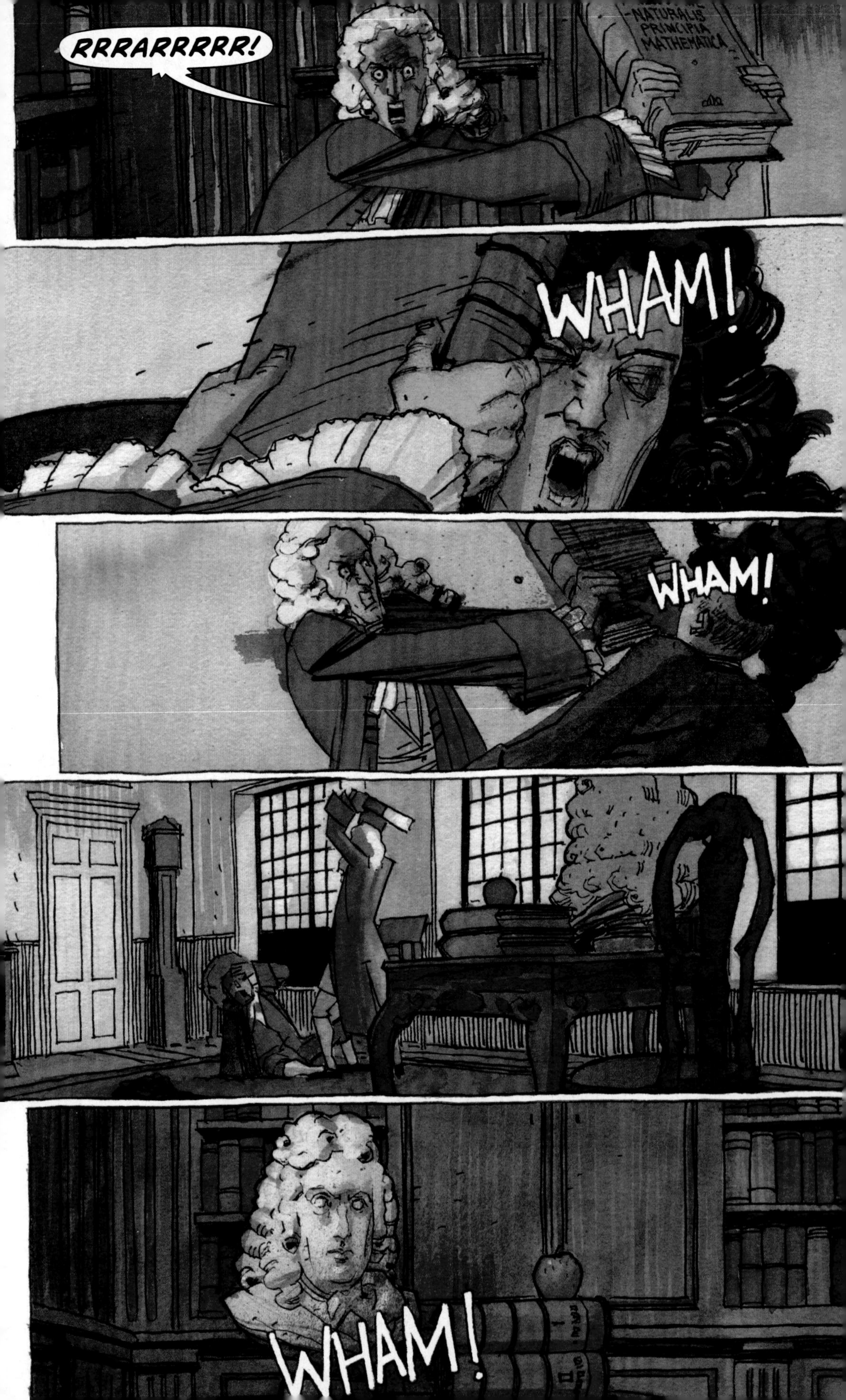
RRRARRRRR!
NATURALIS
PRINCIPIA
MATHEMATICA
WHAM!
WHAM!
WHAM!

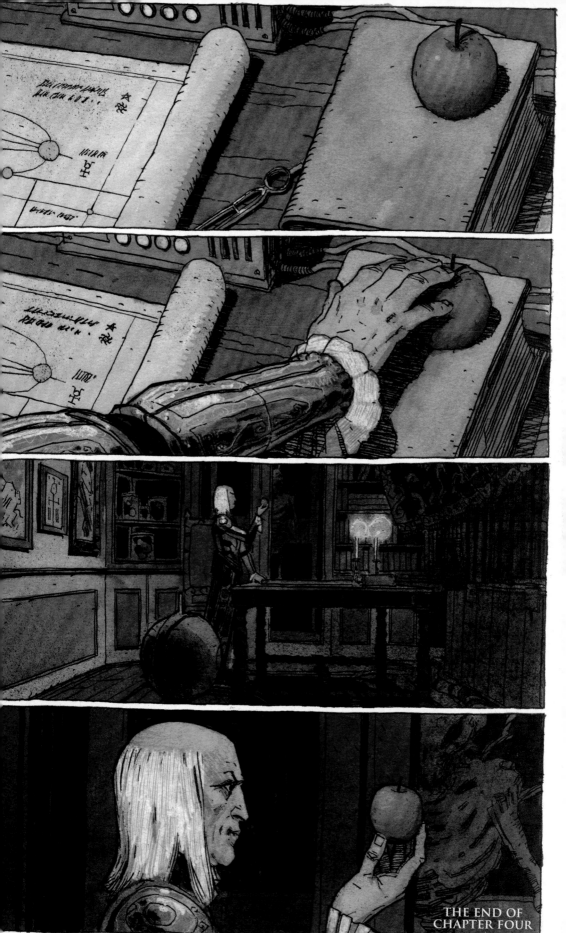

THE END OF
CHAPTER FOUR

Cover Gallery

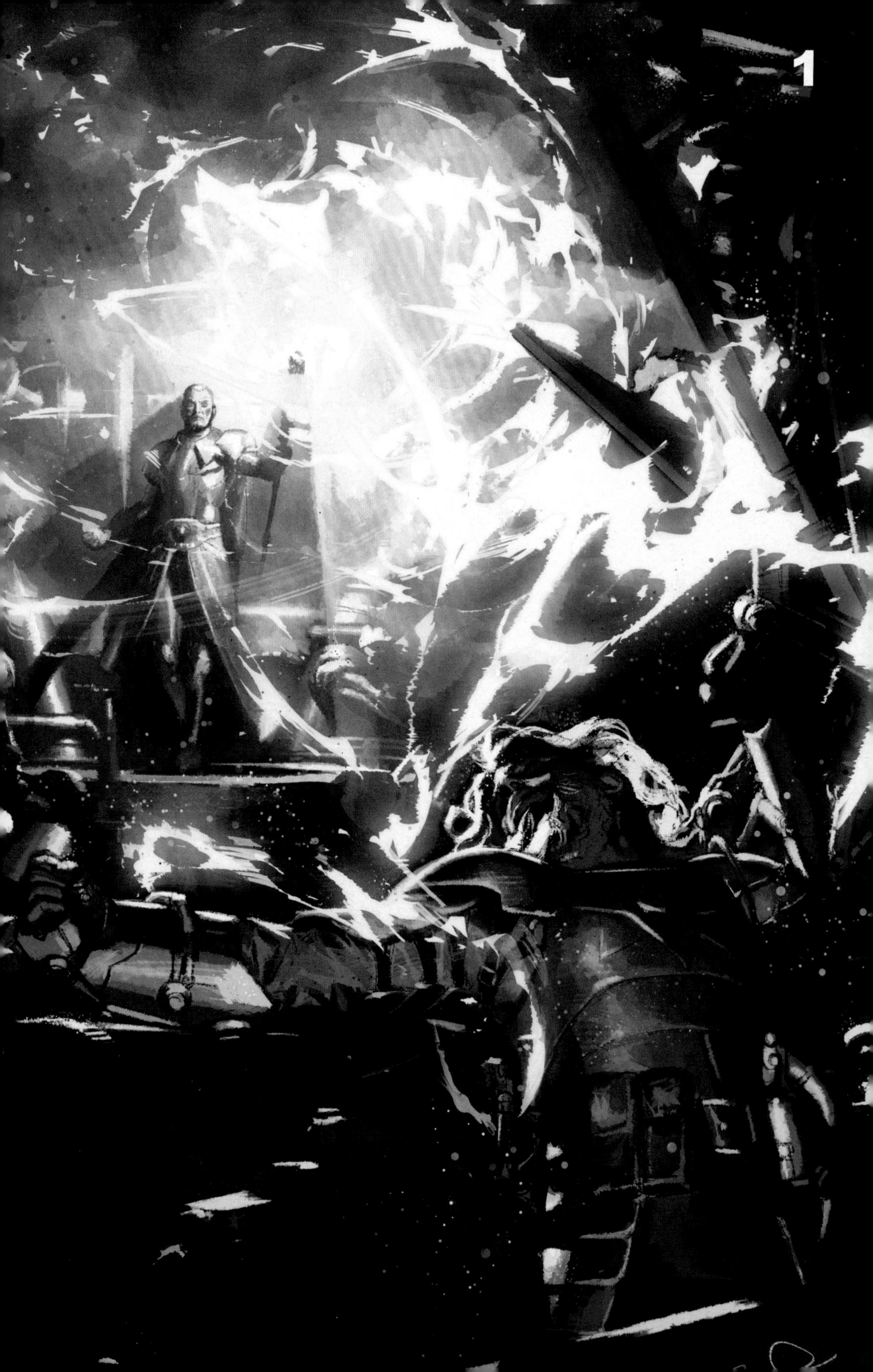
1

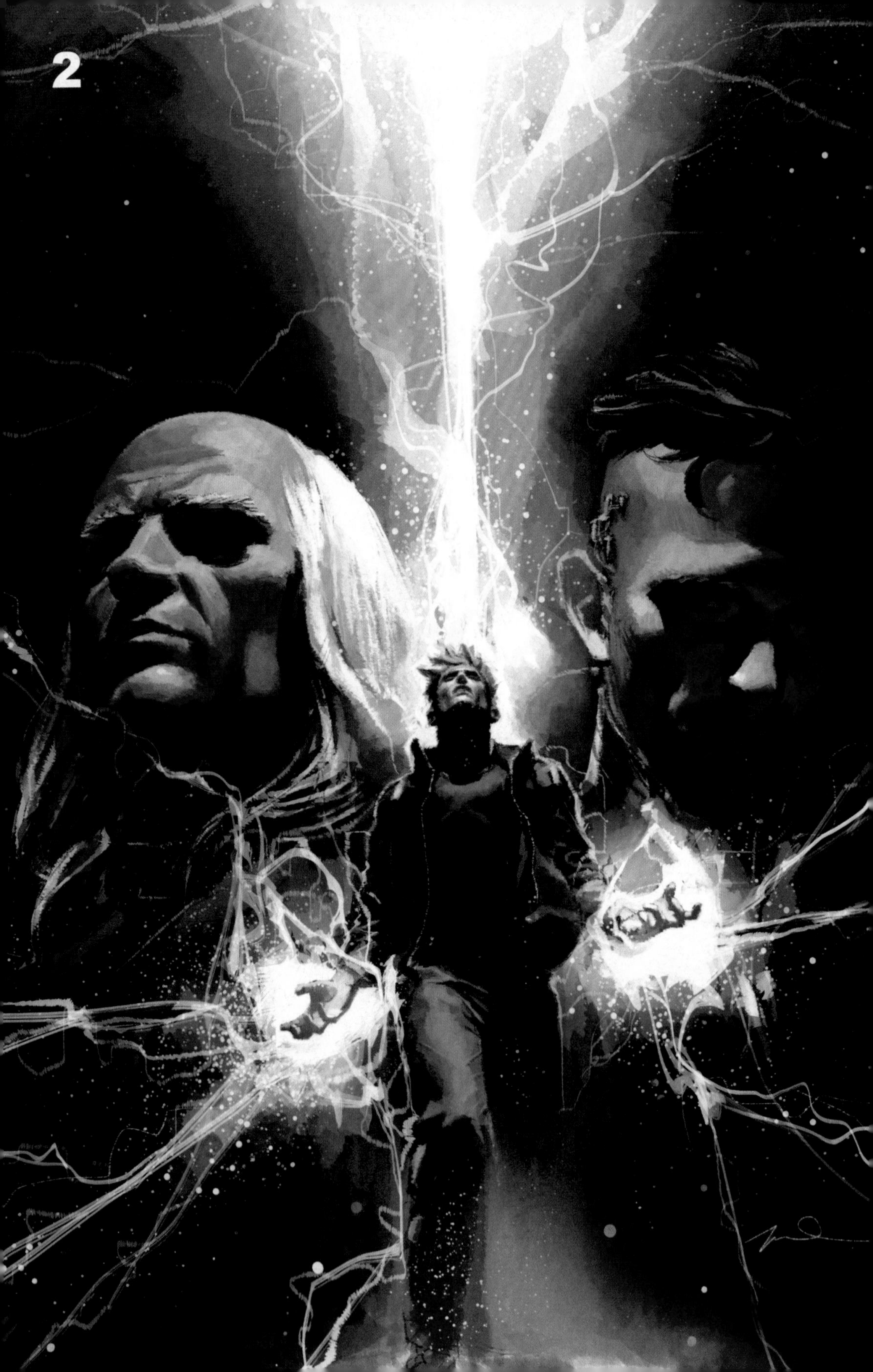
2

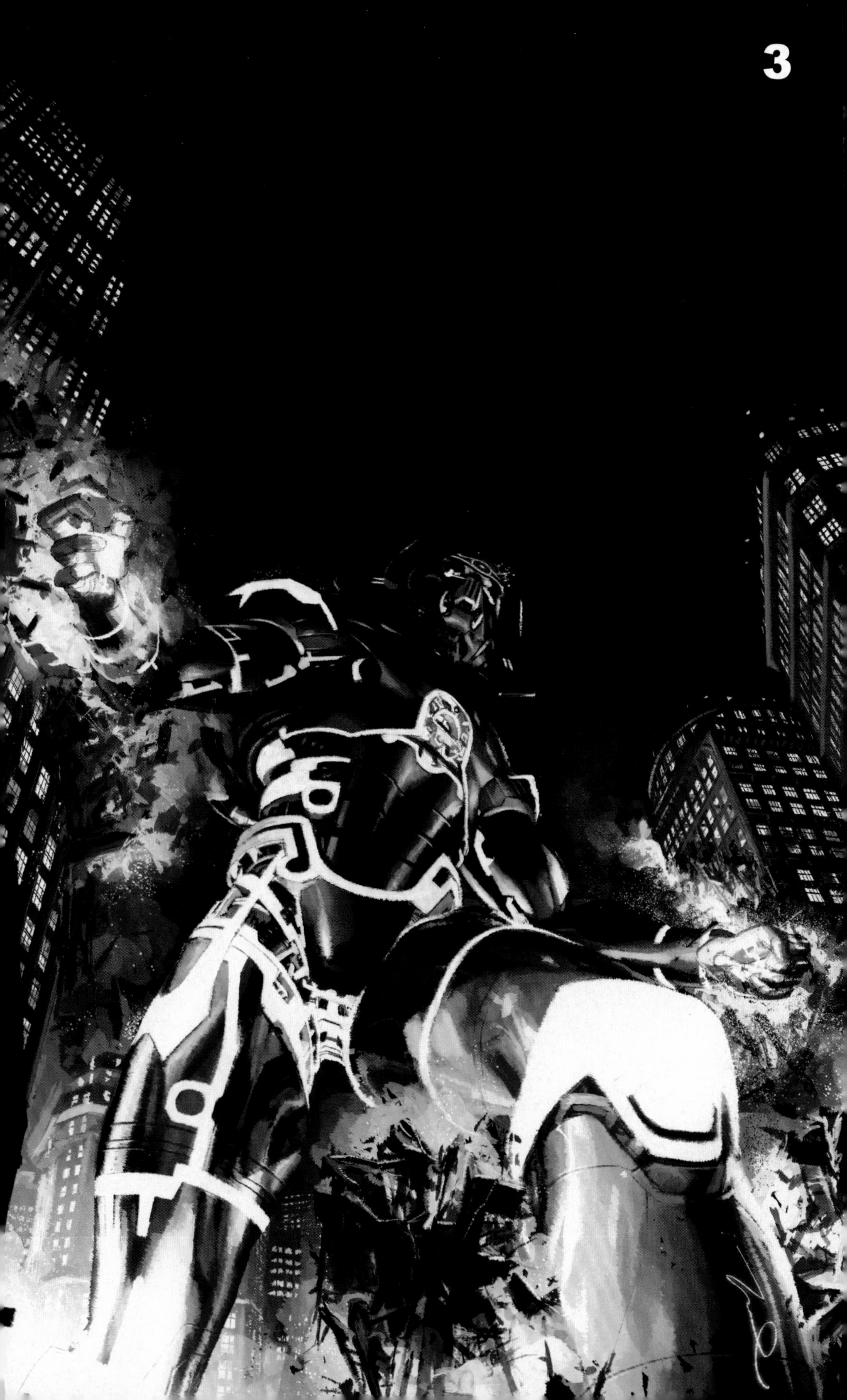
3

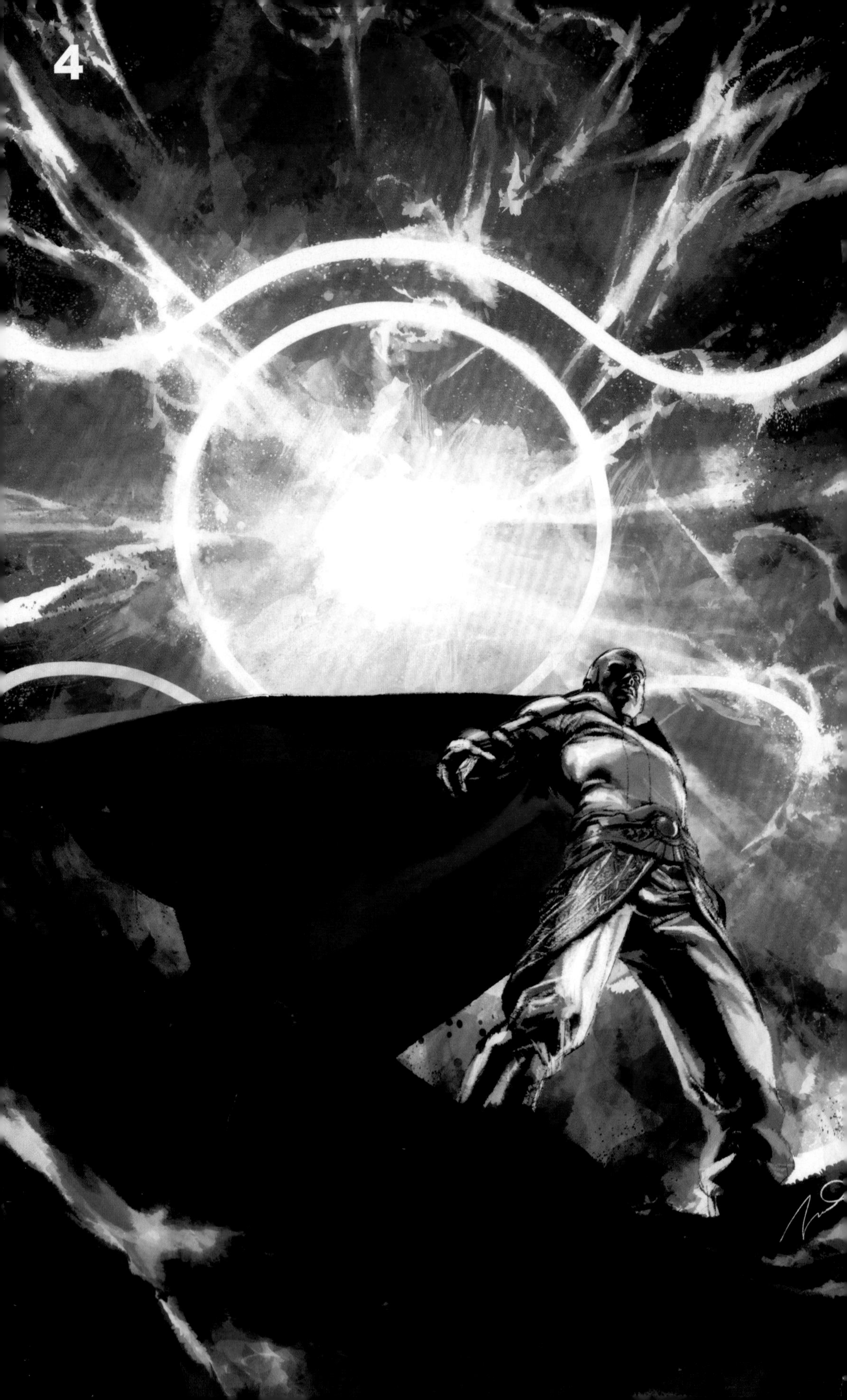
4

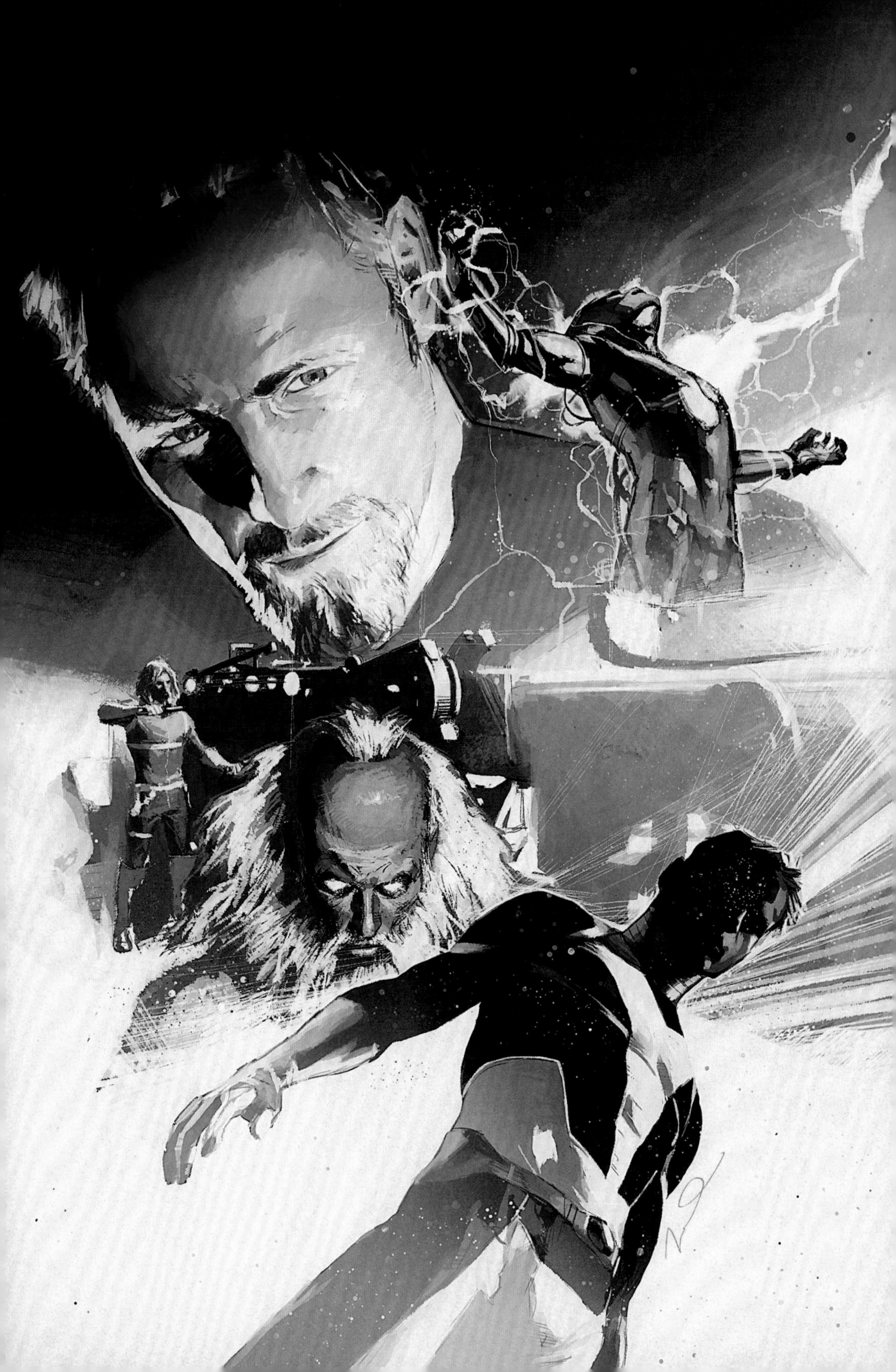

6

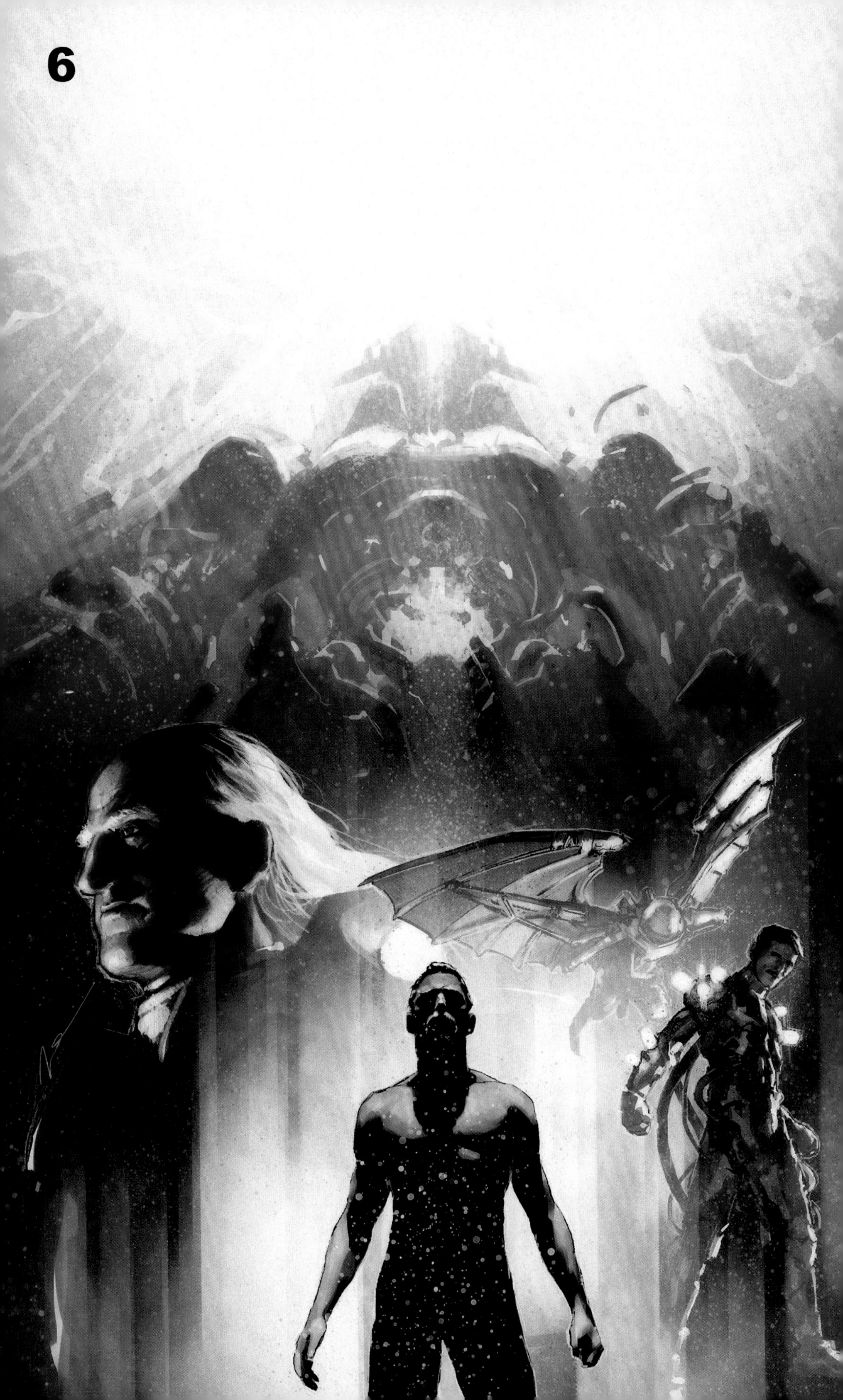

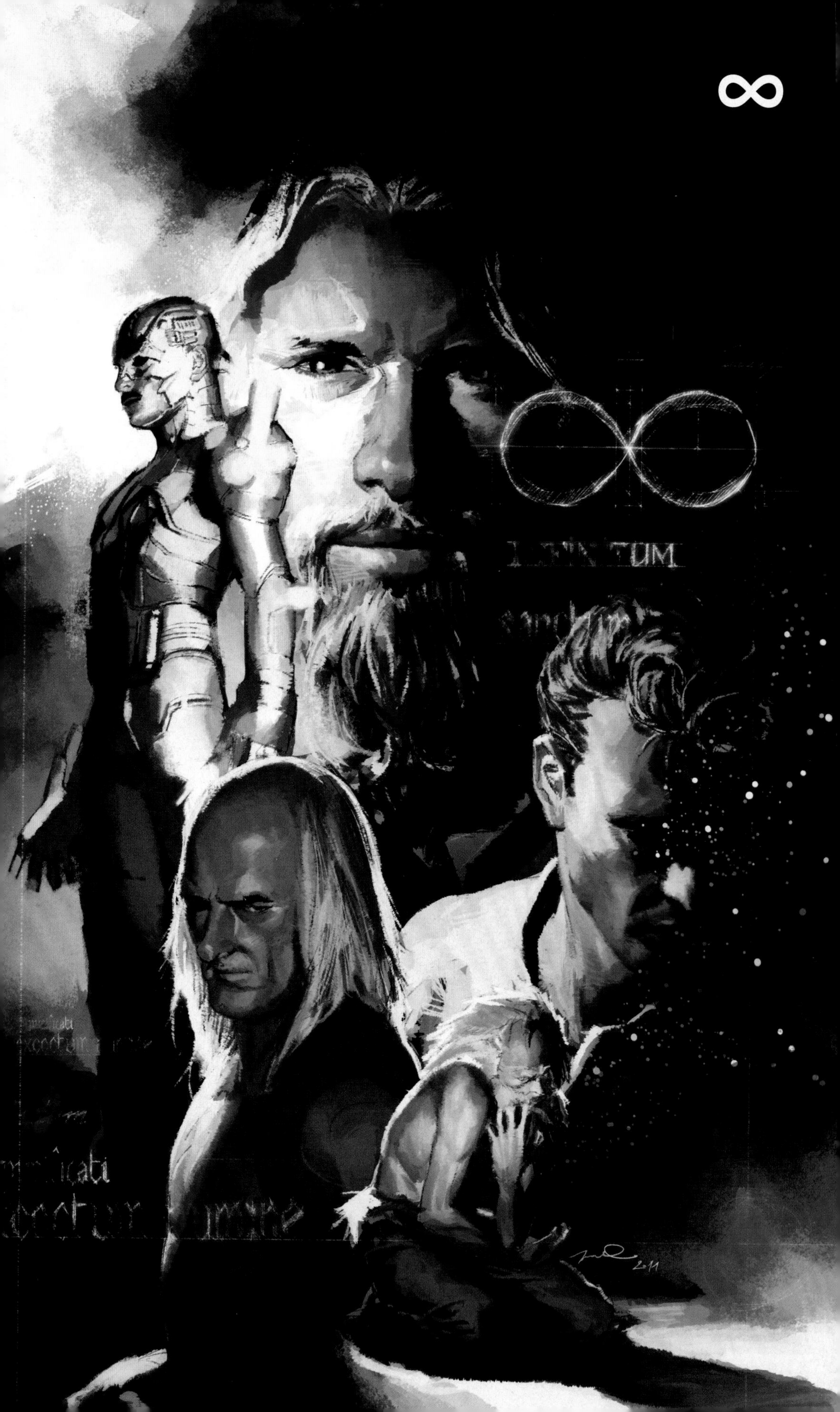

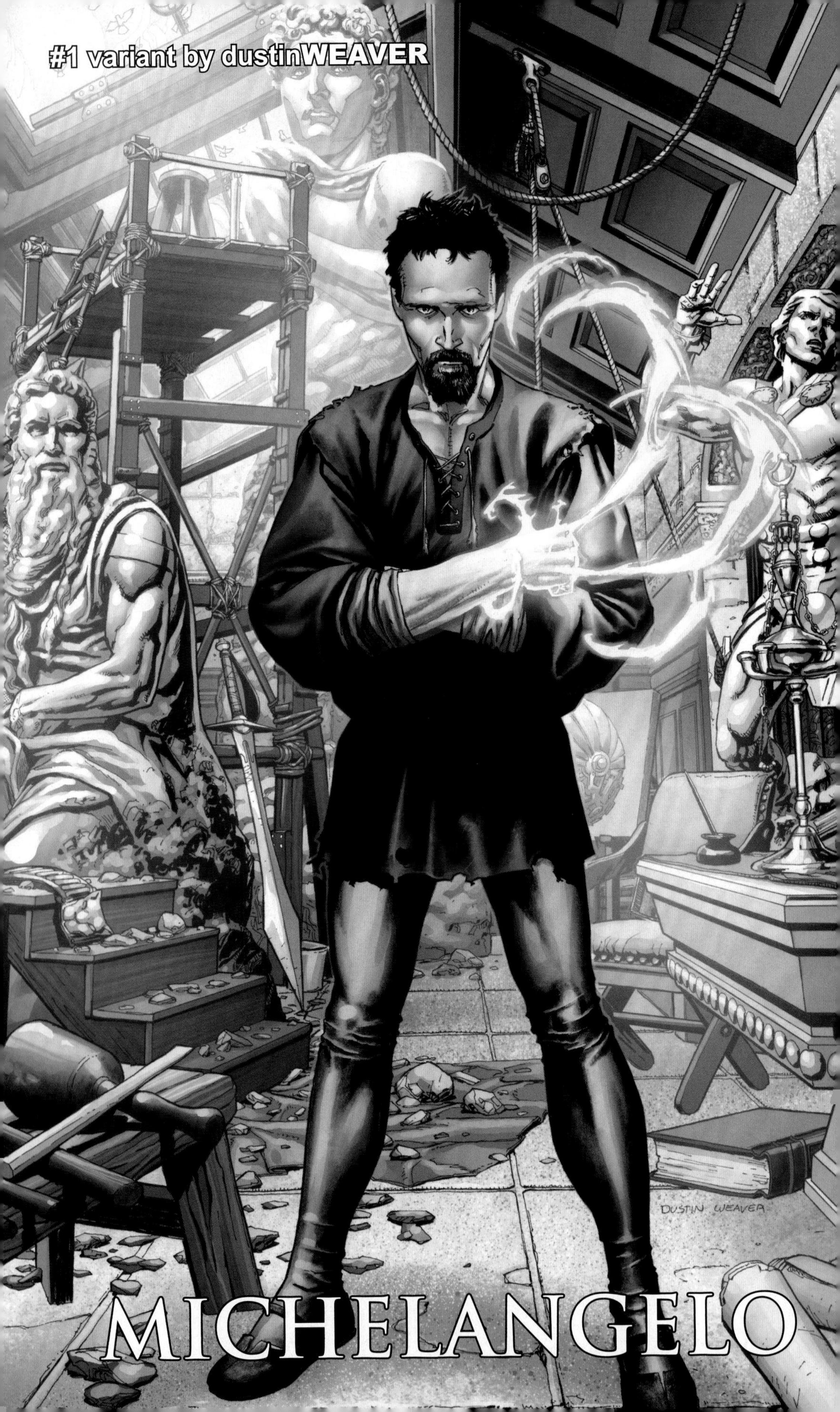
DUSTIN WEAVER
MICHELANGELO

#1 variant by dustinWEAVER

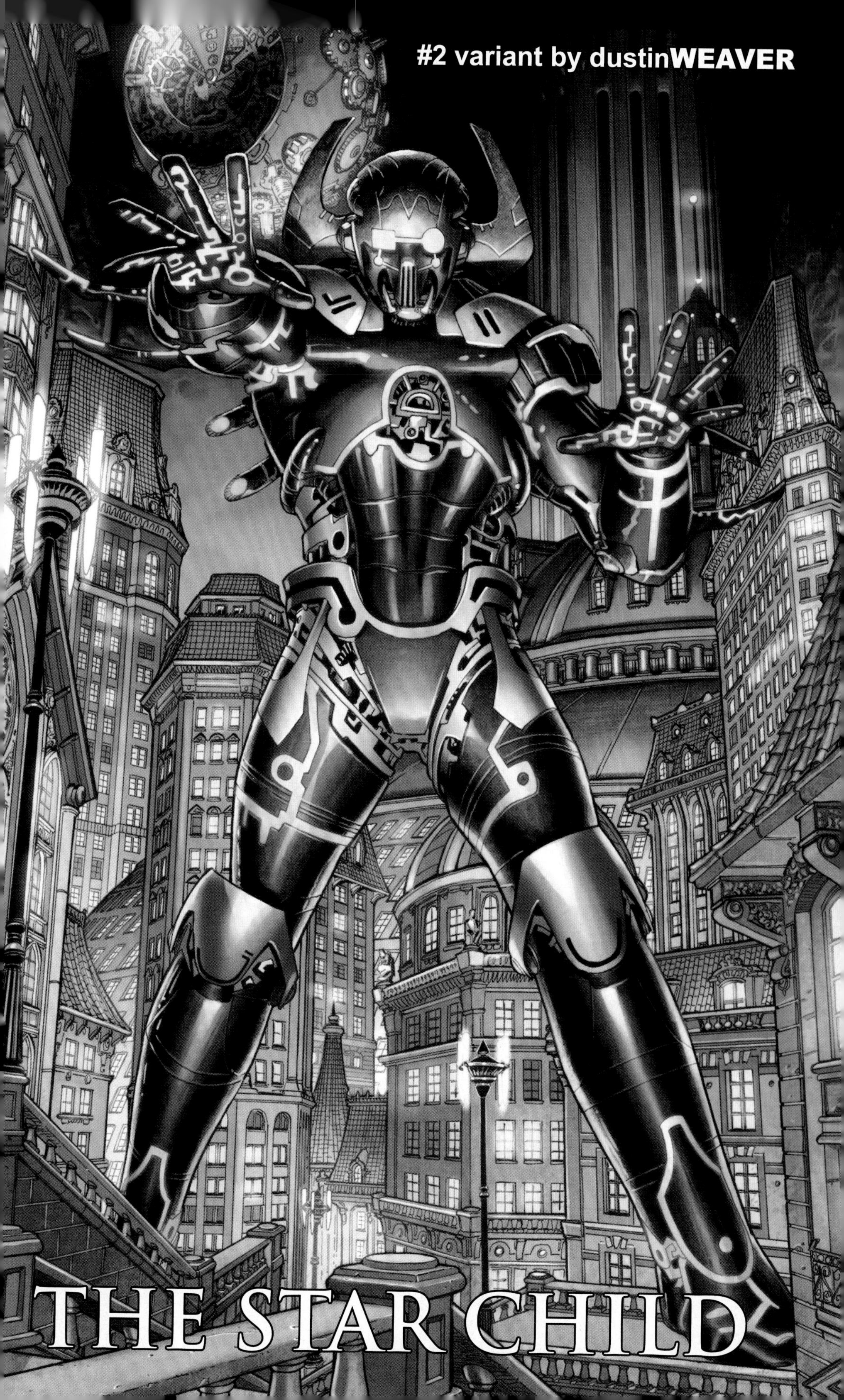
#2 variant by dustinWEAVER
THE STAR CHILD

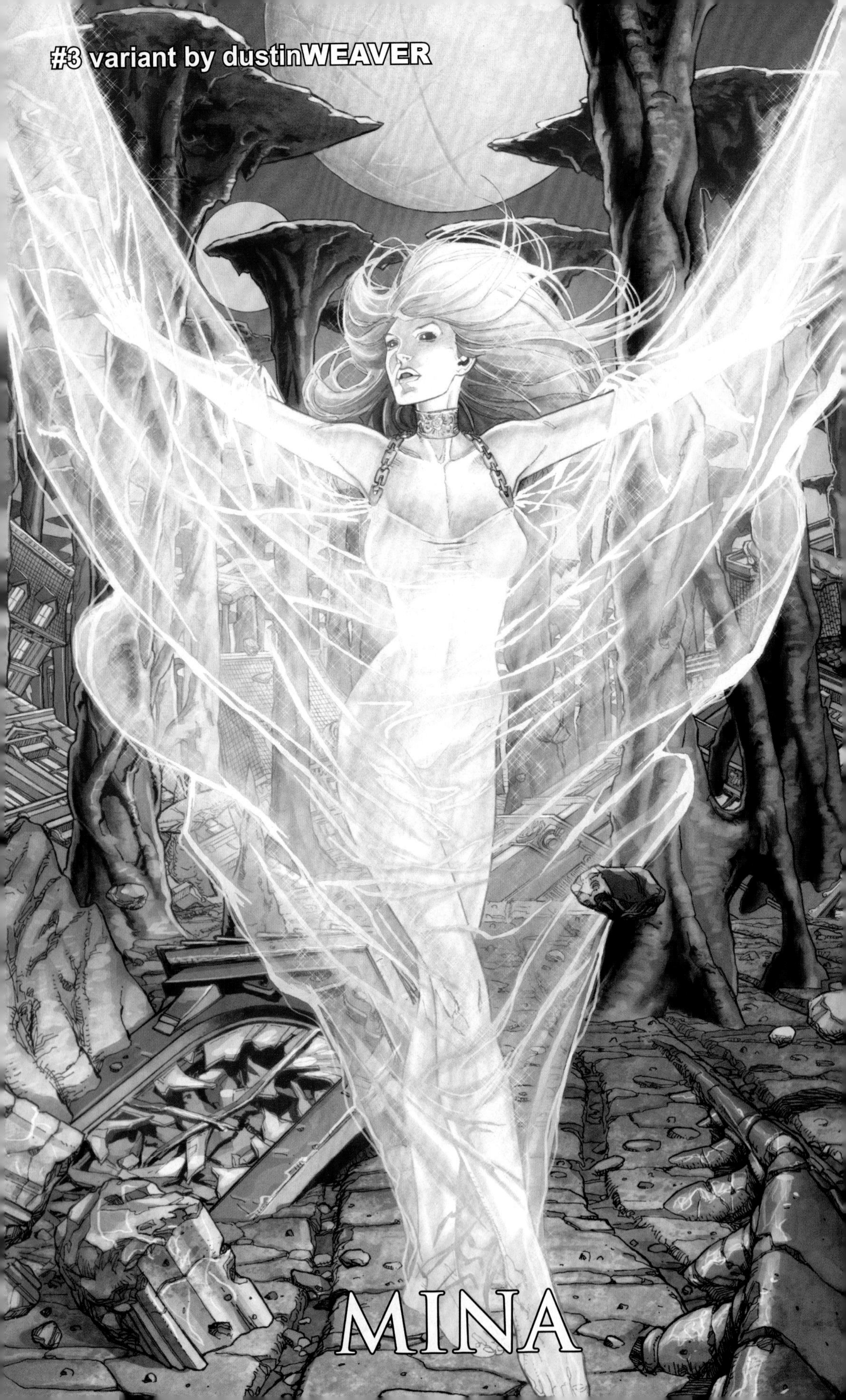
#3 variant by dustinWEAVER
MINA

∞ variant by dustinWEAVER

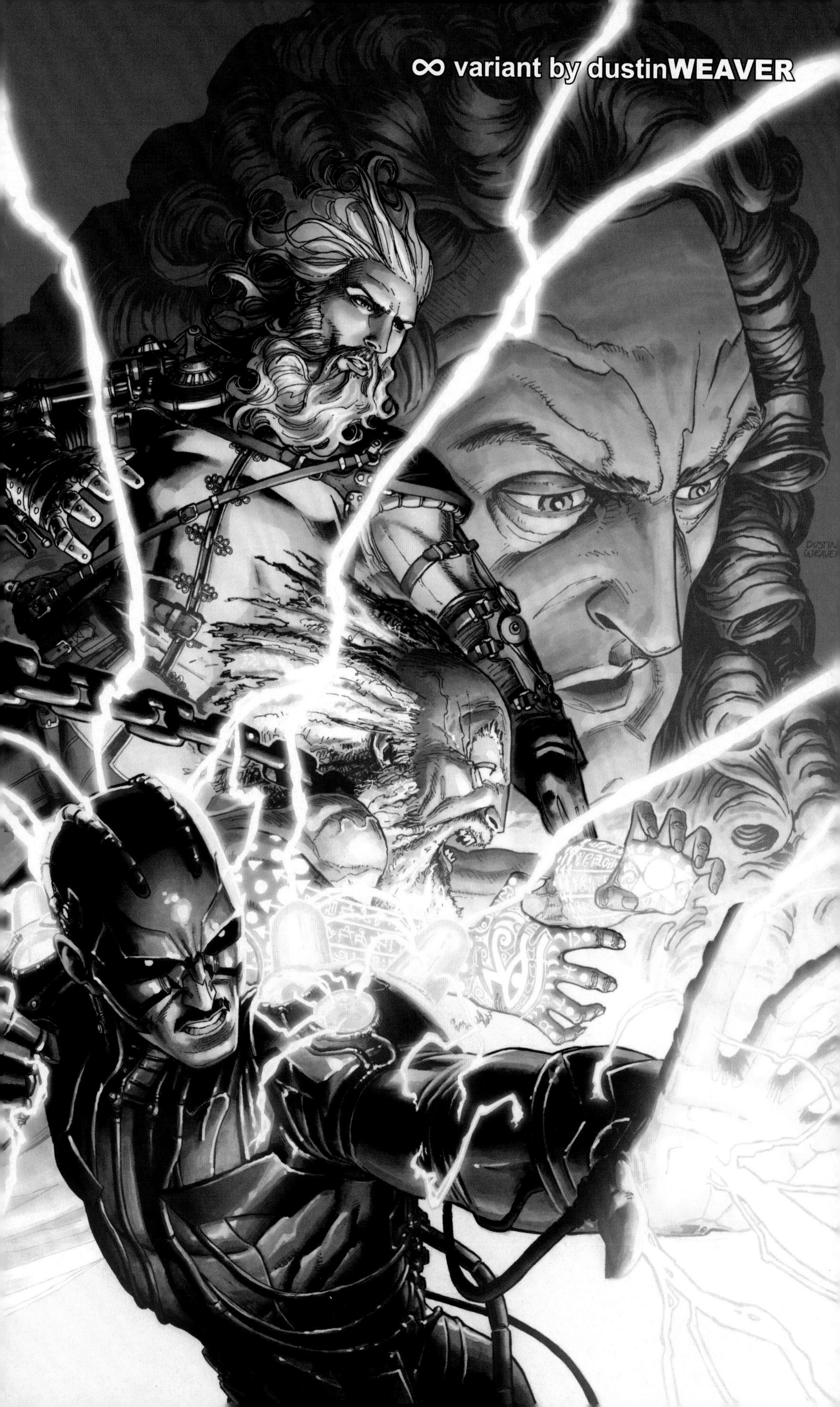
DUSTIN WEAVER

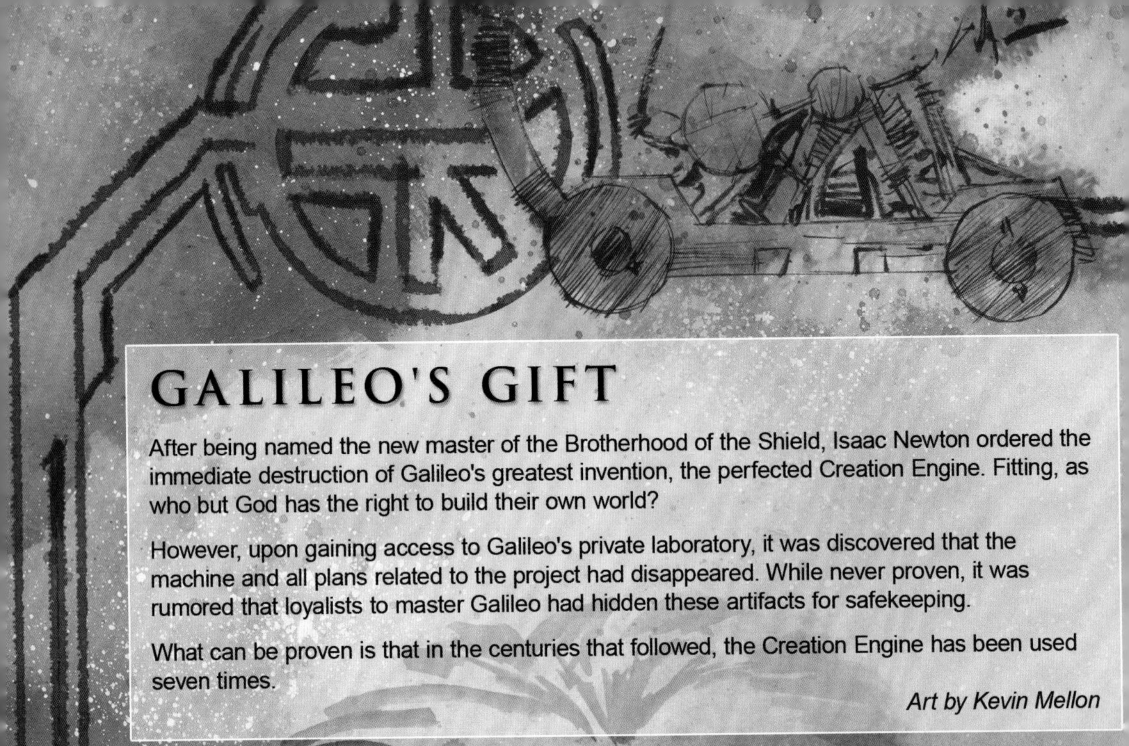

GALILEO'S GIFT

After being named the new master of the Brotherhood of the Shield, Isaac Newton ordered the immediate destruction of Galileo's greatest invention, the perfected Creation Engine. Fitting, as who but God has the right to build their own world?

However, upon gaining access to Galileo's private laboratory, it was discovered that the machine and all plans related to the project had disappeared. While never proven, it was rumored that loyalists to master Galileo had hidden these artifacts for safekeeping.

What can be proven is that in the centuries that followed, the Creation Engine has been used seven times.

Art by Kevin Mellon

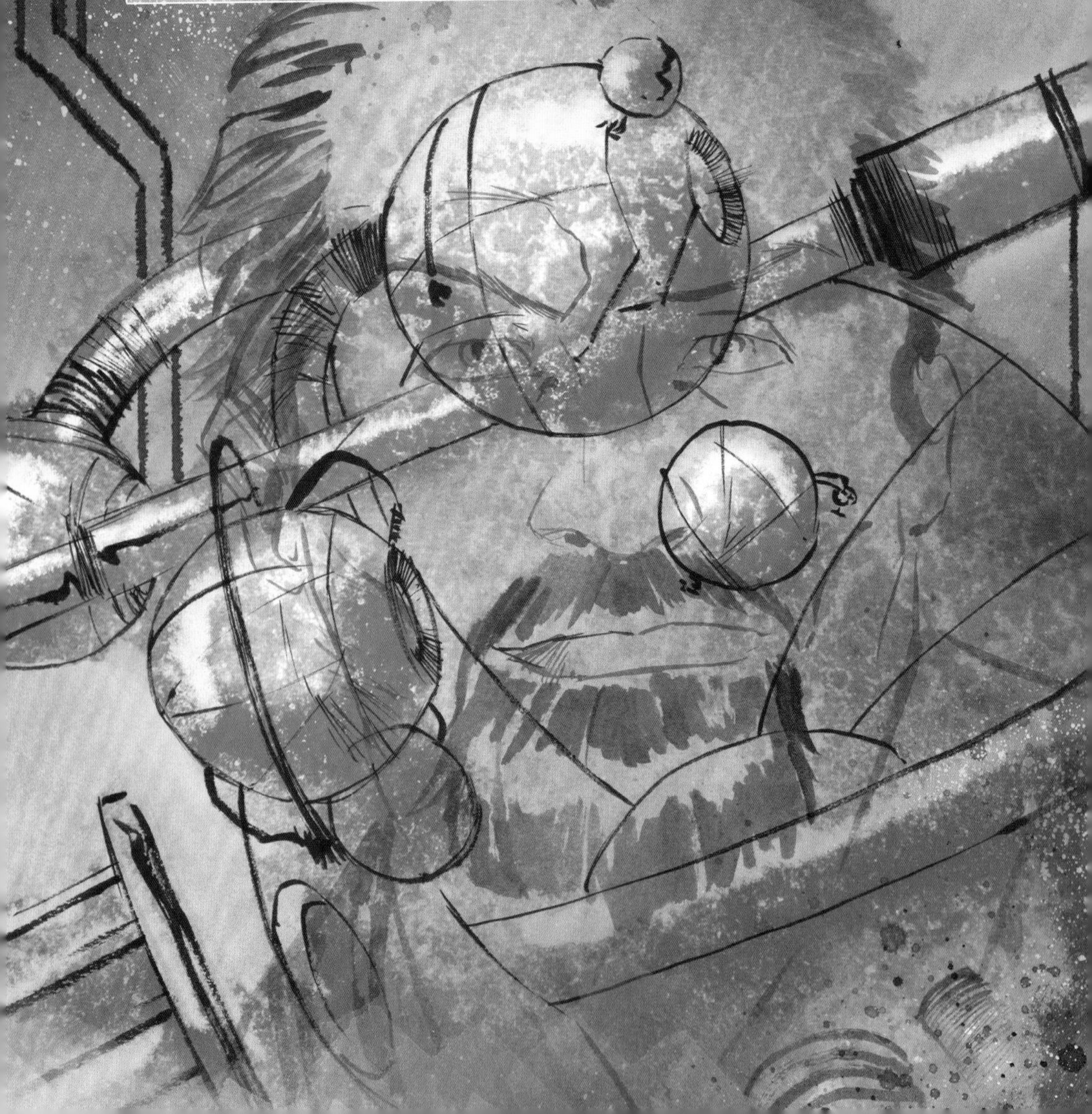

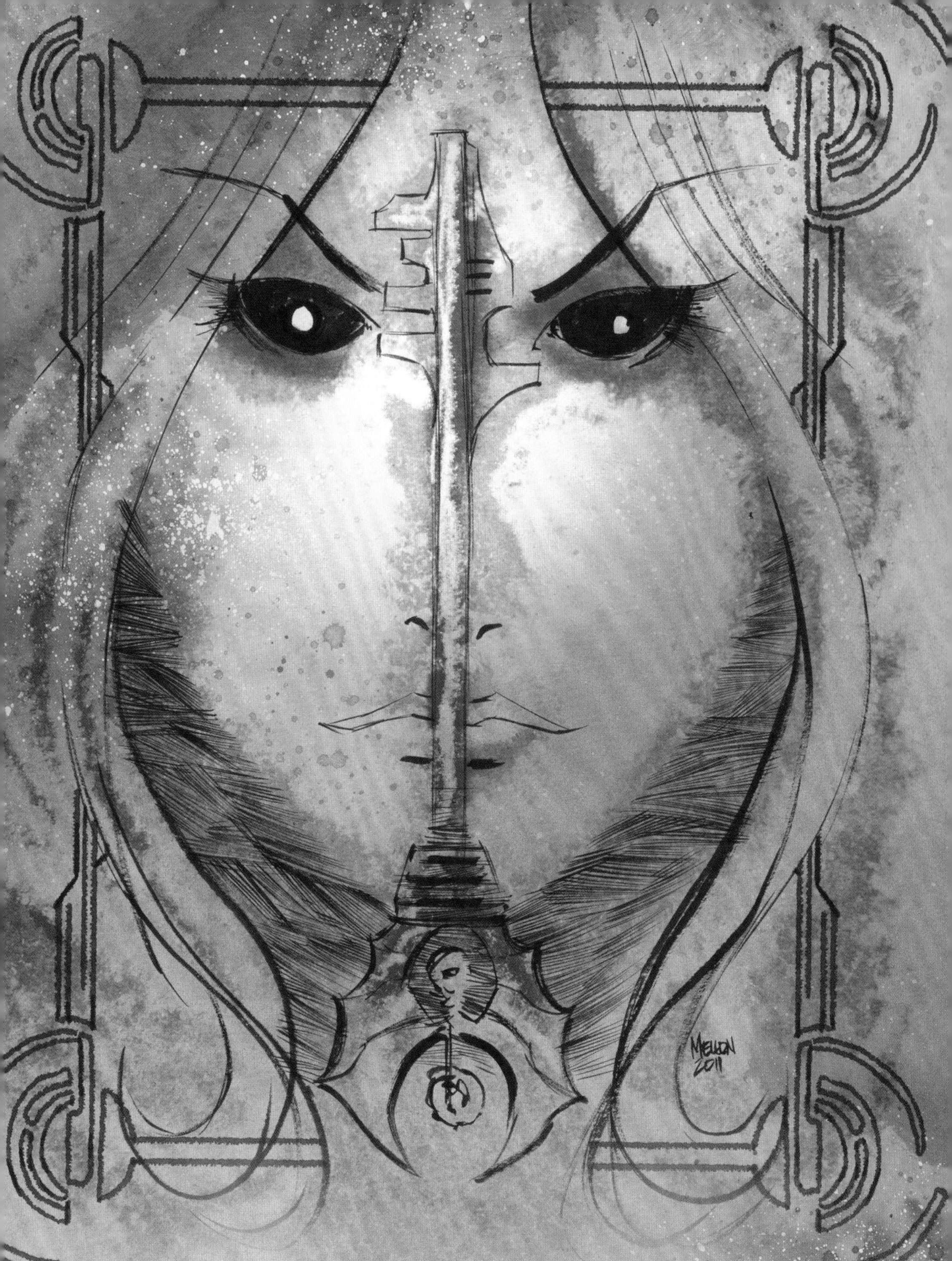
MELLON
2011

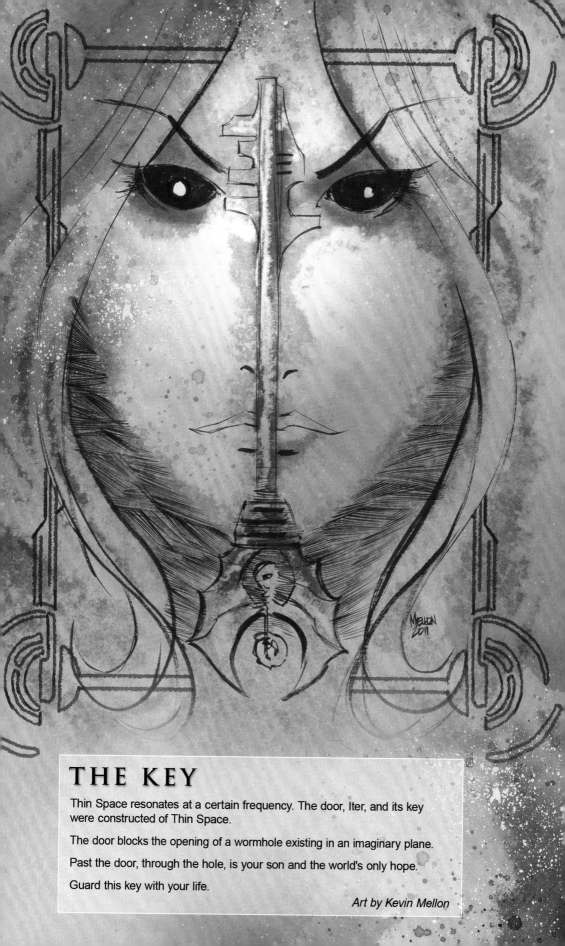

THE KEY

Thin Space resonates at a certain frequency. The door, Iter, and its key were constructed of Thin Space.

The door blocks the opening of a wormhole existing in an imaginary plane.

Past the door, through the hole, is your son and the world's only hope.

Guard this key with your life.

Art by Kevin Mellon

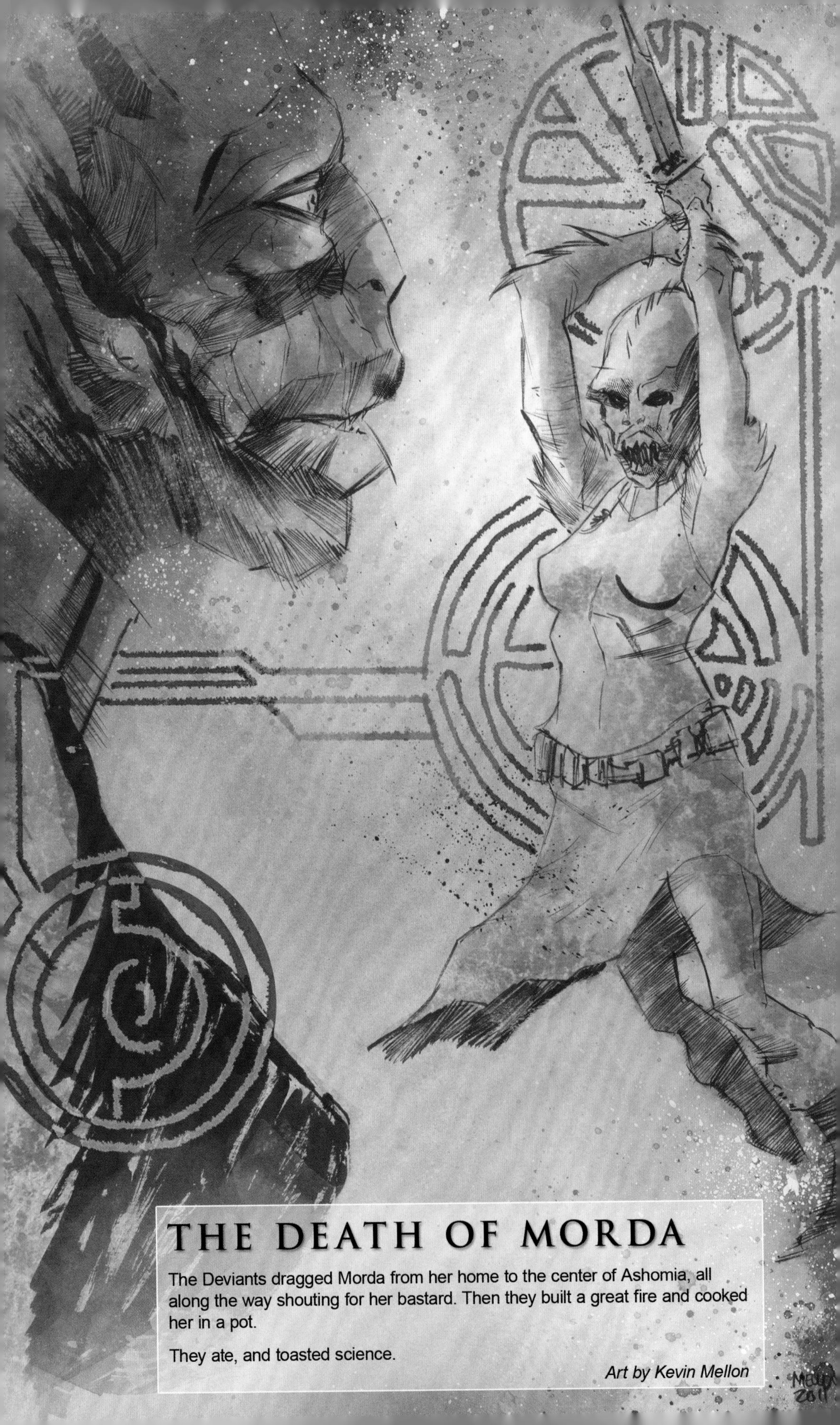

THE DEATH OF MORDA

The Deviants dragged Morda from her home to the center of Ashomia, all along the way shouting for her bastard. Then they built a great fire and cooked her in a pot.

They ate, and toasted science.

Art by Kevin Mellon

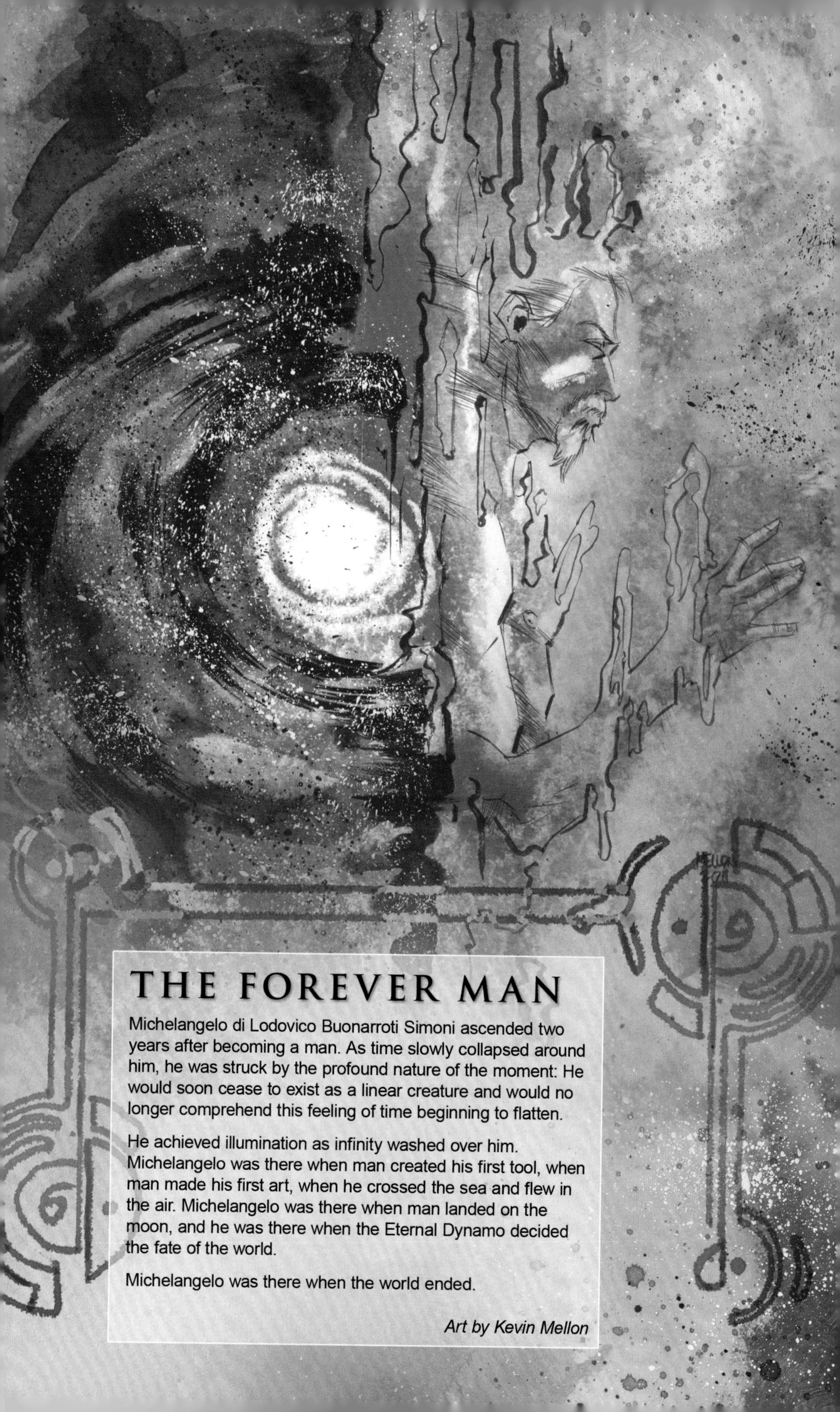

THE FOREVER MAN

Michelangelo di Lodovico Buonarroti Simoni ascended two years after becoming a man. As time slowly collapsed around him, he was struck by the profound nature of the moment: He would soon cease to exist as a linear creature and would no longer comprehend this feeling of time beginning to flatten.

He achieved illumination as infinity washed over him. Michelangelo was there when man created his first tool, when man made his first art, when he crossed the sea and flew in the air. Michelangelo was there when man landed on the moon, and he was there when the Eternal Dynamo decided the fate of the world.

Michelangelo was there when the world ended.

Art by Kevin Mellon

LEONARDO DA VINCI

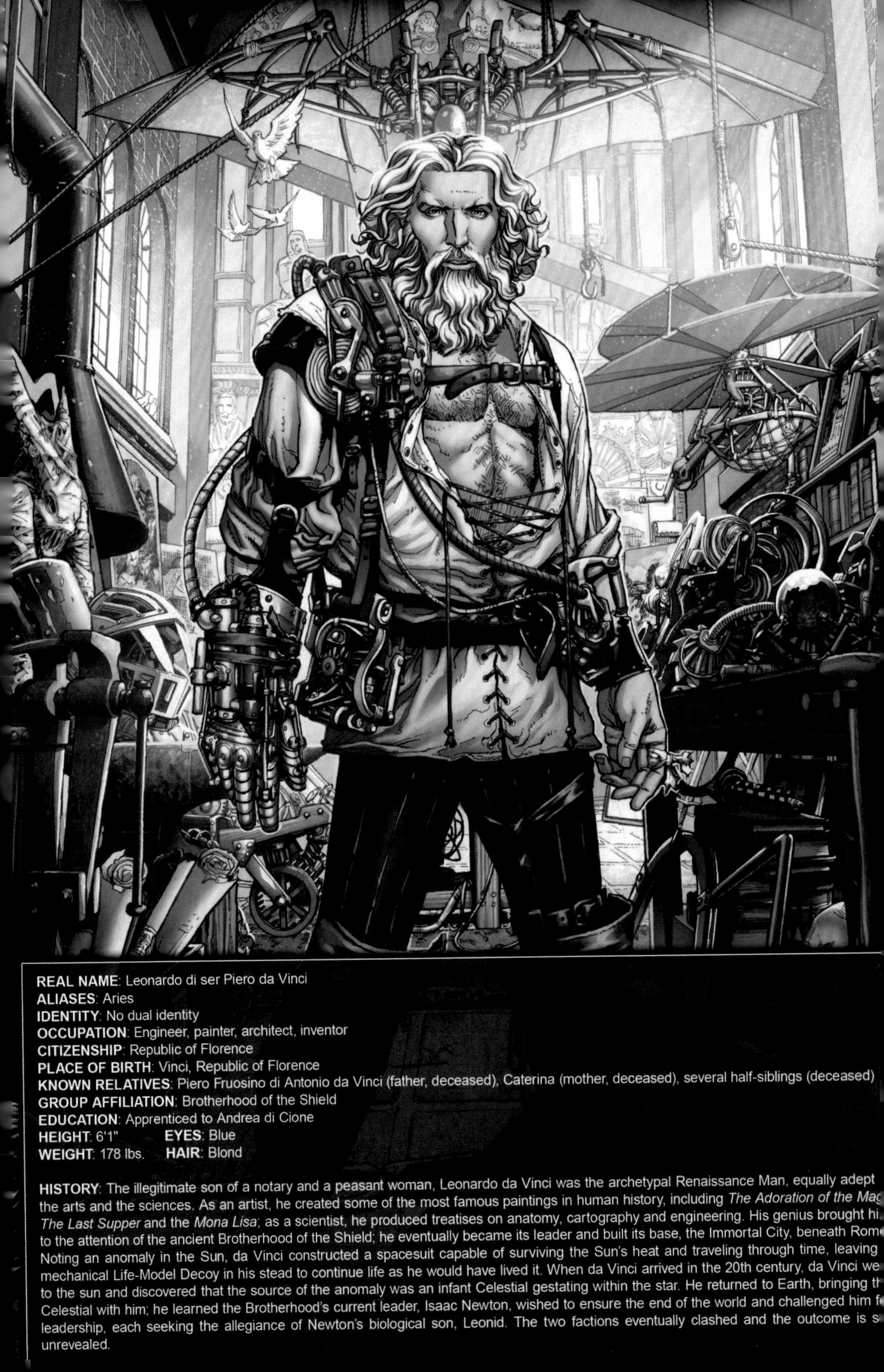

REAL NAME: Leonardo di ser Piero da Vinci
ALIASES: Aries
IDENTITY: No dual identity
OCCUPATION: Engineer, painter, architect, inventor
CITIZENSHIP: Republic of Florence
PLACE OF BIRTH: Vinci, Republic of Florence
KNOWN RELATIVES: Piero Fruosino di Antonio da Vinci (father, deceased), Caterina (mother, deceased), several half-siblings (deceased)
GROUP AFFILIATION: Brotherhood of the Shield
EDUCATION: Apprenticed to Andrea di Cione
HEIGHT: 6'1" **EYES**: Blue
WEIGHT: 178 lbs. **HAIR**: Blond

HISTORY: The illegitimate son of a notary and a peasant woman, Leonardo da Vinci was the archetypal Renaissance Man, equally adept the arts and the sciences. As an artist, he created some of the most famous paintings in human history, including *The Adoration of the Mag The Last Supper* and the *Mona Lisa*; as a scientist, he produced treatises on anatomy, cartography and engineering. His genius brought hi to the attention of the ancient Brotherhood of the Shield; he eventually became its leader and built its base, the Immortal City, beneath Rom Noting an anomaly in the Sun, da Vinci constructed a spacesuit capable of surviving the Sun's heat and traveling through time, leaving mechanical Life-Model Decoy in his stead to continue life as he would have lived it. When da Vinci arrived in the 20th century, da Vinci we to the sun and discovered that the source of the anomaly was an infant Celestial gestating within the star. He returned to Earth, bringing th Celestial with him; he learned the Brotherhood's current leader, Isaac Newton, wished to ensure the end of the world and challenged him f leadership, each seeking the allegiance of Newton's biological son, Leonid. The two factions eventually clashed and the outcome is s unrevealed.

ISAAC NEWTON

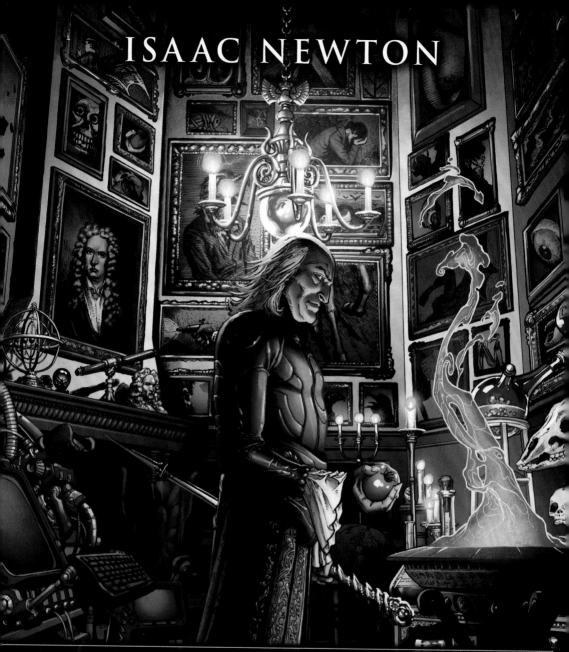

EAL NAME: Isaac Newton
LIASES: None
DENTITY: No dual identity
CCUPATION: Leader of the Brotherhood of the Shield; former Warden of the Royal Mint, Member of Parliament, university professor, athematician
ITIZENSHIP: UK
LACE OF BIRTH: Woolsthorpe Manor, Woolsthorpe-by-Colsterworth, Lincolnshire, England
NOWN RELATIVES: Isaac and Hanna Newton (parents, deceased), Barnabas Smith (stepfather, deceased), Leonid (son)
ROUP AFFILIATION: Brotherhood of the Shield
DUCATION: MSc in Mathematics from Cambridge University
EIGHT: 5'7"   **EYES**: Blue
EIGHT: 144 lbs.   **HAIR**: Gray (originally brown)

STORY: Born to illiterate farmers, Isaac Newton was a star pupil at school and took a keen interest in mathematics and science. As a young an, Newton was recruited by the ancient Brotherhood of the Shield and schooled in their secrets by Galileo Galilei. Newton sought more owledge than the Brotherhood could provide, and in 1625 he entered the Deviant city Ashomia, where he was granted access to their secrets becoming one of their society and mating with a Deviant woman, Morda; once he had learned all he could, he betrayed Morda and the eviants, destroyed Ashomia and fled. In time, Newton discovered the Elixir of Life, which granted him immortality. He published his magnum us, the *Principia Mathematica*, in 1687, which outlined universal gravitation and the laws of motion. He also discovered calculus, although other mathematician, Gottfried Leibniz, independently discovered it almost simultaneously; amid accusations of plagiarism, the two became ter enemies and Newton later took his rival's life. In addition to his scientific pursuits, Newton also wrote extensively on theological matters, hough he refrained from publishing those writings that expressed his heretical beliefs. Using the promise of his Elixir, Newton eventually ined total control of the Brotherhood. Unbeknownst to Newton, the son he bore with Morda, Leonid, survived and was eventually inducted o the Brotherhood. In 1956, Leonardo da Vinci, long thought dead, returned to the Brotherhood and challenged Newton's leadership, leading a violent schism.

NOSTRADAMUS

REAL NAME: Michel de Nostredame
ALIASES: "The Architect of Revelation"
IDENTITY: Publicly known
OCCUPATION: Apothecary, author, translator, astrological consultant
CITIZENSHIP: France
PLACE OF BIRTH: Saint-Rémy-de-Provence, France
KNOWN RELATIVES: Jaume and Reynière de Nostredame (parents, deceased), Jean de St. Rémy (maternal great-grandfather), Delphine (sister, deceased), Jean I, Pierre, Hector, Louis, Bertrand, Jean II, Antoine (brothers, all deceased), unidentified wife (deceased), Anne Ponsarde (wife, deceased), three daughters, three sons and two other children (all unidentified and deceased)
GROUP AFFILIATION: None
EDUCATION: Unfinished studies in medicine
HEIGHT: 5'6" **EYES**: Blue
WEIGHT: 125 lbs. **HAIR**: Gray

HISTORY: Born in 1503 to a grain dealer and notary, Michel de Nostredame's childhood remains mostly undocumented until he entered the University of Avignon at age 15. The school was closed shortly after, due to the plague, and Nostredame traveled the countryside and became an apothecary. He married an unidentified woman and had two children who died, presumably of the plague. Years later, Nostredame remarried a rich widow who bore him six children. Moving away from medicine to the occult, he changed his name to the Latinized version Nostradamus and wrote an almanac that contained the first of his prophecies. Persons of nobility and other prominent status began asking him for "psychic" advice, amongst them the immortal Sir Isaac Newton of the Brotherhood of the Shield. When Nostradamus refused to give Newton the prophesies he demanded, Nostradamus was enslaved in an underground chamber beneath the Immortal City and periodically injected with a variation of the Elixir of Life that kept him alive but caused his body and mind to decay. Imprisoned for centuries, Nostradamus persevered until Newton's son Leonid released him in time to witness a violent battle between Newton and a time-traveling Leonardo da Vinc

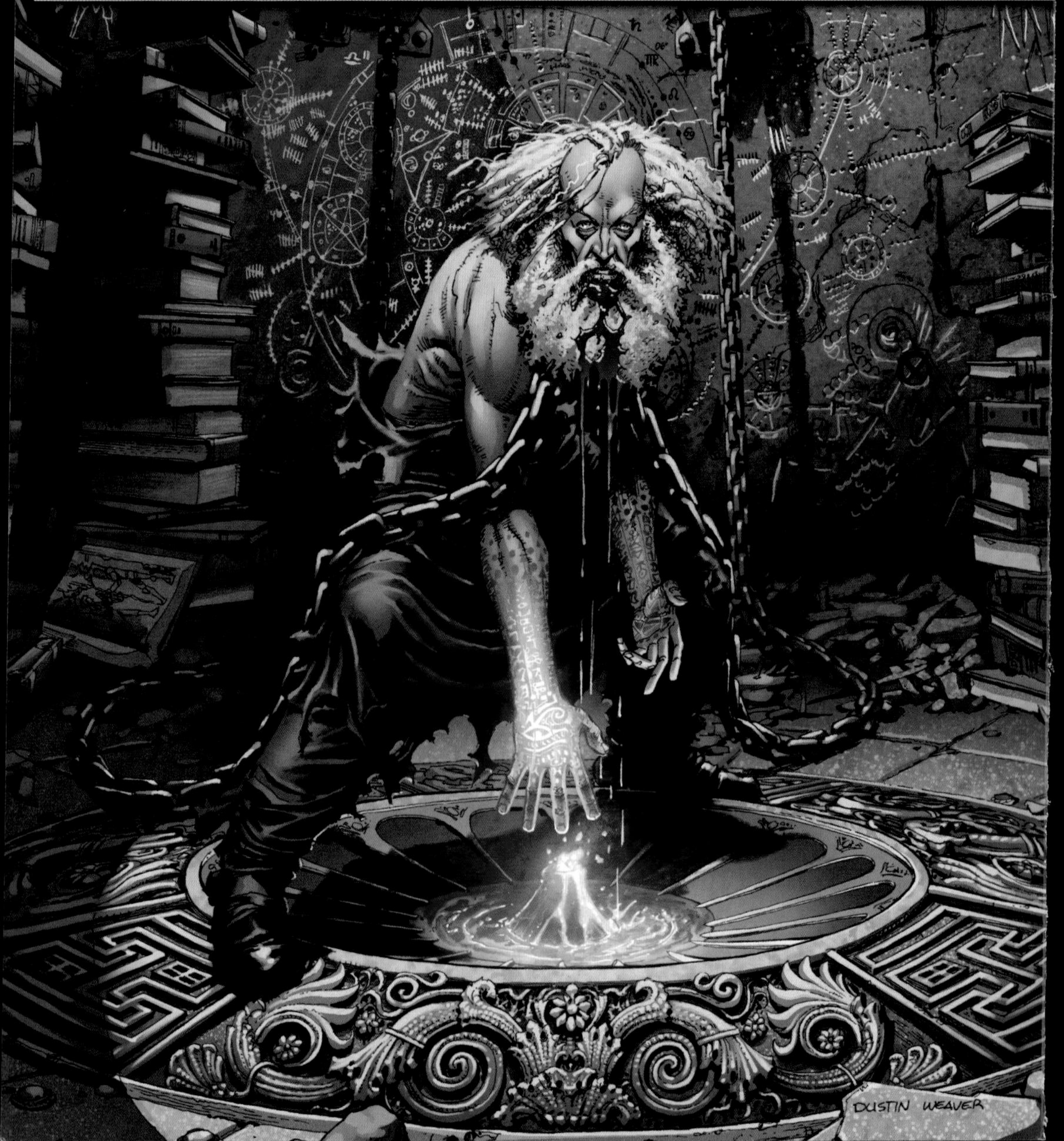
DUSTIN WEAVER

ZHANG HENG

REAL NAME: Zhang Heng
ALIASES: None
IDENTITY: No dual identity
OCCUPATION: Astronomer, administrator, engineer, poet
CITIZENSHIP: China
PLACE OF BIRTH: Luoyang, China
KNOWN RELATIVES: Zhang Kan (grandfather, deceased)
GROUP AFFILIATION: None
EDUCATION: Graduate of Imperial University
HEIGHT: 5'3"   **EYES:** Brown
WEIGHT: 153 lbs.   **HAIR:** Black

HISTORY: Born in China's Eastern Han Dynasty, circa 78 AD, Zhang Heng studied to be a writer, becoming a noted poet until he turned his attention to astronomy at 30. A skilled inventor, Heng created the first seismograph, capable of detecting earthquakes thousands of miles away; the first odometer, allowing for the production of highly accurate maps; and a water-powered armillary sphere that he used to make the most accurate star maps of his era. His genius brought him to the Emperor An-Ti's attention, soon being appointed the Emperor's chief astronomer. During this time, his astronomical observations assisted in reconfiguring the Chinese calendar, although his uncompromising stances prevented him from rising any further in the court's ranks. In 114 AD, Heng encountered a Celestial, who informed him that she carried an infant Celestial inside her. Told the energy required to birth the child would destroy the planet, Heng instead suggested the Celestial let the infant gestate within the Sun, where it remained in infancy for centuries until discovered by Leonardo da Vinci in 1956. Political intrigues with the court's eunuchs during Emperor Shun's reign eventually prompted him to step down; he later served as administrator of the city of Hejian, though he briefly returned to the Emperor's court before his death in 139 AD.

NATHANIEL RICHARDS & HOWARD STARK

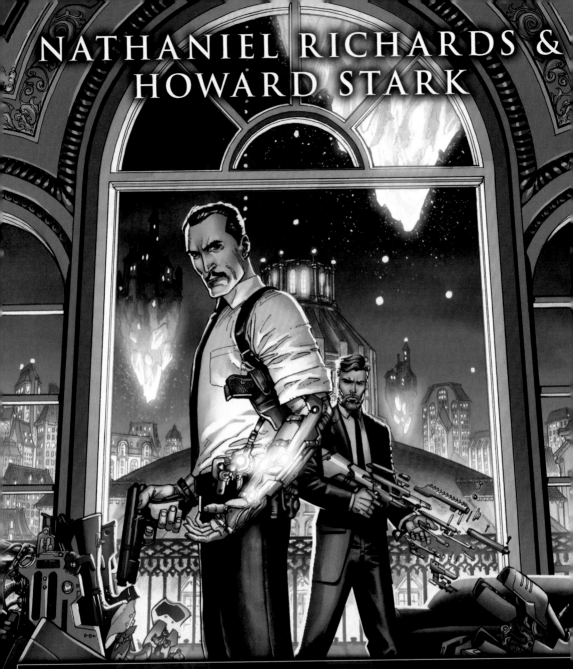

REAL NAME: Nathaniel Richards/Howard Anthony Walter Stark
ALIASES: (Richards) None; (Stark) none
IDENTITY: (Both) No dual identity
OCCUPATION: (Richards) explorer; (Stark) businessman; (both) Brotherhood of the Shield enforcers, scientists
CITIZENSHIP: USA
PLACE OF BIRTH: (Richards) Riverside, California; (Stark) Richford, New York
KNOWN RELATIVES: (Richards) Evelyn Richards (wife, deceased), Reed Richards (Mr. Fantastic, son), others; (Stark) Maria Colli
Carbonell Stark (wife, deceased), Anthony Edward "Tony" Stark (Iron Man, son), others
GROUP AFFILIATION: (Both) Brotherhood of the Shield; (Stark) Hellfire Club, Control, Project Tomorrow
EDUCATION: (Richards) extent unknown; vast scientific intellect; (Stark) advanced degrees in physics and mechanical engineering
HEIGHT: (Richards) 6'2"; (Stark) 6'
WEIGHT: (Richards) 180 lbs.; (Stark) 168 lbs.
EYES: (Richards) Brown; (Stark) blue
HAIR: (Richards) Brown; (Stark) black

HISTORY: Partnered together in the early 1950s as Brotherhood of the Shield agents, Nathaniel Richards and Howard Stark were tasked w
retrieving Brotherhood leader Isaac Newton's biological son Leonid from Nikola Tesla, who recently resurfaced after disappearing nearly
decade earlier. Tesla attacked them in a suit that could discharge electrical bolts. Richards instinctively fired his weapon, killing Tesla, but t
body was taken by a time-traveling Michelangelo and revived by merging him with his suit. Years later, they located Leonid and brought him
the Brotherhood's Immortal City beneath Rome. Stark and Richards were forced into battle again when Tesla broke into the Brotherhoo
home. In the battle Tesla's power core was damaged. The resulting explosion coupled with Richards' time-travel abilities and shunted the t
approximately 600,000 years into the future. Stark and Richards repaired Tesla's power core, the three agreed to a truce, and combining th

NIKOLA TESLA

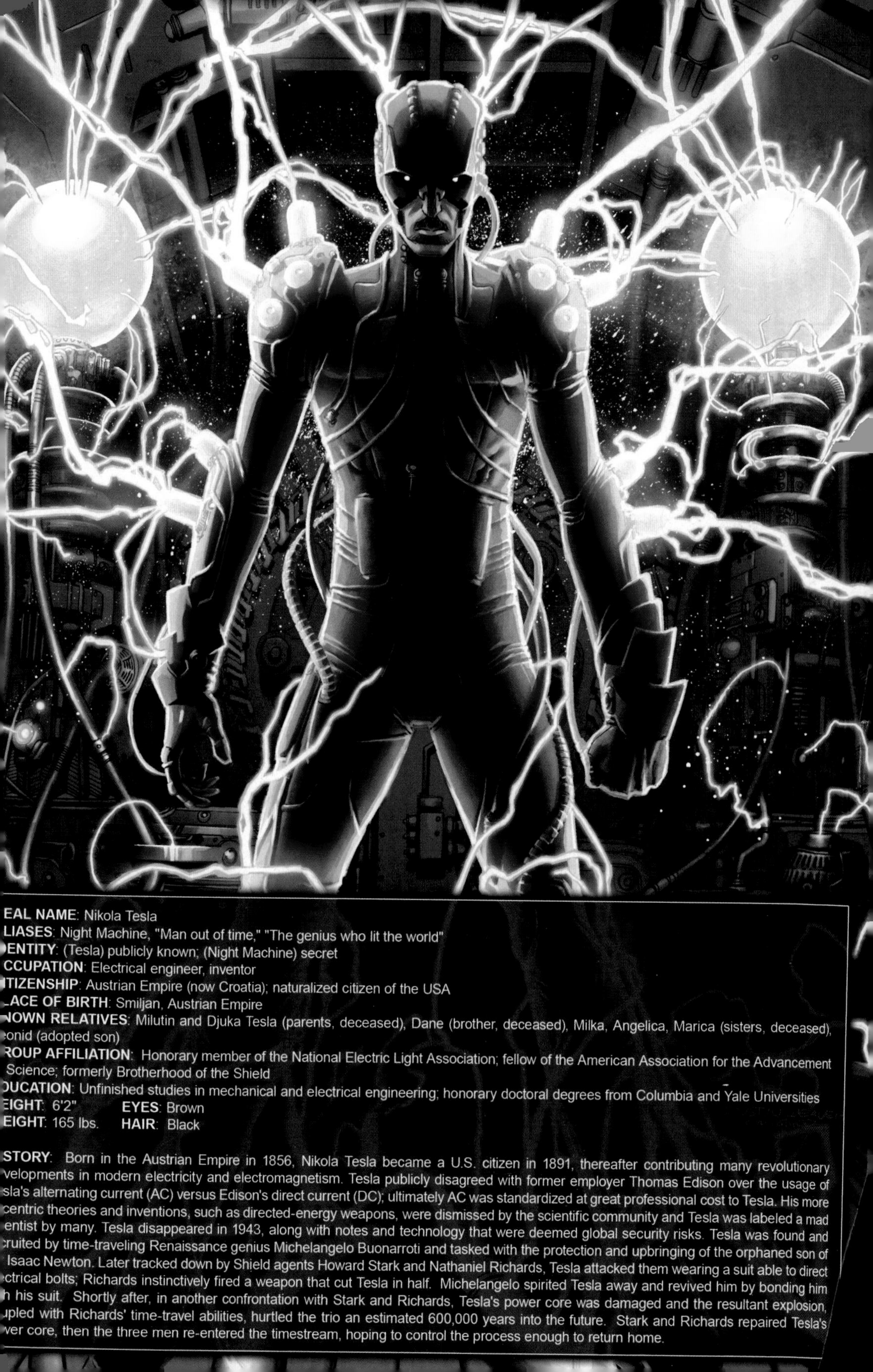

EAL NAME: Nikola Tesla
LIASES: Night Machine, "Man out of time," "The genius who lit the world"
ENTITY: (Tesla) publicly known; (Night Machine) secret
CCUPATION: Electrical engineer, inventor
ITIZENSHIP: Austrian Empire (now Croatia); naturalized citizen of the USA
ACE OF BIRTH: Smiljan, Austrian Empire
NOWN RELATIVES: Milutin and Djuka Tesla (parents, deceased), Dane (brother, deceased), Milka, Angelica, Marica (sisters, deceased), onid (adopted son)
ROUP AFFILIATION: Honorary member of the National Electric Light Association; fellow of the American Association for the Advancement Science; formerly Brotherhood of the Shield
UCATION: Unfinished studies in mechanical and electrical engineering; honorary doctoral degrees from Columbia and Yale Universities
EIGHT: 6'2" **EYES**: Brown
EIGHT: 165 lbs. **HAIR**: Black

STORY: Born in the Austrian Empire in 1856, Nikola Tesla became a U.S. citizen in 1891, thereafter contributing many revolutionary velopments in modern electricity and electromagnetism. Tesla publicly disagreed with former employer Thomas Edison over the usage of sla's alternating current (AC) versus Edison's direct current (DC); ultimately AC was standardized at great professional cost to Tesla. His more centric theories and inventions, such as directed-energy weapons, were dismissed by the scientific community and Tesla was labeled a mad entist by many. Tesla disappeared in 1943, along with notes and technology that were deemed global security risks. Tesla was found and cruited by time-traveling Renaissance genius Michelangelo Buonarroti and tasked with the protection and upbringing of the orphaned son of Isaac Newton. Later tracked down by Shield agents Howard Stark and Nathaniel Richards, Tesla attacked them wearing a suit able to direct ctrical bolts; Richards instinctively fired a weapon that cut Tesla in half. Michelangelo spirited Tesla away and revived him by bonding him h his suit. Shortly after, in another confrontation with Stark and Richards, Tesla's power core was damaged and the resultant explosion, upled with Richards' time-travel abilities, hurtled the trio an estimated 600,000 years into the future. Stark and Richards repaired Tesla's ver core, then the three men re-entered the timestream, hoping to control the process enough to return home.

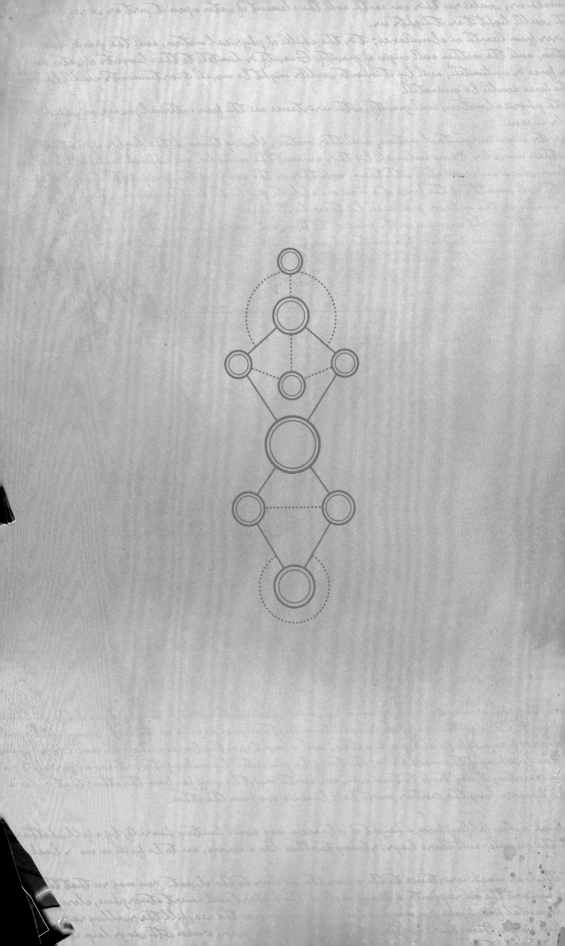